SHADING & DRAWING TECHNIQUES

by Jasmina Susak

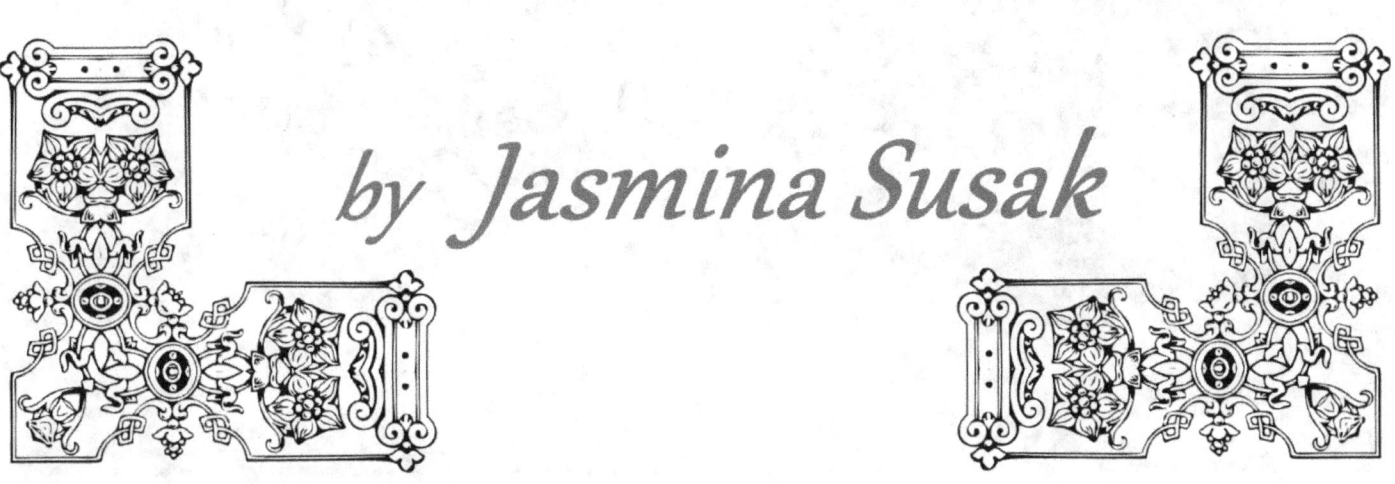

Copyright © 2020 by Jasmina Susak

www.jasminasusak.com

Text and artwork © Jasmina Susak

Page layout and cover design by Jasmina Susak

All rights reserved. No part of this publication may be reproduced, distributed, or transmitted in any form or by any means, including photocopying, recording, or other electronic or mechanical methods, without the prior written permission of the author. For permission requests, contact the author via email: jasminasusak00@gmail.com

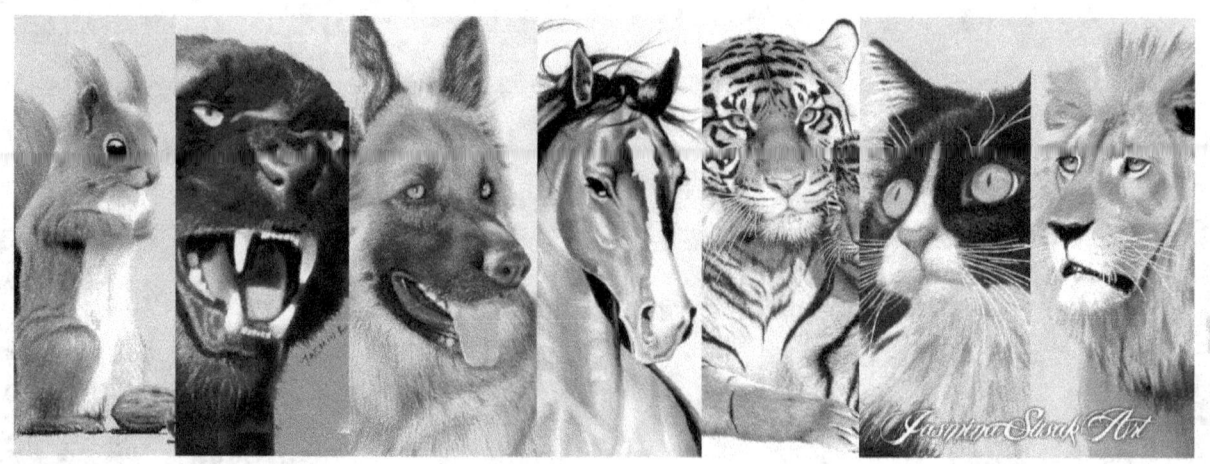

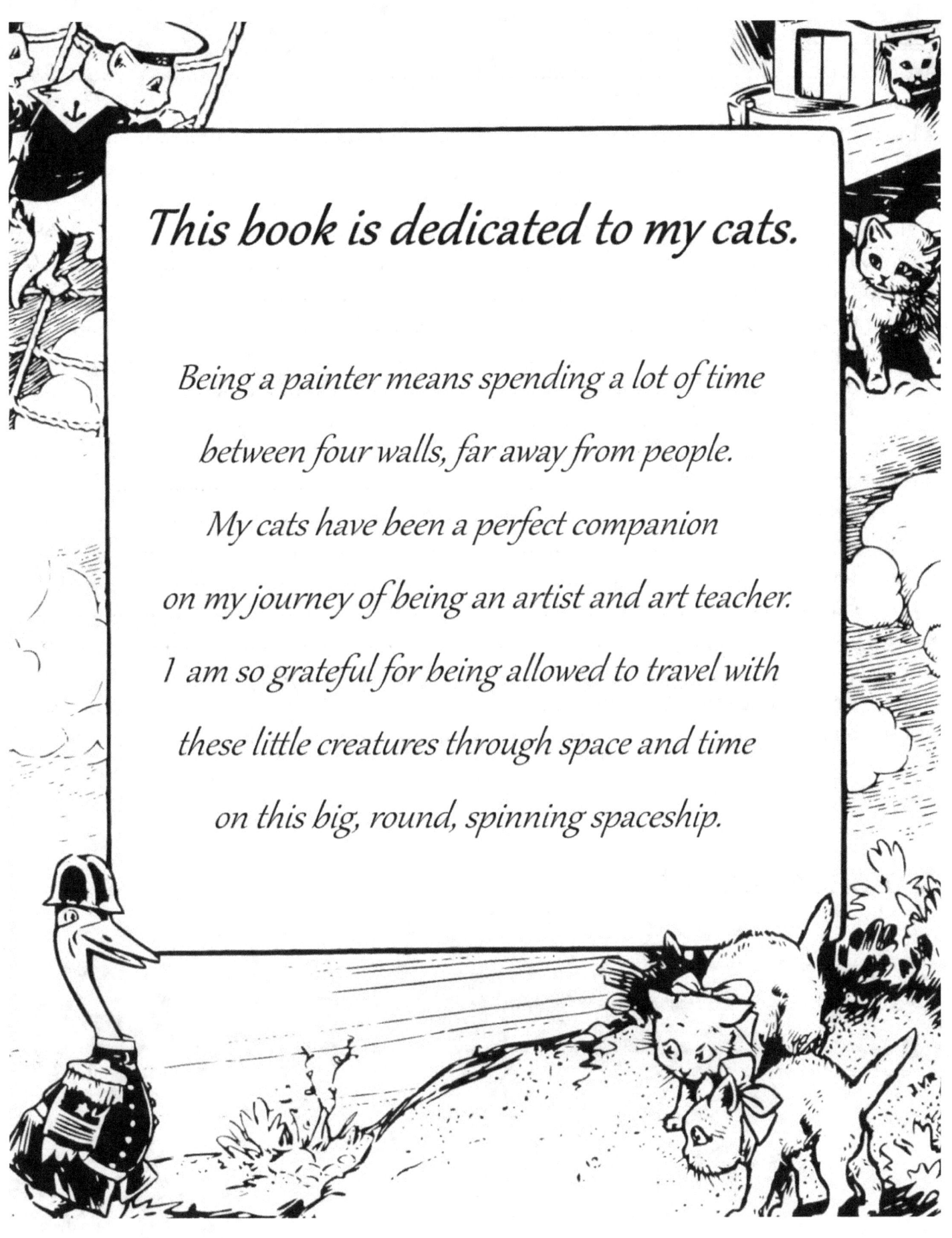

This book is dedicated to my cats.

Being a painter means spending a lot of time between four walls, far away from people. My cats have been a perfect companion on my journey of being an artist and art teacher. I am so grateful for being allowed to travel with these little creatures through space and time on this big, round, spinning spaceship.

Table of contents:

Art materials 10
Drawing Tutorials:
A butterfly 24
Water droplets 35
A Rubik's Cube 41
A glass cup 59
A football ball 70
Knitted fabric texture 81
A palm tree on a beach 87
An umbrella 108
An apple 118
A teaspoon 133
An ear 140
A half-cut orange 150
How to draw realistic eyes 158
Black hair 179
Brown hair 184
Hyperrealistic lips 187
Kissing lips 201
Glitter lips and teeth 212
How to draw a smokey glitter eye 224
About the Author 250

More tutorials at:
WWW.PENCILDRAWINGTUTOR.COM

FOREWORD

I have created this book to give some advice on the things I have learned from my experience with drawing. I create a lot of realistic drawings, which is a style of working among all the others out there. It's not the only way of working. There is a wide variety of different styles. Whether you are interested in a realistic style of drawing or not, I hope that the advice I give in this book can be of some use.

To get started, you don't need any previous experience—just to pay attention and to do thorough work with patience. You must practice to become better and better at drawing. By regularly drawing, you develop your muscle memories, the ability to see the things that only artists can see, and the skill. You have to gain experience through repetition and mistakes. With time and practice, you will become more self-confident, willing to try new things, and develop your own style. You will get inspiration and passion, and this is where your creativity will come from. The most important thing in being an artist is knowing what real quality looks like. Then, you can look at your own work and decide how far you have to go and, more importantly, what you need to do to get there. Just remember: the only time you will never become a good artist is when you give up trying. The only way to fail at something is to give up on it. Don't compare yourself to others who are more advanced than you are. They've been working for years, or even decades. Take each step, read, and learn from those who have more experience and practice. I believe that if you create the belief in yourself first, then your art will emerge faster.

Drawing is a complex skill that is impossible to learn overnight. However, sometimes you just want to draw something without waiting months to get decent results. And you should neither expect too much nor get discouraged and frustrated when the things go wrong. You have to enjoy the process—to sit and be with yourself, present in your surroundings. The point is that you understand and experience the essence of realistic drawing. Even if you can't take it to the professional level in a few weeks, you can get there through regular practice. How long it takes depends on the individual. how long it takes.

These simple step-by-step tutorials will help. You can do them with little or no previous experience. Good results are guaranteed if you follow the instructions carefully.

How to use this book?

Prepare all the tools, relax, and work without expectations.
Work on a simple step, with patience, and don't move to the next step until you finish the current one. Don't rush. The next step will happen eventually. But, if you skip the steps, you might get lost and frustrated.
Don't worry about results—just sketch and try to have fun with it.
Try to draw 30 minutes to 1 hour a day. It's just enough; you don't have to work for hours.
Put your drawing aside and take a look at it the next day. You might be able to see the things with "fresh eyes" that you missed the day before. When you return to your drawing after the break and look at it, you will immediately recognize the mistakes. There may be times when you feel stuck. You are not getting along with a certain section, somehow you can't find a flow with it. You don't like something about it, it's not what you want it to be. Do not force it any further! That's when it's time for a little rest.
Take a look at your drawing from a larger distance. Is the shape of your drawn object proportional enough? Is your smooth gradient flawless? Is your object recognizable when you step far away from it? Take a look at your drawing in the mirror or upside down to check up on symmetry and to see it from a different point of view. You will be surprised by the new things that you can notice that way.
Study images of the objects before you start to draw them.

Through these tutorials, I will teach you...
To draw facial features:

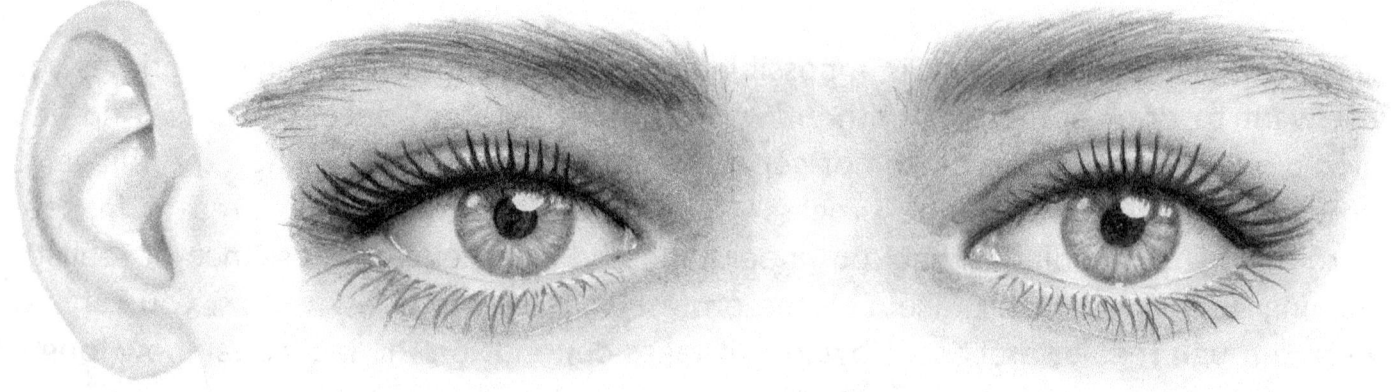

To shade three different pairs of lips:

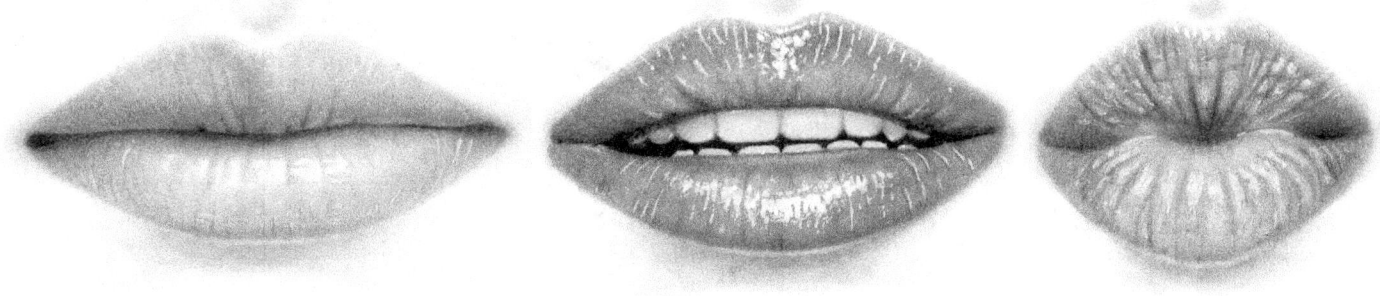

To draw realistic fruits:

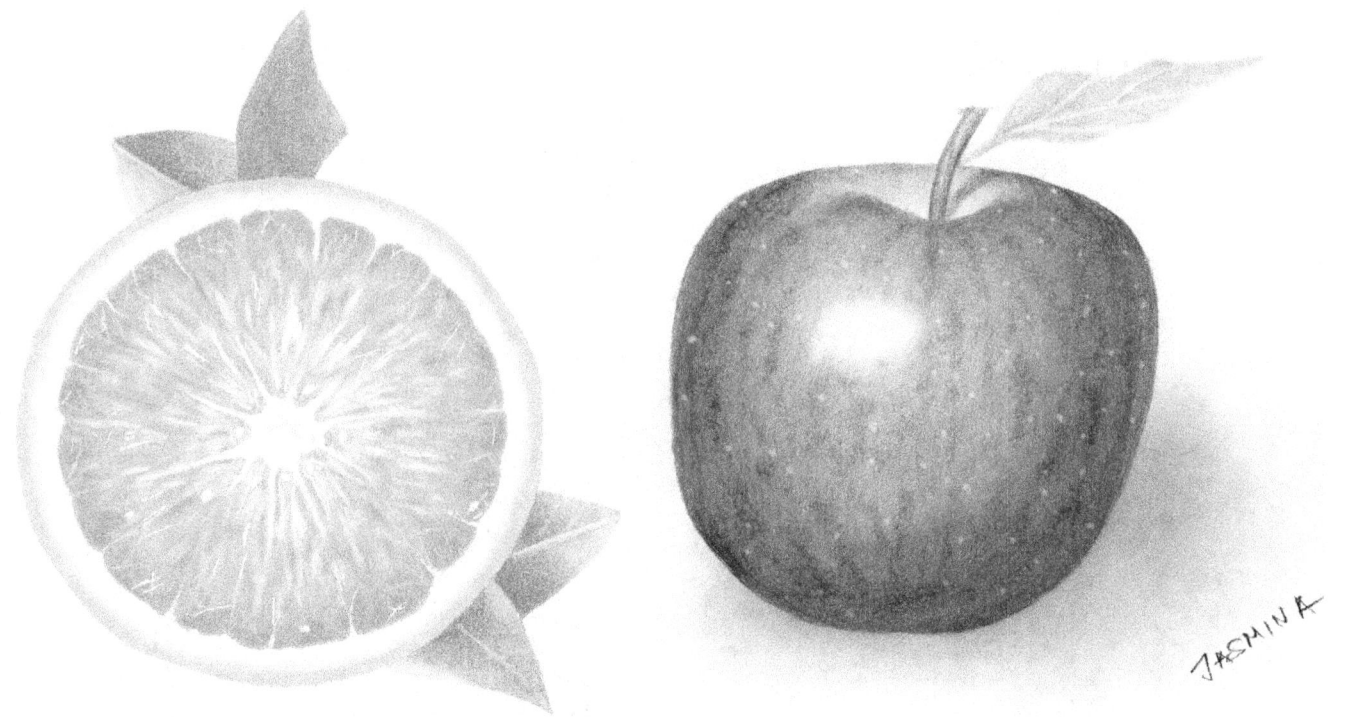

To draw human hair:

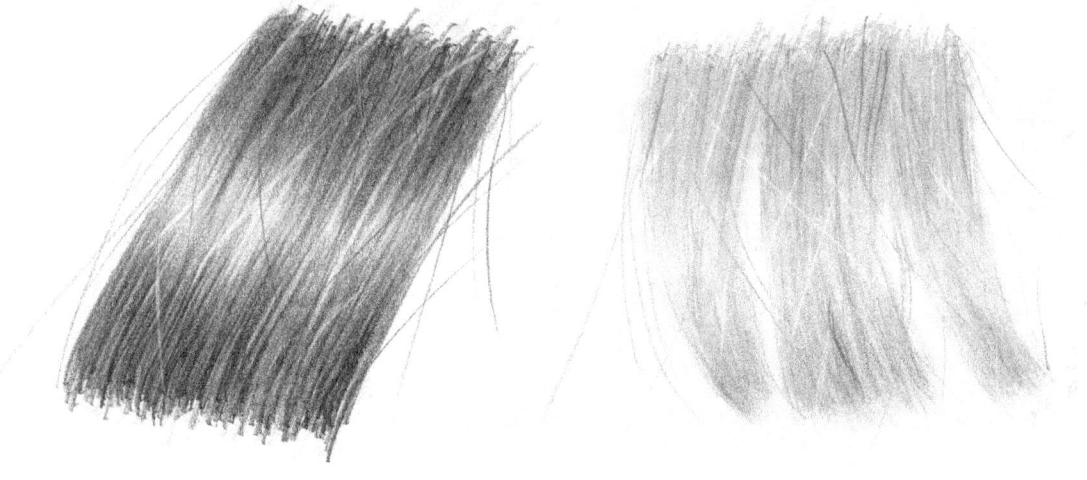

How to make your drawings look 3D:

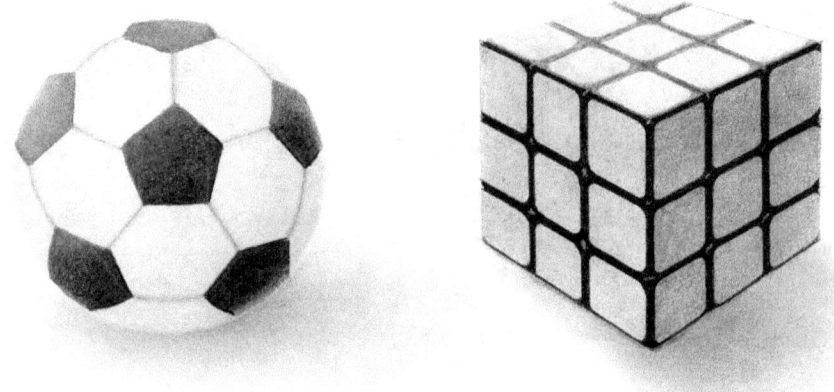

How to make objects shine:

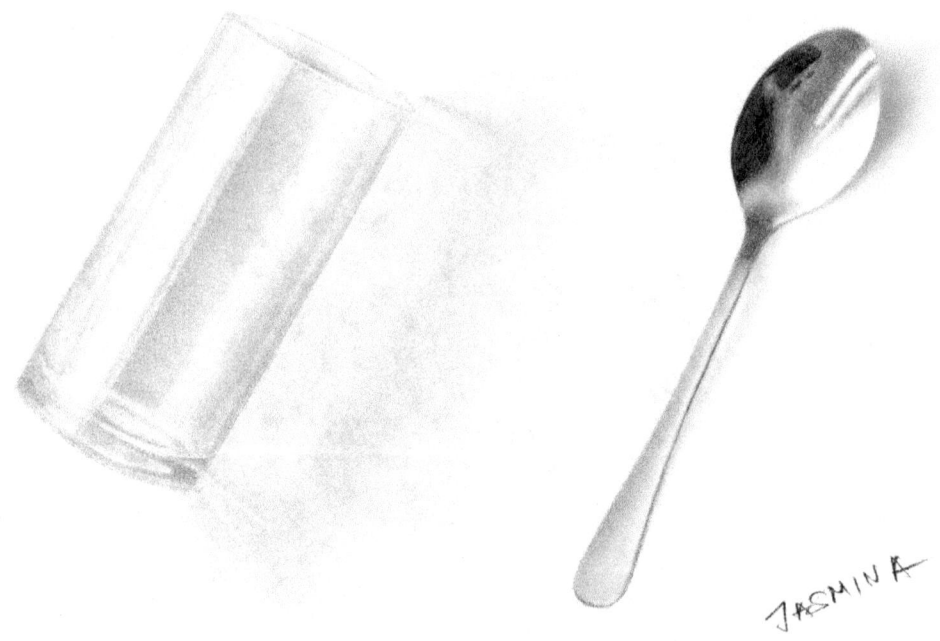

How to make your drawing pop on the page:

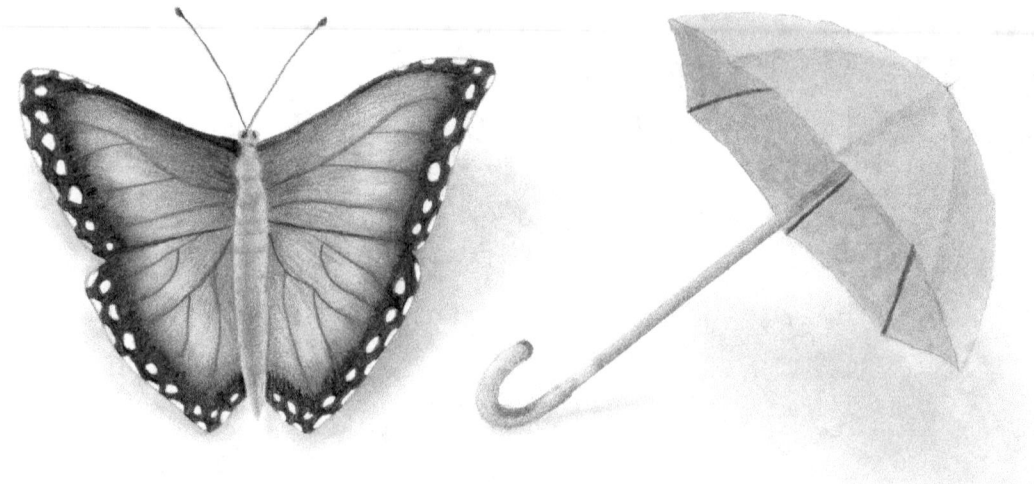

How to draw landscapes:

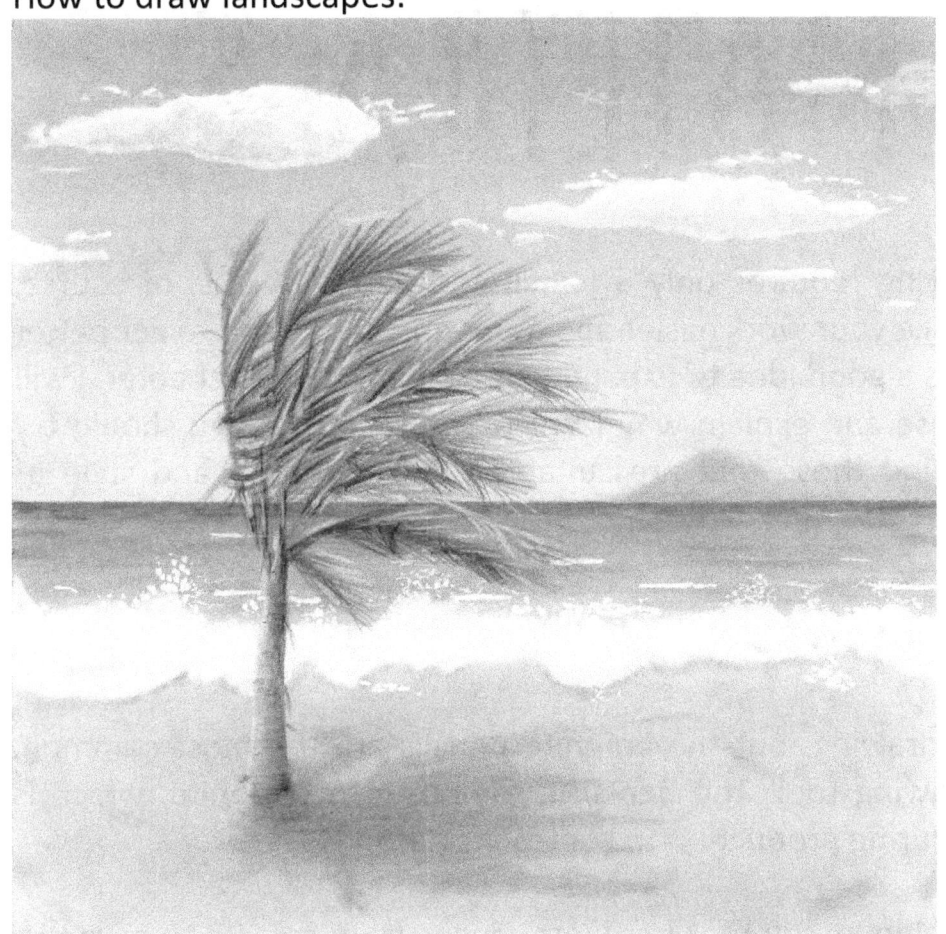

And even to draw on grey paper:

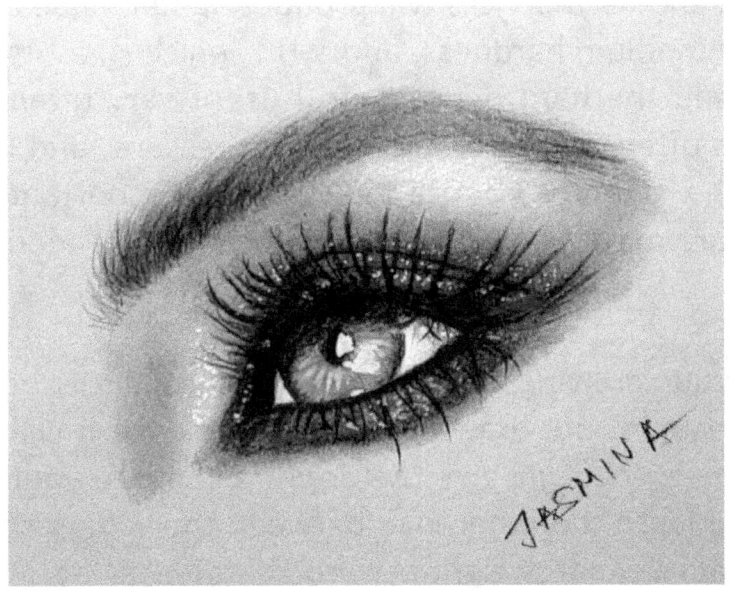

If you are ready for these, let's get started!

ART MATERIALS

Many people think that drawing requires only a pencil and paper. This is, of course, basically true. However, to make your work easier and more enjoyable, and to get better results in a shorter period, it is a good idea to expand your toolbox. In this chapter, I will talk about everything that I use and explain why I use them. However, you should try other tools too in order to find those that are suitable for your hands and style of drawing.

Pencils

There are so many tools for drawing, but the graphite pencils are the most common, popular, and quite cheap drawing tool. The pencil is composed of graphite, which is mixed with various additives during production to control its hardness.

The graphite pencils are available in different hardness ranges from soft 9B to hard 9H. The numbers and letters at the end of the pencil indicate the hardness of the pencil. The letter H comes from the English word hard, which means hardness, and letter B is derived from black. Soft pencils are darker, and hard pencils will produce lighter values. There is also an F (fine) pencil, which has a medium hardness, and a HB, which is, as its name says, something between the soft and the hard pencils and I use it very often because I don't have to change the pencils often; I have to change the pressure, and I can create the values from a 5H to a 2B with a single, HB pencil. However, it is important to use both hard and soft pencils as there are many shades of an image, and they need to be reproduced on the paper.

To make sure you get the right tone for your drawing, I recommend using pencils of different hardness. The more values you create in your drawing, the more realistic it will be. Never be afraid of using the darkest tones; they will give the depth and life to your drawings. Always use at least 3-4 pencils to learn the difference between the values of your drawing. Although it sounds elementary and straightforward, it takes a lot of practice to make a really nice tone scale. The beauty of your drawing will depend on it. So, it is crucial to consider which pencil you use for a particular area of your drawing.

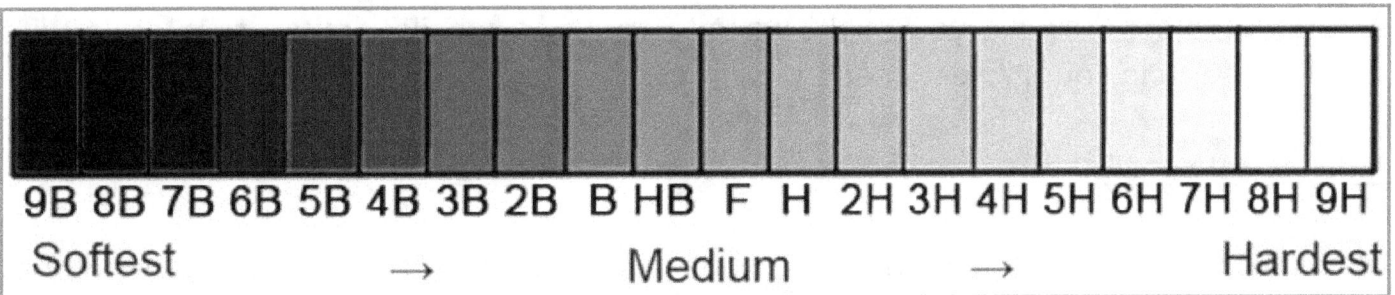

Soft (dark) pencils are great for shading and drawing the darkest areas of, which will give the depth and life to your drawings. While soft pencils run out faster, harder ones can last for such a long time, if not forever, particularly if you have the full scale from an H to a 9H because you don't have to sharpen them often. I can't even remember the last time I sharpened my pencils.

There are many brands of high-quality graphite pencils and they are, more or less, of the same quality. I use Castell 9000 by Faber-Castell, but you can choose any other brand, such as Staedtler Mars Lumograph, Koh-I-Noor or pencils by Prismacolor, Caran D'Ache, Derwent, and so on.

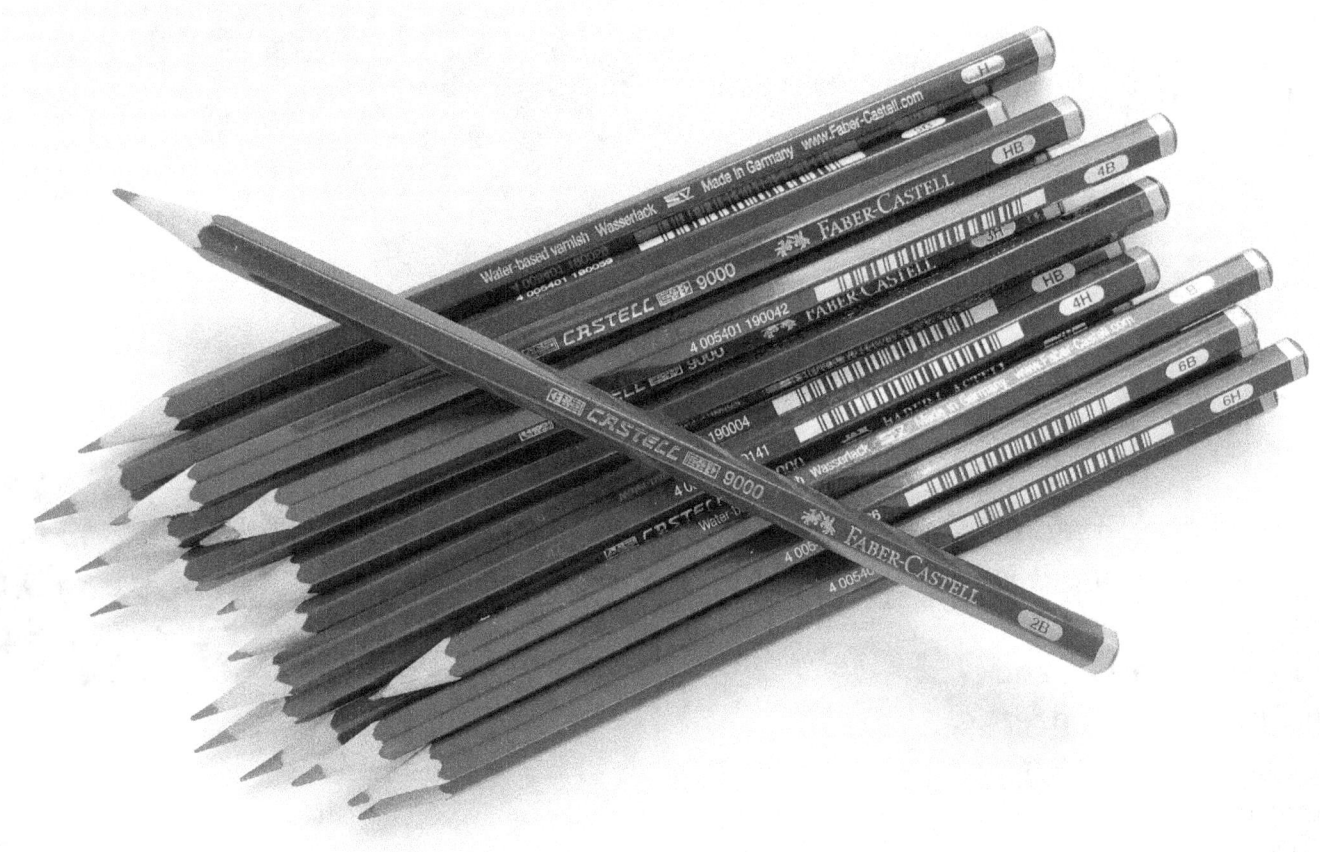

Before you start drawing, you might want to try your pencils, draw a tone scale with them to see tone your project needs.

Mechanical pencils

Mechanical pencils, also known as "Rotring" pencils (but Rotring is a brand name, not the official name for these pencils), can be useful in drawing. I use them often when I draw hair because I can create the hairs of the same thickness without sharpening the pencils. The leads for these pencils are also available in a wide variety of hardness ranges. Also, creating a little detail can make our job easier with this tool. Some people love them very much, and some less, everyone has to experience it for themselves.

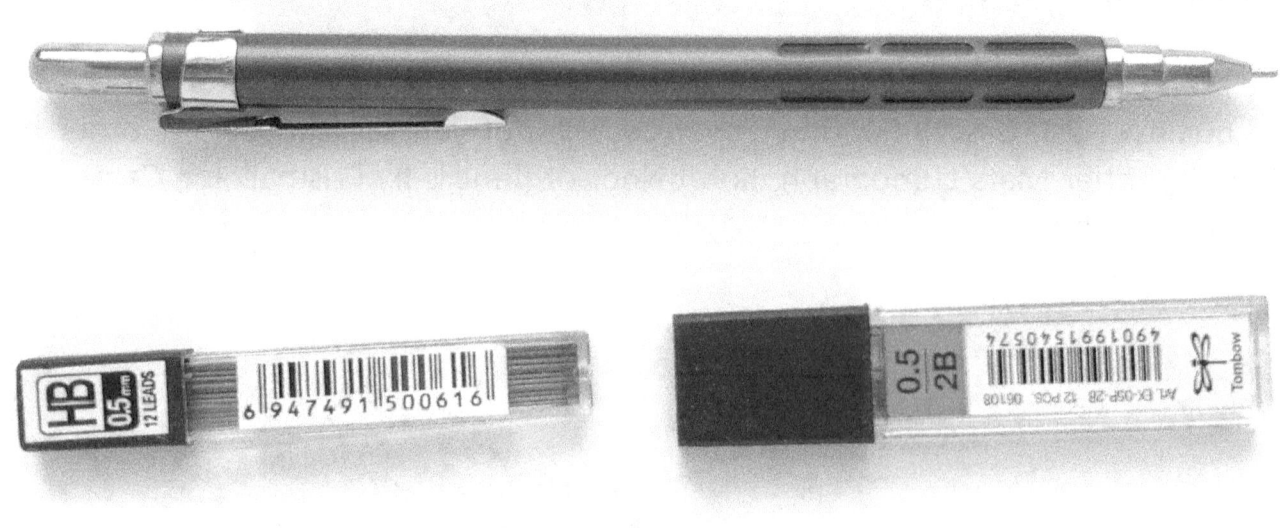

Charcoal pencils

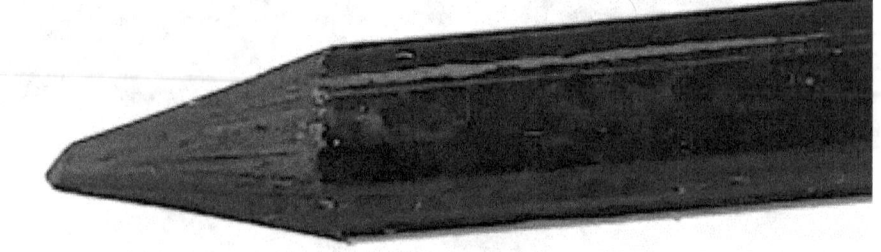

As I mentioned before, for a good drawing it is essential to work out the dark parts and achieve a really deep black color. It is often a problem with the graphite that the more layers are applied, the more the area will gloss. Of course, it's not visible from a certain angle and with proper lighting, but its glitter can be a little distracting and annoying.

A charcoal pencil can be a good solution in this regard. With a charcoal pencil, you can achieve incredible deep black tone, and the advantage is that it doesn't shine. Of course, for the rest of the values in your drawing, you can use graphite if you find it hard to work with charcoal. Anyway, every tutorial from this book can be done in charcoal too, so you should try them both and see which medium you like more.

Paper

Do you think that all the paper is the same and it doesn't matter what you use for your drawings? That's not quite the case. If you have drawn on a simple print (computer) paper, you might have experienced how frustrating and demotivational it can be to draw on thin, low-quality paper. Different types of drawing sheets are made for different types of drawing or painting tools. In this chapter, I want to help you to easily navigate through the paper issue and to know what to look for when choosing the right paper.

Paper size

Today, international standard paper sizes are used in all countries except the United States and some other countries.
We distinguish the 5 most used sizes:
A1 -- 594 x 841 mm -- 23.4 x 33.1 in
A2 -- 420 x 594 mm -- 16.5 x 23.4 in
A3 -- 297 x 420 mm -- 11.7 x 16.5 in
A4 -- 210 x 297 mm -- 8.3 x 11.7 in
A5 -- 148 x 210 mm -- 5.8 x 8.3 in.

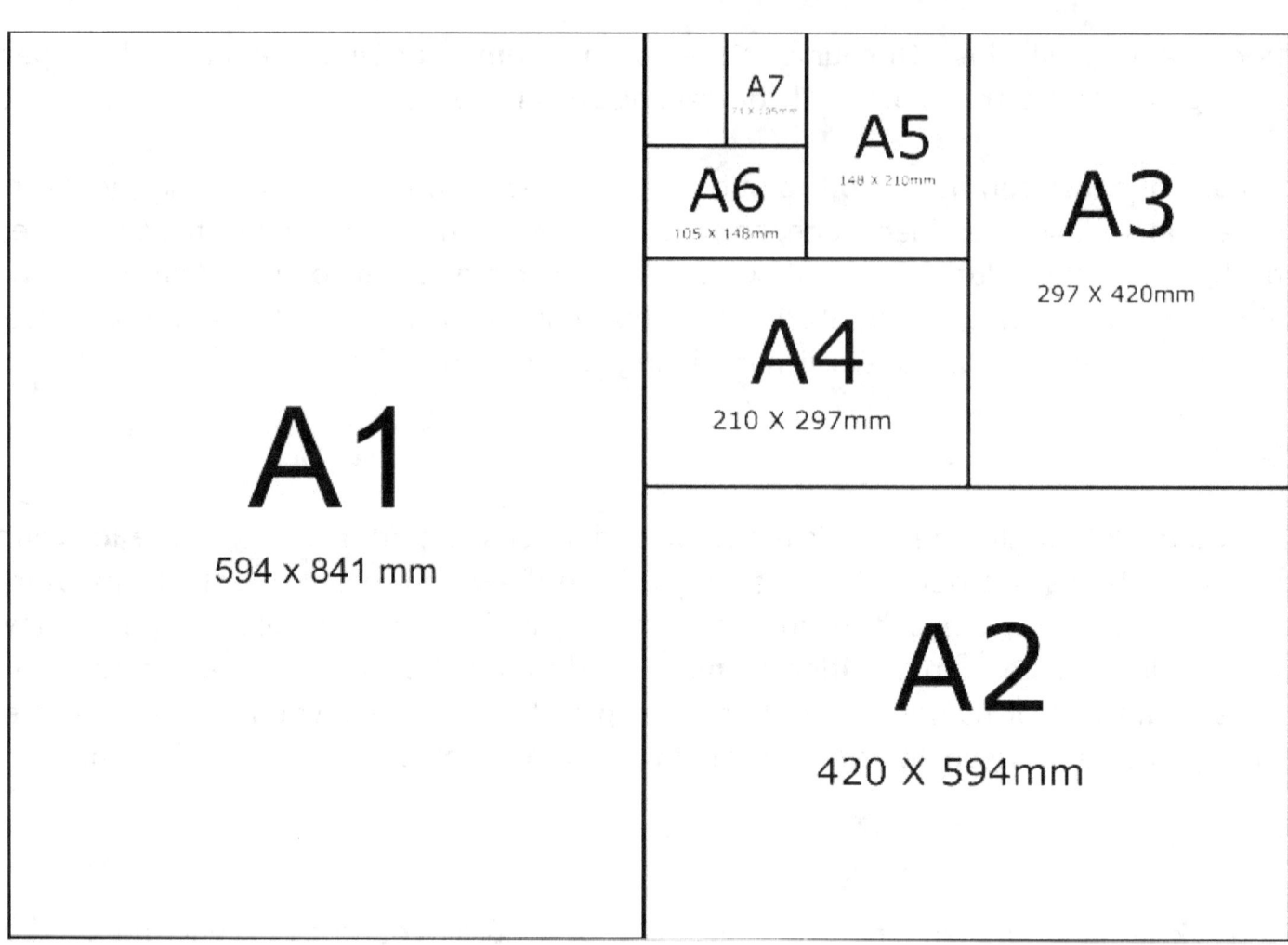

Usually, everyone starts to draw on A4 size, but if you want a detailed drawing, you might want to try the larger drawing sheets as well.

The weight of the paper

The weight of the paper is one of the most important things to keep in mind. The thickness of the paper is determined by its weight per square meter. A common printing paper weighs 80 g/m2 and it is pretty thin and will wrinkle under the pressure of the pencils and after erasing. That's why it is worth choosing heavier paper for drawing. Because a sheet with a weight of about 180-250 g/m2 has much less chance of tearing, crumpling, etc.

The texture of the paper

In addition to the weight of the paper, we must also pay attention to its texture, keeping in mind the medium we will be working on.

We distinguish three types of paper by way of their manufacturing:

- Hot-pressed papers: hot-pressed, high-pressure sheets. They have a much smoother surface and less or no texture.
- Cold-pressed papers: pressed at low pressure and no heat was used. This gives them a much rougher, and a much more textured surface.
- Rough: the paper with the most textured surface.

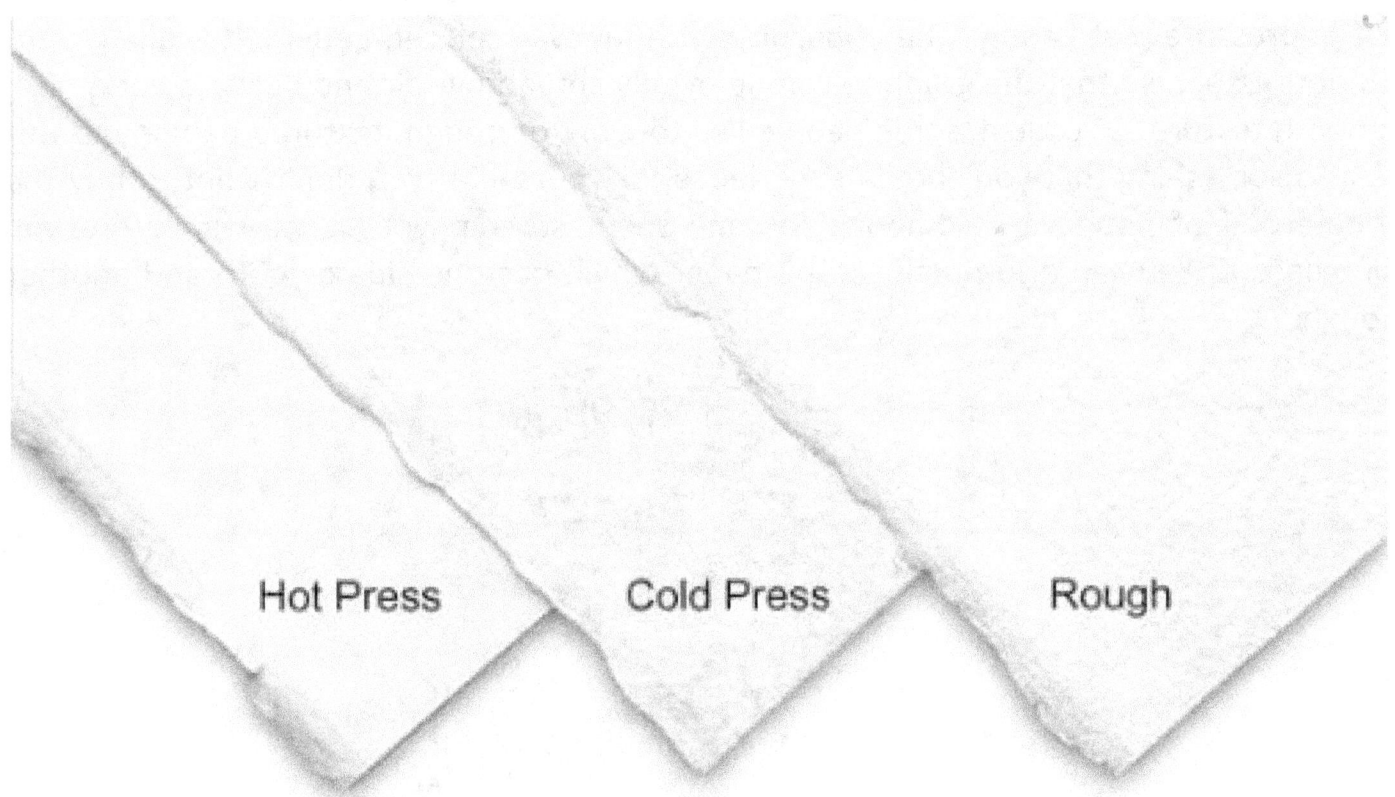

Which paper to use?

For sketches: thinner, lighter papers (approx. 80 g/m2) are also suitable. These are no longer sufficient for more elaborate drawings, as they are easily damaged. You can use graphite very effectively on a traditional printer paper, which will do it perfectly if you are still practicing. However, when you start a more serious artwork, you should get a quality drawing sheet, because it will not only make the artwork easier, but it will be more durable and more beautiful.

Watercolor paper: They usually have a rough, grainy texture and are the heaviest sheets because they have to withstand the use of water. Their weight is usually 200-300 g/m2. Smoother, hot-pressed watercolor papers can also be ideal for drawing.

Graphite, charcoal or colored pencil drawing paper: It doesn't need the same durability as watercolor paper, but it should be a heavier sheet than used for sketches. They usually weigh between 180 and 220 g / m2. But the weight of the card you choose should also depend on your drawing style. So, if you use wax colored pencils with the burnishing technique, you should choose the paper that weighs at least 220 g / m2.

My favorite and the only paper I use for both graphite and colored pencil drawing is Fabriano Bristol, usually A3 or A4 format. This paper is very thick and sturdy. It endures a lot of pressure that I apply when I burnish with my wax colored pencils. It is also a very smooth paper, so that the graphite can be evenly spread over it and I always get a nice, smooth texture. Of course, some people like to work on rough, textured paper, and this is also something that you should experience for yourself. If you don't want to buy the whole pad of paper, ask someone for one sheet so that you can try it before you purchase it. You can also purchase the paper which has one side smooth and another rough.

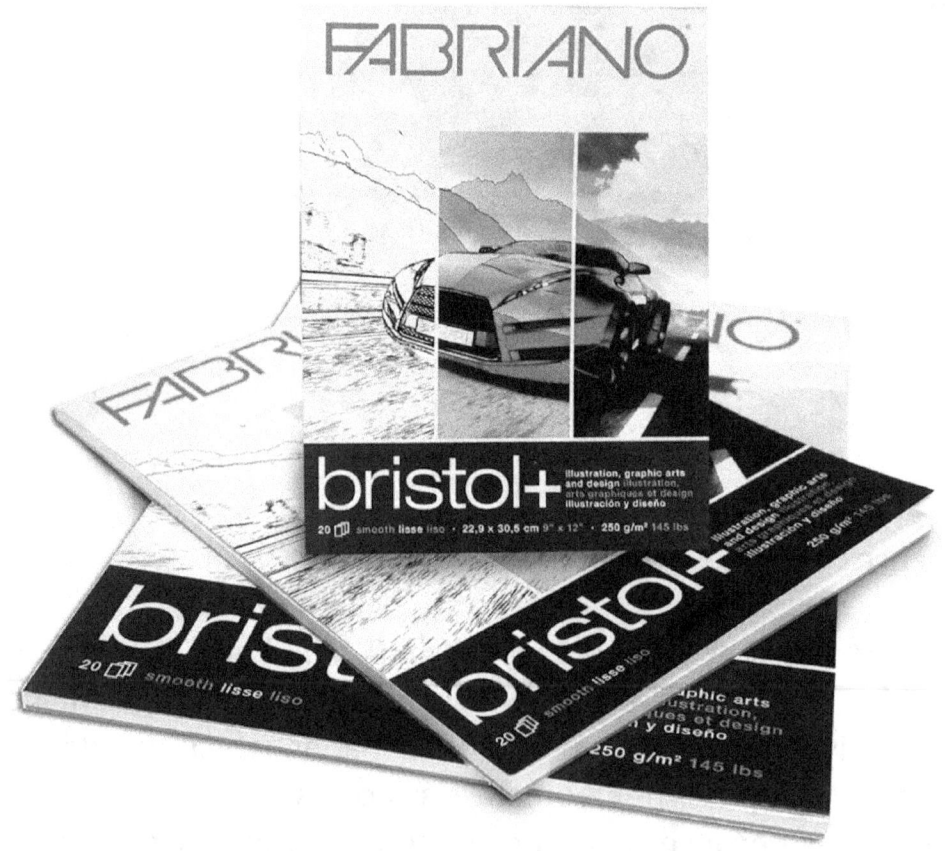

The best known and probably the best drawing paper brands are Strathmore, Stonehenge, Fabriano, Canson.

Erasers

Erasers are needed, not just to eliminate unnecessary lines or to correct errors, but to create the highlights over the drawn area. It is crucial which eraser we use for a particular work, and I suggest getting more kinds of erasers because they are all good for different things. The erasers are cheap equipment, so getting more types is very useful because only one is not good for everything. Choosing a good eraser is also important because a poor quality eraser can damage the paper.

Here are the five main types you may consider getting for yourself:

1. Traditional (plastic) erasers
You may need a standard eraser for larger surfaces. You can even cut them with a knife to be able to create tiny highlights. When the eraser becomes dirty, rub it of some rugs or even sandpaper and you will get to the clean part again. You have to use this eraser very carefully because when you rub it with force on the surface to erase, you may damage the structure of the paper and you cannot restore it. I usually use this for the background or the parts that I wouldn't shade.

2. A kneaded eraser
This kind is soft, easily kneaded, has a high bonding ability (after kneading it "absorbs" graphite and becomes clean again), leaves no greasy stain on the sheet, and does not damage it. We can use it when we want to remove just a little bit of the graphite over the shaded area. So, we have to touch the paper or press it with a quick, tapping motions and the graphite will stick to this eraser. You can break it into small pieces if you wish. You can shape the soft eraser into the shape that suits you if you need small points, or you want to erase a larger surface. Once the surface of the eraser has become black from the stuck graphite, you can re-knead it a bit and continue to erase it with a clean piece.

3. Mechanical eraser
With this handy eraser, you can protect your drawing and really delete only the parts you need; a precision eraser will help you. Such an eraser is the Tombow Mono Zero eraser, which is unique in its class and I often use it for creating the highlights, particularly the highlighted hairs over my drawings. The pen-shaped design makes it even easier to use. The eraser filler comes forward by pressing the end of the pen. So, it is used and can be changed the same way as mechanical pencils.

4. Eraser in pencil

If you have to work with the eraser in small areas, you will benefit greatly from an eraser that you can sharpen like an ordinary pencil with a sharpener. Still, instead of a graphite fill, it contains an eraser. It is also handy because we can hold it and work with it just the way we do with the graphite pencils.

5. Electric eraser

It is good for precision and fast erasing. It can also be used for graphite, colored and charcoal pencils. The great thing about electric erasers is that you can easily erase multiple layers and the small areas without rubbing the surrounding area. Of course, care must be taken not to ruin the paper too much. You may want to "sharpen" the tip of the filler with a blade or sandpaper so you can make quite small highlights or hairs.

In the next image, you can see all the erasers that I have and that I'll be using throughout the tutorials in this book.

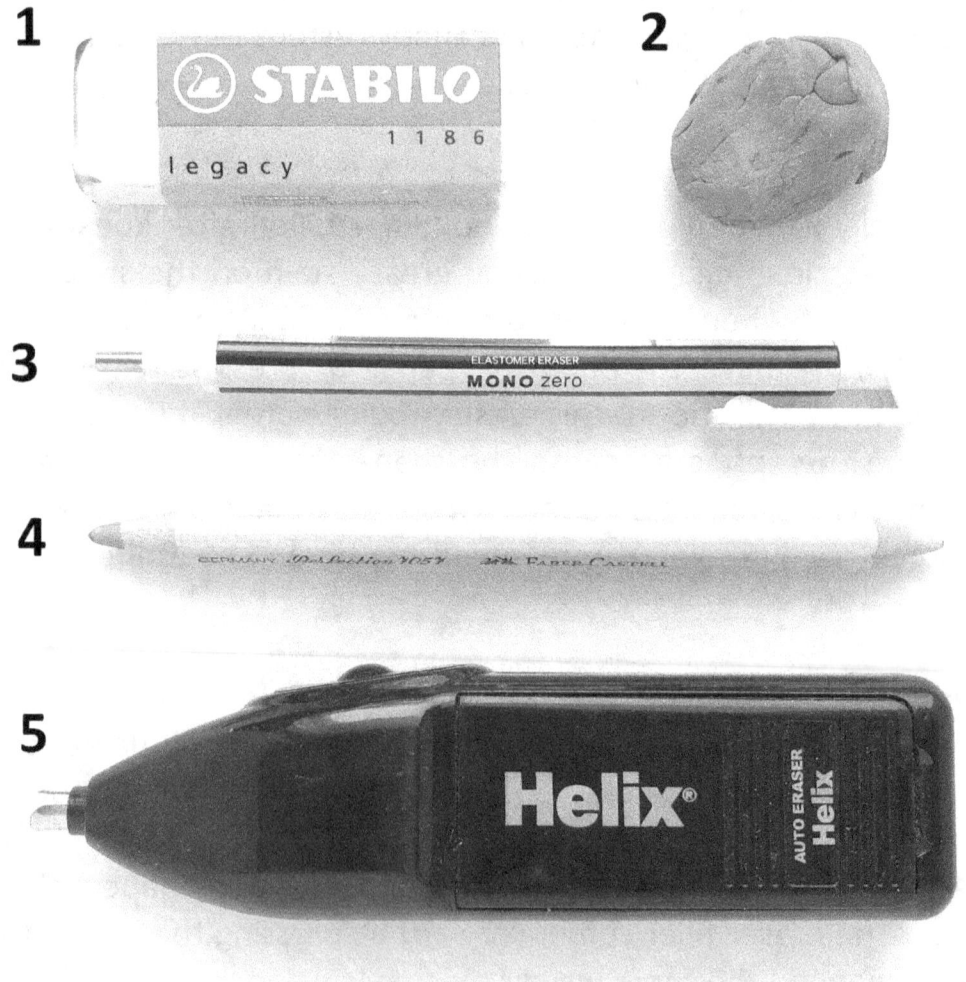

A white ink gel pen

Often when we draw, we want to create the highlights over the drawn areas but no matter how hard we press, even when we use an electric eraser, we can't bring back the white color of the paper because the graphite has colored the fiber of the paper that can't be eliminated, just lightened up. For that, a white ink gel pen is a great solution. I also often use white markers by Uni Posca, which are high-quality markers, and the most important, they are opaque and can be easily applied over the graphite. I also use them over my colored pencil drawings.

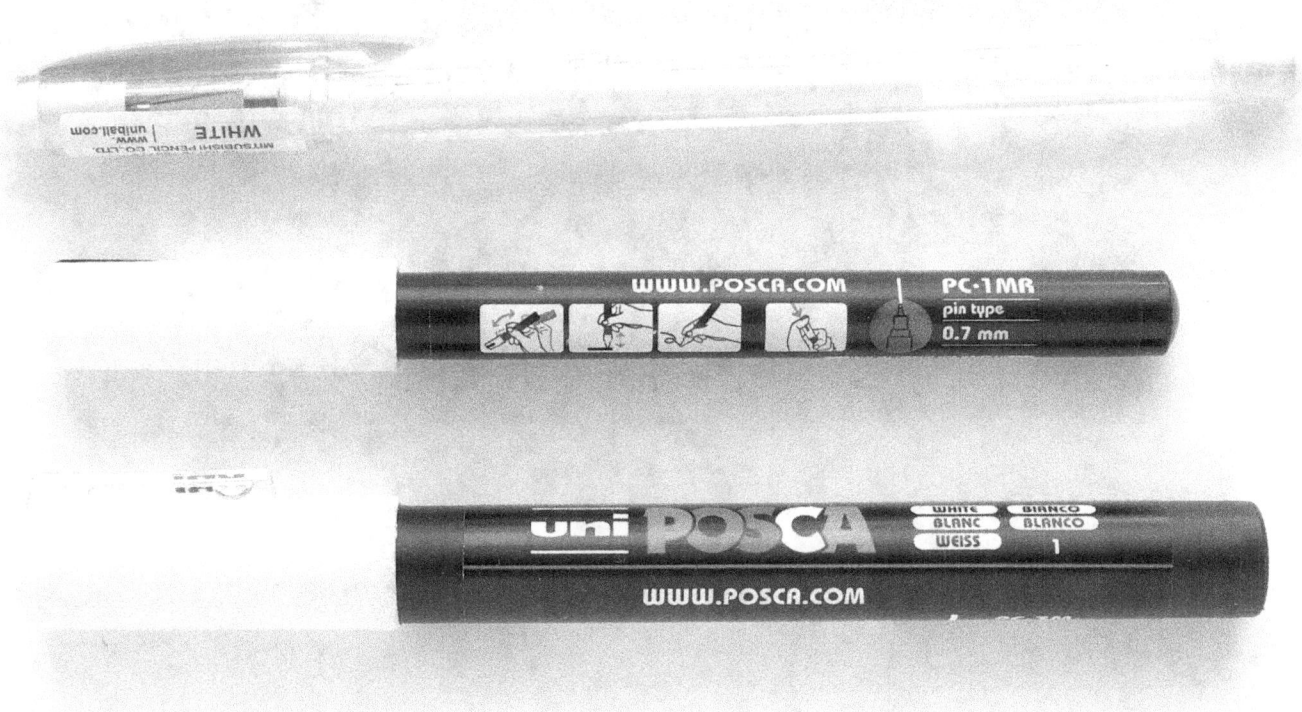

Graphite powder

The graphite powder is ideal for fine, uniform textures, large areas, or backgrounds. It is the same graphite that the graphite pencil is made from, but this is ground to a fine powder. We can use it in many different ways. One of the techniques is the brush technique. Put a little graphite powder on a separate sheet, and then dip our brush and dust off the excess on the draft sheet. Only then can we apply it to the drawing. It is advisable to go through the surface several times and build up the desired color so that the area is not spotted. It is always easier to apply more layers than to erase. You may want to get several brushes of different sizes that you can use depending on the size of the area you want to apply the graphite. I don't prefer this technique, but it is just a matter of habit. I apply it by spreading it over my paper sheet with a piece of tissue that I wrap around my finger. I also use Q-tips to shade with graphite powder.

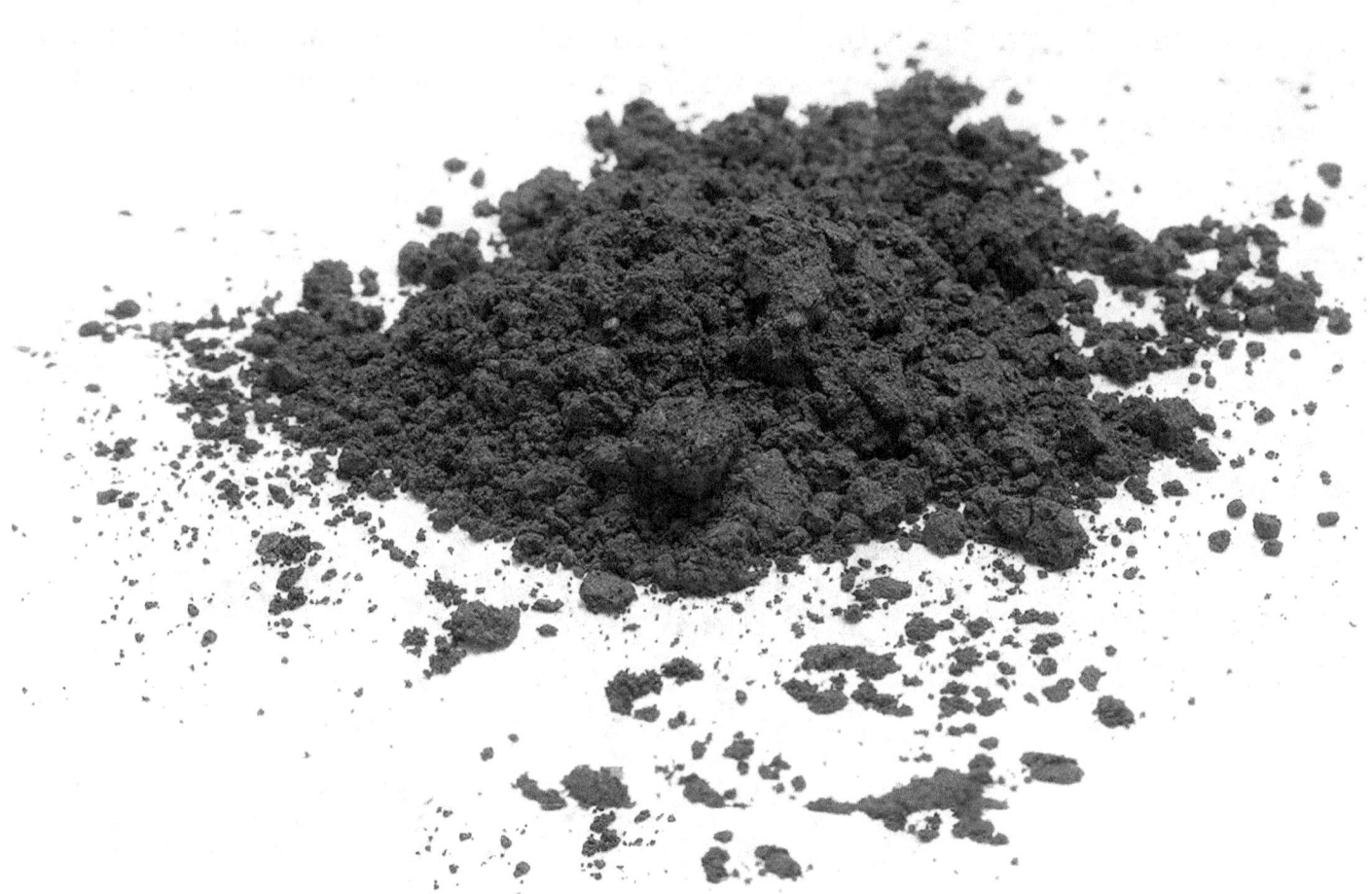

It is not recommended to do with our fingers and also, before applying the graphite powder we shouldn't touch the paper with our bare fingers, not even when we take a sheet of paper out of our pad or sketchbook. The smudged sheet is usually revealed after the graphite powder is spread, just the way the crime scene investigators do with fingerprints. Always wash your hands thoroughly before drawing. Fat and dirt on our fingers can leave a mark on our drawing. This can be really annoying, so precaution is key. It's a good idea to put a protective sheet under your hand to keep your drawing sheet from getting wet or greasy. This is especially important in summer when our hands sweat more. I often use a transparent piece of nylon when I record my drawing processes, so that the viewers can see the entire drawing all the time; meanwhile, I am protecting it from smudging.

Tools for blending

Tissue
You can use a paper handkerchief for spreading the paper, but be careful to choose one that has no odor and it's not moisturizing. As a matter fact, you can even use a kitchen paper towel, or even a toilet paper, which I often use when I run out of the tissues. They will do the same thing. If the surface you want to smear is too small for a tissue, try using the following tool mentioned in this chapter.

A blending stump
These pressed, pointed rod of paper are used to blend the graphite, to create a nice, even tone.

There are two types of this "paper pencil": tortillion, with only one end pointed, and the blending stump with a pointed tip at both ends. Previously, there was a difference in their softness, but now they are of about the same quality and differ only in shape, so it doesn't matter which one you choose. The blending stump will last longer since you have two ends to use. I usually have one end cleaner when I want to blend lighter areas, and another end "dirtier" that I already used a lot for blending, and its tip has accumulated a lot of graphite on it so that I can use it to blend darker areas.

When you have too much graphite on it, rub it a bit on the sandpaper, and it will be clean again. Temporarily, if you can't get it right away, you can wrap a piece of tissue on a mechanical pencil and use it.

Q-tips
Q-tips can also be used for blending, but because they have a bit larger "heads" than the blending stumps, we can use them for a bit larger areas. They are also very good for fine blending when we don't want to apply too much graphite. What's more, clean Q-tips can even remove a lot of drawn graphite, so practice using these on a separate piece of paper first.

Cotton pads
If you don't have any tissues on hand, you can use cotton pads. They will do just the same work.

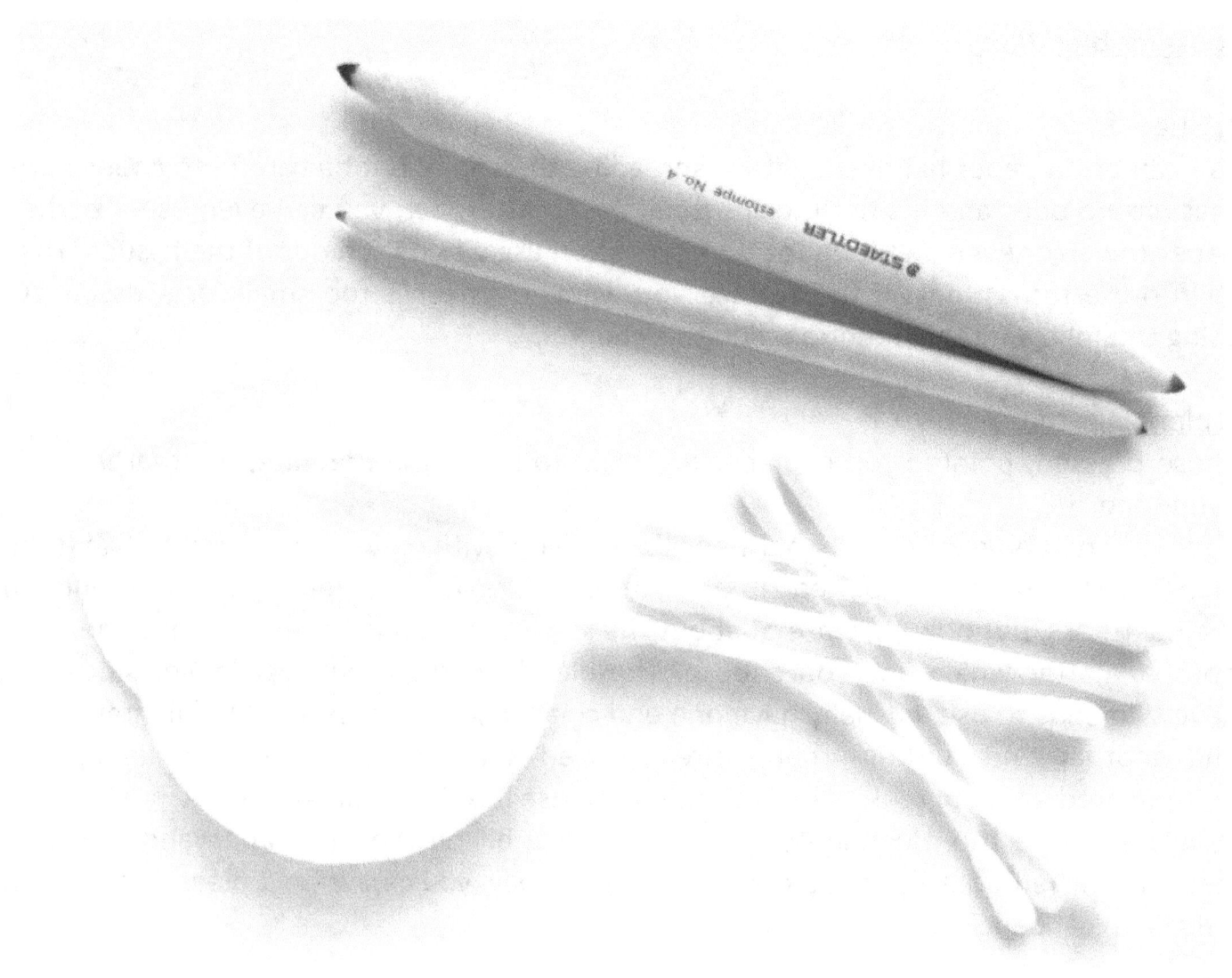

Additional tools

Fixative

You may want to spray it with a fixative to protect it from smudging. There are two kinds of fixatives:
1. Workable fixative that you use in the middle of the work and you can continue working over it.
2. Non-workable fixative when you can't add anything to the paper after spraying it. This one is used at the end of the drawing

Sharpener

If you're not just using a mechanical pencil, you'll need a high-quality sharpener. The more expensive ones tend to stay sharp longer, the cheaper ones need to be replaced more often. When we find that the pencil is no longer capable of sharpening, or especially if the sharpener breaks the tip, it is time for a replacement. I used simple, hand-held ones, but you can also choose electric ones.

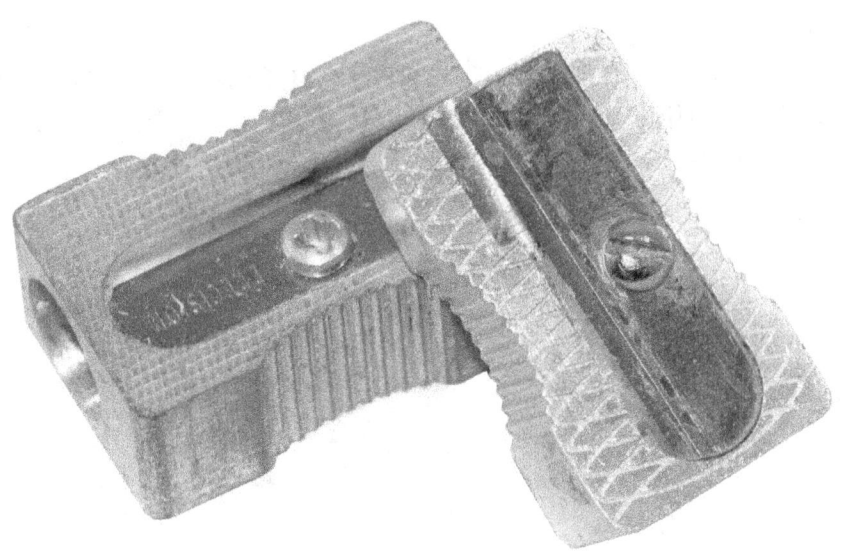

Ruler(s)

A ruler is a useful tool for making a straight line when you are not able to do freehand. Throughout these tutorials, I will often use a ruler for measuring. I suppose that everyone has one at home since it's a very cheap tool.

Drawing compass

You will need a simple drawing compass for some sketches from these tutorials.

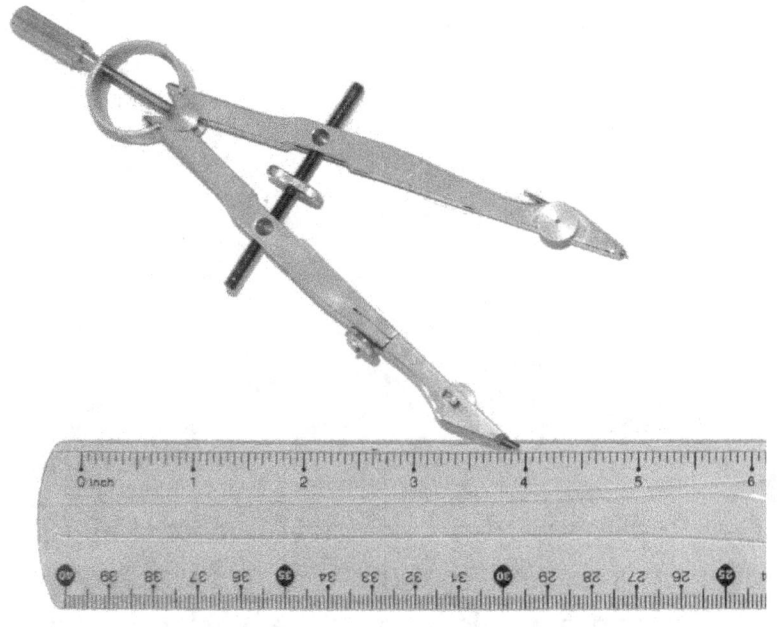

A BUTTERFLY

Let's start with a butterfly.
First, draw its body, or thorax, in the middle of your paper to have the starting points. Then you can draw the outlines of the wings. The shapes can be randomly, but try to make them symmetrical. In the next image, you can see how I started. The outlines don't have to be perfect.

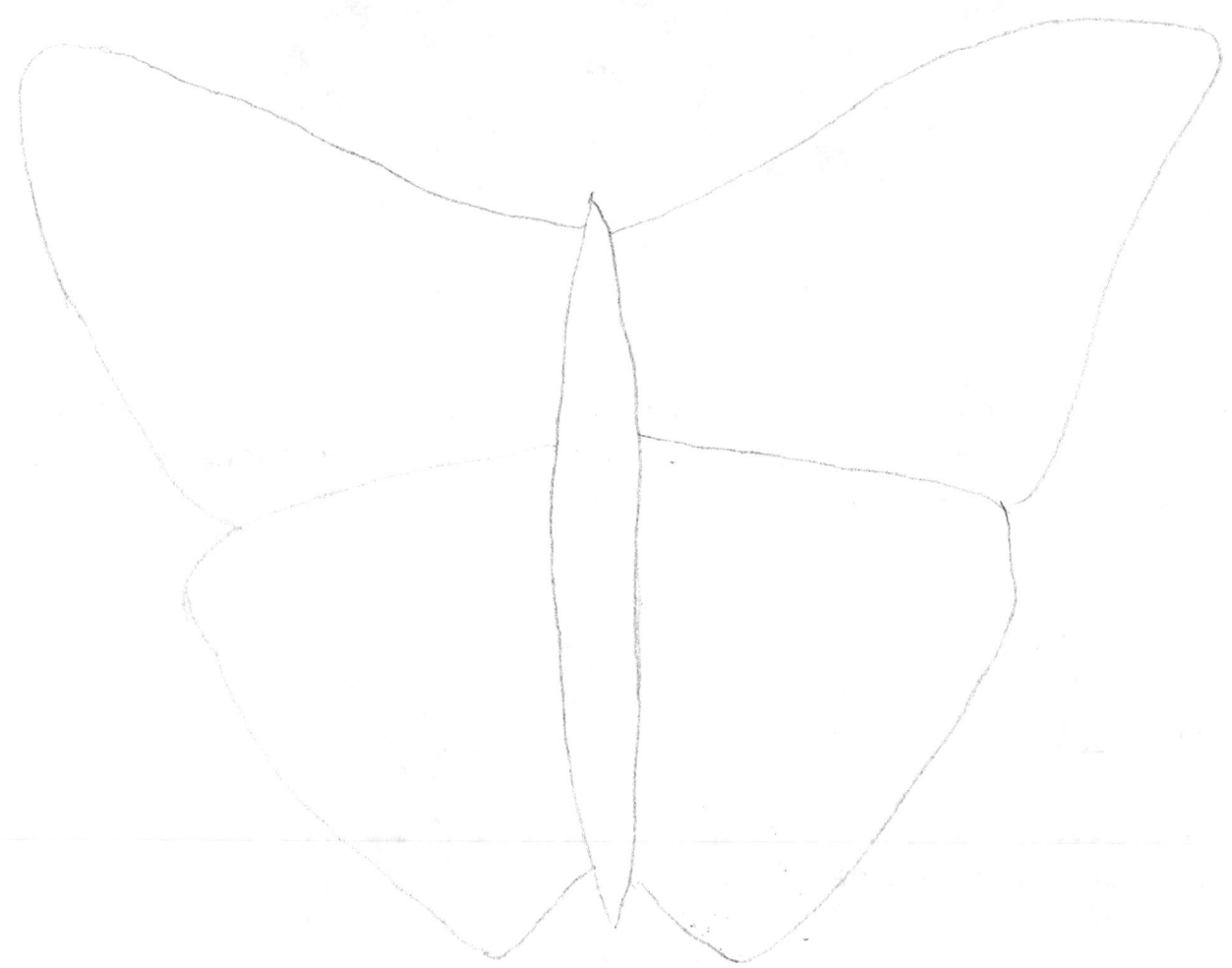

Create some patterns before you start shading. I want to create those typical white dots over the black edge of the wings. If you have a white ink gel pen or a white marker, you can color the whole area with a black pencil, and then you can create them with a white ink gel pen. But for those who don't have these tools, I want to show you how to do that. So, we have to draw around these dots, and they will stay white.

Create the dots next to the edge – as shown in the next image. Do the same all around the wings. The dots don't have to be the same; some of them can be smaller, some of them bigger. The pattern doesn't have to be the same as on the existing butterflies, but we can change something and create it as we wish. Try to do the same to recreate on both the left and right wings, and to make the patterns as symmetric as possible. Draw two antennas at the top of its body.

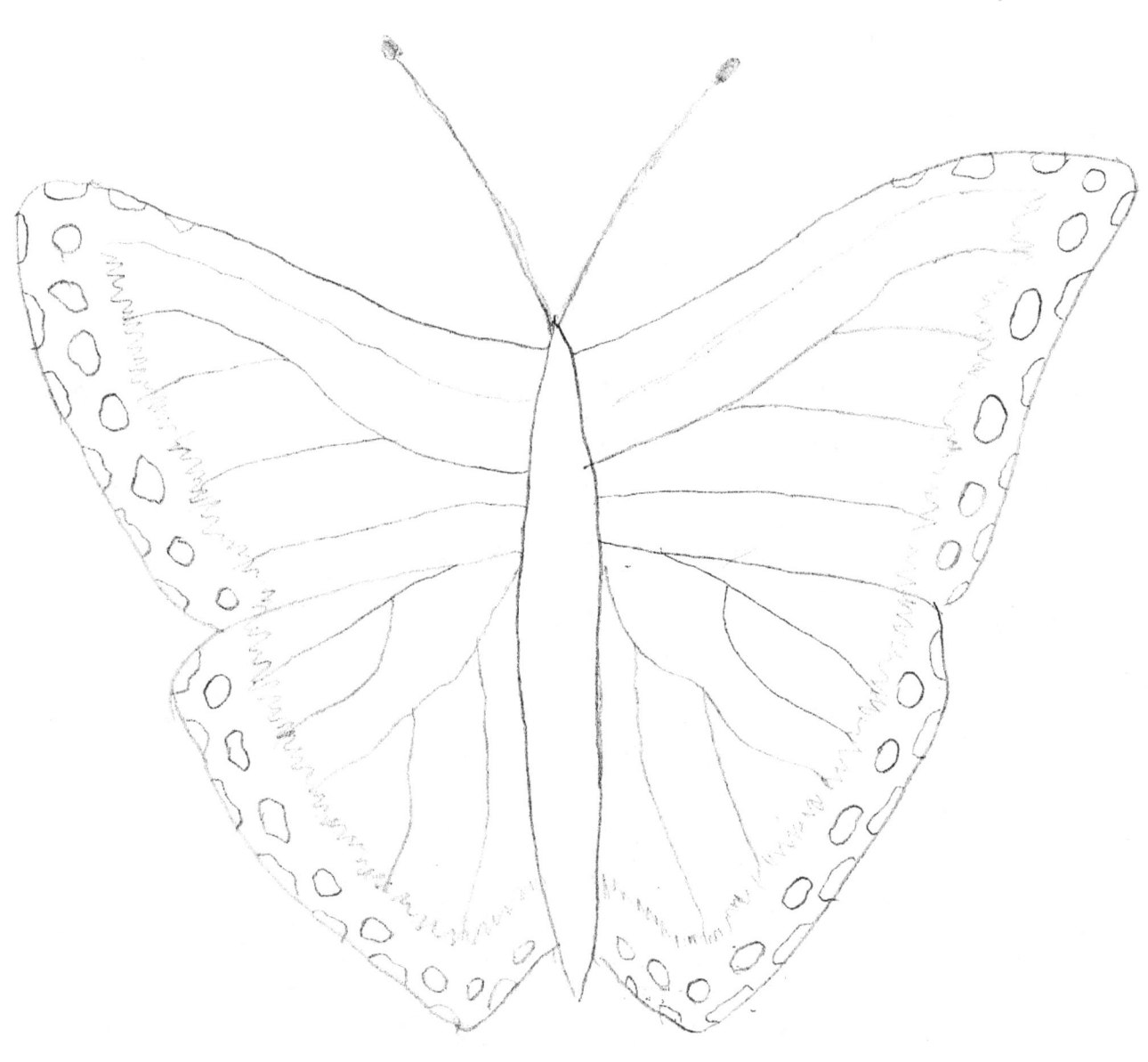

Let's start at shading.

First, shade the body in the middle. I'm using an H pencil for this. In the very middle of the body, create a bit darker area by pressing harder and then press less and less as you shade towards the edges or towards the wings, to make its body look a bit round. So, here, you either press less and less with the same pencil, or you start using a lighter pencil.

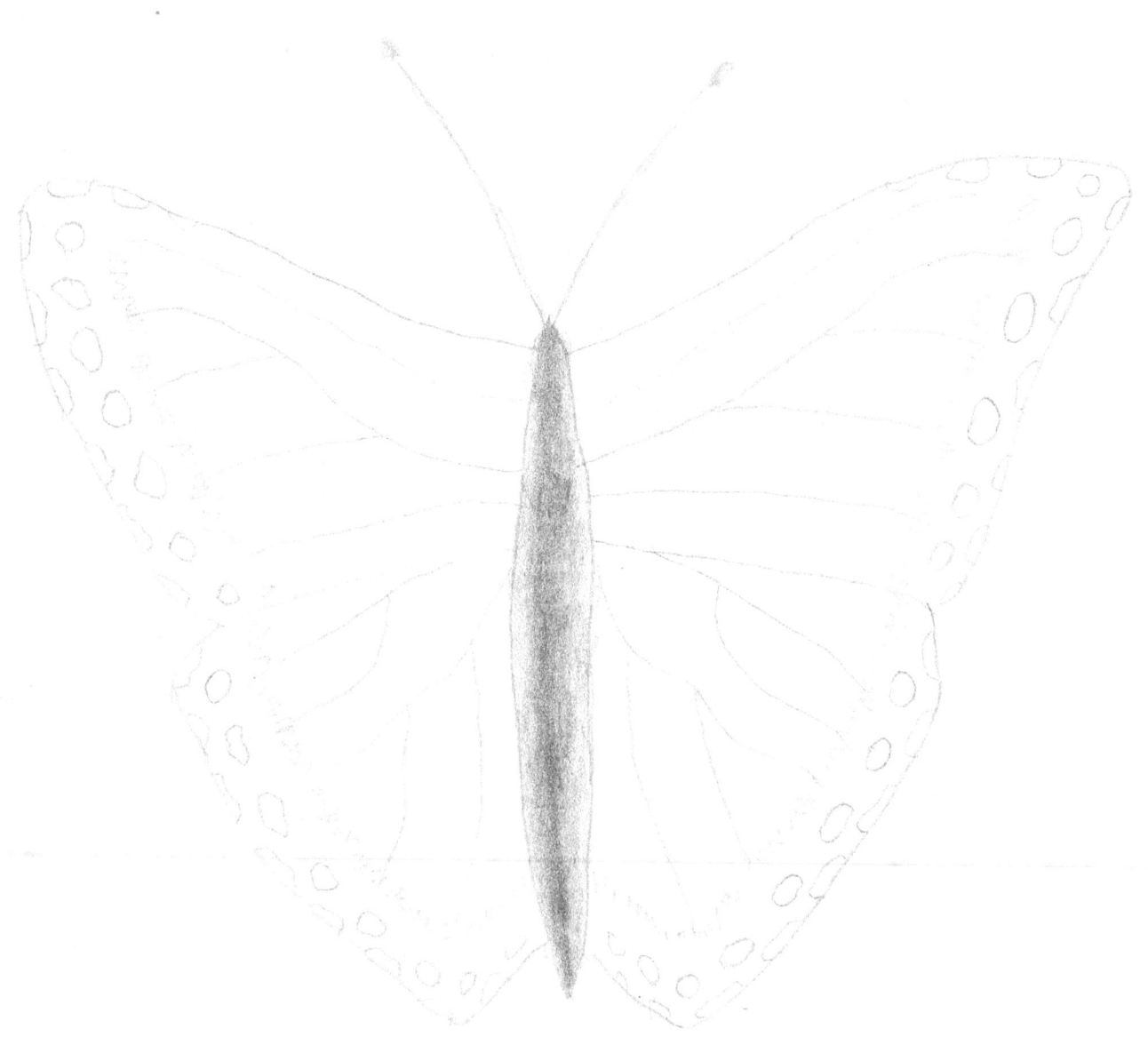

Blend it a bit with a Q-tip to make it look soft, and then you can create some patterns with an HB pencil, something like tiny, horizontal lines, and at random. Also, the head and eyes. Just avoid making it look flat and monotonous and add some randomness. Some patterns can be blended with a blending stump.

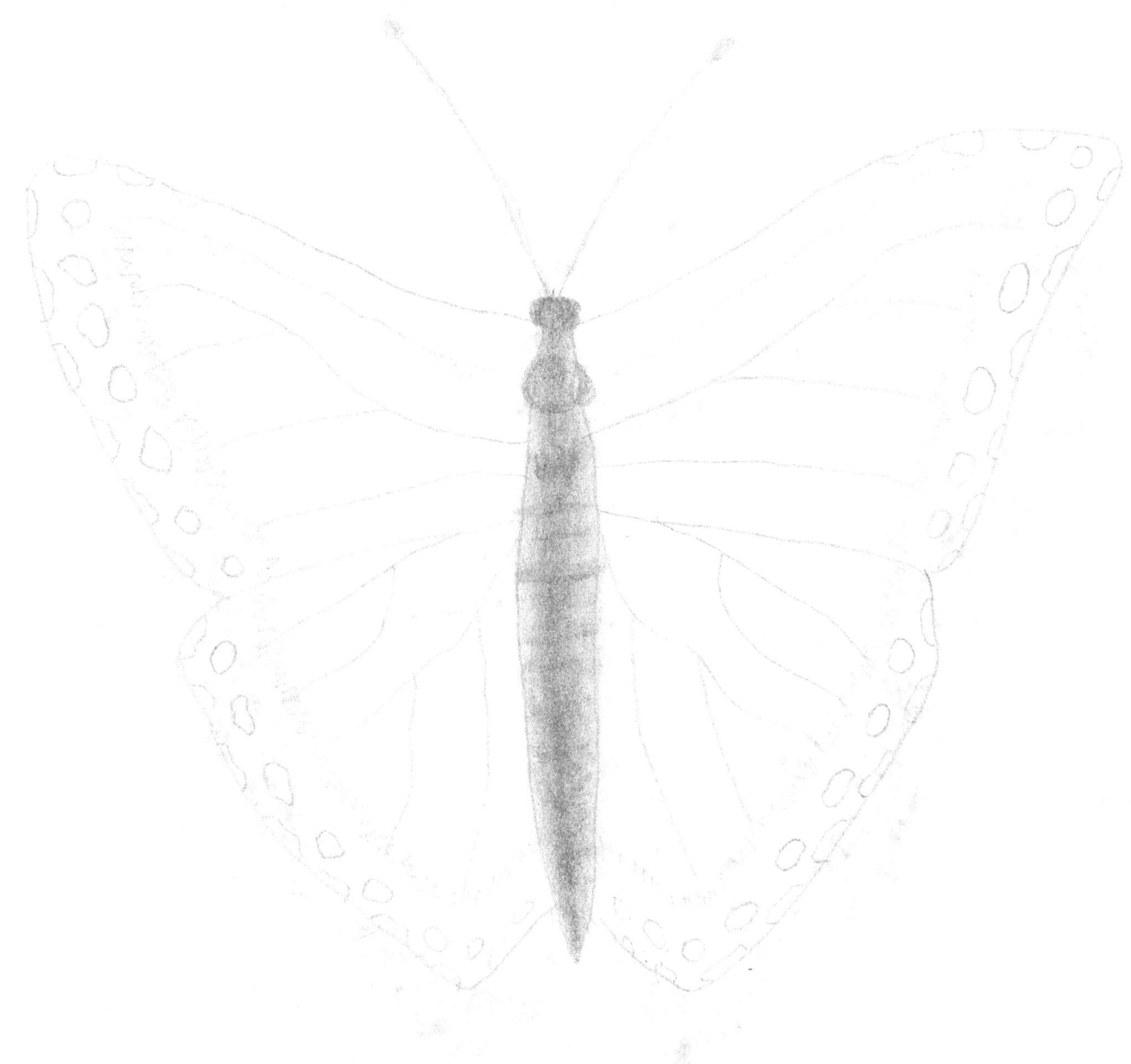

Next, color the edges with a 6B or darker pencil. I use an 8B for the whole step.

As I mentioned before, we have to leave out the white dots and just color around them. Of course, we have to work very carefully next to the edges and next to the white dots and to make the edge between the black and white areas clean and sharp. Press very hard because here you want to create a black color. Here you have to cover everything patiently, and it takes a lot of time.

In this step, you can recreate the shapes of the dots, so when you are drawing around them, you're shaping them, and here you can change their shapes.

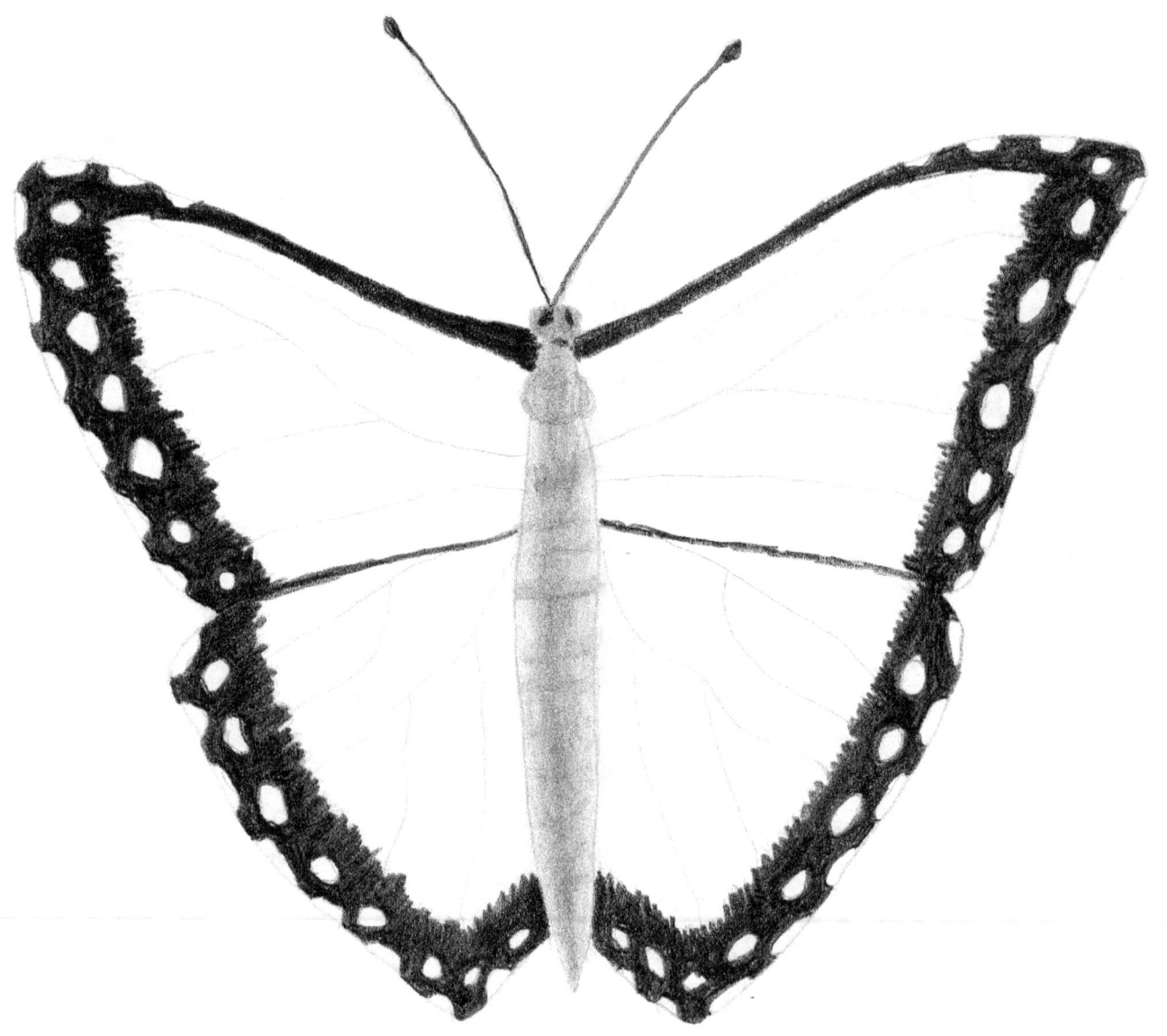

Now we can strengthen the patterns over the wings with a 2B; go over them again and press harder. Then, shade the inner areas of the wings.

I start next to the 8B area using a 2B because I want to make the gradient transition from 8B to a very light pencil. So, start drawing the strokes over the 8B area that you previously drew, pressing harder next to its body and then slightly lift of the pencil as you finish each stroke, a bit further from its body. Study the next image to see what I want to explain. We want to create a smooth gradient because the dark pencil should be continued with the lighter one in the next step. We have to create a bit longer strokes in the upper part, and then to create shorter and shorter lines as we work downwards.

Now you can see that the body is too bright compared to the surrounding area, but we can always go back and darken it later if necessary.

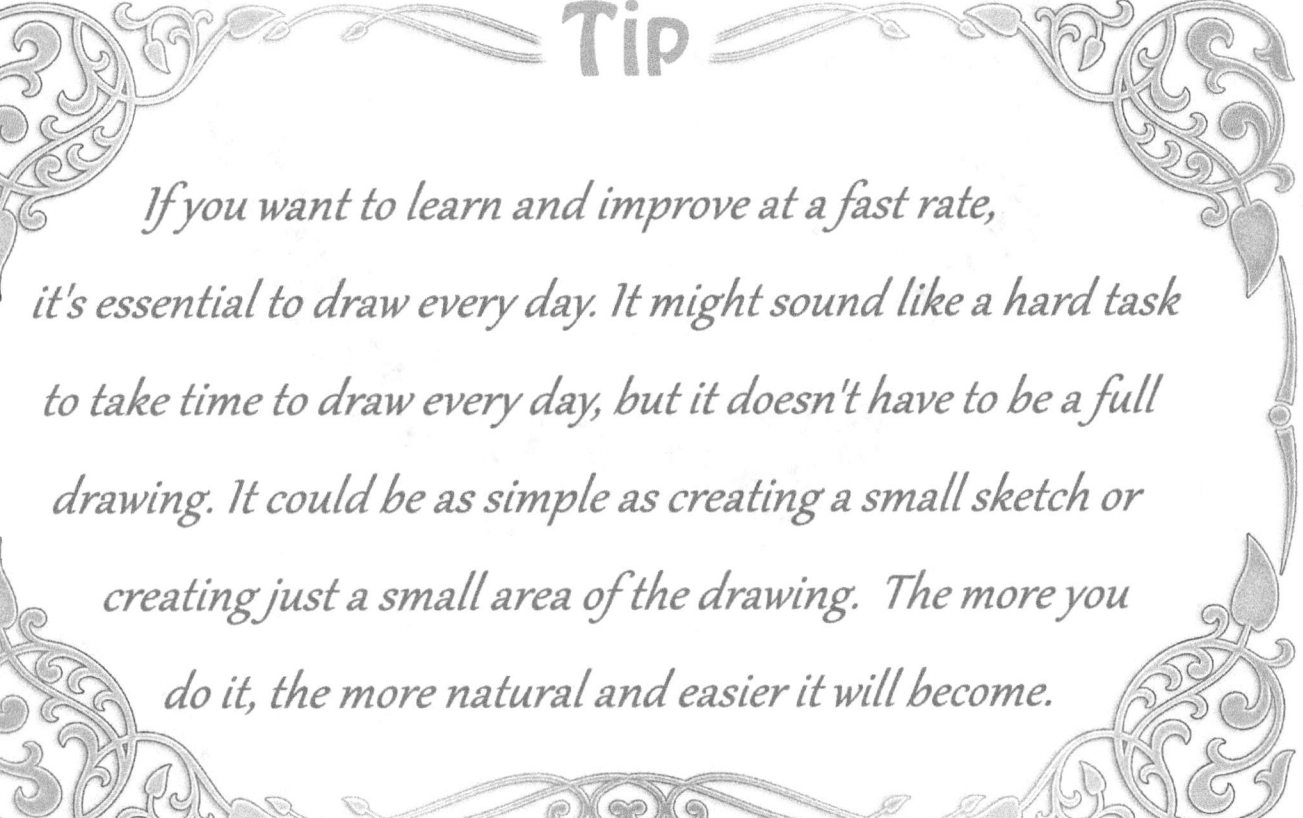

Tip

If you want to learn and improve at a fast rate, it's essential to draw every day. It might sound like a hard task to take time to draw every day, but it doesn't have to be a full drawing. It could be as simple as creating a small sketch or creating just a small area of the drawing. The more you do it, the more natural and easier it will become.

Do the same next to the outer black areas that contain white dots, but here you have to draw very short strokes and make them a bit longer over the lines of the pattern.

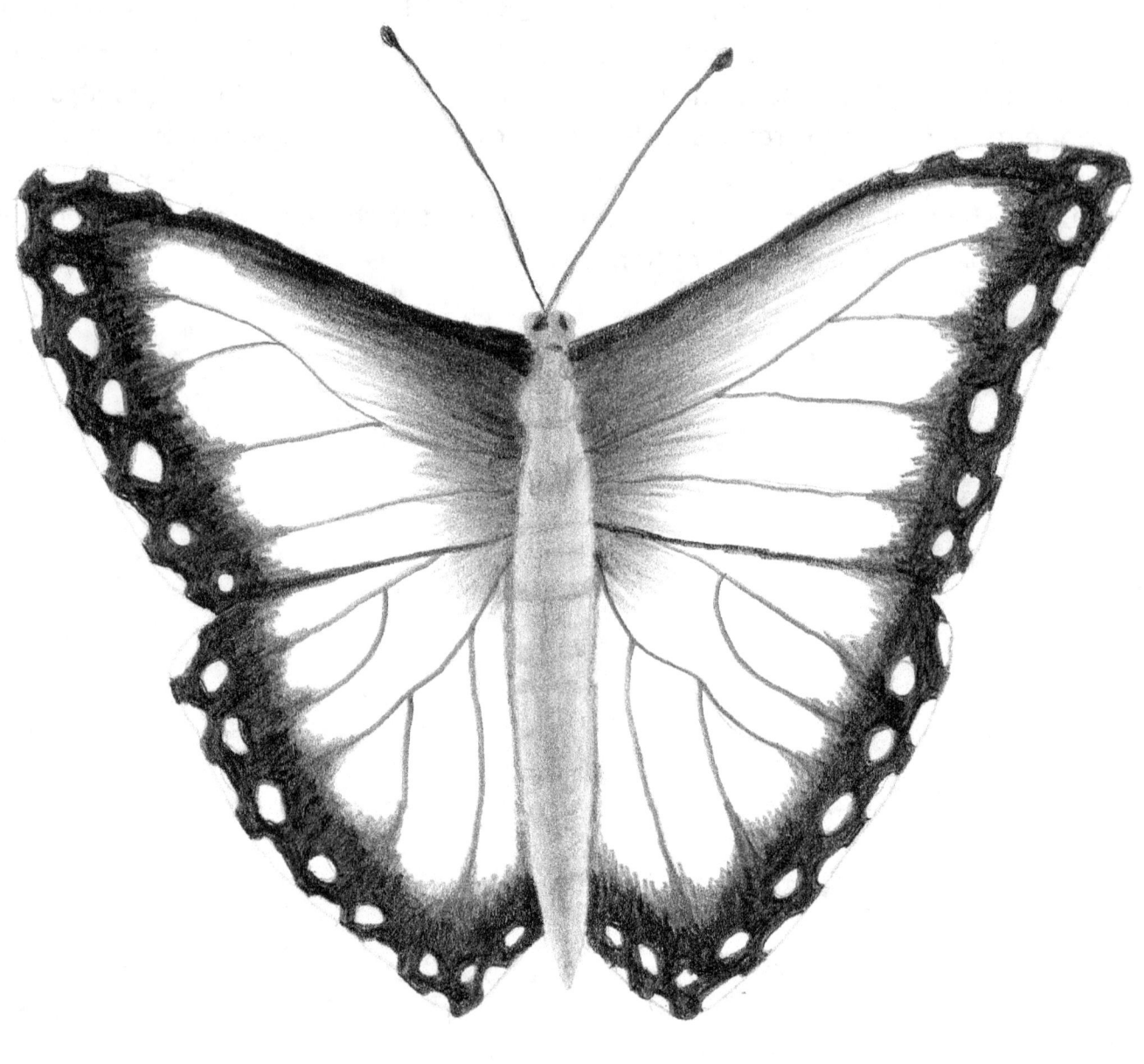

Continue with an HB and go over the previously drawn strokes that you just drew with a 2B and same here: press hard over the 2B strokes and lift off the pencil as you finish each stroke. Do the same from the opposite direction, from this edge that we also shaded with an 8B and after that with the 2B. This step does take a lot of time, and you don't have to do it in one sitting because your hand may hurt.

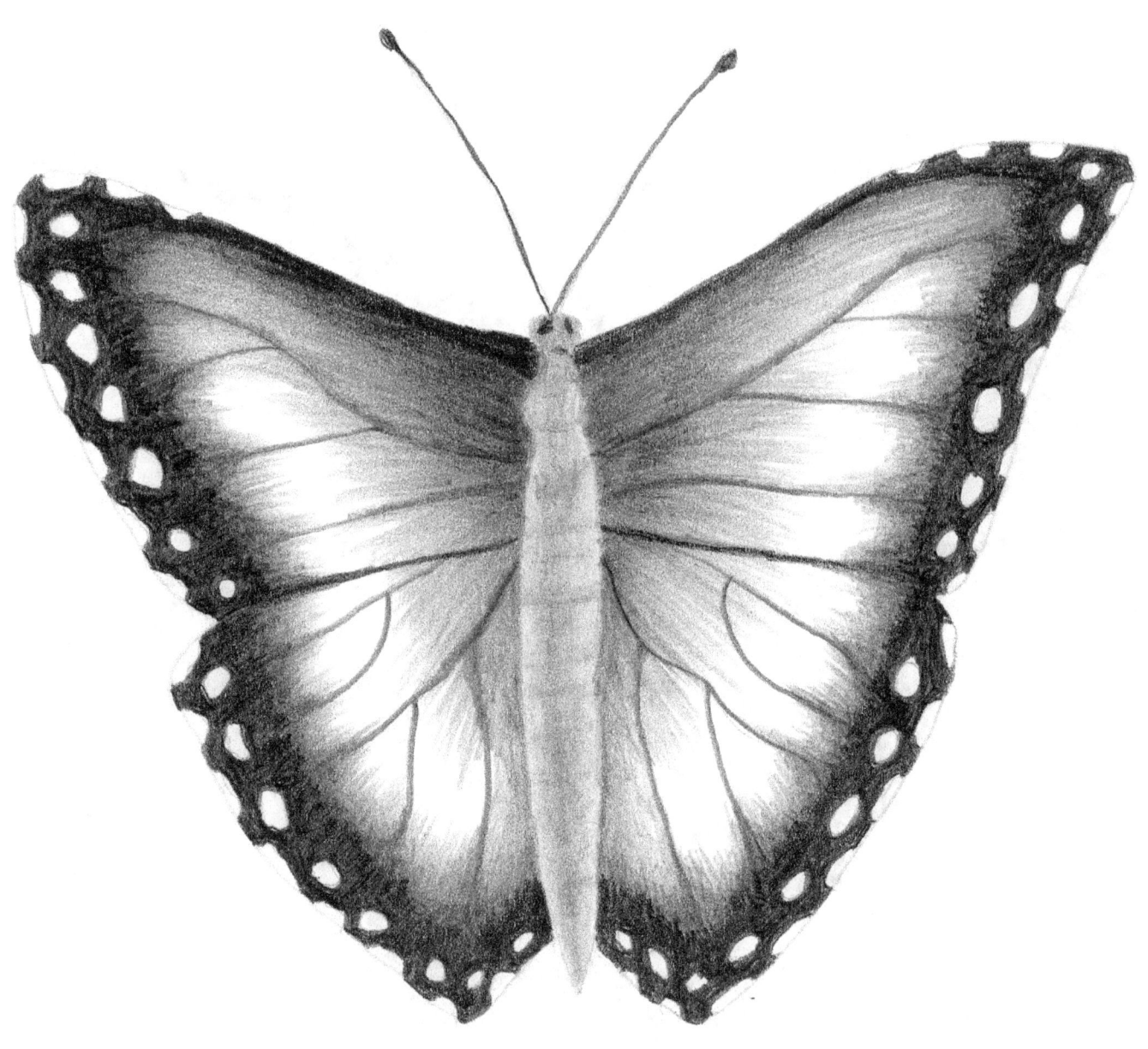

As a continuation, use a 2H for the highlighted parts, actually the parts that we have left uncovered. Go over the previously shaded areas, in the same manner, in the same direction that you did before but with a 2H.

Now you can see that these areas are still pretty highlighted, so they are the brightest parts of the wings except for the white dots.

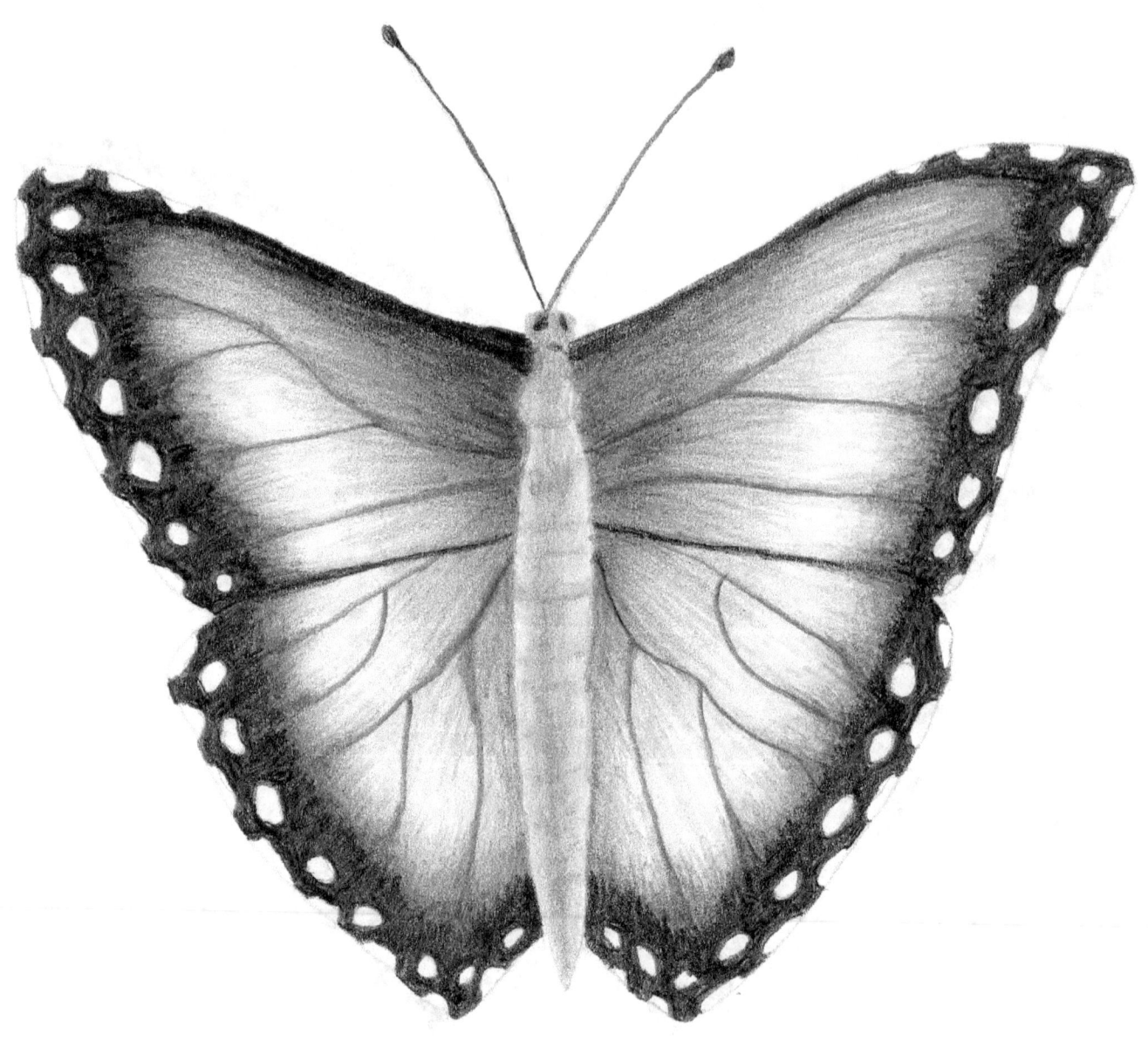

Now we can blend it all carefully with a Q-tip and start over lighter areas and then go towards the darker areas. So, use a clean Q-tip over the lighter areas, and when you get some graphite on its tip, you can apply it over the darker areas, and not in the opposite order. The blending will make the butterfly look soft.

After blending, you'll see whether you need to add more shade.

Also, outline the wings so that the marginal white dots can come to expression because they weren't quite visible; they looked like they belonged to the background. So, separate them from the background by outlining, as shown in the next image. If you accidentally go over these white dots, you can apply a white marker over them and make them white again.

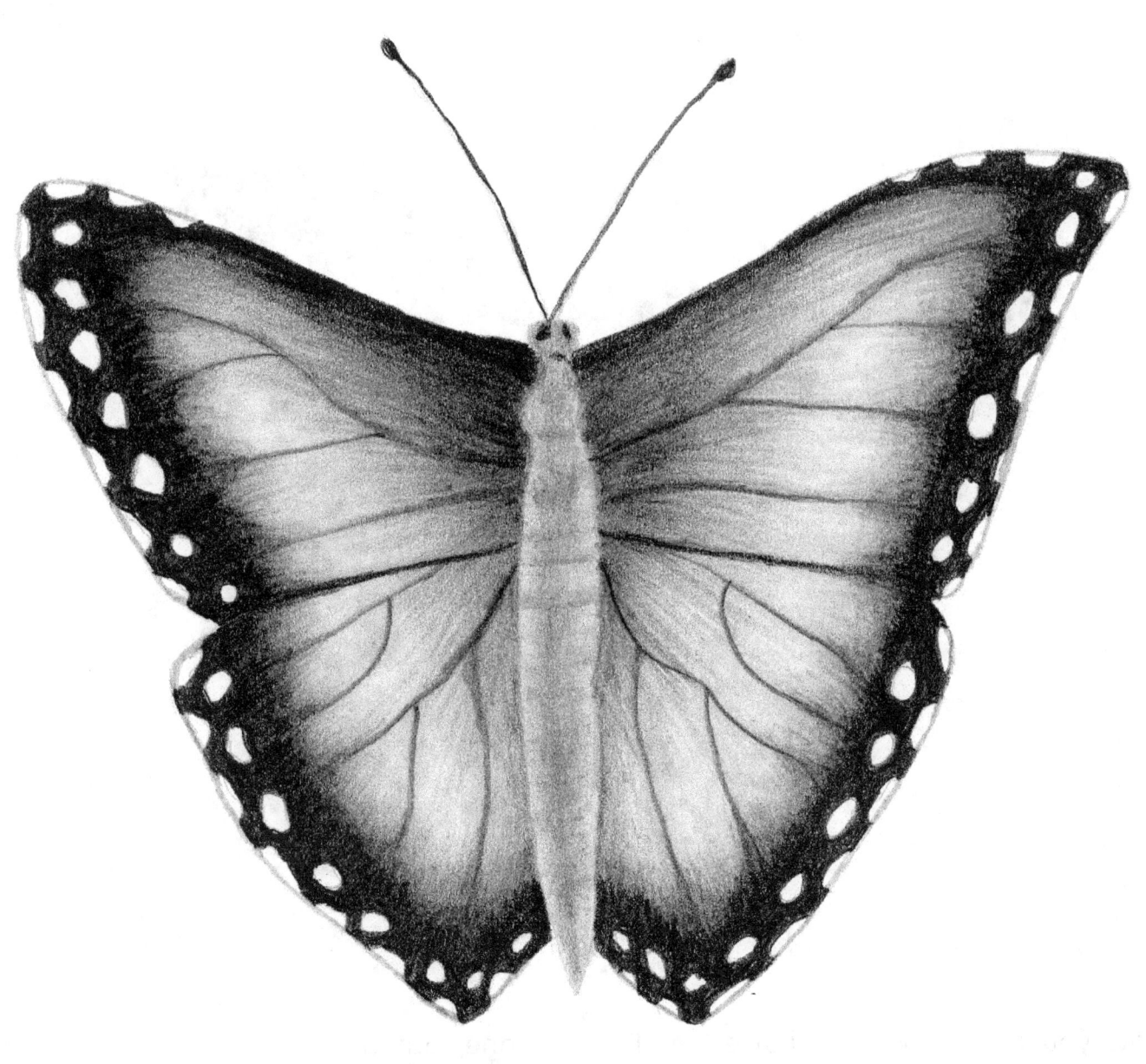

Lastly, create the cast shadow, which will make our butterfly look more 3D. So, the shadow will be cast by the wings over the surface where the butterfly is standing.

I used graphite powder and tissue, and I created the shape similar to the right-wing, as shown in the next image. The upper part can be farther from the butterfly and the lower part closer. I make the shadow cast by the left-wing much smaller so that that wing can appear closer to the surface. Of course, this all also depends on the light source.

As you can see, the cast shadow will enhance the white dots of the wings, and they become more visible. But we can't create the cast shadow all around the butterfly, only over some areas, and it is enough to suggest that all the white dots are the part of the butterfly and not the background.

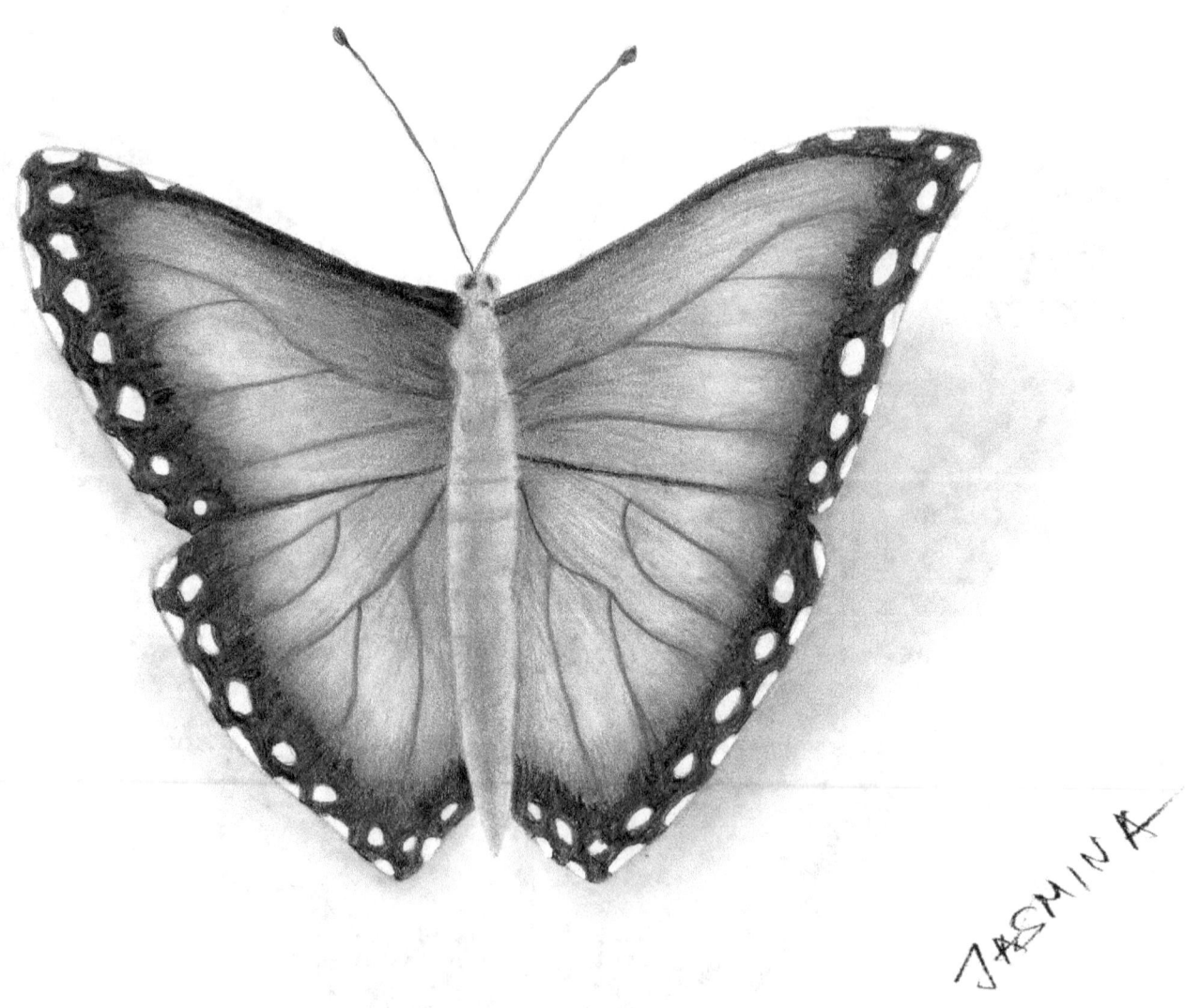

Now you can draw more butterflies like this one, but try it with different patterns, different shapes, and different cast shadows.

WATER DROPLETS

Let's draw water droplets next.
As a first step, shade the whole sheet of paper with graphite powder completely before you start shading and drawing the droplets. Pour a bit of graphite powder on a separate piece of paper, wrap a tissue around your finger and dip it into the graphite powder. Then spread it over the paper with horizontal movements.

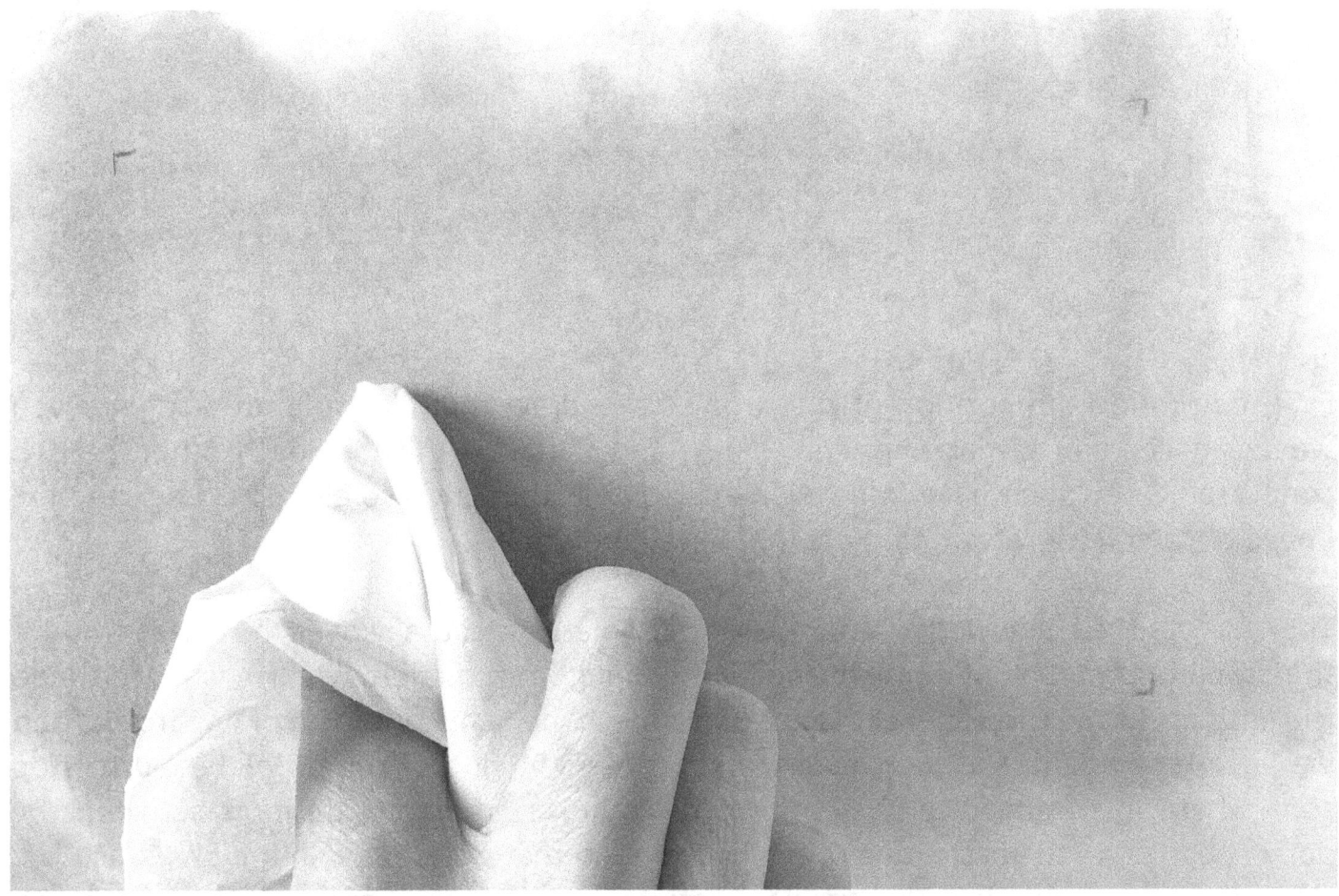

After that, you can also use vertical or even circular motions, press very hard, and try to create the even texture for the background. In the next image, you can see my paper sheet with the graphite spread over it.

First, determine the position of the droplets, so draw them at random wherever you want: smaller and bigger ones, tiny ones, and then two next to each other, or two connected. They don't have to be all in a circular shape, but also elliptic. Study the next image to see the variety of droplets that I have drawn.

Then, create the shadowed areas under the droplets, or actually over the surface where the droplets are found. If our light source is coming from the left side, we want to shade the left part of the droplets next to the side where the light source is coming from. Then we have to shade less as we shade towards the right side of the droplets and to stop somewhere in the middle. So, we have to create a gradient transition between the darkest parts and the basic tone of the background that we created in the previous step. Here also, we should use the circular motions because we want to create a smooth texture. For this step, I'm using a B pencil but you can use an HB or an F pencil, but darker than a B pencil is not good for this.

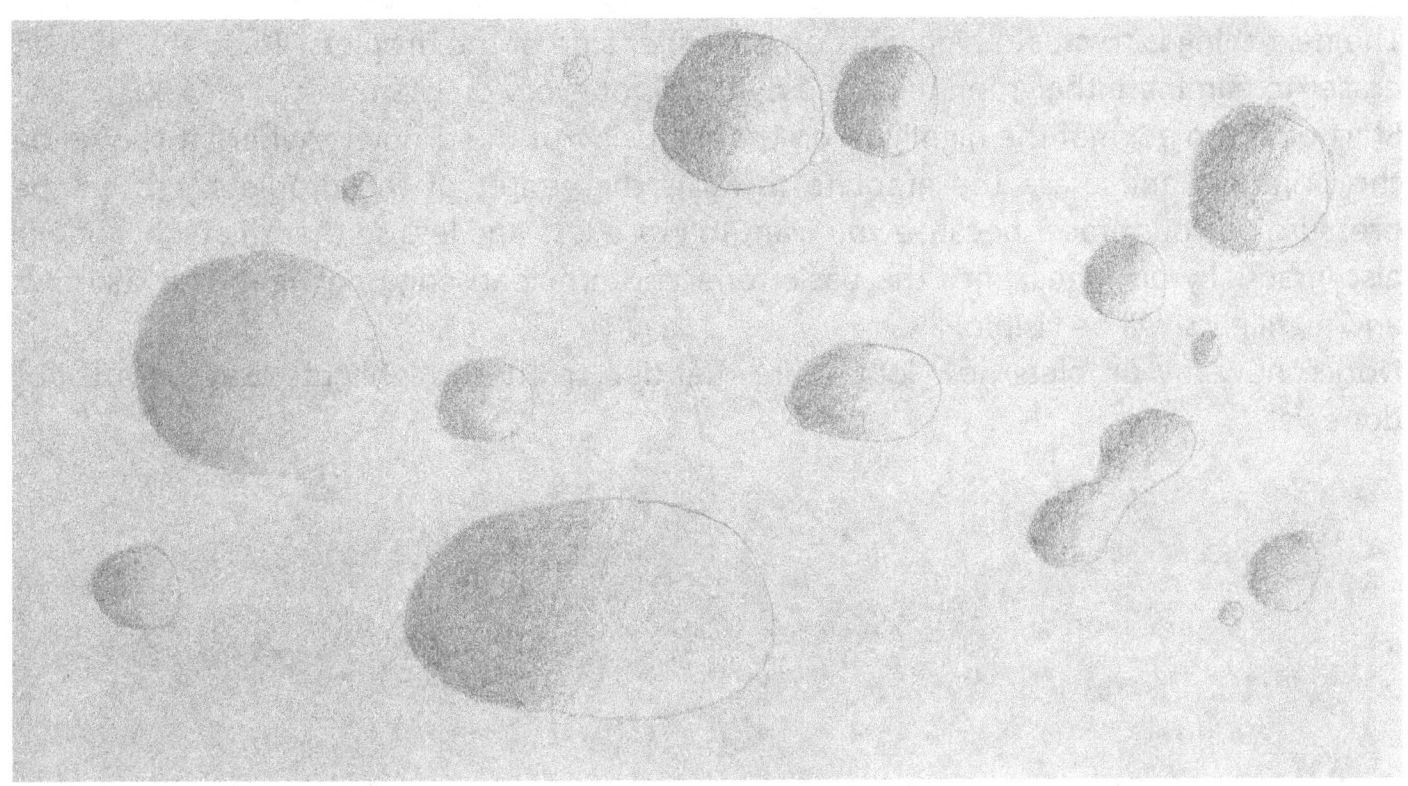

Now we can blend it all with a blending stump. We can use a blending stump to blend the smaller ones and a Q-tip to blend the bigger ones. These areas should be as smooth as possible, so keep on blending until you create a smooth texture.

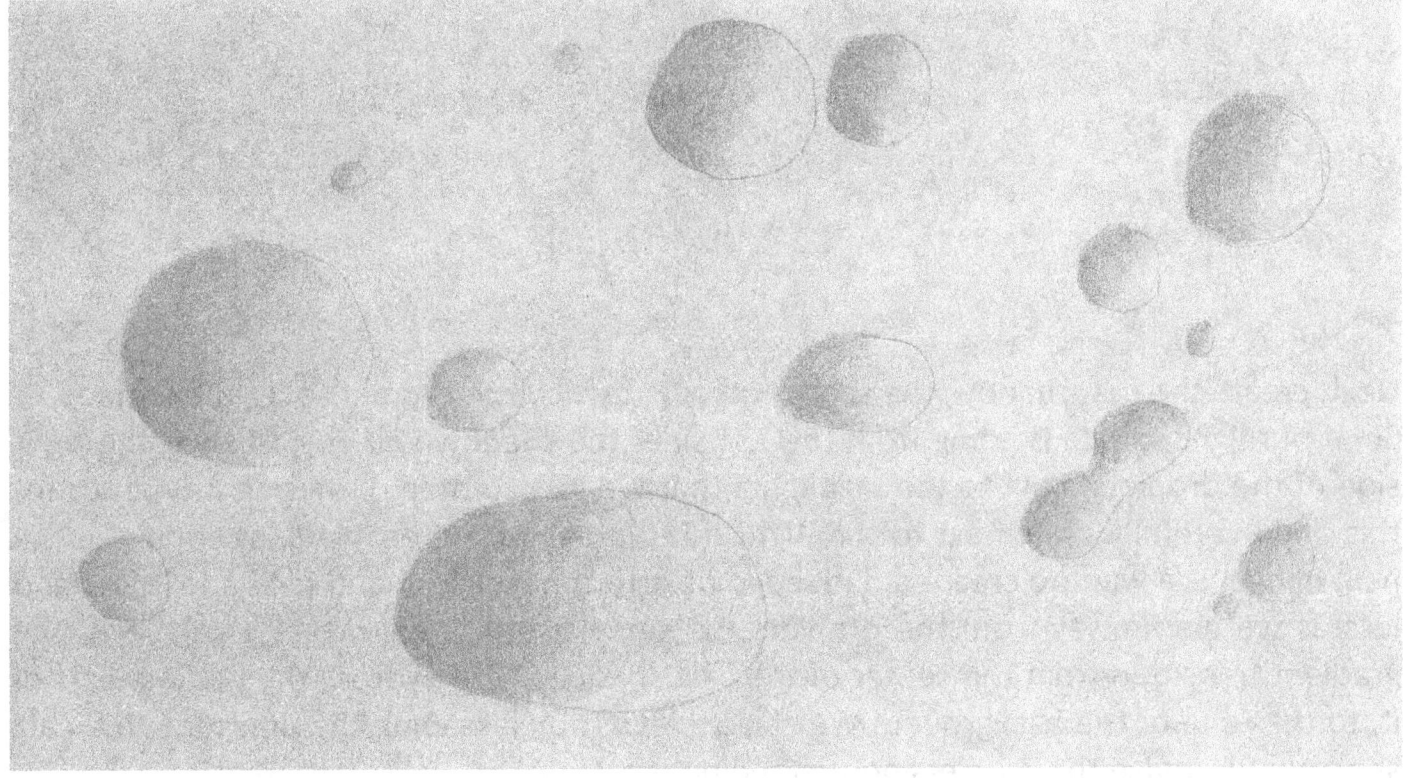

The next thing is to create highlights on the other side of the droplets. To do this, use an eraser to eliminate the graphite on the right side of every droplet.

Start over the edge of the highlight, on the right side of the droplets, where it should be the brightest and erase the graphite towards the center of the droplets. Lessen the pressure on your eraser because you want to erase less and less so that the highlight will also gradually disappear into the basic tone and no clean edge between the shadows and highlights will be visible.

Notice how my droplets now look more real due to these highlights. But we are not done yet.

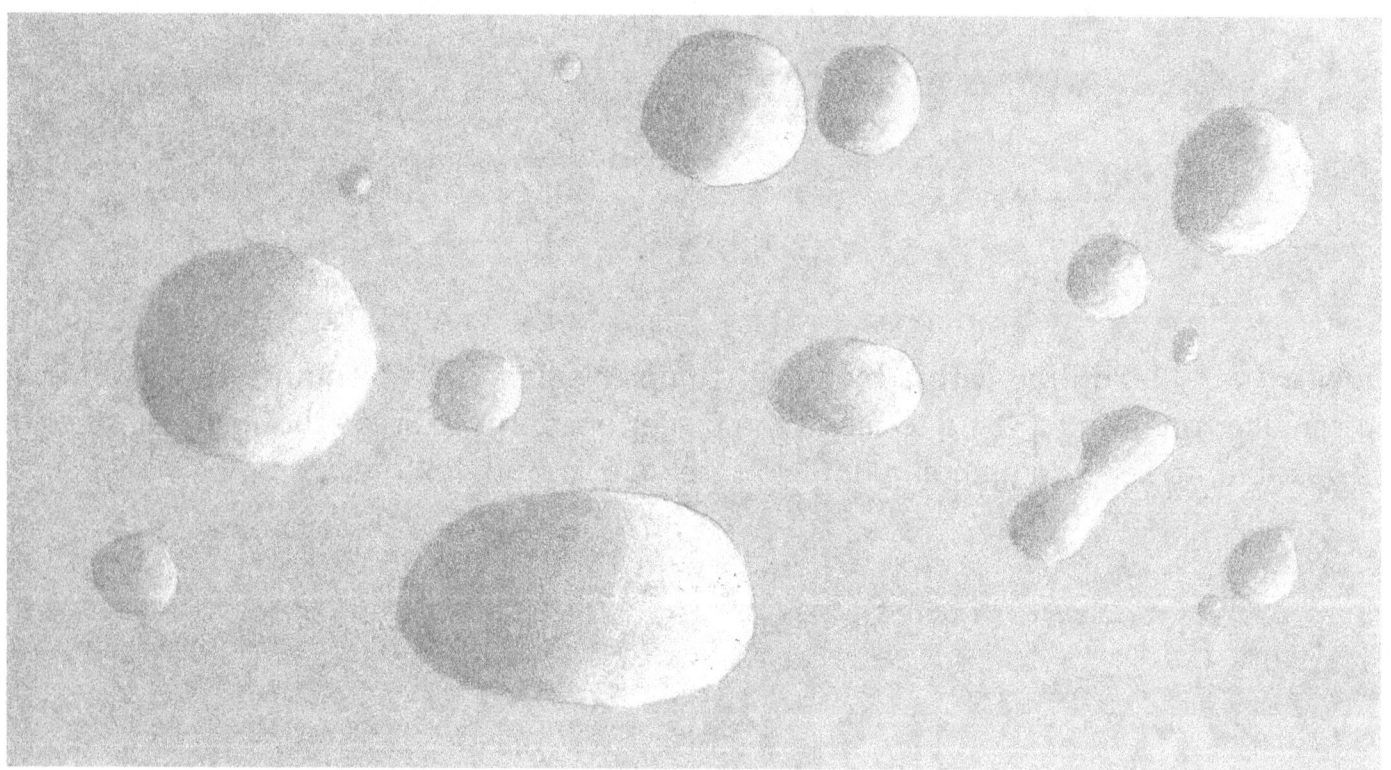

Next, create the cast shadow, the shadow that is cast by the droplets over the surface.

So, if our light source is going from the left side, the shadow will be cast over the right side of the droplets, next to the highlights that we just created. I'm using a B pencil for this and I carefully draw next to the highlighted areas of the droplets, as shown in the next image. We want to create a dark edge next to the highlight and to shade it less and less as we work away from the droplets. So, here also it is important to achieve that gradient transition from the center of the cast shadow, namely from the darkest part of it, to the tone of the background. We can achieve it by lessening the pressure. The cast shadows will make the droplets pop on the paper.

When you are done with them all, blend them with a blending stump and do it carefully next to the edge of the droplets because the edge between the highlight of the droplet and the cast shadow has to be clean and of course the cast shadow should be the darkest right next to the droplets. I use a B pencil all the time but you can use a B pencil next to the droplet and then start using an HB farther from the droplet, and then make the outer edges of the cast shadow with a 2H. But you can also learn to change the pressure on your pencil and to achieve a smooth gradation containing a lot of values with a single pencil.

Now you can see that the droplets look three-dimensional after the cast shadows are added and the highlights seem to be brighter because the dark value of the cast shadow will enhance the highlight.

Don't forget the rule of thumb that the bigger droplets will cast a bigger shadow and they will spread wider than the shadows cast by the small droplets.

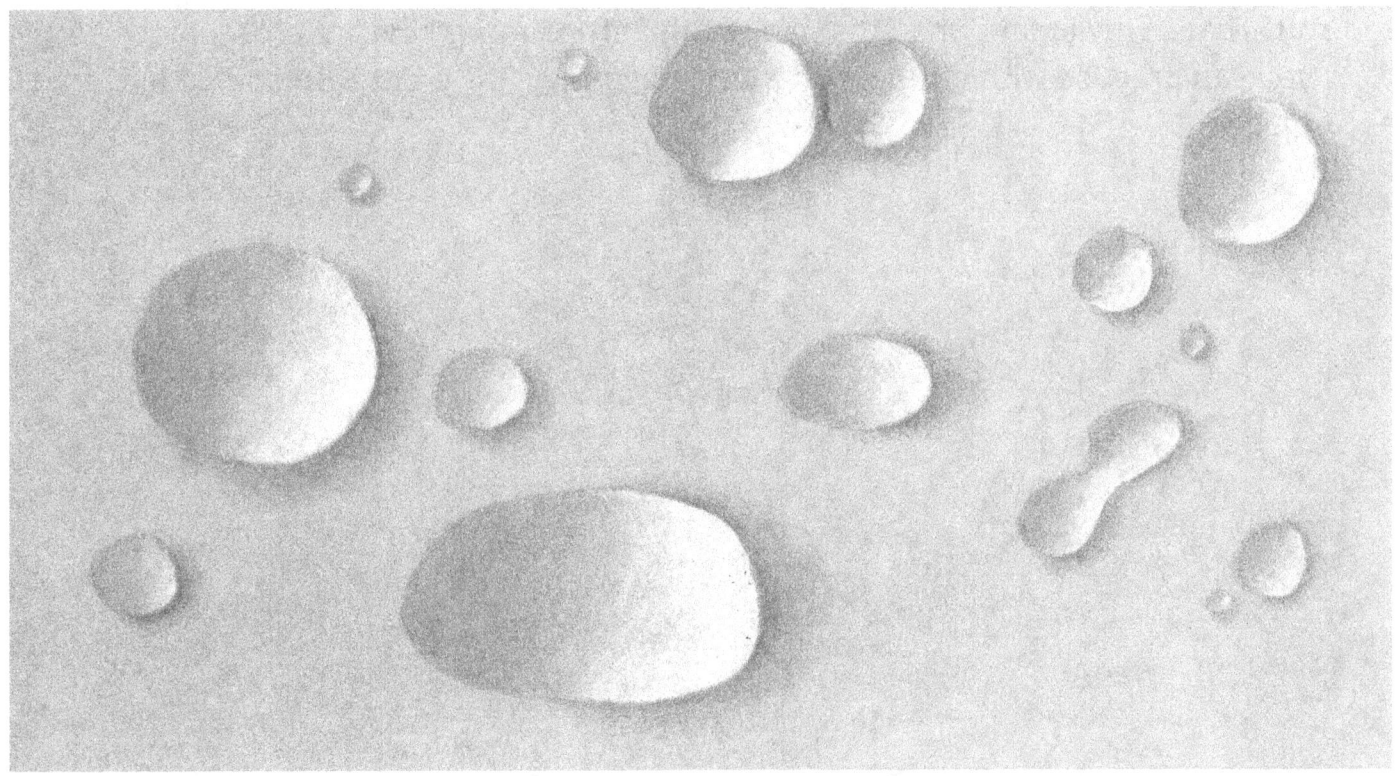

Now we can create the second kind of highlights, the reflected light which will indicate some light sources that are reflecting over the droplets. If we have created the droplets and the cast shadows as if our light source is coming from the left side, we have to create the reflected lights over the left sides of the droplets, namely the shadowed areas that we created in the right after determining the position of the droplets.

We can either make the reflected lights by cleaning the graphite with an eraser, or we can draw them with a white ink gel pen or a marker.

If you try to do that with an eraser, particularly a kneaded eraser, you will see that you can't create a bright area, but we need a white tone here. We can even try with an electric eraser which actually can erase much more and easier, yet it won't make the areas white again. That's why we can get some help from a white, opaque medium. I used a white marker by Uni posca, 0.9-1.3 for larger droplets, and a pin type 0.7 mm for the small droplets. I have applied 2-3 dots over each droplet. Analyze the next image before you start doing it. Notice how the droplets look shiny and wet now.

Lastly, add some glossy effects and for that use a ruler and a mechanical eraser. Place the ruler with its edge over one of the reflected lights (a white dot) and create a line from the center of the reflected light outwards, with an eraser, with a quick, confident movement. Then place the ruler crosswise and do the same. See the next picture to note where I have created these lines.

The kneaded eraser is not really good for this, I mean it won't erase enough because it is too soft. That's why I mentioned that it's worth getting more kinds of erasers.

Now you can practice with different shapes, imagining a different light source and shade accordingly.

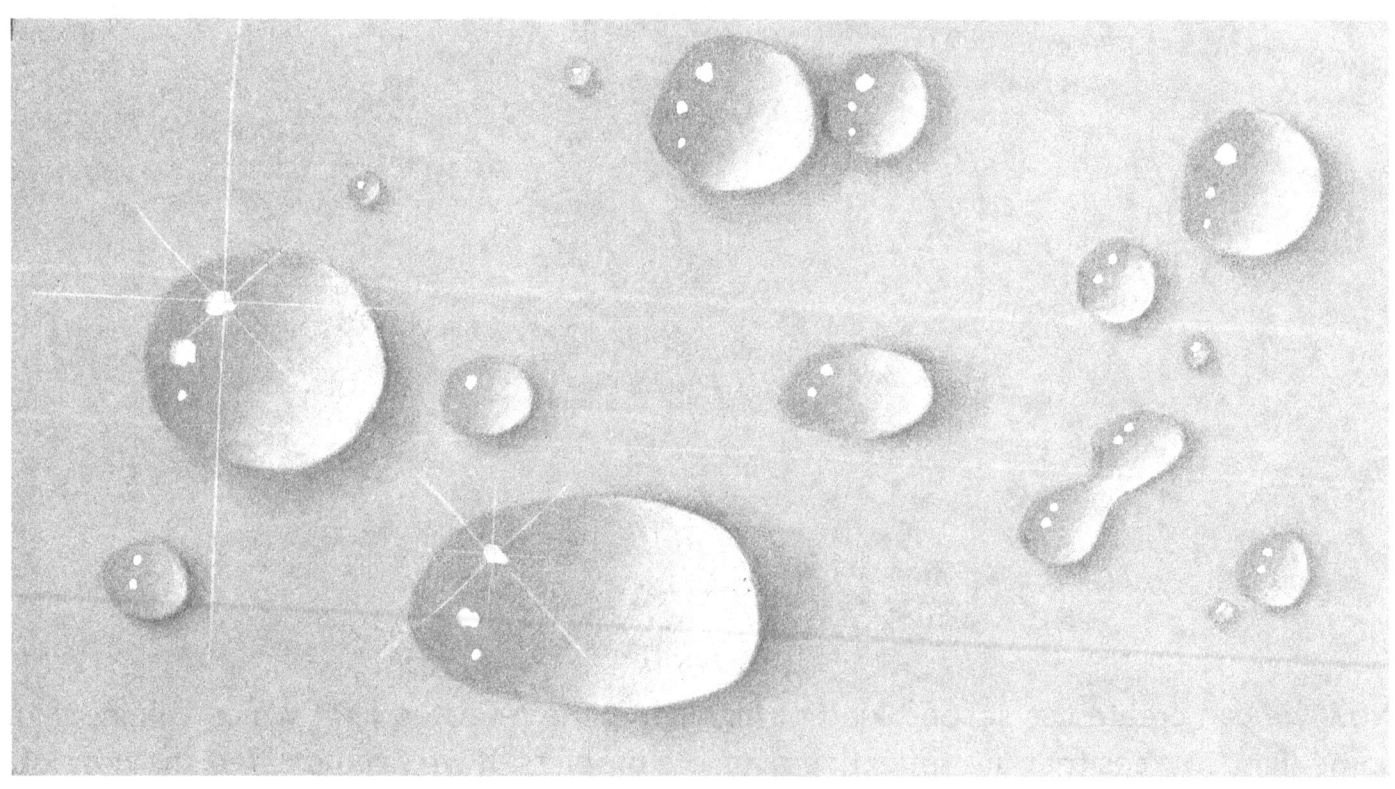

A RUBIK'S CUBE

Next, let's draw a Rubik's Cube. For sketching it, we will have to do some math and geometry. Start with a vertical line in the middle of your paper to create the edge between the right and left sides, or so-called faces. I draw on A4 paper format (210 x 297 mm -- 8.3 x 11.7 in), and my line in the middle is 6.5 cm (2.5") long. Then we have to draw two more lines on the left and the right sides to determine the edges of the cube and to place them much higher them the midline. Since the line in the middle is 6.5 cm (2.5") long, these two can be 5.5 cm (2.2"). I'm using a B pencil for sketching it, but you can use an HB or any other pencil.

Let's connect the ends of these lines as shown in the next image, and we will get two sides of the Rubik's Cube.

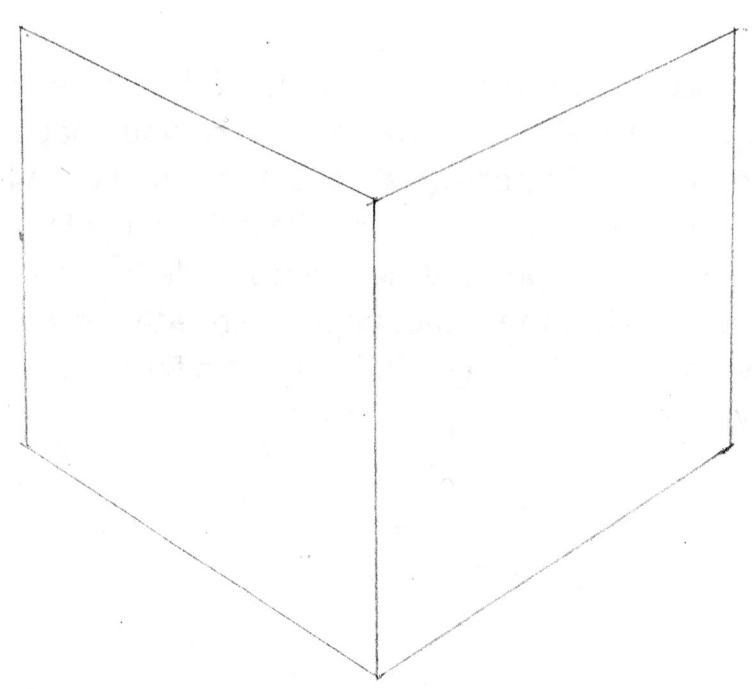

Tip

A drawing where you only use similar tones (close to each other on the hardness scale) will look flat, lifeless and won't get anyone's attention. Include as many values to your drawings as possible. All the tones should be found in your artwork: from deepest black to pure white.

Now we only have to determine the position of the upper face. To determine the top corner, where the two upper edges will meet proportionally we have to place our ruler over the line in the middle and to mark the line above the upper plane; don't draw over this area because we're going to use a very light pencil and it would be visible even if we erase it, it will damage the paper. In the next image, I have placed a dashed line digitally which shouldn't be drawn, only the tiny, vertical line above it (in a circle).

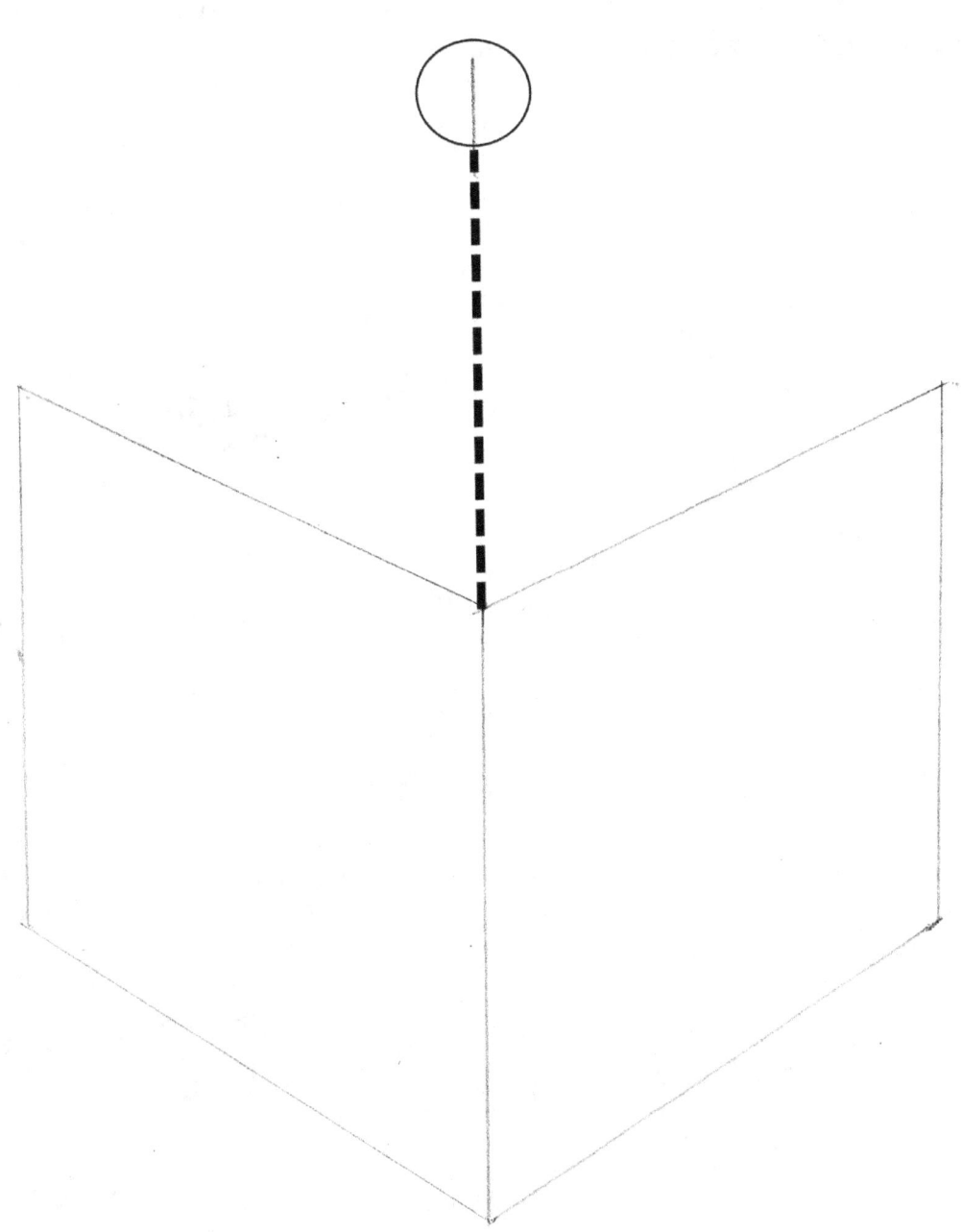

The next thing is to determine the point where the two upper lines of the upper face will meet. The line between the side faces and top faces in my case is 5.2 cm (2.0"). I want to create a little bit shorter lines so that the edges or these sides can appear closer to the viewer's eye. We have to take the measure with our drawing compass as shown in the following diagram, and keeping the needle in the same place, reduce the distance between the needle and the pencil lead to 5.0 cm (1.9") and mark over the tiny line that we created in the previous step. Do not draw the line that I marked with the dashed line yet because we are not sure where it should be placed. Do the same on the left side and you will get the crosspoint of these two lines.

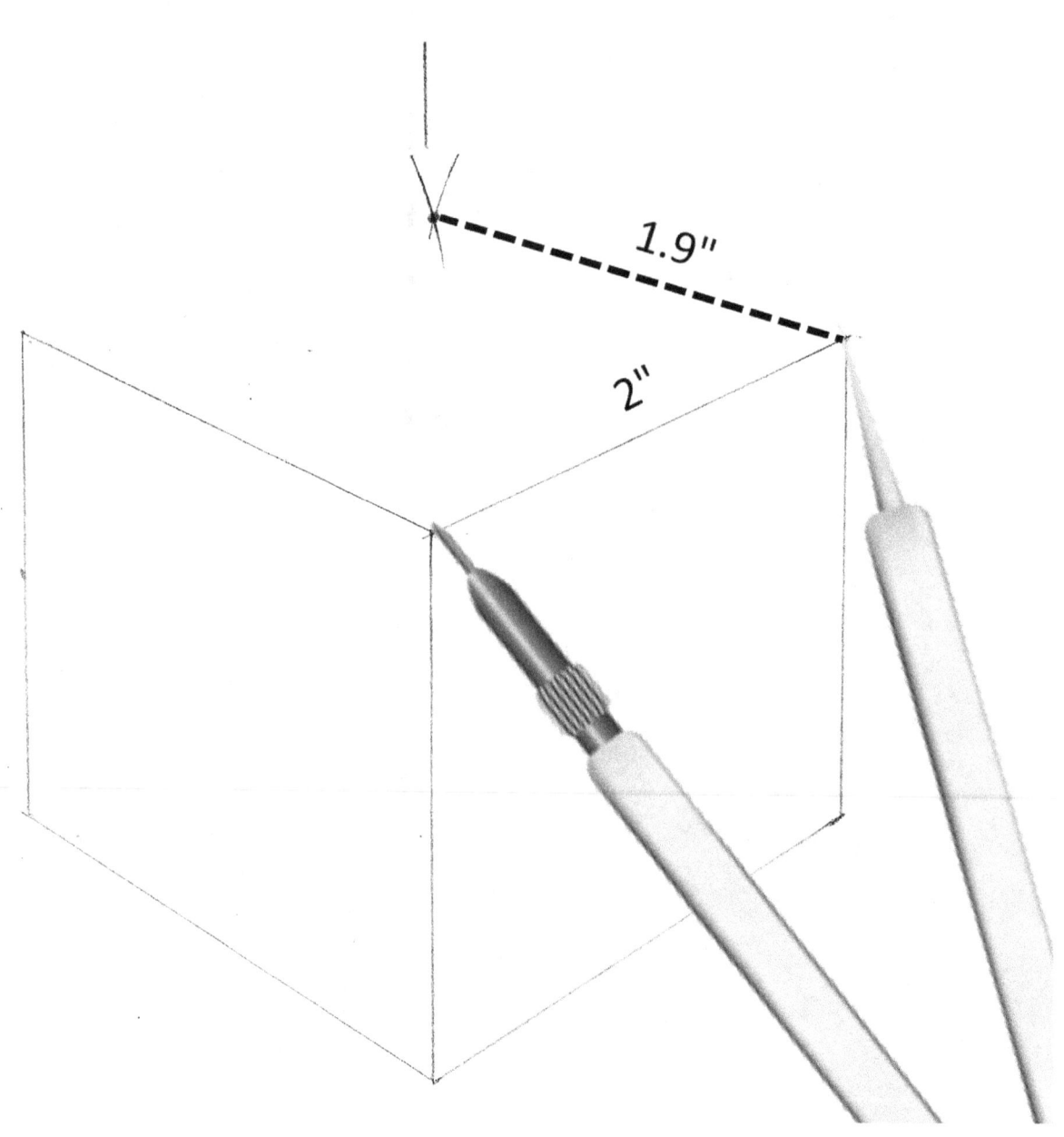

Since we have our crosspoint where all those tiny, marked lines meet, we can create the two upper lines. Just connect the left and the right corners with it, and erase all the tiny lines that are not part of the Rubik's cube.

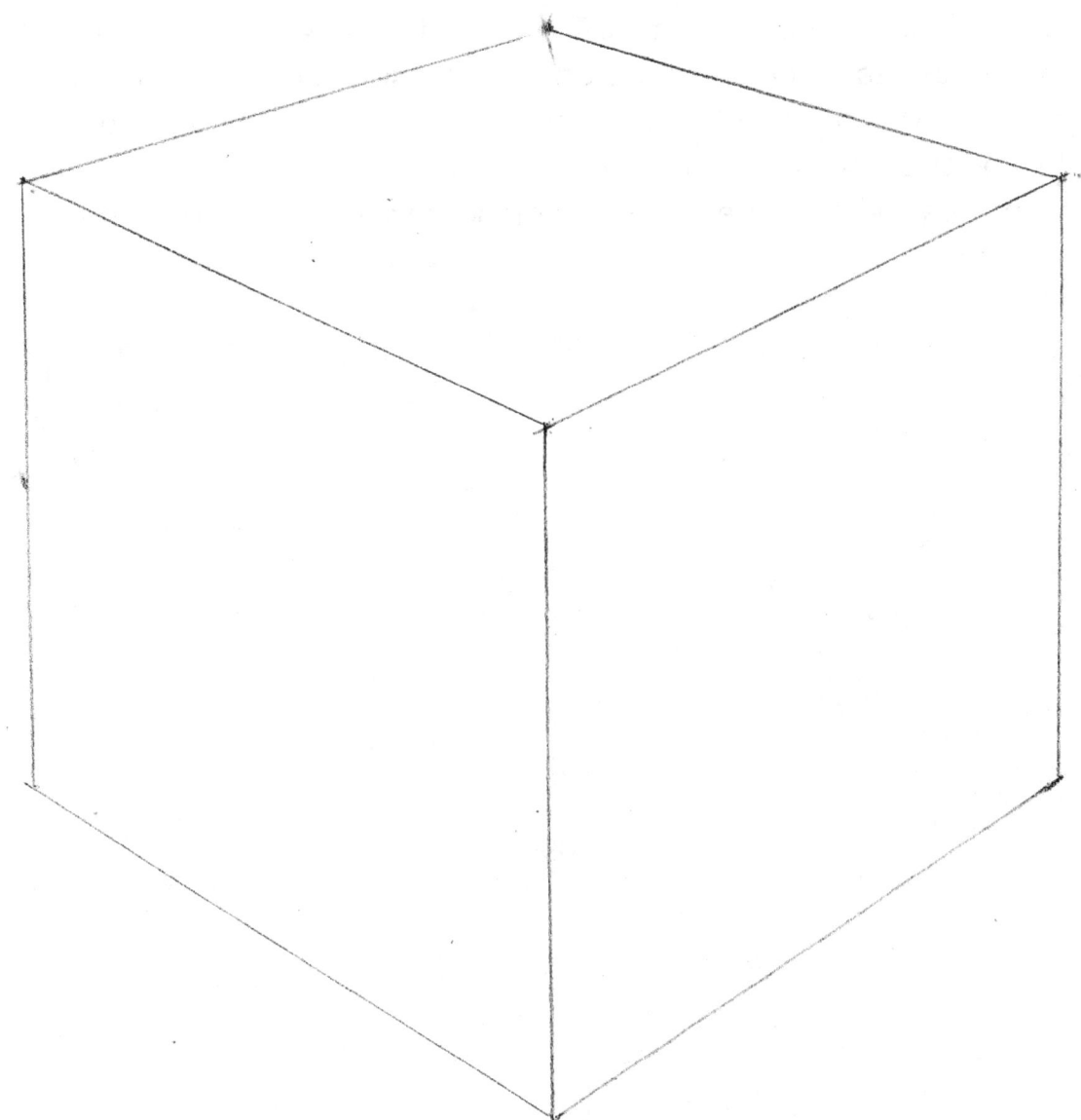

Now we have to create the nine parts of each face of the Rubik's Cube. If the height of the vertical line in the middle is 6.5 cm (2.5"), the upper squares have to be the longest, so mark 2.4 cm (1.0") and then for the next line 2.1 cm (0.8") so it has to be less than the upper one. Then we have 1.9 cm (0.75") for the lowest row. Next, mark the lines between the rows on the vertical lines on the left and the right sides. The height of that line is 5.5 cm (2.2"), so we have to mark the first upper square 2.1 cm (0.8"), the lower line of the mid-row at 1.9 cm (0.75"), so that we have left 1.6 cm (0.6").

Lastly, we have to mark the position of the vertical lines between the squares. They have to be the widest next to the vertical line in the middle and they have to be smaller and smaller towards the left and the right edges of the Rubik's cube. So, let's mark it at 2.1 cm (0.8") on both sides, then 1.9 cm (0.75") and the marginal column is 1.7 cm (0.6") wide. You don't have to mark the upper edge of the side faces but you lean the bottom part of your ruler to another ruler and move it to draw lines parallel to the one in the very middle, and this is what we will do in the next step.
Study these images and measurements and mark the same areas to connect the lines.

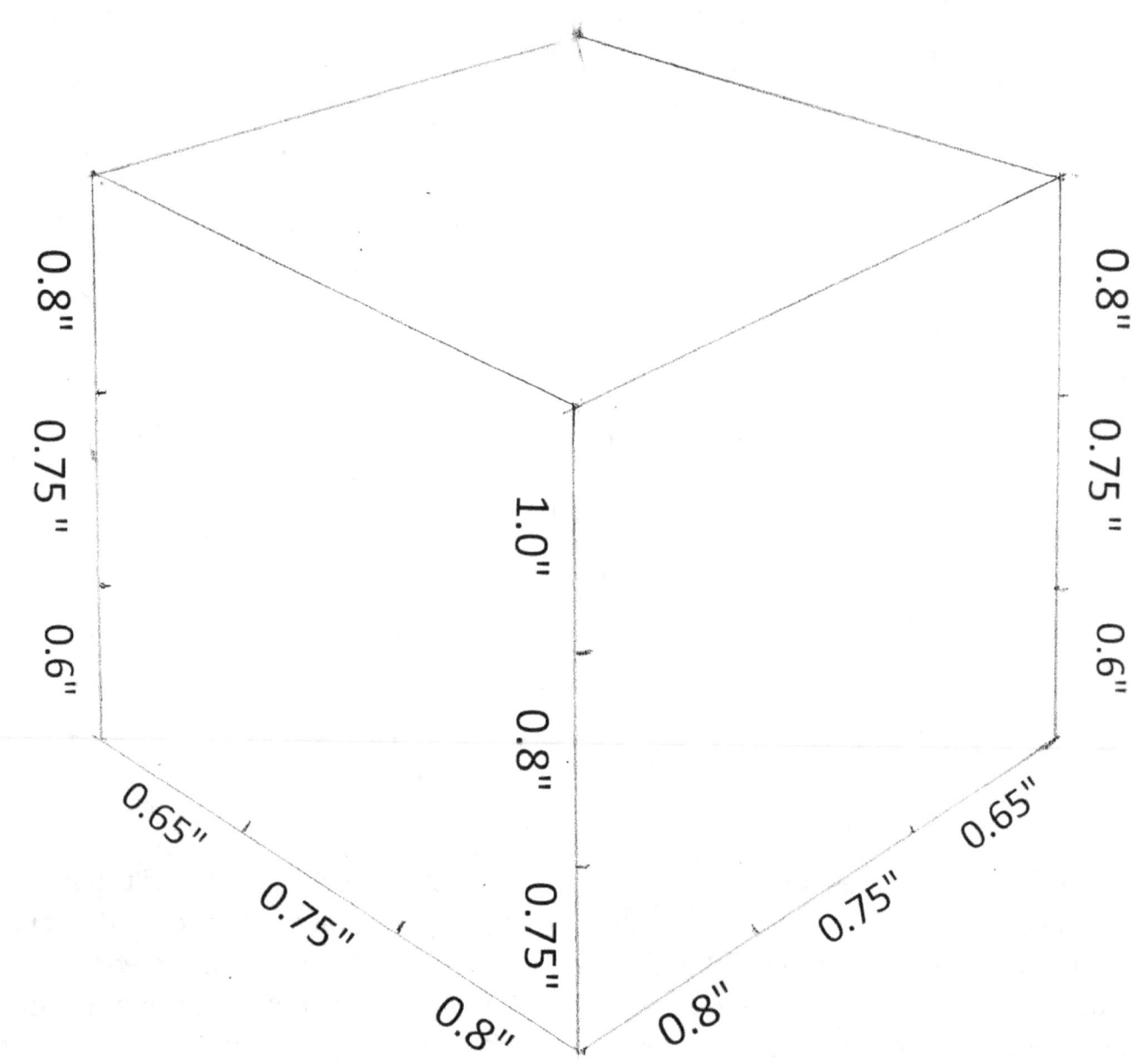

Connect these marked lines to separate the left and the right sides into nine squares. Now you can see that these tiny squares are not squares from this point of view, but they are rhomboids. Also, we're going to make very thick lines over these, but only after we have shaded all the sections.

I used a 2B to create these lines and I pressed hard because I want to have them visible under the layers of graphite. After all, we are going to shade over them. But we are not done yet here. We have to split the upper face into nine sections. For that, we already have the starting points of the squares from the upper sides.

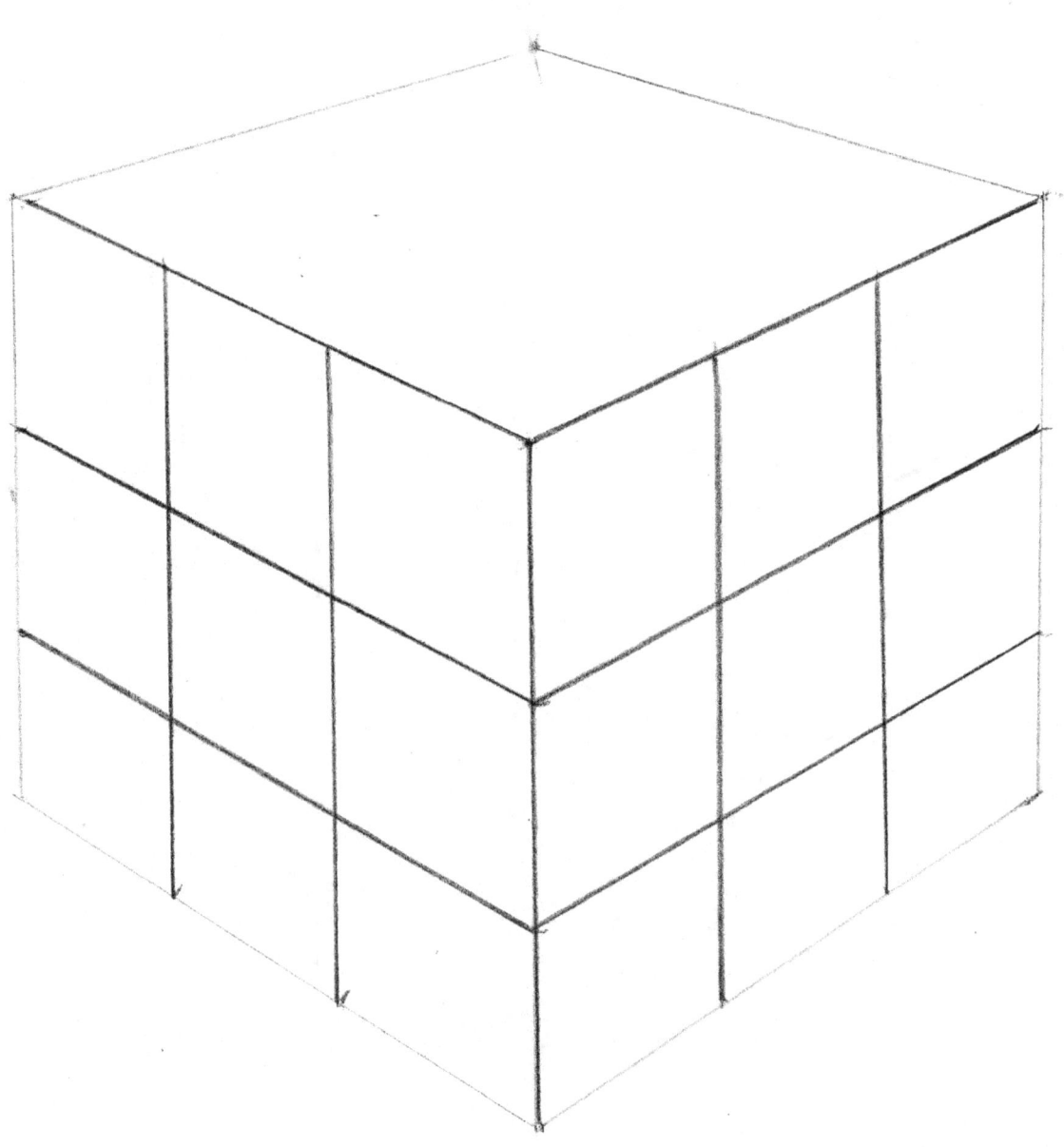

Since the upper edge is 5.0 cm (1.9") long, we have to divide it into three parts that are not equal, but the ones on the side should be longer and the square in the middle, next to the upper edges should be the shortest: 1.9 cm (0.75"), 1.6 cm (0.6") and 1.1 cm (0.4").

Finally, connect these marked points to get nine sections over the upper side of the Rubik's cube as shown in the following picture.

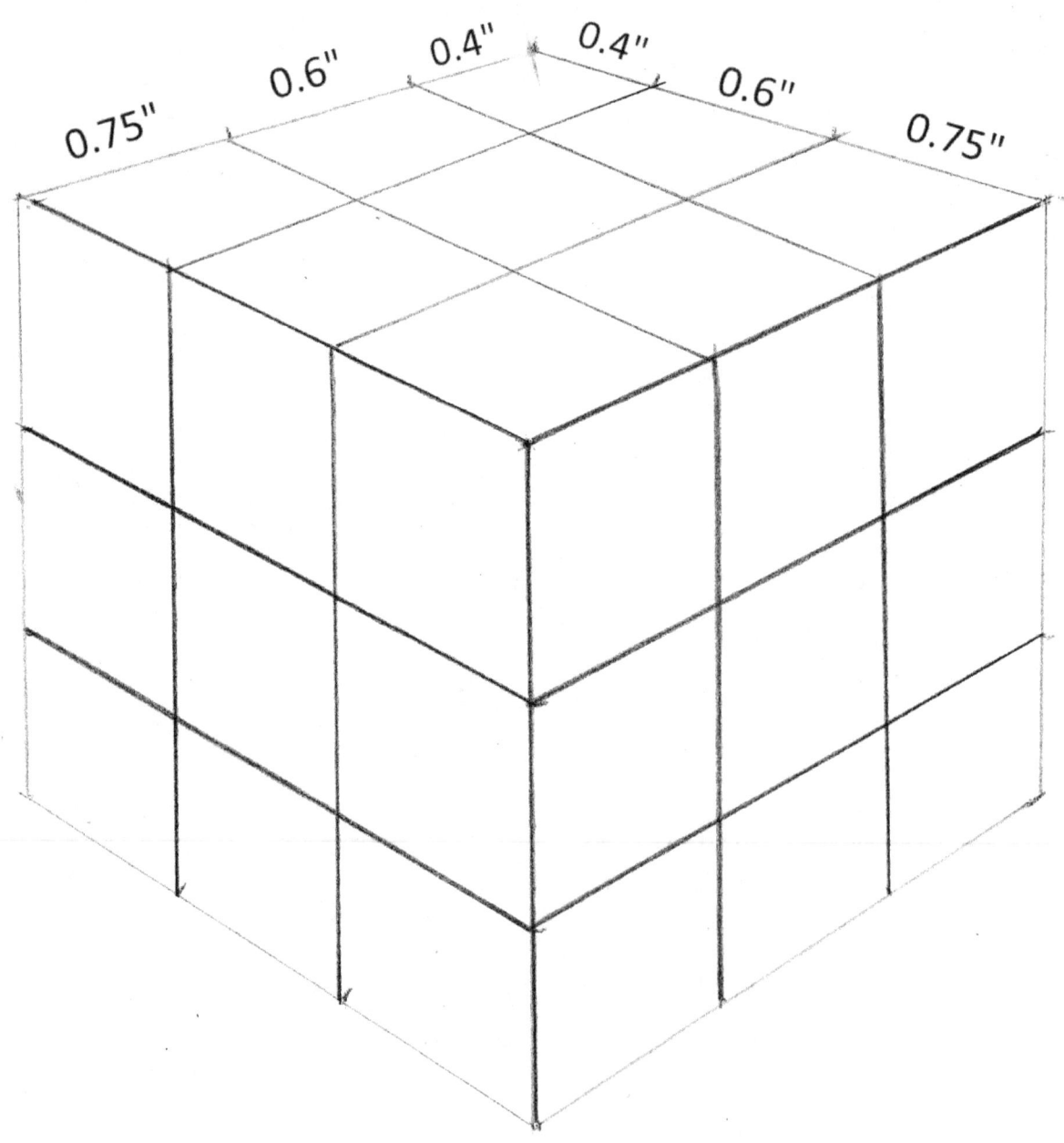

Now we are done with math, and we have to shade next.

Let's start with shading the upper face using a 6H pencil because the upper area always gets most light, and let's suppose that these squares are yellow. You can use any other H pencil such as 4H or harder. Make sure to put another piece of paper or tissue under your hand to avoid touching the paper with your hand because you will have to shade the areas under this one. Here we have to use the Circulism method to apply circular motions and create tiny, overlapping circles because we want to create a very smooth texture. You will still see the lines between the squares, and we're just going to strengthen them later and to make them thicker. You don't even have to blend this pencil with a tissue, go over and over again until you create a smooth texture. Take your time and carefully shade next to the outer edges and next to another face, or side of the Rubik's Cube. Apply normal pressure here; don't press too hard or too lightly. We want to apply the same pressure all the time in order to create a smooth texture.

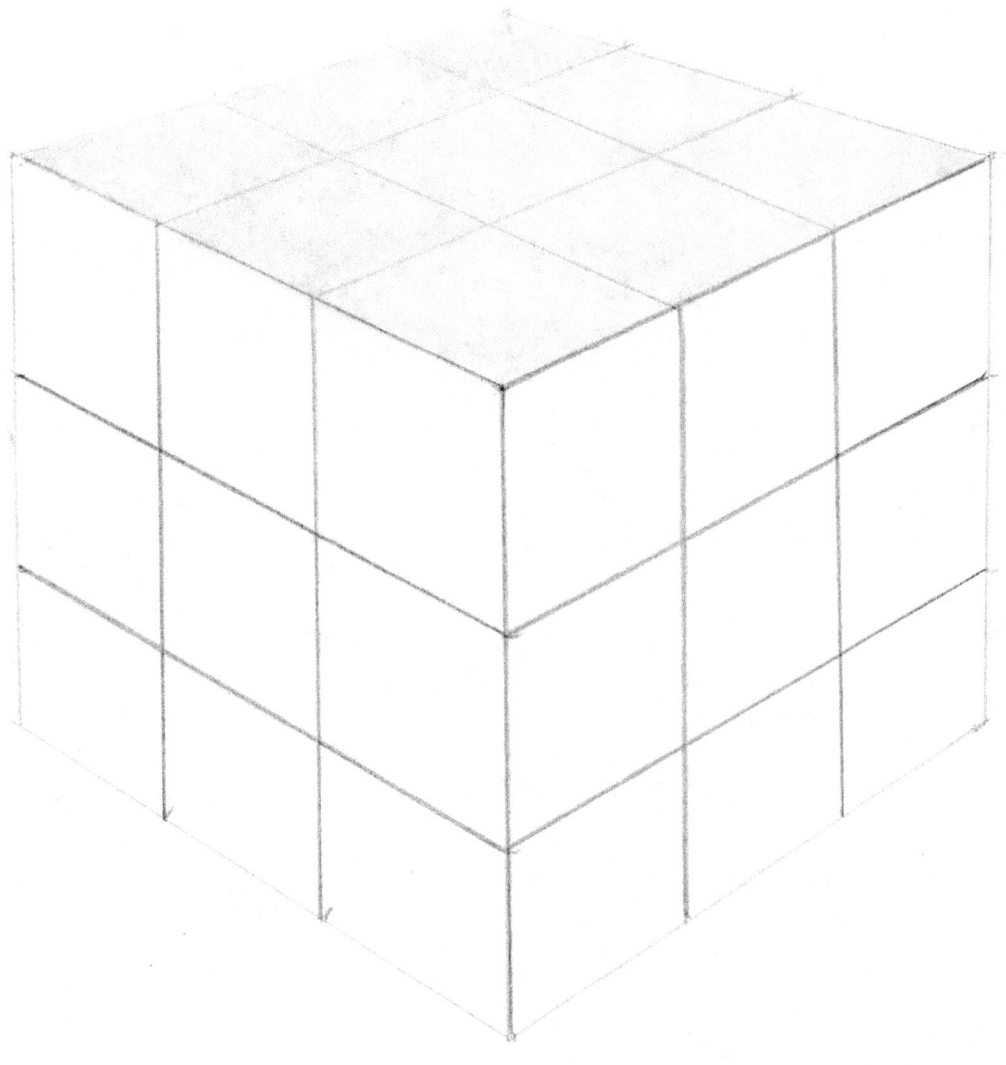

Shade these two lower faces with two different values because we have to create red and blue squares, which are quite darker than the upper area, and they are also less illuminated. I want to use an H pencil for the left side, and let's do the same here, so just circular motions all the time and try to cover the areas evenly, go over the lines between the squares, and you will still be able to see them through. Try to use a round tip of your pencil since it will make progress faster, and the area will be smoother. The flat side of a chisel-shaped tip of the pencil is also good for this. You can create by rubbing the lead on the sandpaper. A sharp point of the pencil is not good because with a well-sharpened point we will create a lot of different tones and it will take a lot of time to cover the areas. It is good for details but not for shading these areas.

Blend it all carefully with a tissue.

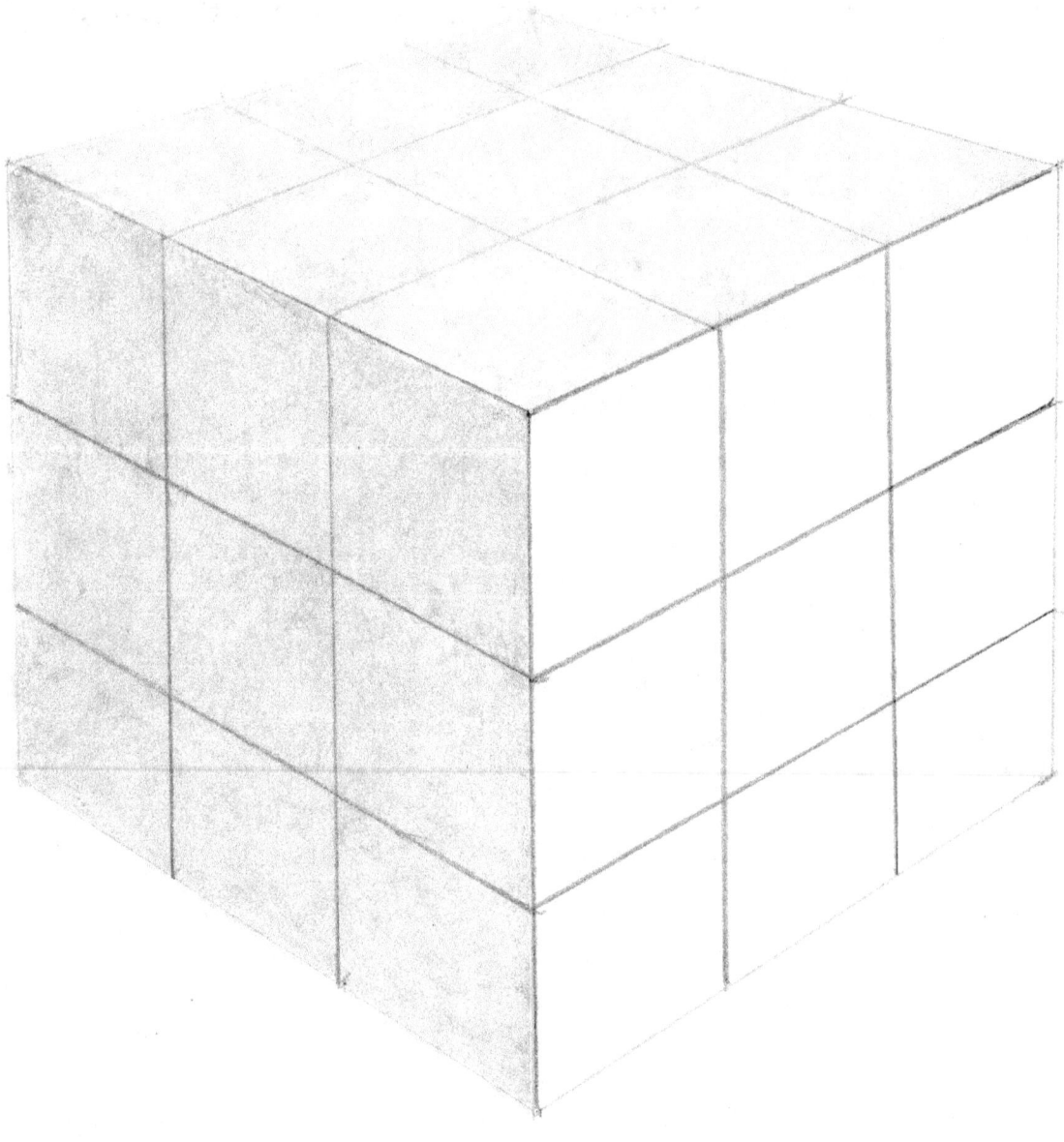

Shade the nine squares on the right side with a darker value. I use a 2B pencil for this.
Same here: try to create a smooth texture by applying the pencil evenly.
Blend it a bit with a tissue. If you apply some of the graphite around the rubic's cube, just erase it with an eraser to get a straight, clean edge between the background and the cube.

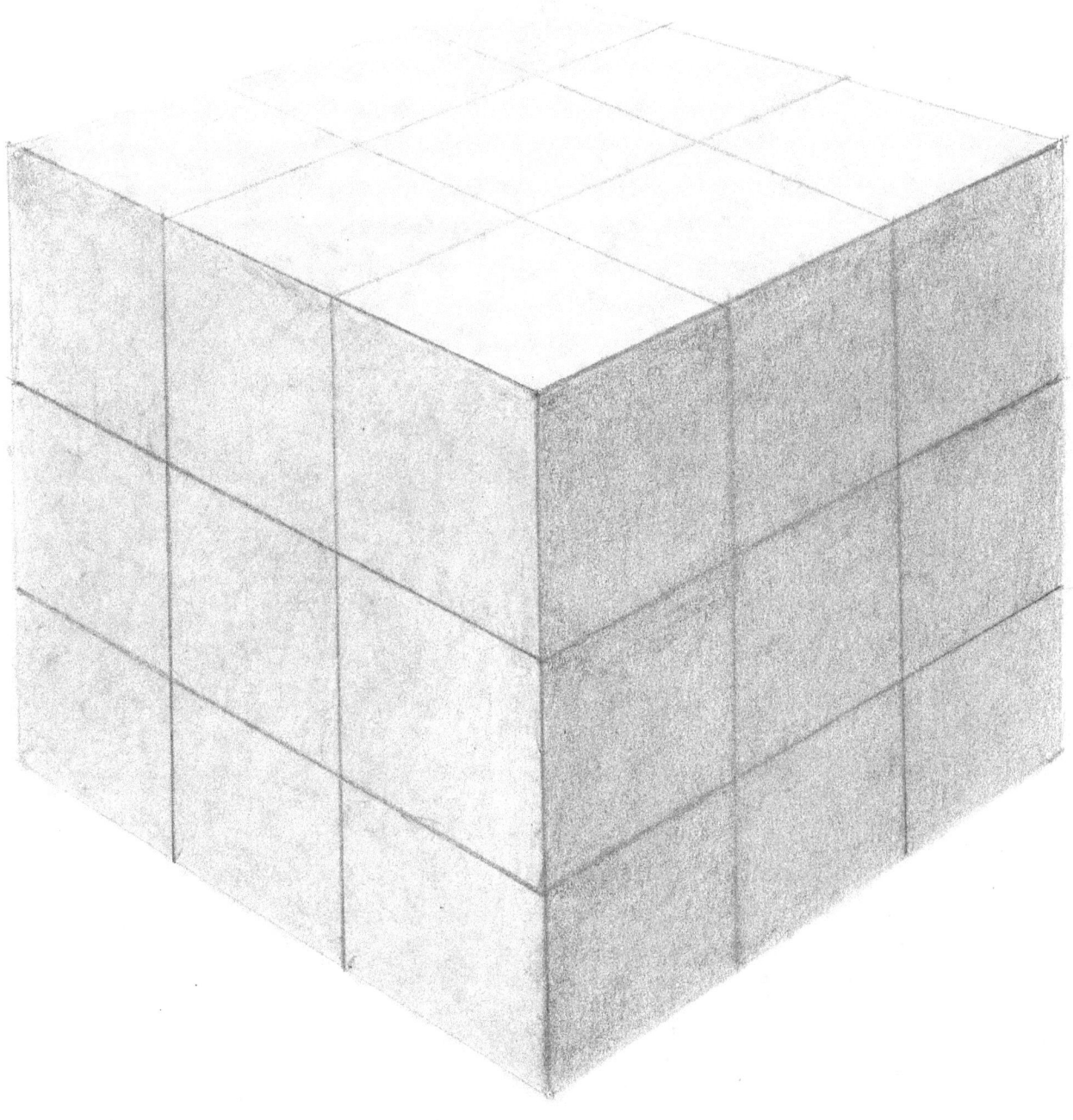

As a final step, we can create the edges between these tiny squares. Strengthen the lines that you created while sketching, as shown in the next image. Create very thick lines, and I suggest using a ruler.

Even the areas that are black will be also more illuminated over the upper face, so I suggest using an H pencil and go over the lines. You can create two parallel lines next to the initial lines and fill the space between them. Just make sure to make them straight, not wavy.

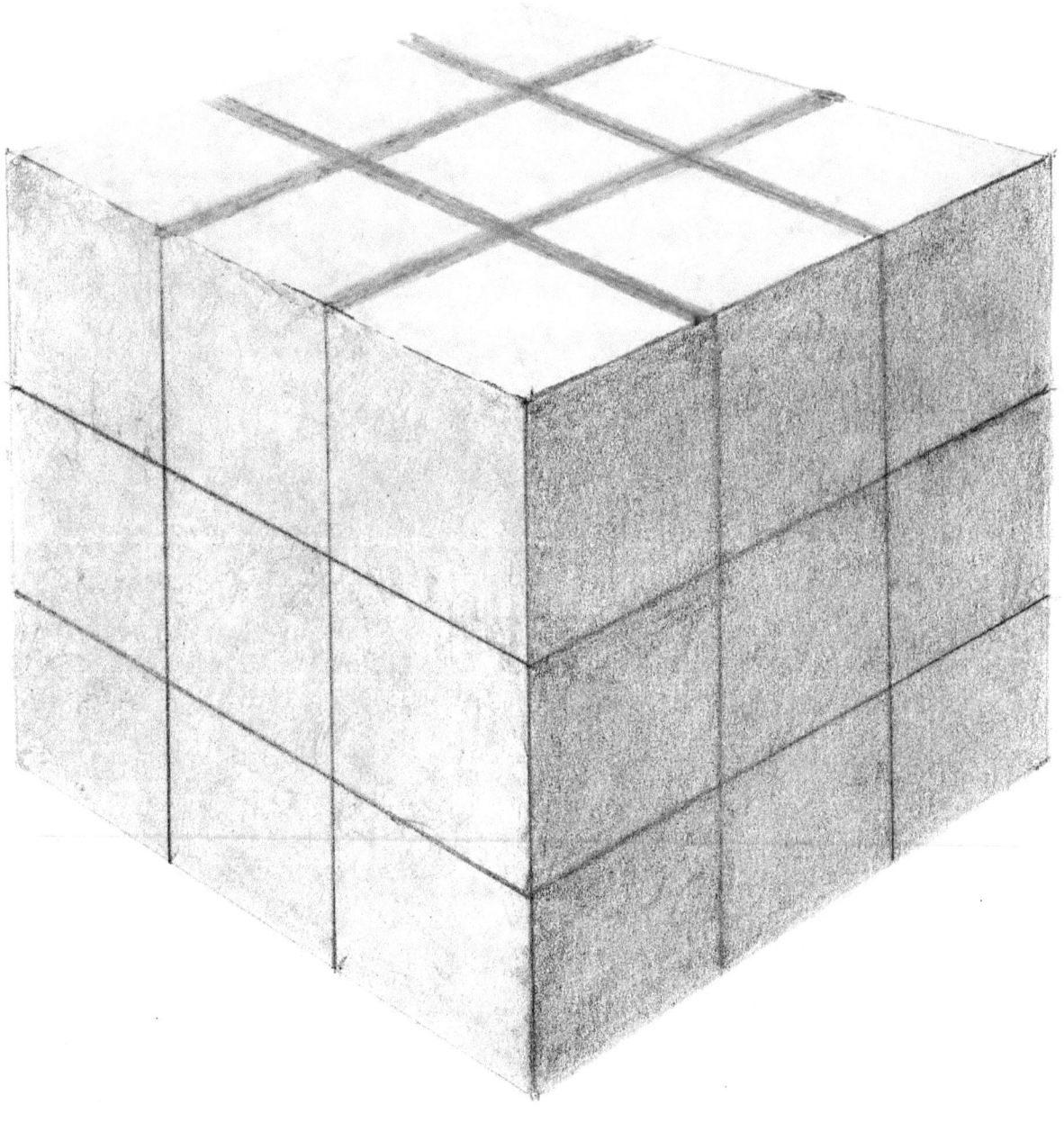

Do the same with the rest of the lines but use a 4B or darker pencil. I use an 8B in this step because these lines have to be absolutely black.

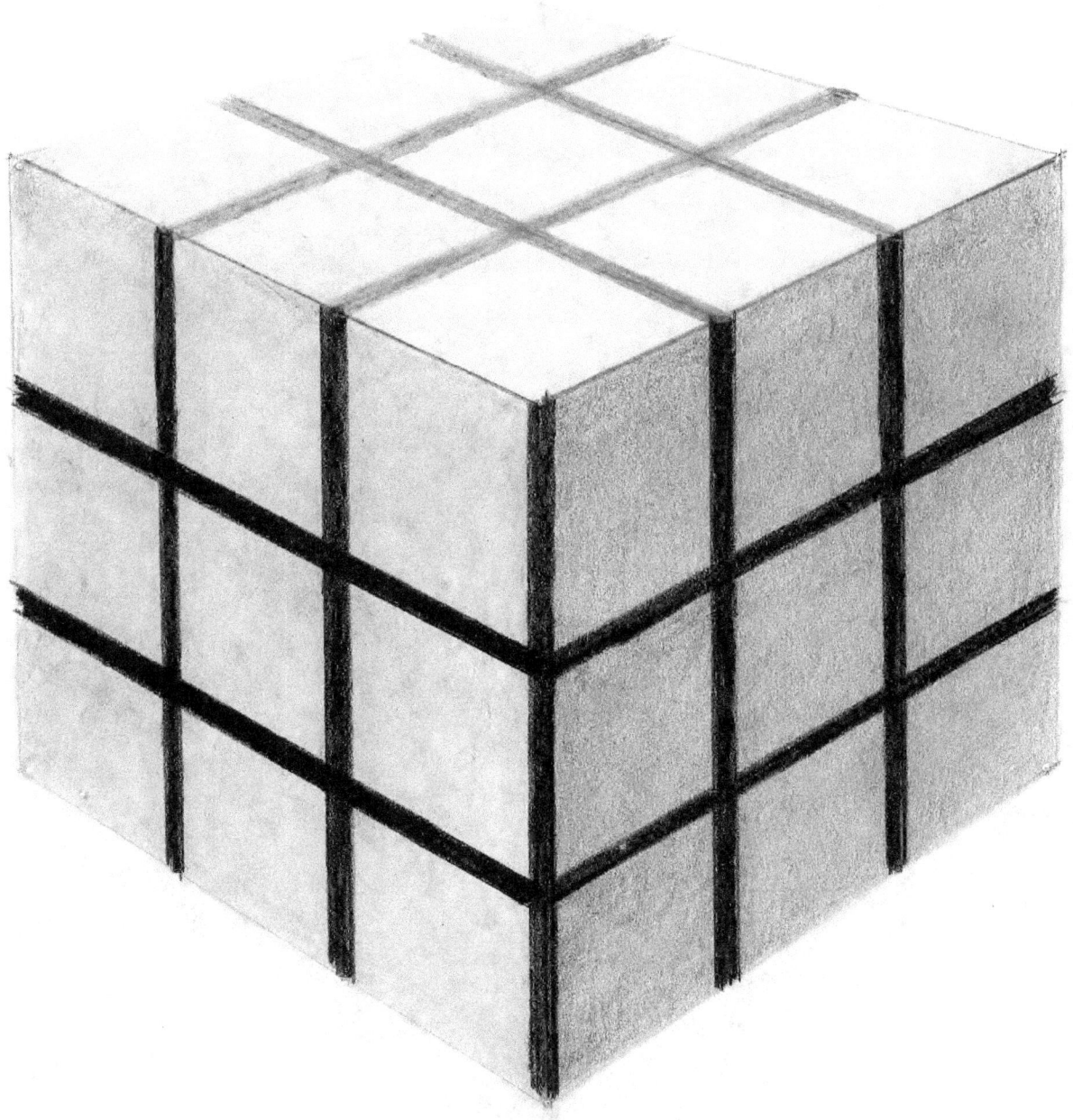

Do the same with the two edges between the upper part and the side parts. The lower part of these lines has to be drawn with an 8B and the upper part has to be drawn with an H pencil. Use a 2H in between to make these two values flow into each other so that the edge can appear round.

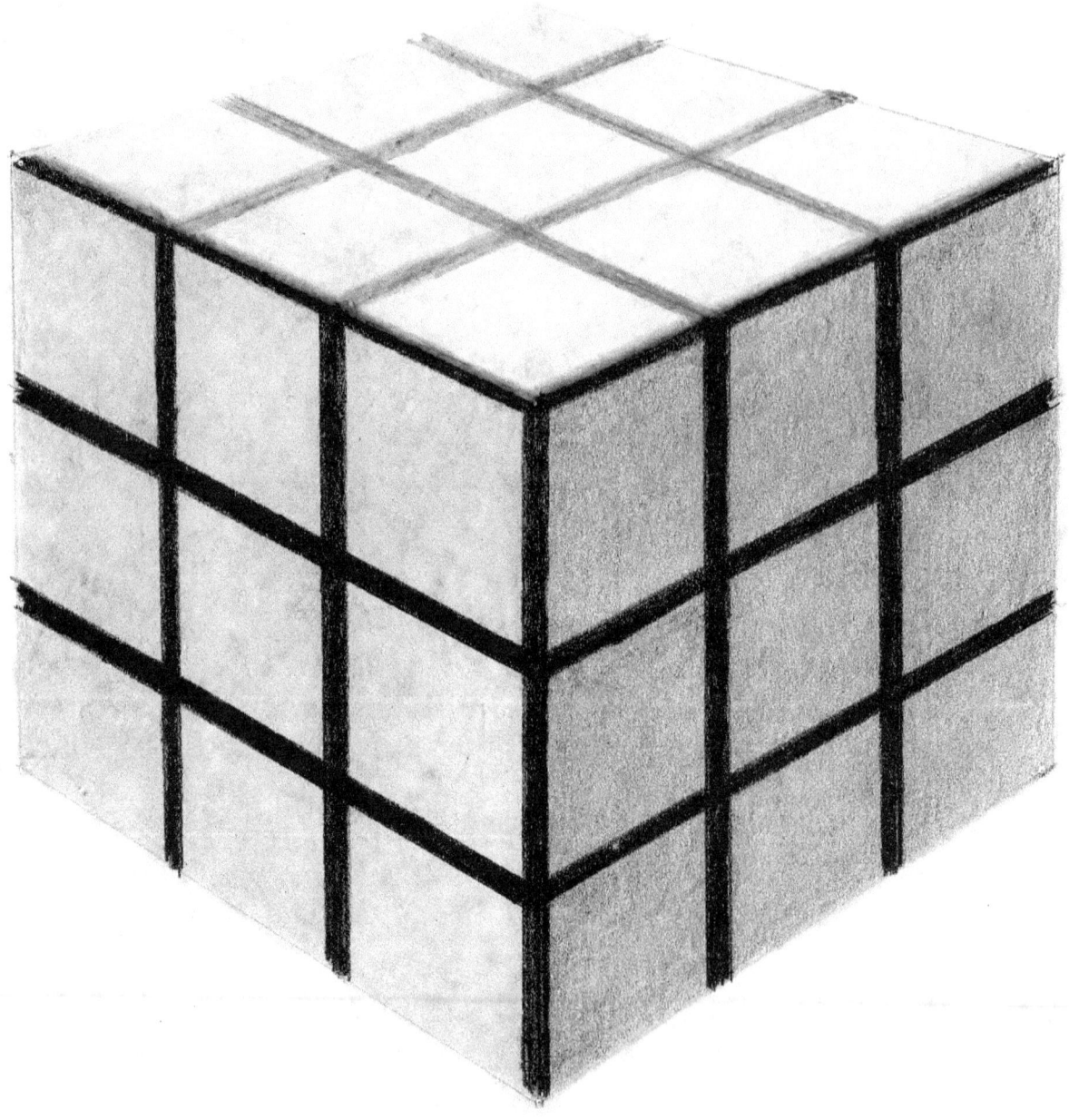

Now we can create some details, for example, make the corners of these tiny squares round. Use an H for the upper area, and a 4B or darker for the rest of the squares.

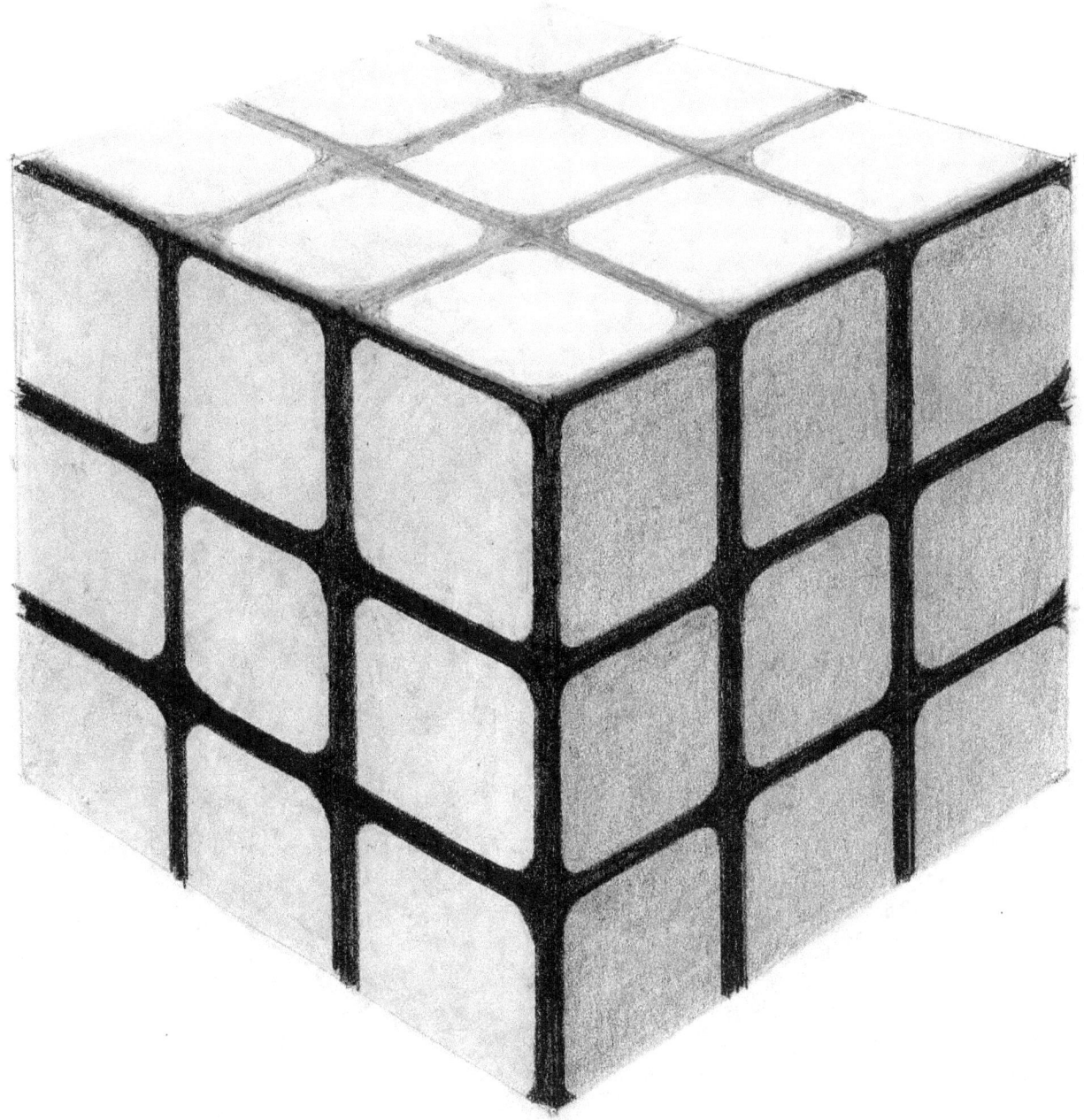

Create the cast shadow or actually the lower edge of the lower two sides using a 2B. Here also, make the corners round and draw very carefully to preserve the sharp and straight edge. Use a ruler if necessary.

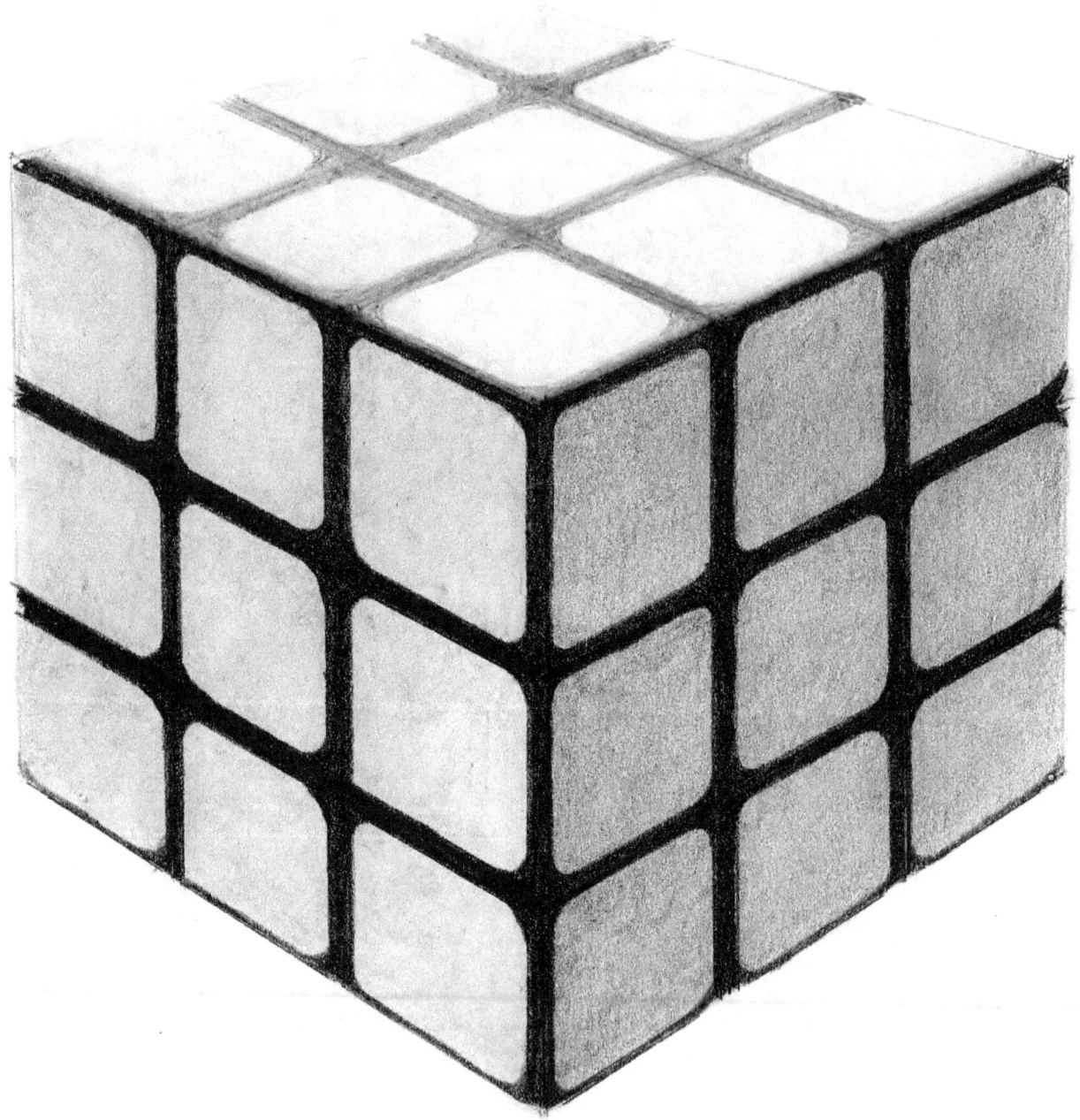

Next, create the highlights over the protruding areas between the tiny parts for a Rubik's Cube. Do it by erasing over the thick, dark lines, over the crosspoints between the squares. You shouldn't remove the graphite completely, lighten it up a bit. You won't be able to do it with a kneaded eraser, particularly if you used an 8B, like me. I used an electric eraser for this because I could remove the graphite effectively over the tiny areas. If you erase too much, go over it with a pencil again.

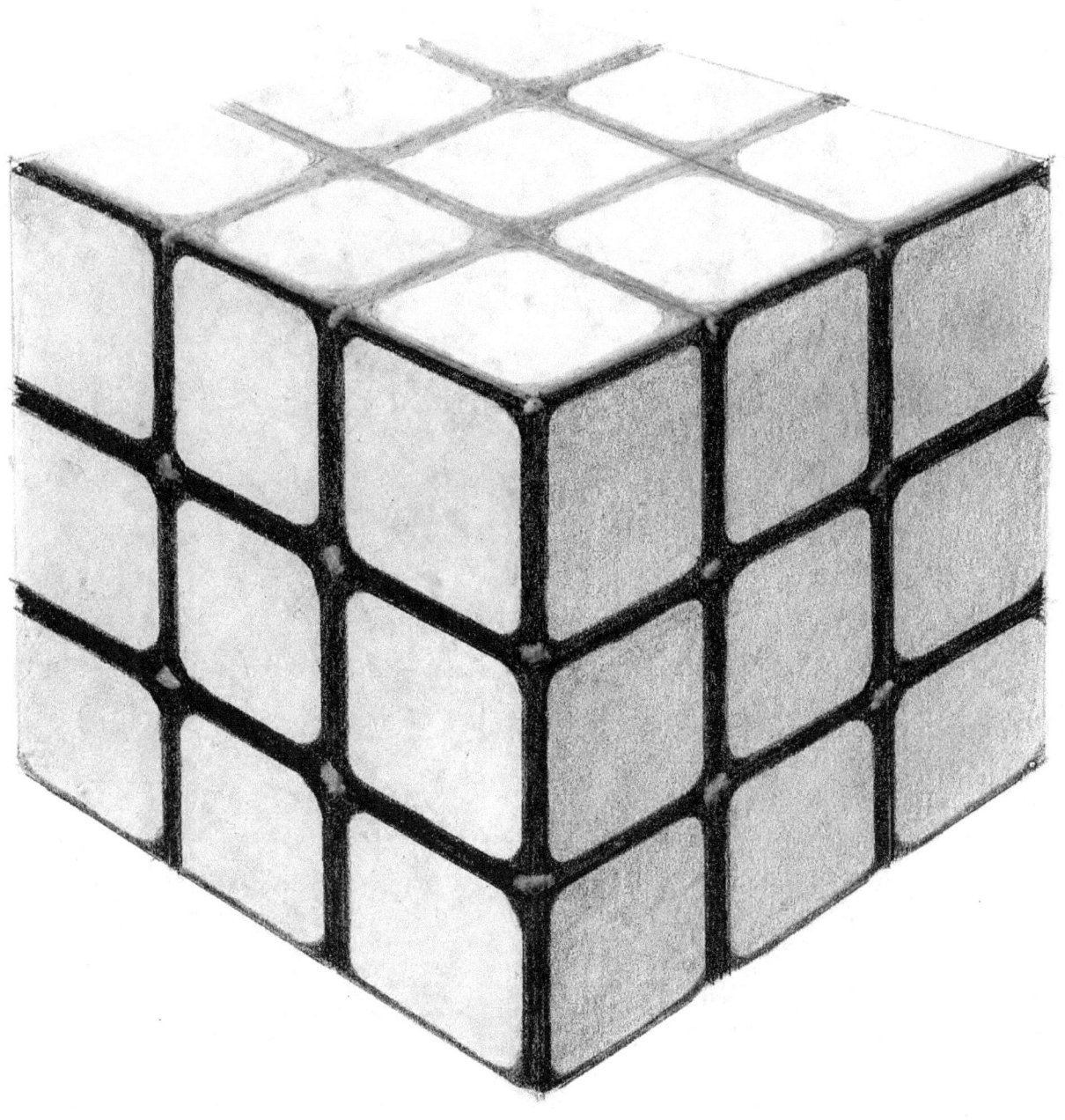

Lastly, create the cast shadow. Let's suppose that our light source is coming from the upper-left corner. Place two pieces of paper over the Rubik's cube, dip a tissue or a cotton pad into the graphite powder and spread it over the right-lower area next to the Rubik's Cube.

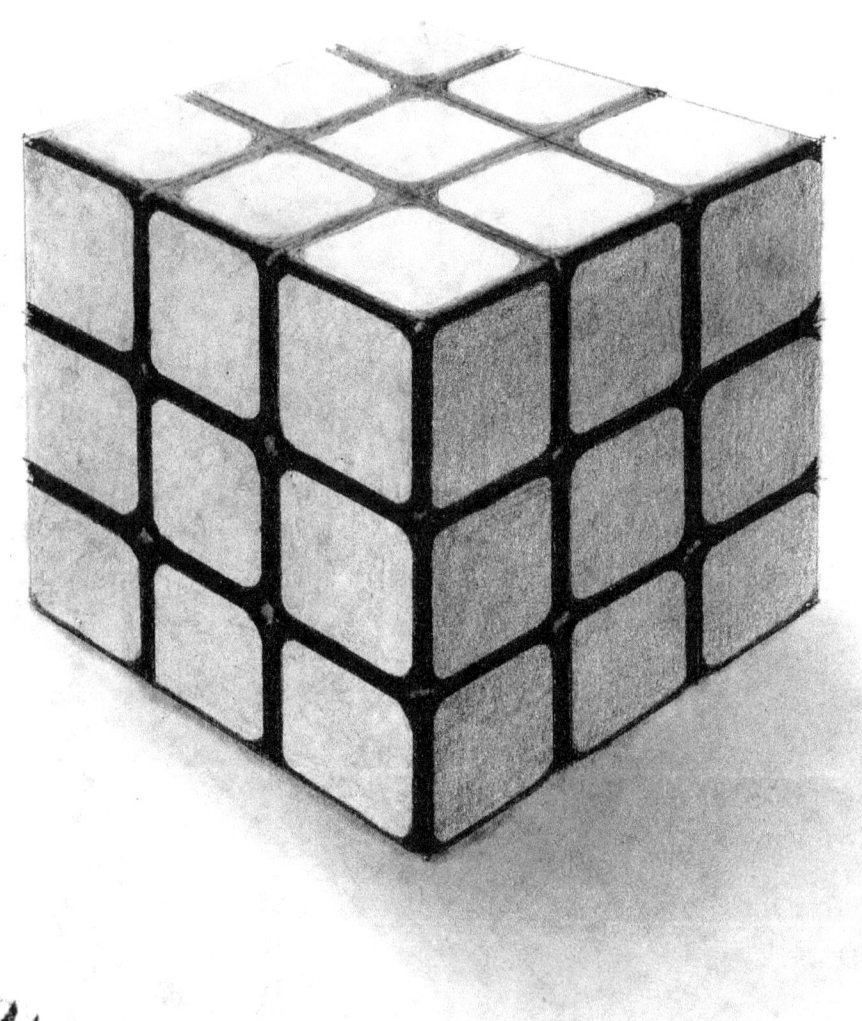

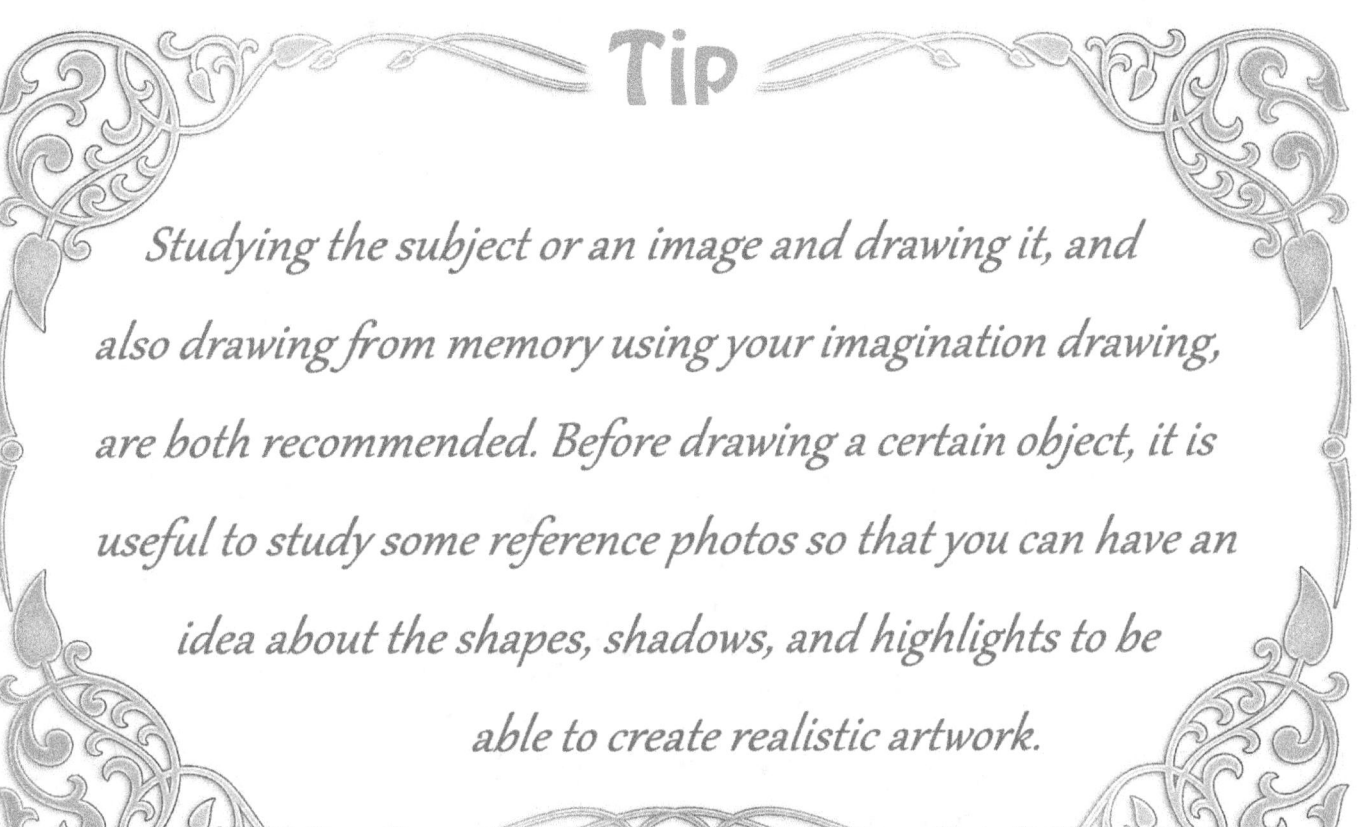

Studying the subject or an image and drawing it, and also drawing from memory using your imagination drawing, are both recommended. Before drawing a certain object, it is useful to study some reference photos so that you can have an idea about the shapes, shadows, and highlights to be able to create realistic artwork.

A GLASS CUP

Let's draw a glass cup using the reference photo that I have taken for us. You can take your own picture with a different shape of a cup, just make sure to place it under the strong light to get a nice cast shadow, and also the highlights over the cup.

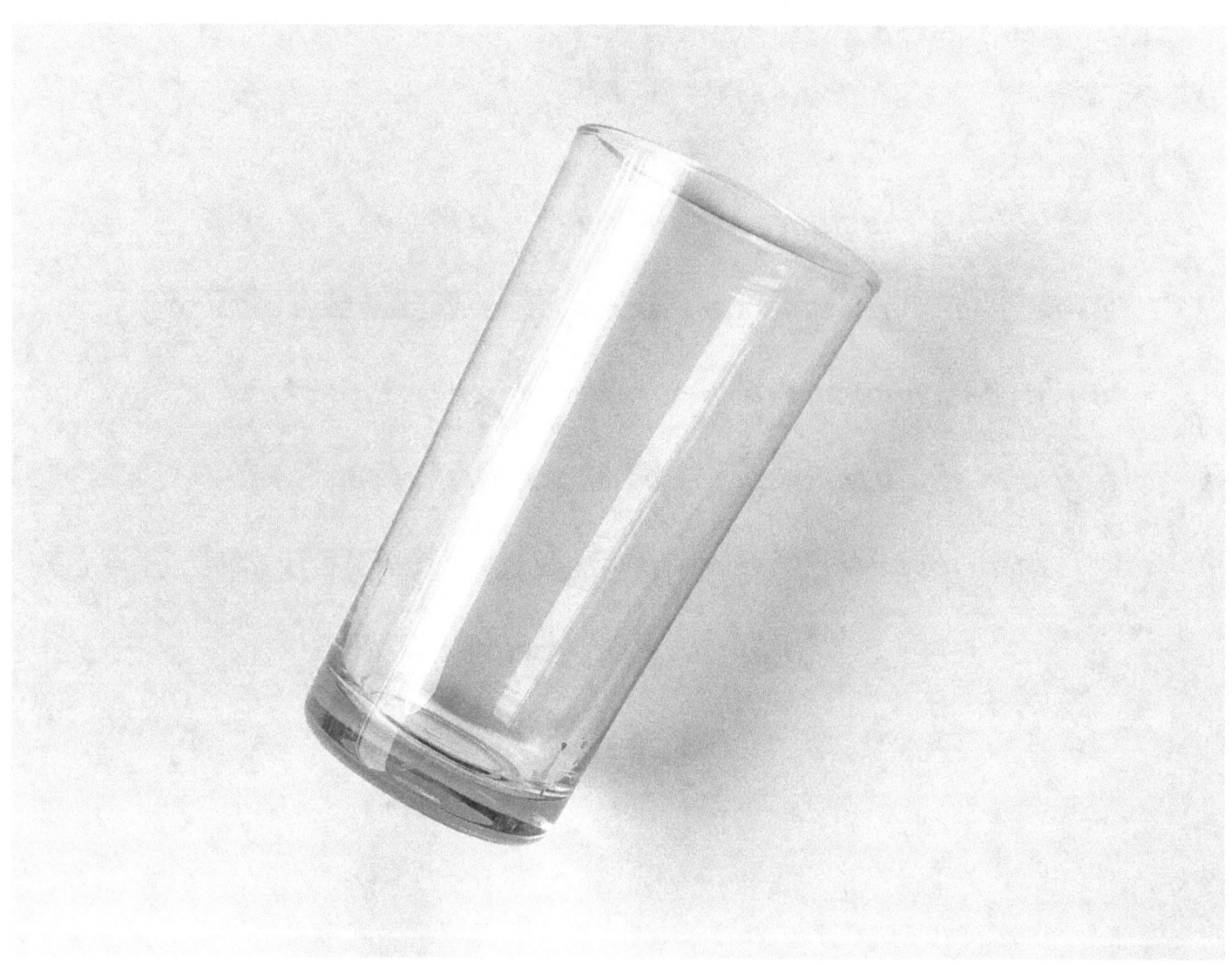

First of all, we have to draw two parallel lines. The length and the width don't have to be the same as in the reference photo. We need the photo just to see the highlights, shadows, and cast shadow. Use a ruler and an HB or lighter pencil to sketch it. My lines are about 8.0 cm (3.0") long if you want to draw the same size as mine.

Next, outline the upper and the bottom parts of the glass cup as shown in the next image. We should check it out in the mirror because we have to make it symmetrical, and we can figure it out only when we take a look at it in the mirror. Only then we can see whether our cup is symmetrical enough.

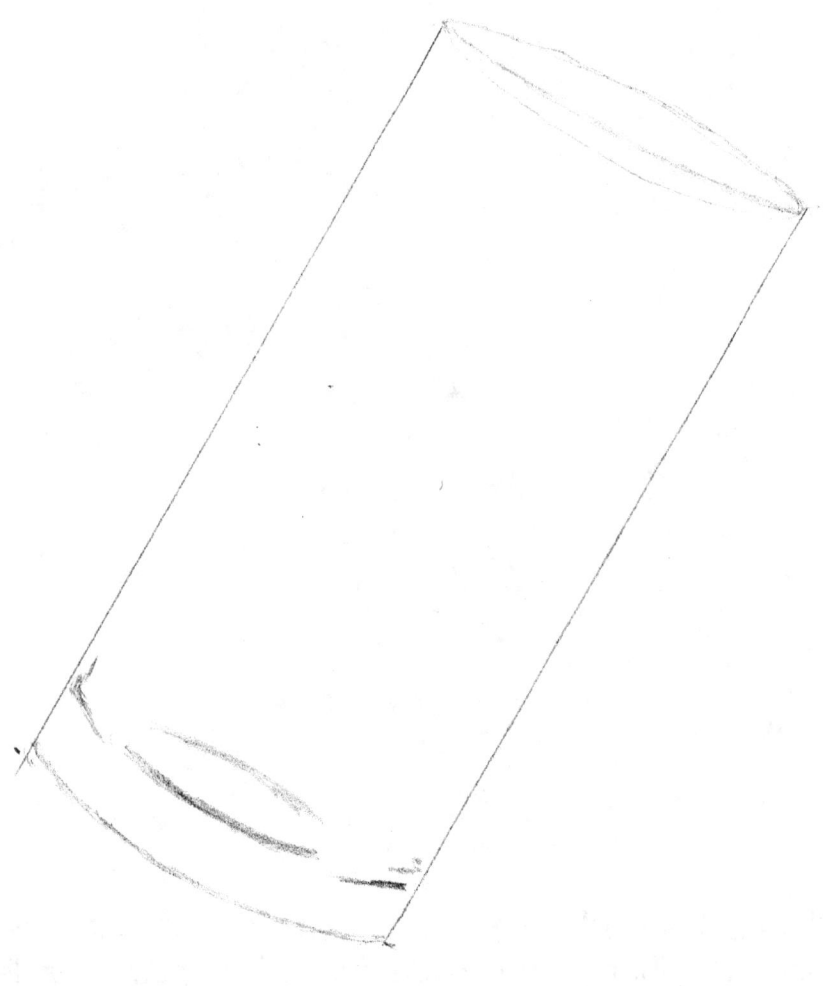

I suggest shading it all with graphite powder because we can create a much smoother texture than to draw it with a pencil. So, wrap a tissue around your finger, dip it into the graphite powder, place a piece of paper over the part that you want to be highlighted and shade over the edge of that, paper and, of course, over the cup. You can see how I do it in the following picture. If you have applied the graphite over the background, too, as I have, don't worry, we're going to erase it. We have to go even over the edges to apply the graphite over the whole length of the cup evenly.

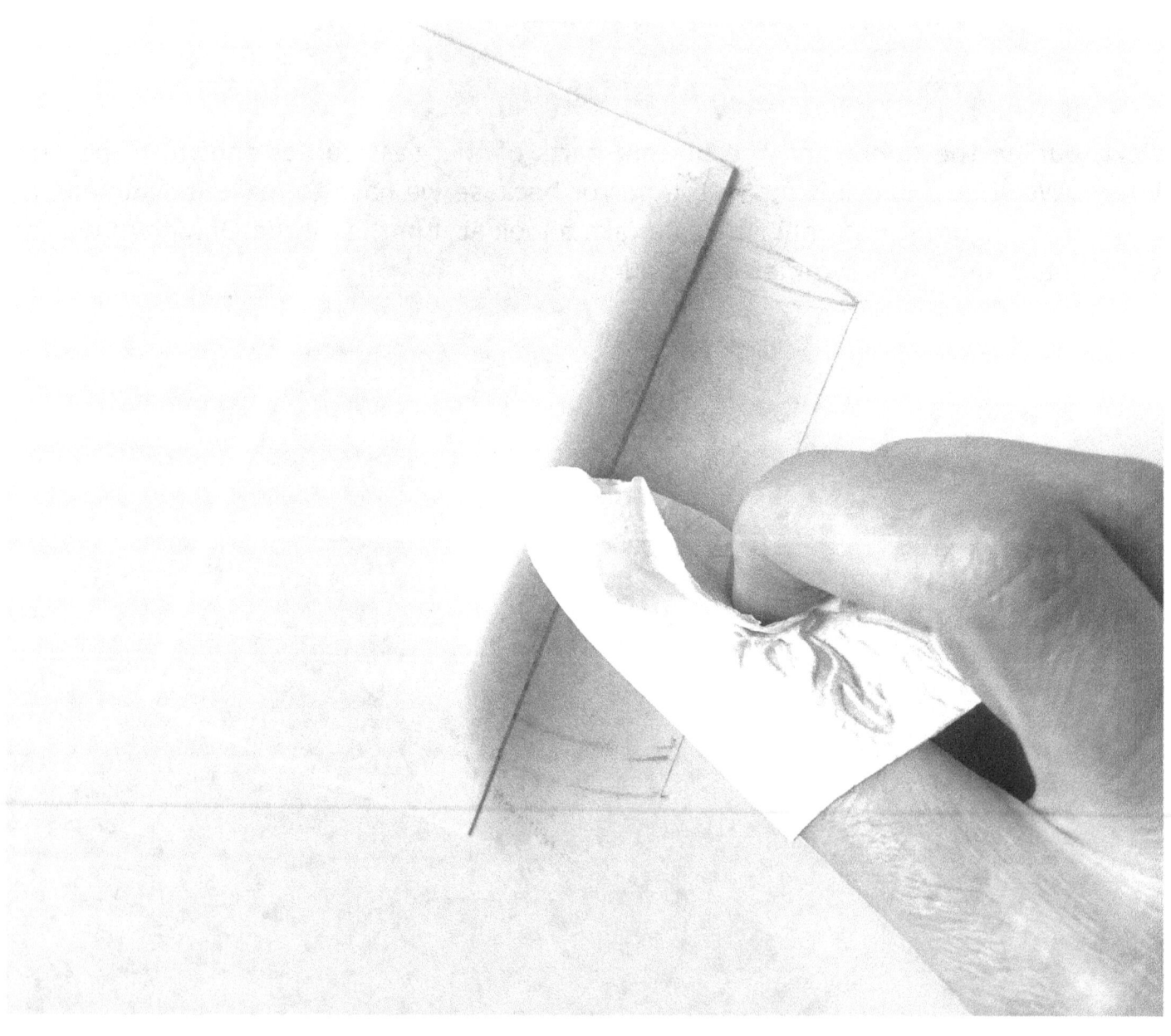

Do the same on the right side of the glass, place a piece of paper over the background, where the cast shadow is found, and shade over the paper. Press less and less as you shade away from the edge to create a smooth gradient.

When you lift off the separate piece of paper that you used to isolate the background, you get something like this:

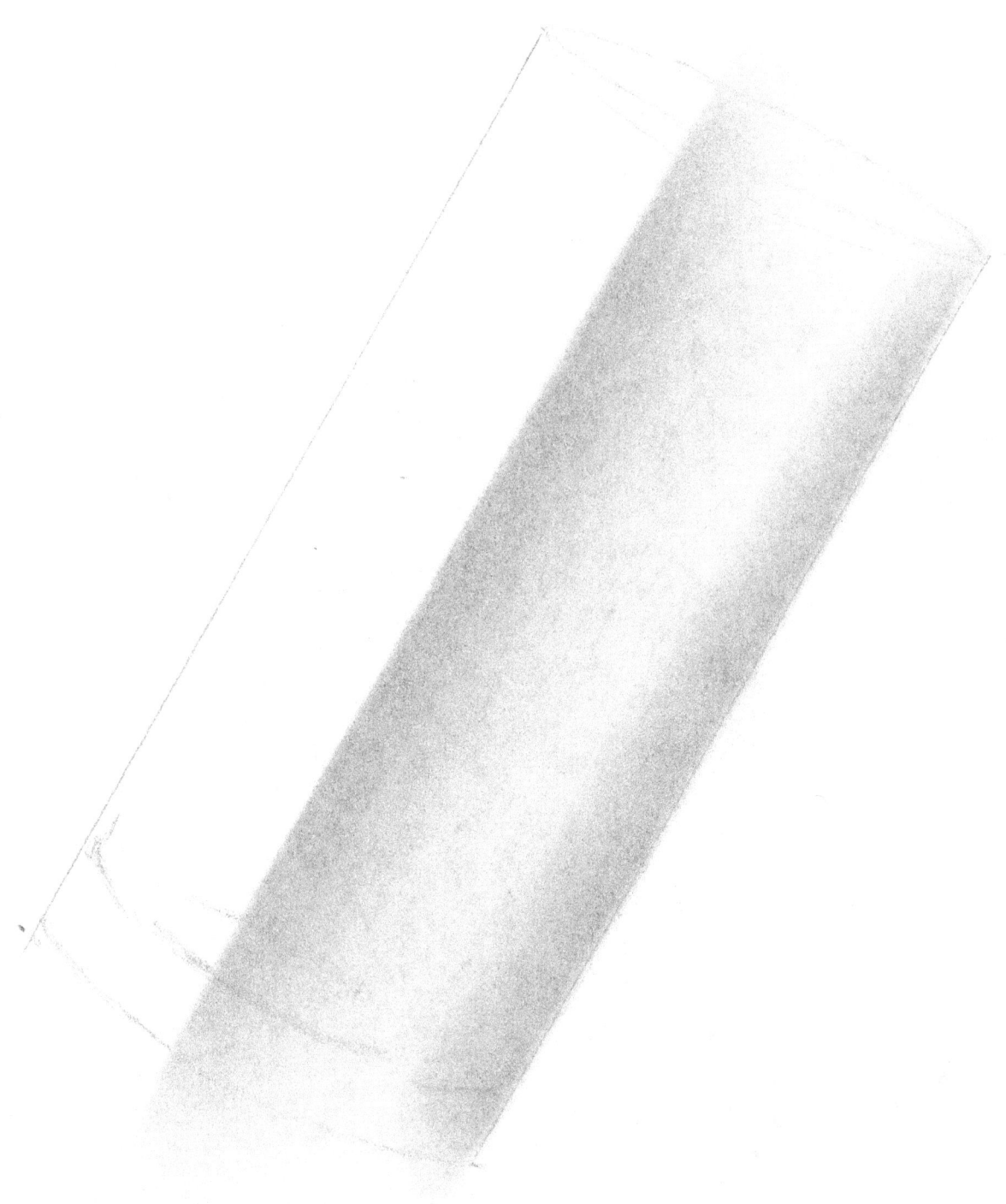

Now place a separate piece of paper over the background on the left side and shade that edge of the cup which should be much lighter, so don't dip a tissue into the graphite powder but use what you have on your tissue and just shade next to the separate piece of paper.

Let's create a cast shadow too, and then we are done with the graphite powder.
Place another piece of paper over the glass to isolate it and have only the background approachable. Create the cast shadow, the shadow that is cast by the cup. As you can see in the reference photo, the cast shadow has to be a bit lighter next to the glass, and darker a bit farther from it. We can also use a bit of a Q-tip to shade tinier areas.

Now that we have basic shadings done, we can create the details.

Erase the graphite that you applied over the background, of course, except for the cast shadow on the right side.

Start creating highlights by erasing the shaded areas where necessary. You don't have to create the same highlights from the reference photo, just approximately.

Compare my previous and next image to see where I have erased the graphite for the highlights.

Now we can create tiny highlights at the bottom of the glass. I'm using a mechanical eraser to erase these details. So, wherever you see it in the reference photo. If you can't create bright enough highlights, and you can use a white ink gel pen or a white marker. Do the same in the upper area next to the rim. It's still not quite visible, but we're going to shade next to it to enhance the highlights. To make it simpler, take one step and use one tool at a time.

I use a B pencil to create dark at the top and the bottom of the cup. We have to develop dark areas too, to give the picture depth and to make the highlights next to them look brighter. So, the whole bottom area has to be quite darker than the rest of the cup, but the other dark areas can be shaded with an HB, for example, around the rim of the cup.

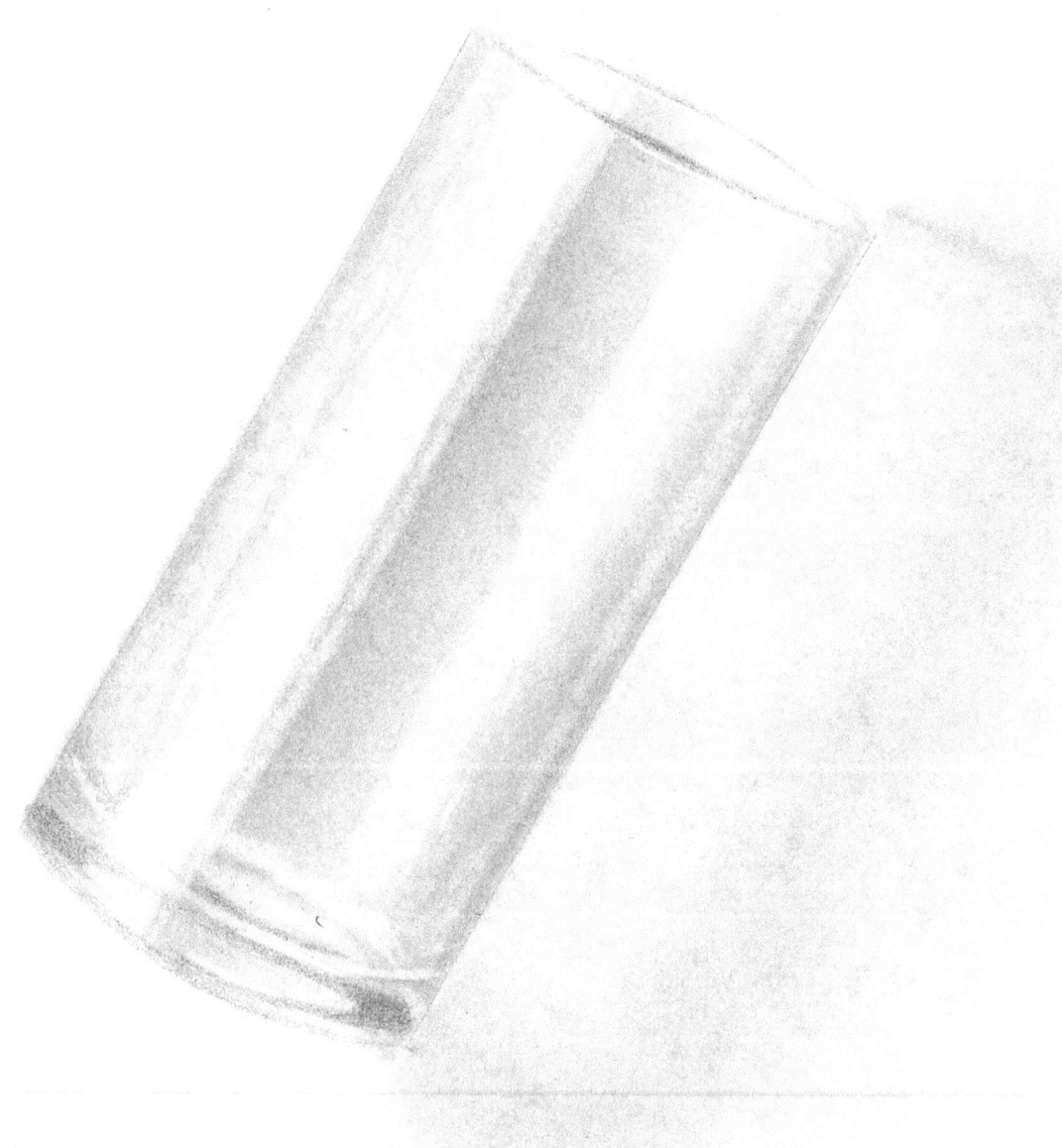

Blend it with a blending stump and shade more where necessary. You can and more details if you want, and as I mentioned before, take your own pictures and practice shading and drawing different cups by following the steps from this tutorial.

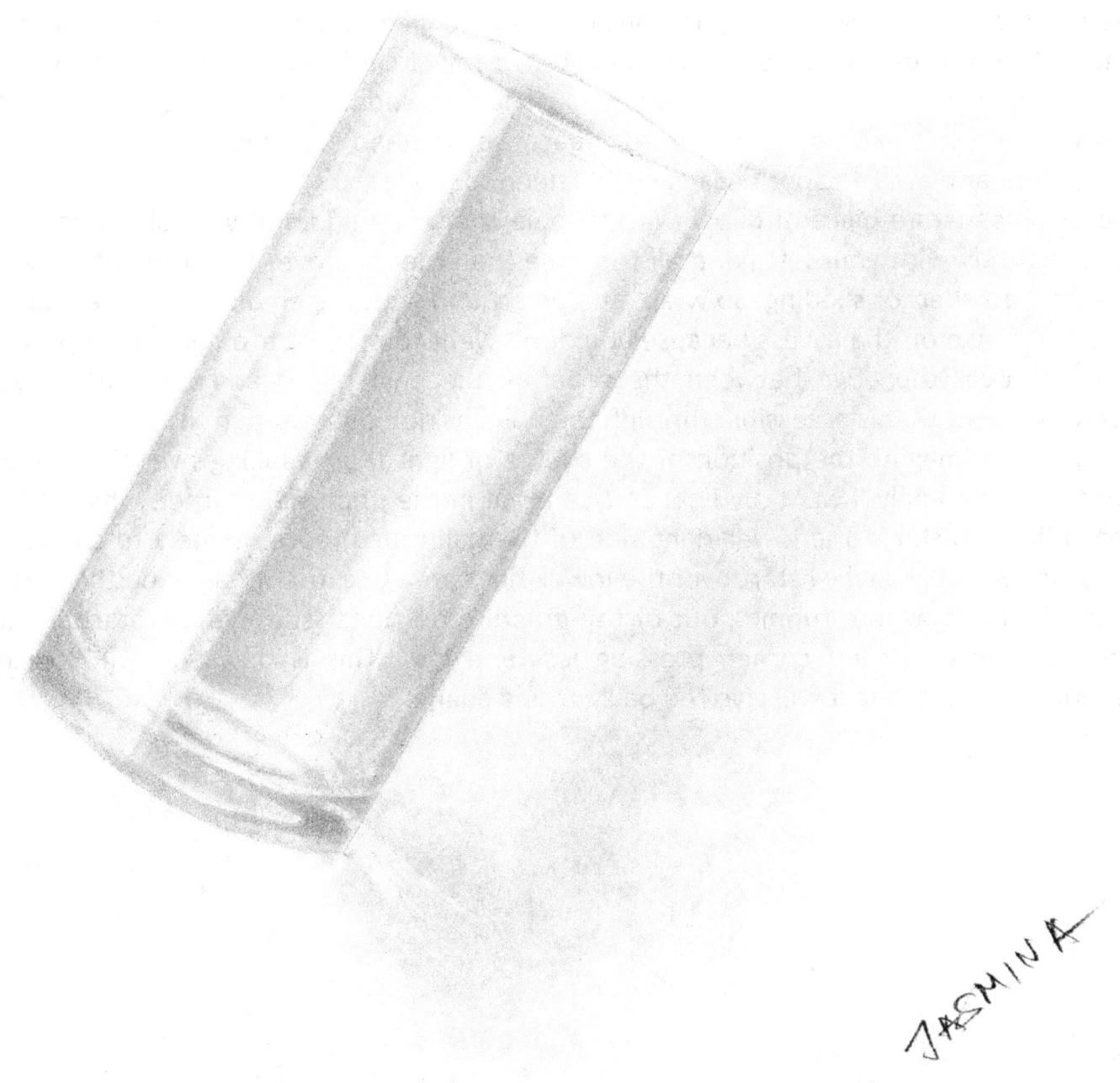

A FOOTBALL BALL

Now let's draw a football ball, and of course, we have to start with a circle. That's why we have to use a drawing compass, but let's draw a circle on a separate piece of paper and not on our drawing sheet. The diameter of my circle is about 8.0 cm (3.0") if you want to draw the same size as me. Create a circle on a separate piece of paper and cut it out with the scissors. Do it very carefully because we need a perfect circle. Don't throw out a circular piece of paper because you'll need that later.

Place the separate piece of paper with its hole over the middle of your sheet of paper. Hold it firmly with your left hand all the time, don't let it move. I want you to use the graphite powder for shading. So wrap a tissue around your finger, dip it into the graphite powder, shake off the excess because you don't want to make it too dark, and apply the graphite over the edge between the separate piece of paper and the part of your drawing paper that is accessible through the hole, as demonstrated in the next image.

We have to imagine the position of the source of light that is falling over the ball and shading accordingly. I want my light source to be in the upper-left corner, which means that I have to shade the lower-right side of the ball much more, namely to create the self-shadow. That's why I start over the lower-right area because it has to be the darkest here. Then, as we are running out of the graphite on our tissue, we can start shading towards the upper-left corner, pressing less and less. This is how you will create a smooth gradient, and it will give the ball a round shape.

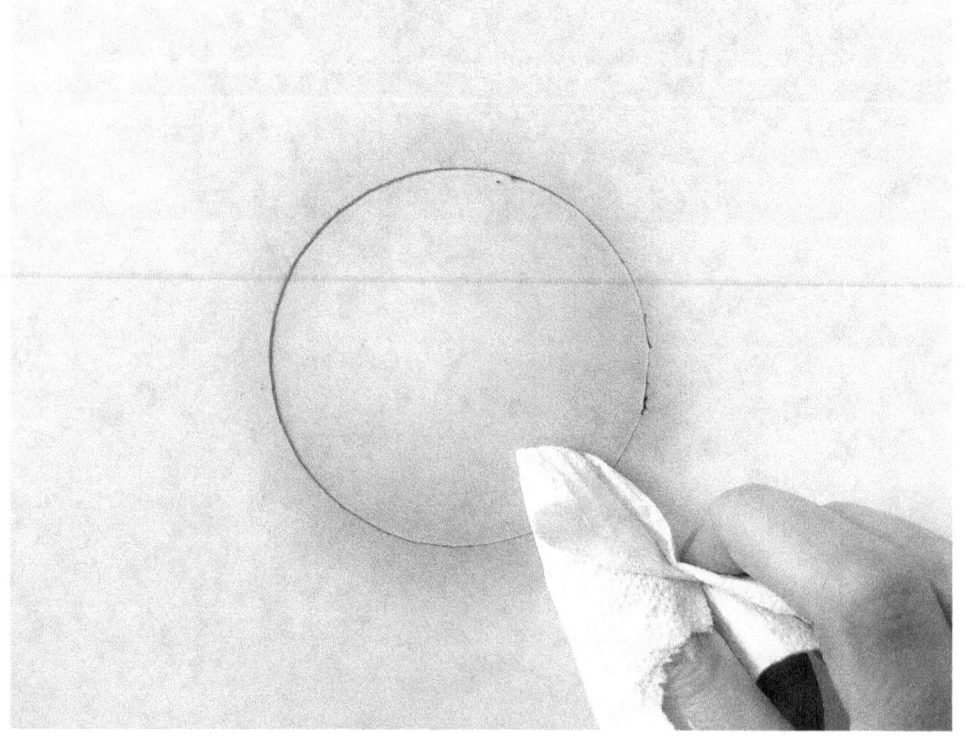

When we remove a separate piece of paper, we get something like this:

You can see how it now looks like a ball and has a round shape.
Now we can draw the patterns typical for the football ball containing black pentagons and white hexagons. Of course, you can draw any other patterns, but let's start with this one. Although it might sound simple to do, it isn't, and you have to measure and pay attention to proportions. Anyway, any kind of pattern is very useful to create because it will teach you patience and make you train your observational skills.
Start with a black pentagon in the very middle of the ball to keep it simple for now. A pentagon has five equal sides and the five equal corners. Start with a smaller line and draw four more. Then you can measure the sides to see if they are of the same length. You don't have to make it perfect at the first try, try to make it approximately

proportional.

In the next image, you can see my attempts to draw a pentagon from the smallest one to the final one. Since I would color the inner area of the pentagon with dark pencils, I didn't mind having all those lines visible. It is difficult to draw a perfect pentagon at first without having more lines applied to find their right positions. You can practice on a separate piece of paper first if you want.

So, each black pentagon is surrounded only by white hexagons, which means that we have to draw the lines from the outer corners of the pentagon, as shown in the next picture. These will represent the edges between the neighboring hexagons. Keep in mind that the ball is round, so the pentagons and hexagons won't have their correct shape next to the edge, from this point of view.

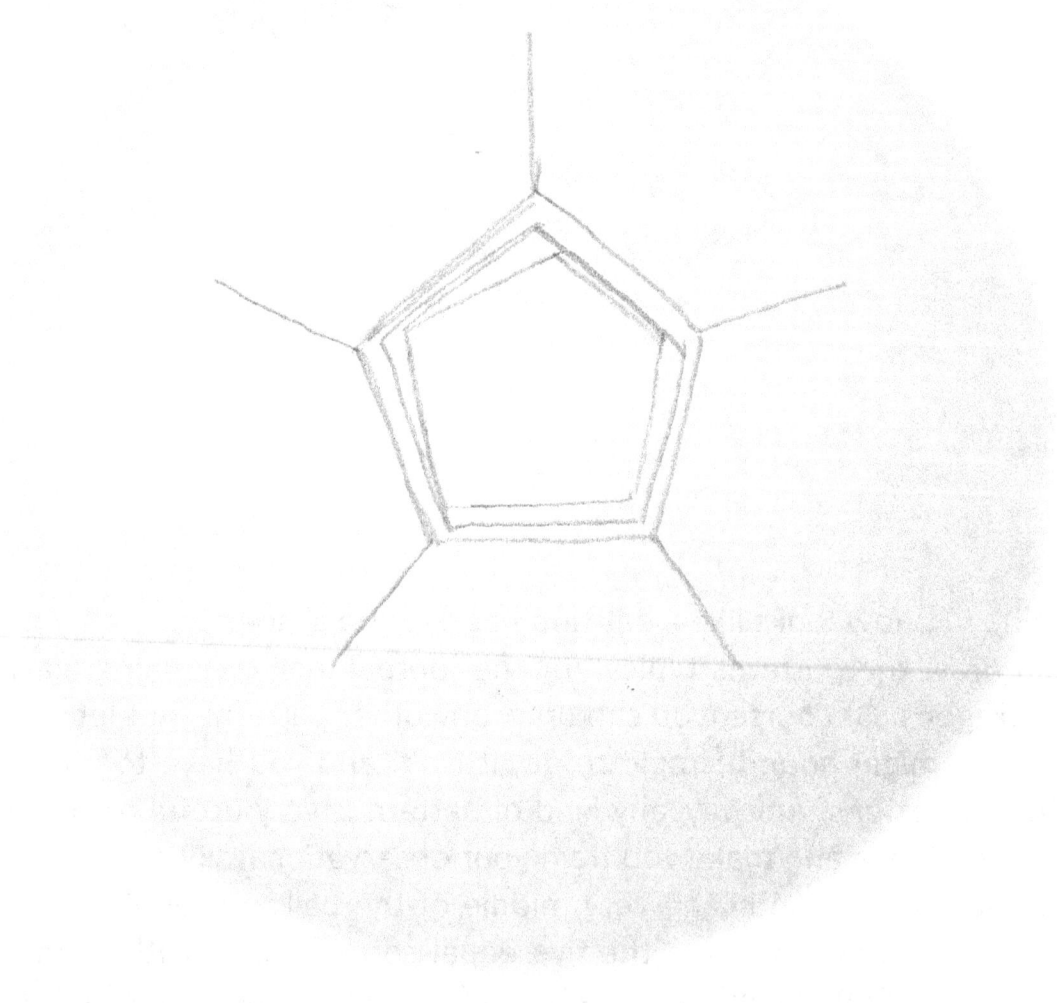

On the other side of these lines, we have to draw pentagons whose two sides will start at the end of the previously drawn lines. Then, draw two curvier lines, and the fifth line doesn't have to be visible.
Make sure that everything is in the right place and where you want it before you start shading, or actually coloring the pentagons because the dark pencils can't be completely erased.

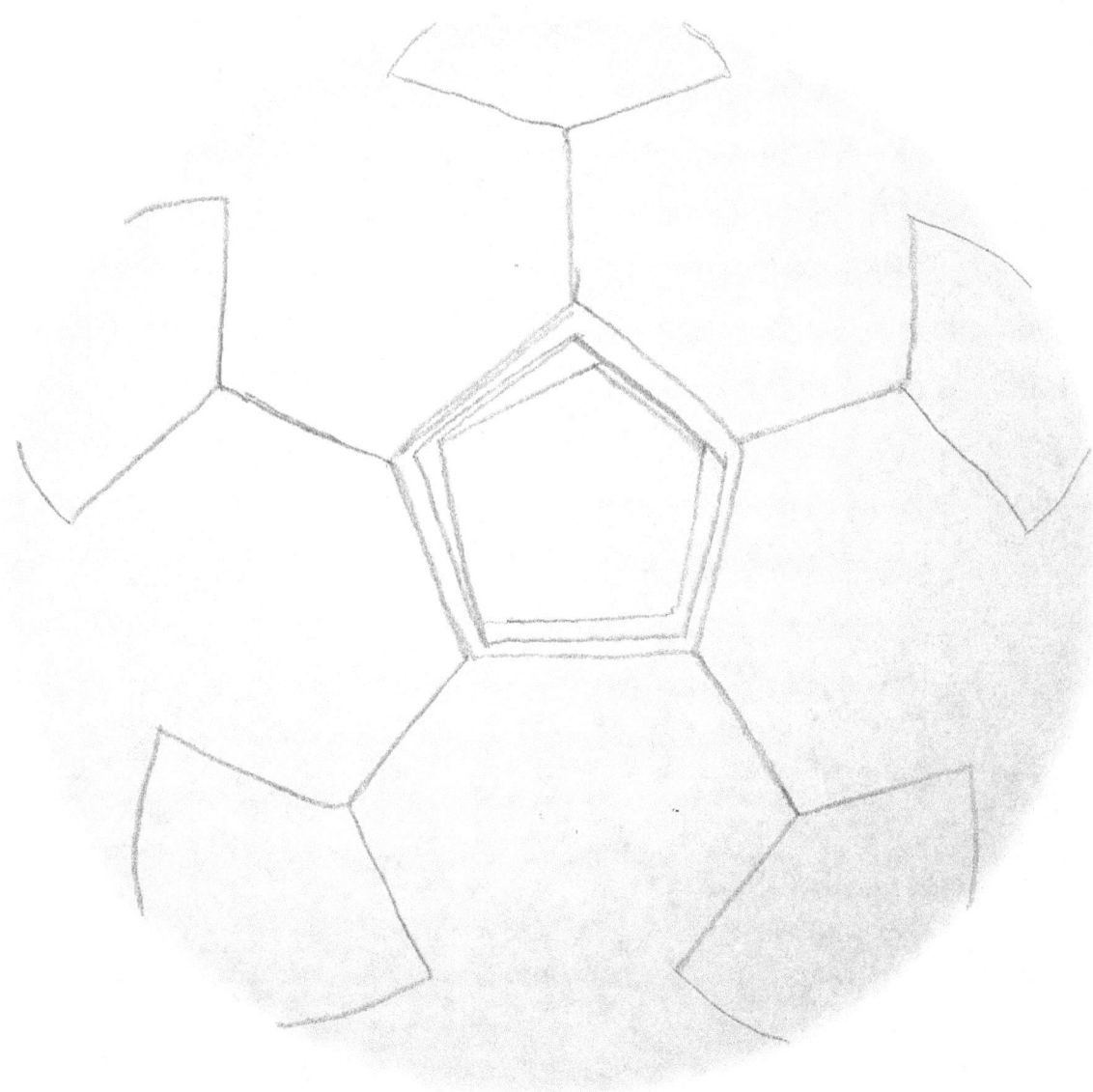

Here you can see that the hexagons are forming after having drawn all the pentagons. Just draw the sixth line of the visible hexagons and you are done with sketching.
Lastly, mark each pentagon with an X or as you wish, to make sure that these are the areas that you want to color.

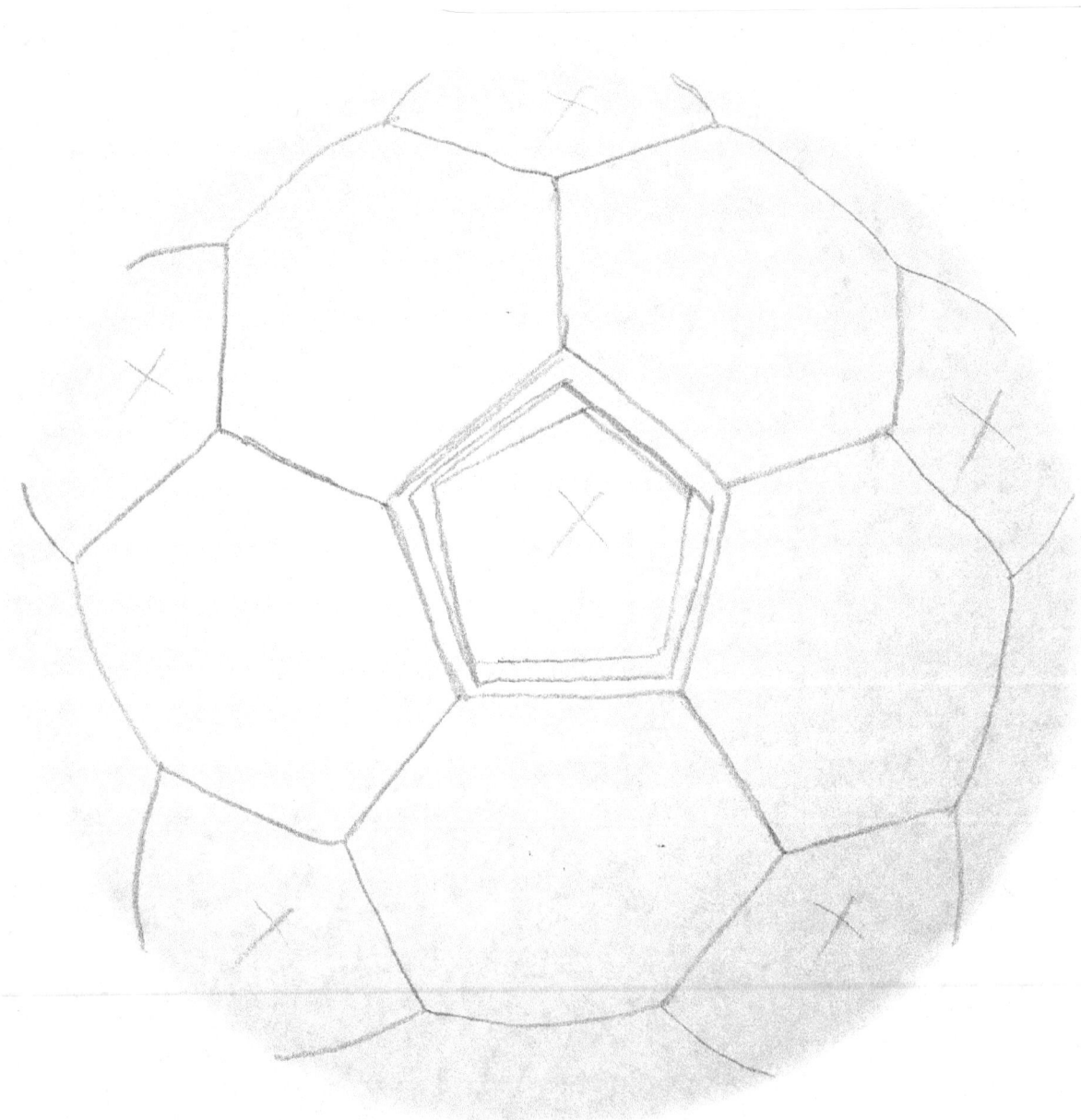

Now we can create the values of the pentagons. As we know, these parts are black, but the black color will also change the value when illuminated. That's why it is important to use different values for these pentagons, depending on their position.
So, if our light source is coming from the top-left corner, the pentagons over the top-left area of the ball would be the brightest. I use an H pencil and circular motions to create a smooth texture over these pentagons. Shade carefully next to the edges.

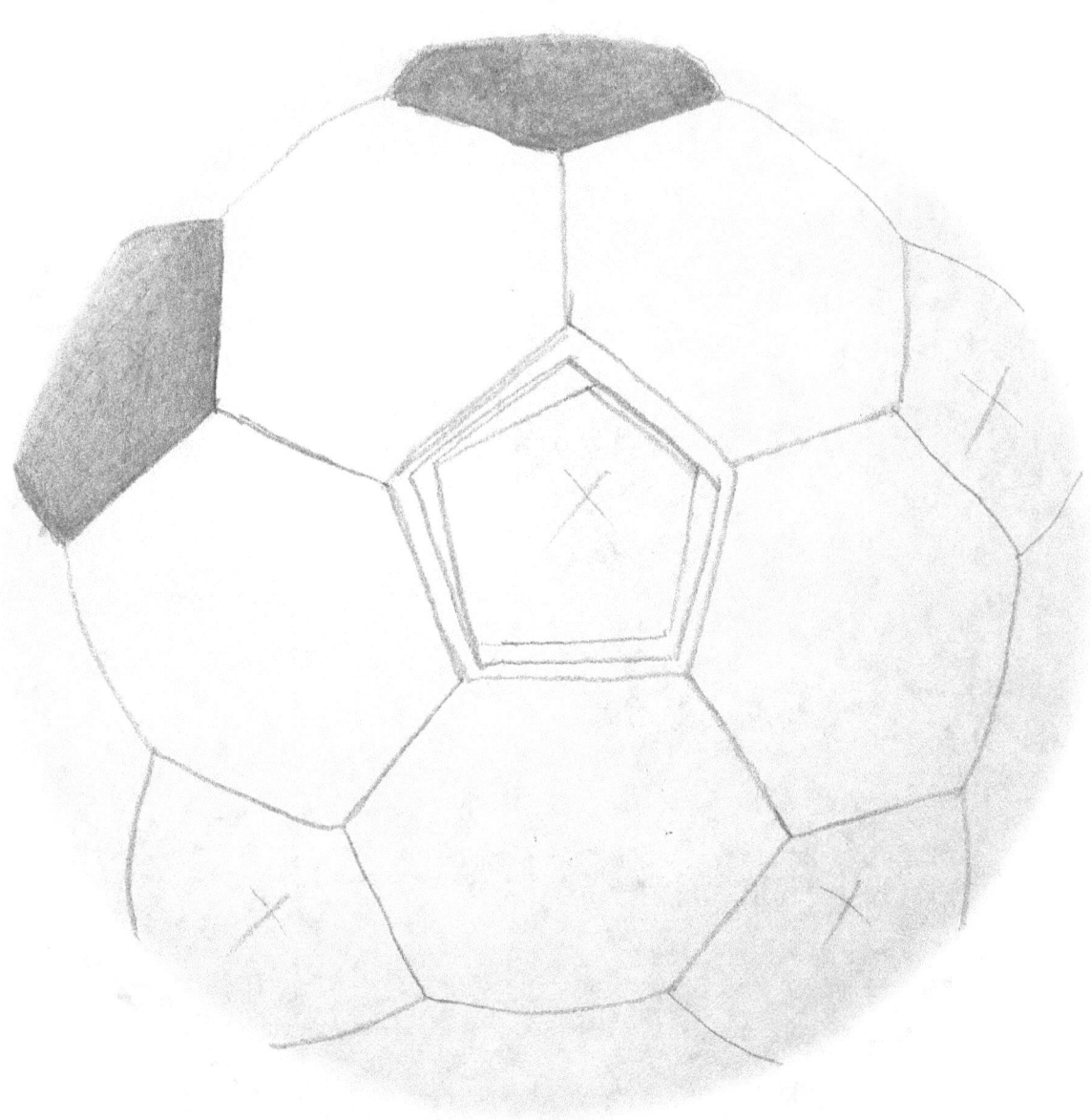

Continue with an HB to cover the upper-left part of the Pentagon in the middle because this part is more illuminated, and then we are going to continue with the darker pencil. Here also, apply the same pressure all the time and circular motions.

Also, shade the parts of the marginal pentagons that would get more light, still using an HB and the edge of the pentagon that is found in the self-shadowed area. The edge of a ball is always more illuminated, and this is called reflected light.

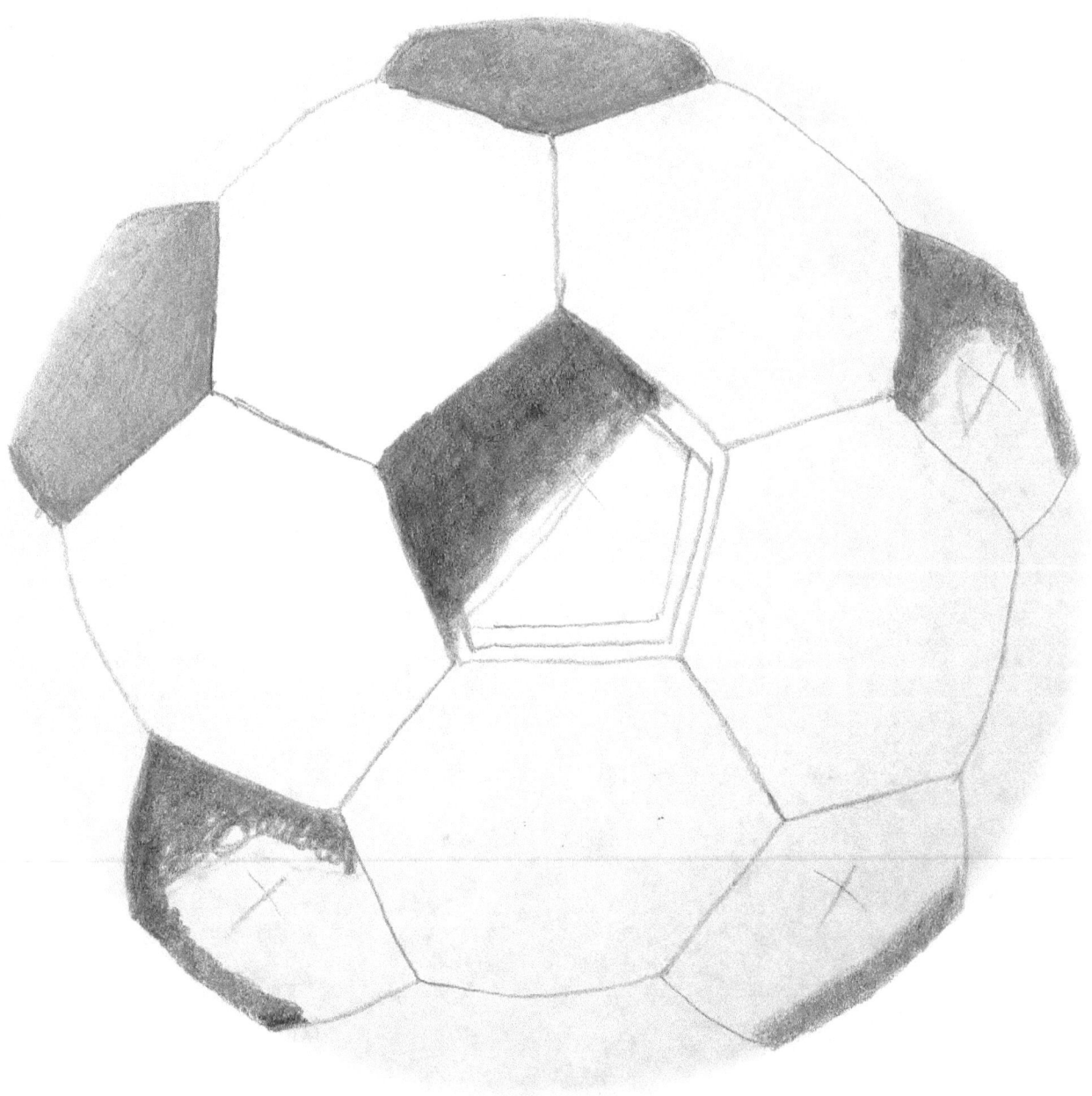

Use a 6B or darker pencil to color the rest of the pentagons. As you can see, the lighter area that we created over the outer edge of the pentagon in shadow, with an HB, represents the light that is reflecting from the table where the ball is placed. It will also indicate the roundness of the ball, and it comes to expression after the darkest pencil is applied.

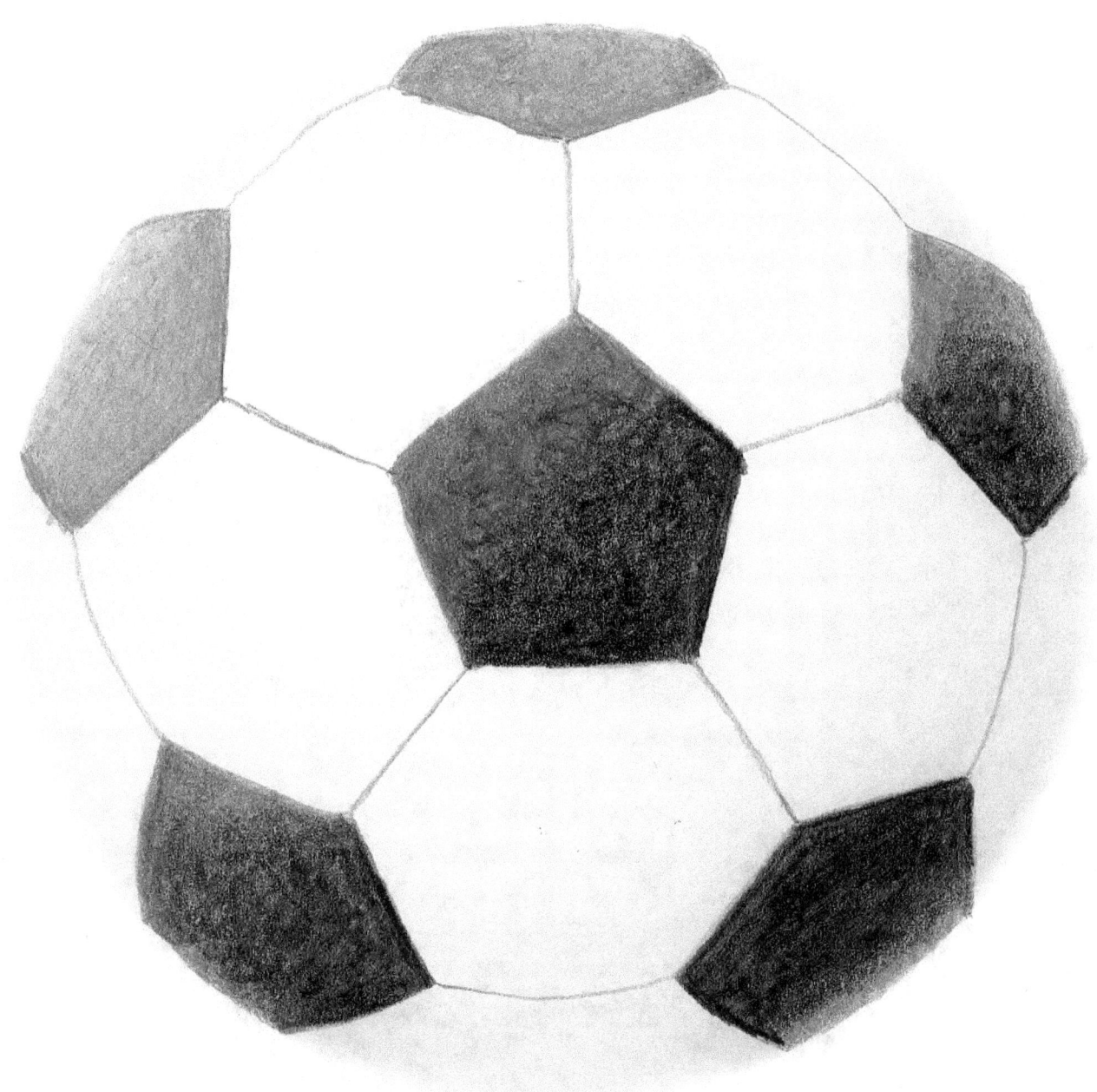

Next, blend the edges between the white hexagons with a blending stump to make them look a bit bent inwards. Try not to make these too dark, so you don't have to dip the dip of your blending stump into the graphite powder, but apply just as much as you have left on it from the previous blending.

Next time, try to draw a ball with different patterns, or even basketball ball, tennis ball, or even billiard balls by following the shading steps from this tutorial.

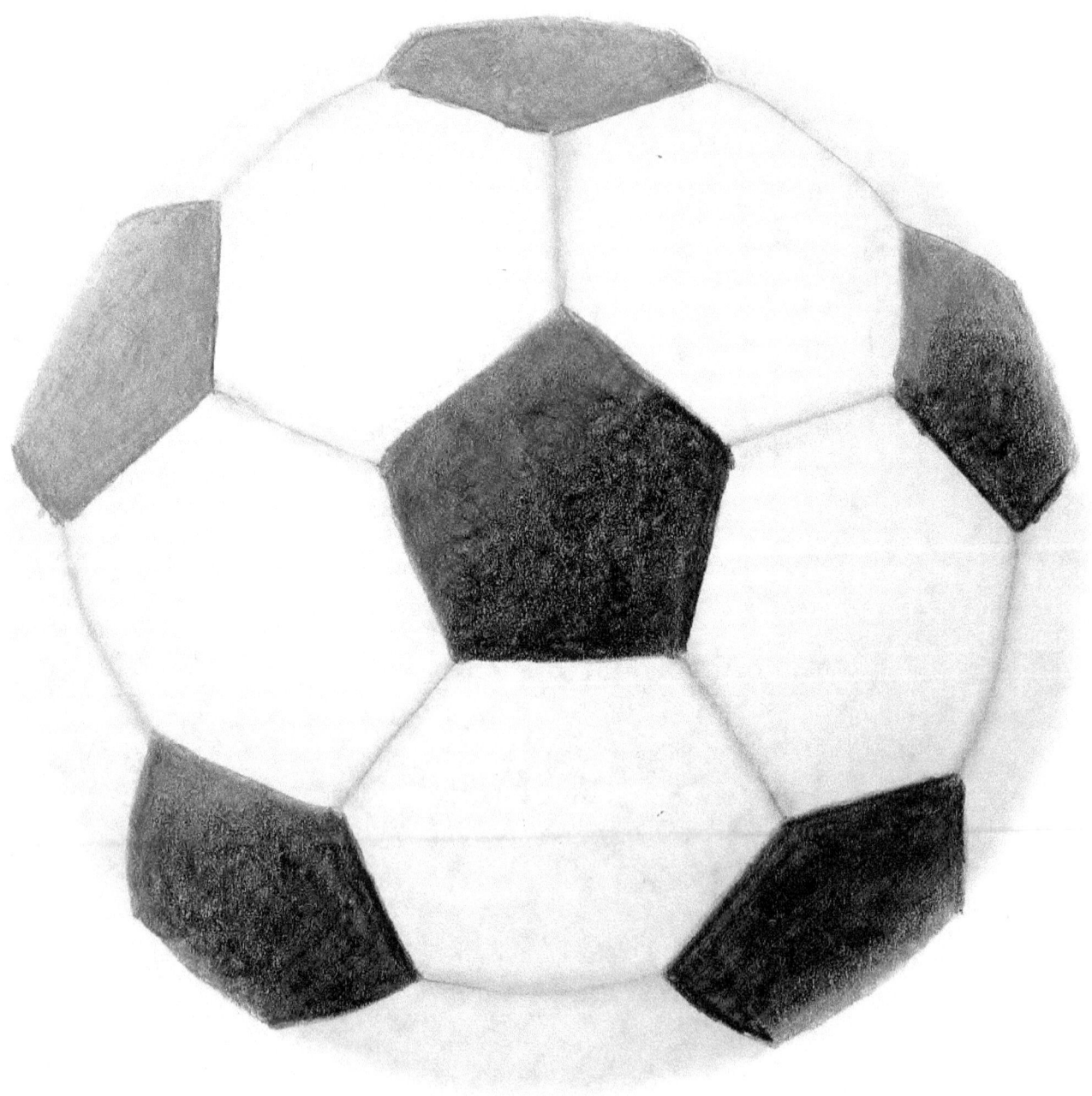

Lastly, create the cast shadow with graphite powder. Take that circular piece of paper that I told you not to throw out, that you cut out at the very beginning, place it over the ball covering it completely.

If our light source is coming from the upper-left corner, the cast shadow will fall over the table, next to the lower-right edge of the ball.

Wrap a tissue around your finger, dip it into the graphite powder and create the cast shadow by applying horizontal movements, over the circular piece of paper too. The cast shadow has to be the darkest next to the ball, so go over this area more often, and also lessen the pressure as you shade away from the ball. The cast shadow, as always, has to disappear into the background/table gradually.

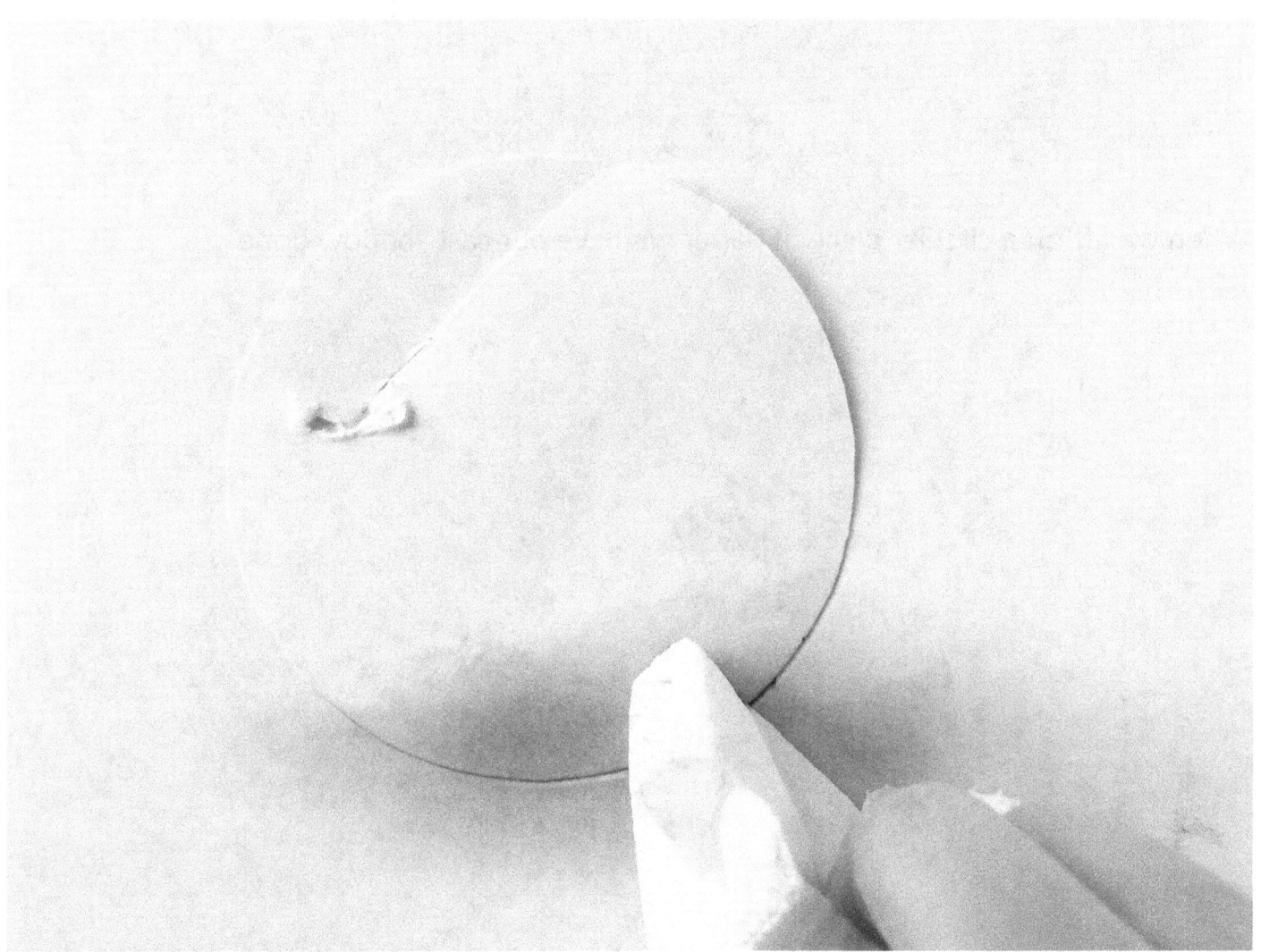

Tip

Don't worry about not being happy with a drawing or how it looks. The result doesn't matter because it's a process. Just draw and keep drawing and over time you'll improve. On the other hand, it is also not good if you are solely satisfied with your drawings. This means that you have no reason to improve and practice.

Be realistic and keep working hard.

When we lift off a circular piece of paper we have our cast shadow done.

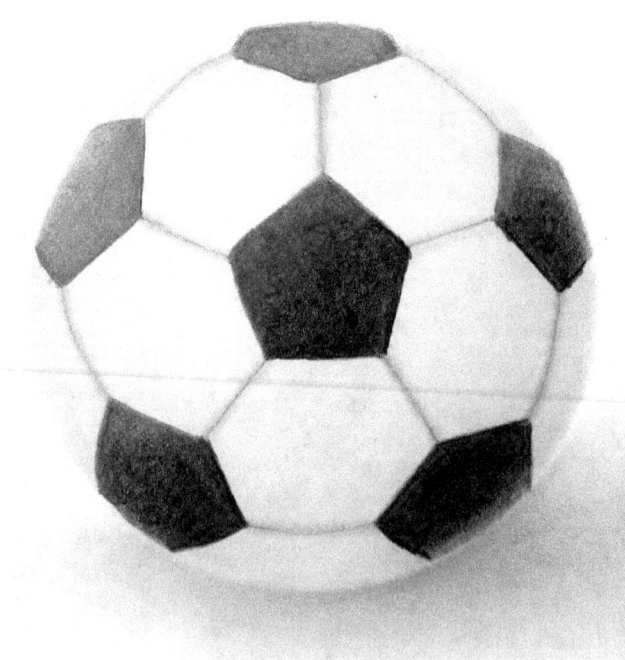

KNITTED FABRIC TEXTURE

Let's draw needed fabric texture, something like a wool thread that interweaves, the material that the wool clothes are made off. You will see this pattern when you zoom in the fabrics.

I suggest drawing repetitive patterns because they are very good for you to practice drawing. Not only this pattern but any pattern, like mandalas and anything repetitive, so that you can practice your observational skills, gain patience, and take measures with your eyes. When you create the same pattern again, you will make it better because you will have more experience and you will know better where and how to draw.

Start creating the rows that contain four units, as shown in the next image. A single unit is marked with bold lines. This is similar to the "V" letter, but it has to be created with two parallel lines, which will indicate the thickness of the wool. The bottom lines shouldn't be connected. Try to make each unit and the distance between the units the same, as much as possible.

Then draw three more columns, so that you can have at least four rows and four columns. 2-3 are not enough for the texture to be recognizable, and it's not enough for practicing.

When you take a look at it upside down, you should see the same pattern. Then you will know that the pattern is good. Rotate your paper often to check it up. Of course, we can't make it like perfectly the same, but just approximately, so try your best. It may not be successful at the first try, but if you try it again and again, you will make it better. In the next image, you can see that my pattern is also not perfect, but it's okay.

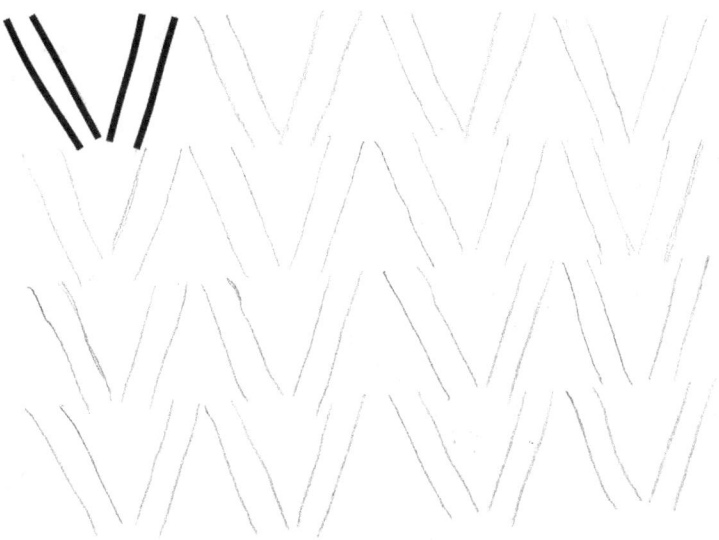

Now we can connect these threads with curvy lines. I have marked what I do in this step with bold lines that you can see in the next image. Draw double lines and try to make the same distance between these lines all the time, namely the same thickness of the thread.

In the first row, these are fully visible, but in the second, third, and fourth row, they have to be drawn behind the upper areas of the units, as shown in the following diagram.

When you create one unit, take a look at the upper one to make it the same as that one, and on the left and the right side, when you have drawn them already, and try to do the same, as much as possible.

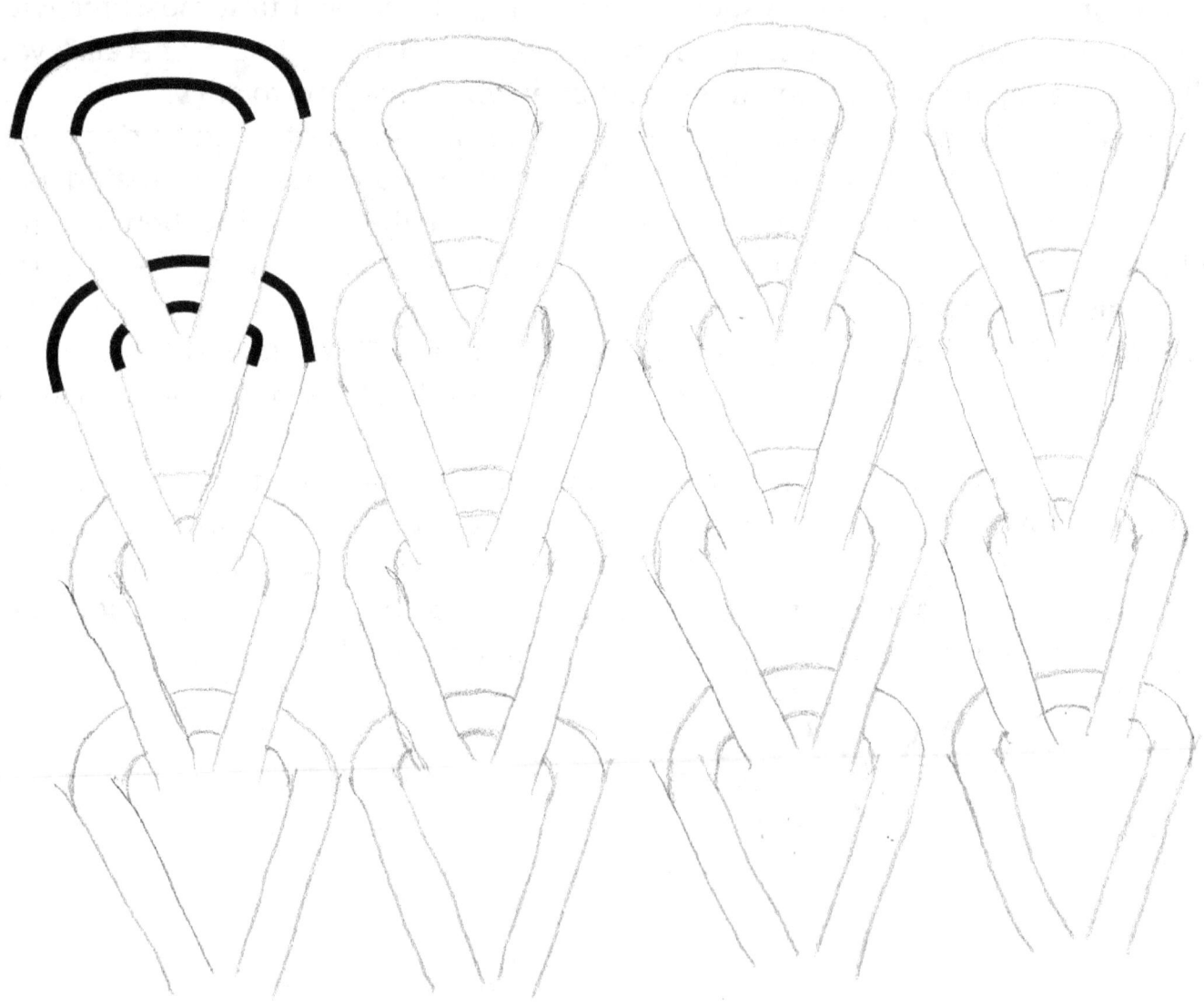

Next, we actually have to do the same, but with the paper turned upside down. Of course, you don't have to rotate it, but rather practice different strokes and movements this time. So, draw the curvy lines to connect the lower parts of the units, and go behind the upper areas of the units. I have placed the bold lines over the connections that I am creating in this step. Analyze the image before you start drawing.

Now you see how they are interwoven. The marginal units would have their connections cut, so leave them the way I have done, or draw more units next to them.

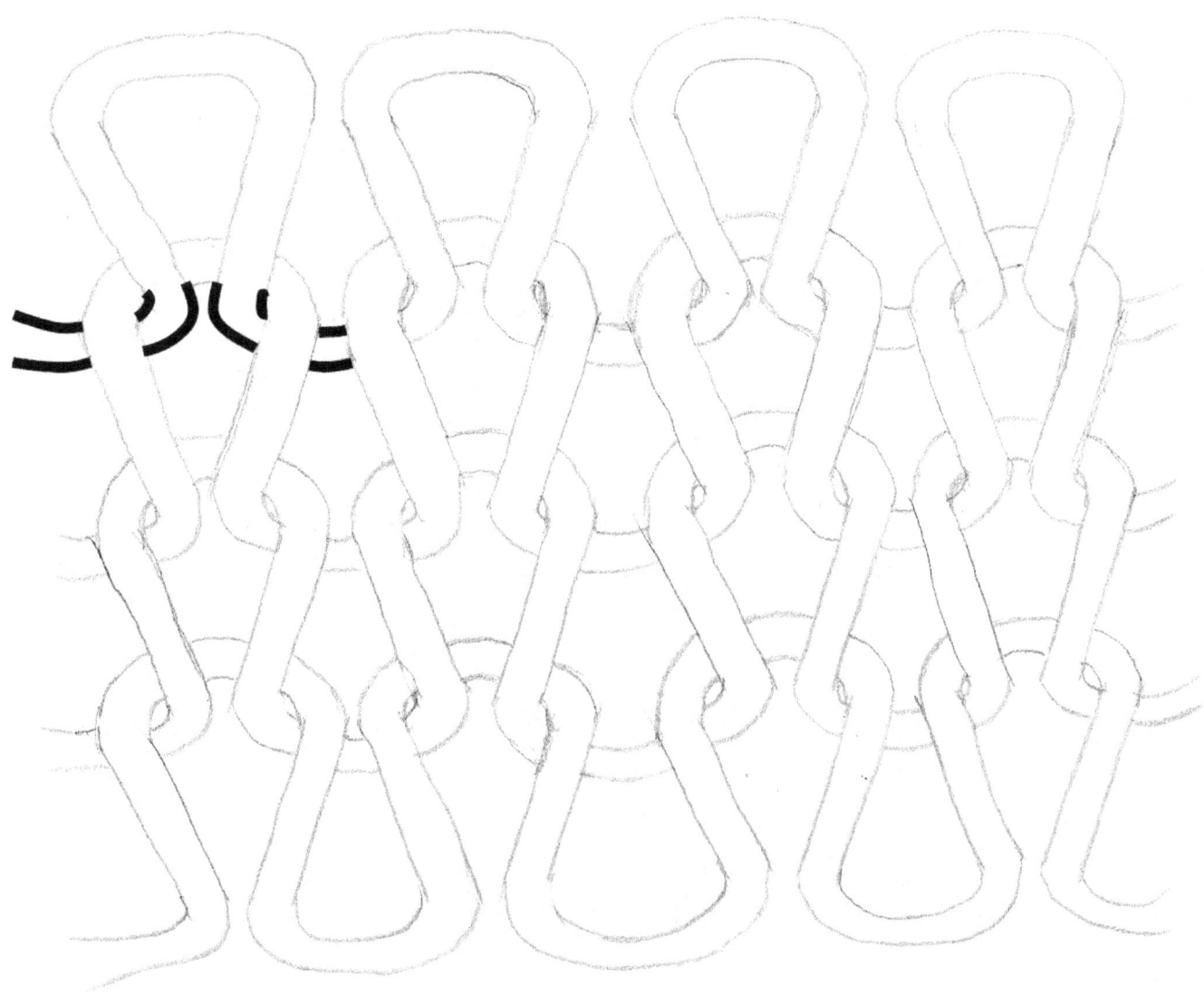

Erase the unnecessary lines, if you have them drawn around the main lines.
Now we can start shading. I want to use a blending stump and to shade next to the edge, within the thread. It will make the thread look round and less flat. You can do it even with a pencil and then blend it with a blending stump. To make the shading simpler, do this only with the straight areas, for now.
Erase the graphite that you have applied over the background, next to the thread to make the edges clean and sharp.

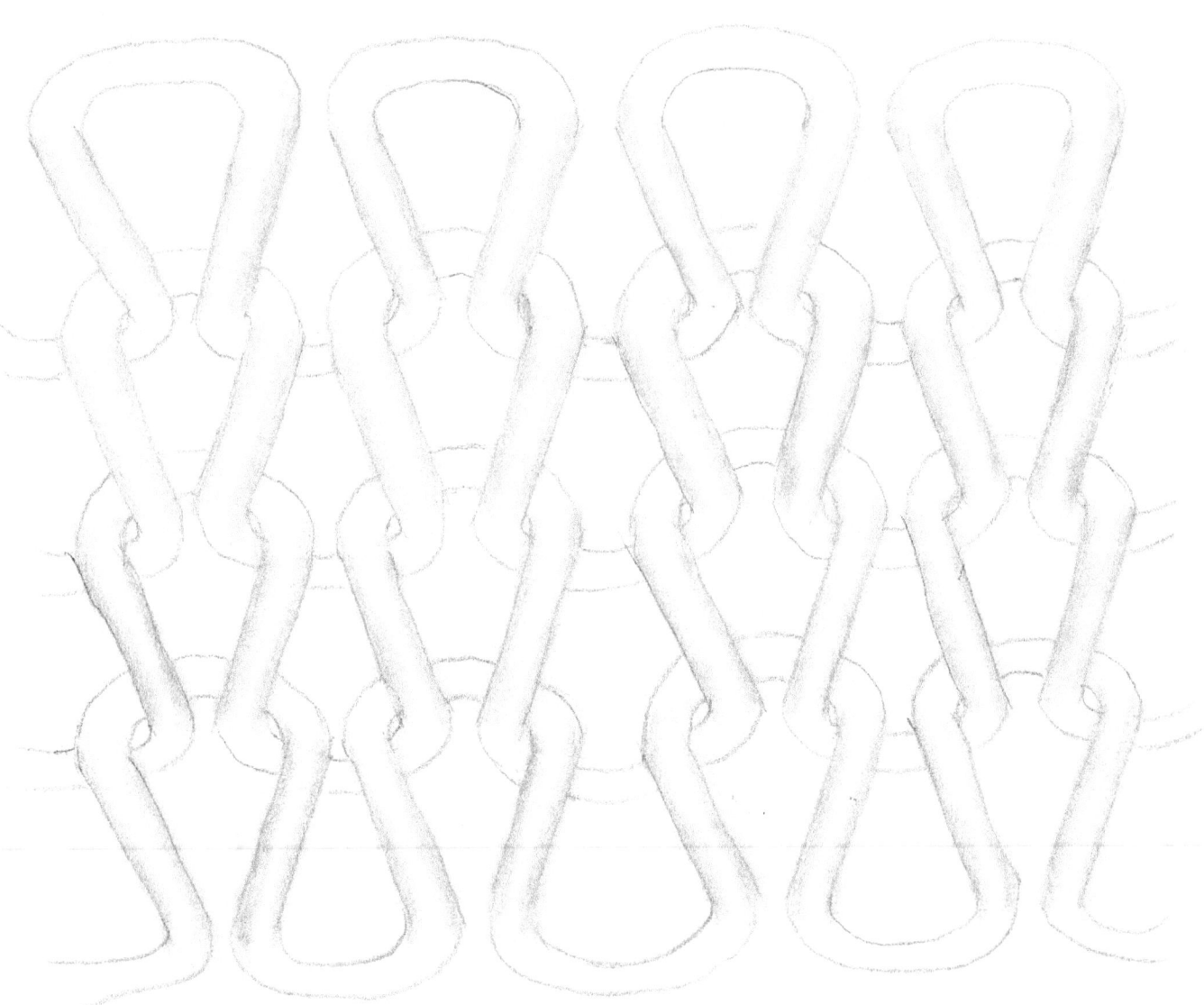

Next, shade the parts of the thread that receive less light, namely the parts that go behind the thread. We can actually shade them whole, using an HB. You can use an H, or a 2H also.

Study the next image and compare it to the previous image to see the difference and which areas I have shaded.

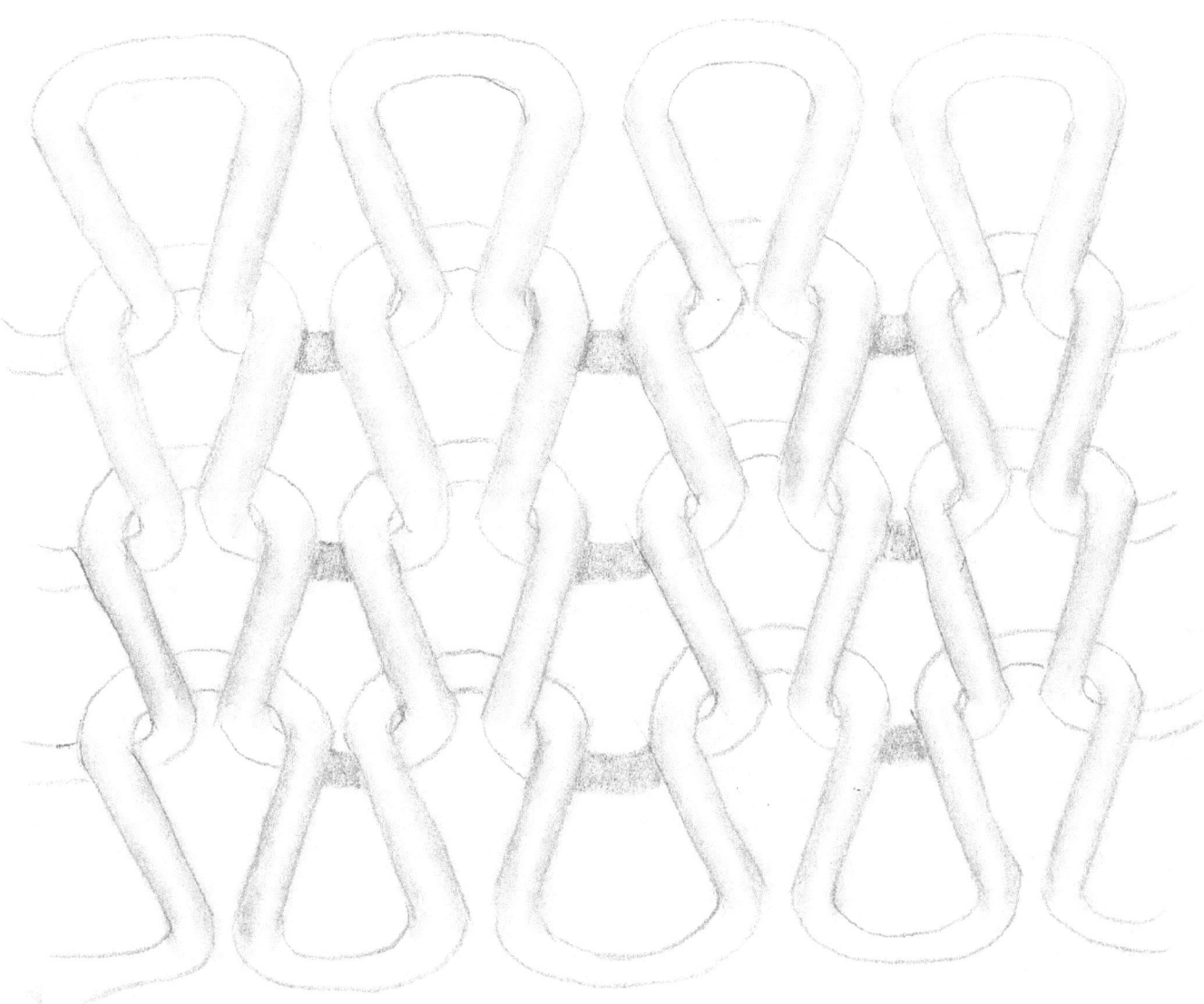

Next, let's shade also the upper parts of the units that are found behnd he lower parts of the units. For his, we can use a blending stump or we can even use a lighter pencil and to shade them. Particularly in the lower area to shade more and then a bit less in the upper area. It will also make the thread look round. I'm using a 2H for this. Fill the upper areas of the units completely and then press harder in the lower area, or you can even use two different pencils for this.

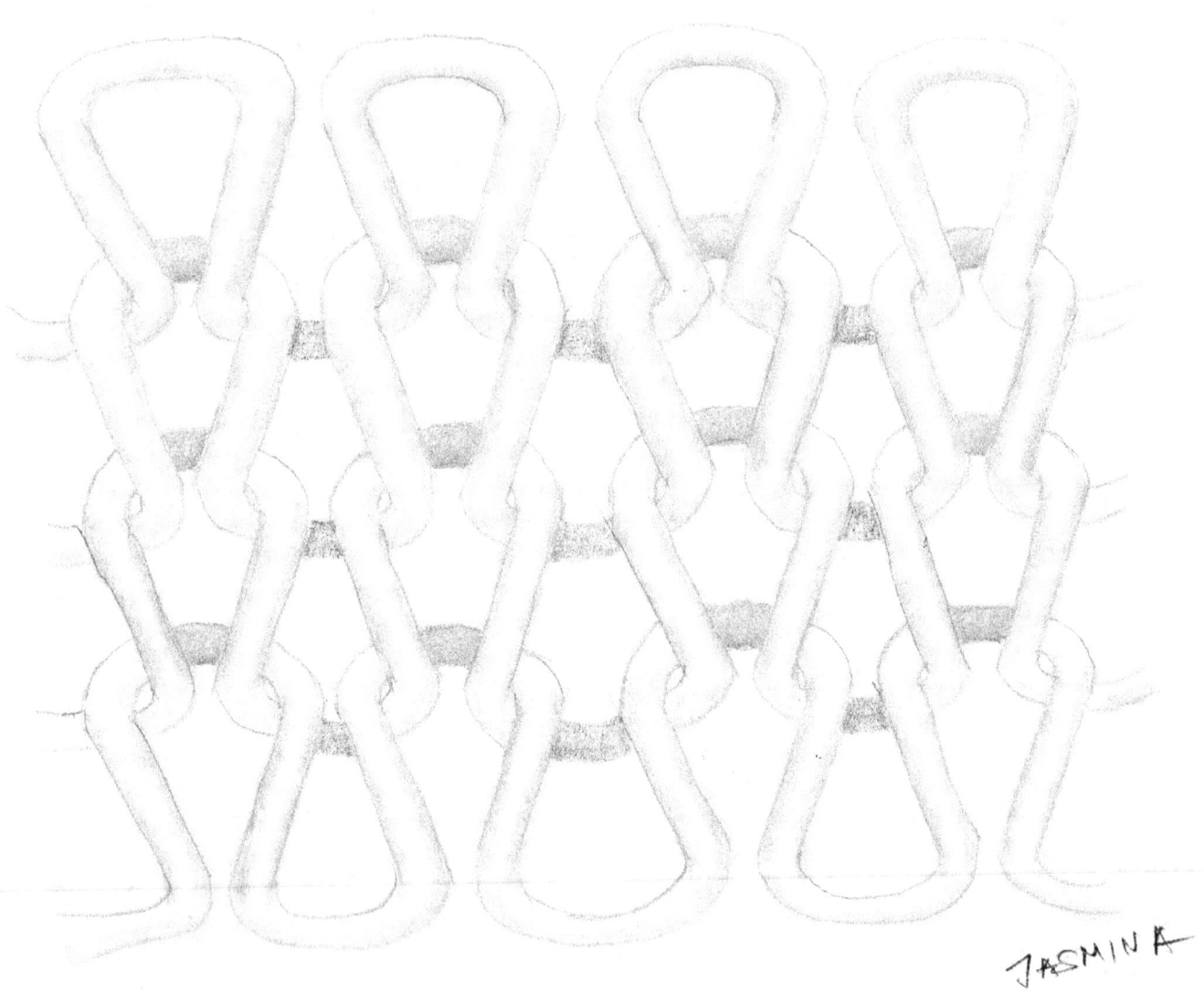

A PALM TREE ON A BEACH

Let's draw a landscape next. I want to draw a palm on the beach and to use a square orientation, 21 cm x 21 cm (8" x 8").

Mark the horizon, the edge between the sky and the sea/ocean with a straight, horizontal line using a ruler. Then apply the graphite powder with a tissue to shade the upper half of the paper for the sky. Start at the top because the sky should be darker there and apply only horizontal movements. As you shade downwards, you will run out of the graphite and this way you will create a smooth gradient between the darker and lighter tones because the sky is always a lighter next to the horizon.

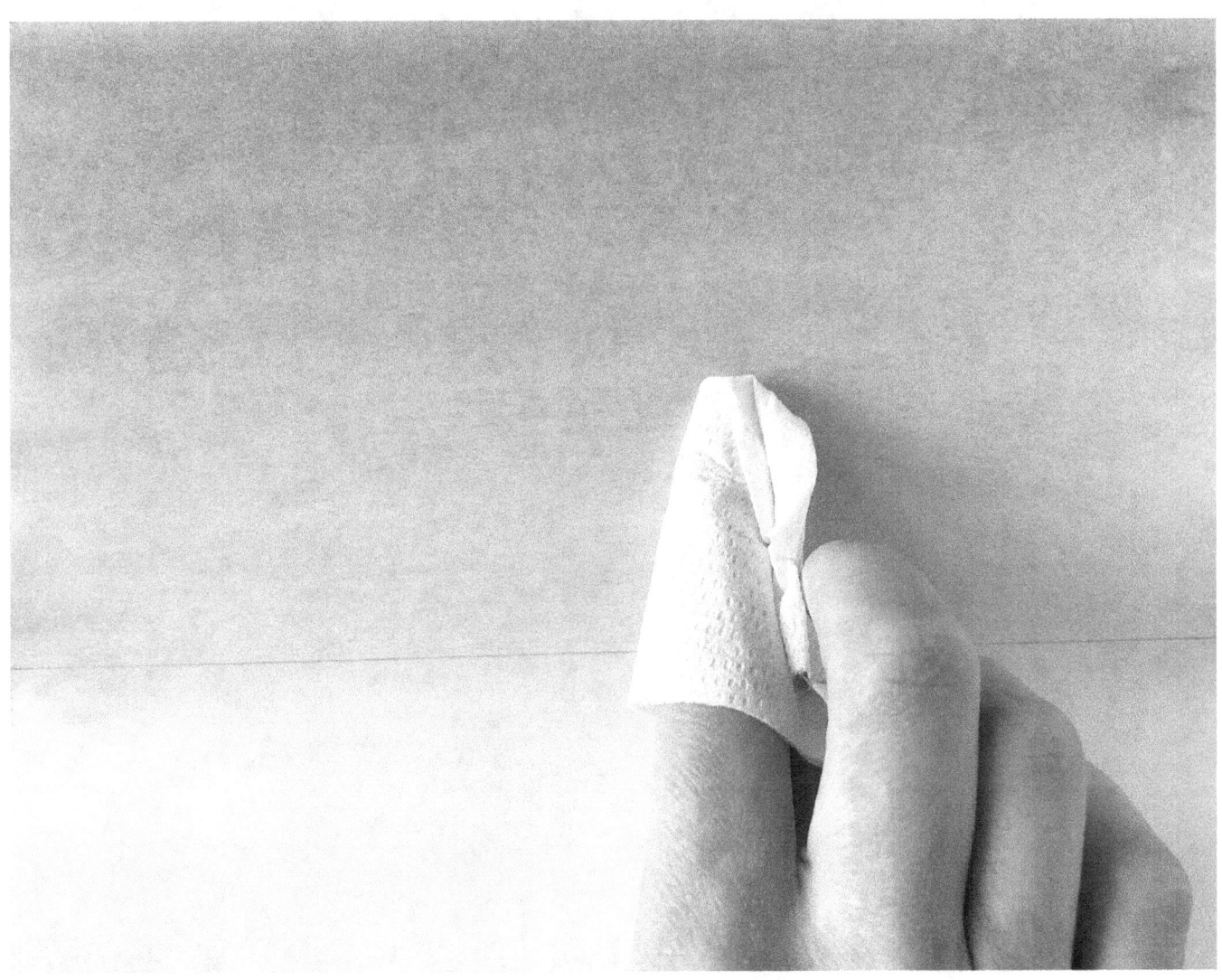

The next thing is to create clouds over the sky. You can skip this step, but I think it's a good idea to practice creating the clouds and it's pretty interesting to do. Not to

mention that the sky will look interesting and less boring with some clouds around.
I want to use an electric eraser because this tool allows me to clear most of the graphite and I won't smudge anything around so that the edges of my clouds can stay clean. You can use any other eraser, and only a kneaded eraser is not hard enough to remove a lot of graphite. Create your clouds anywhere you want. In the next image, you can see where I have placed mines. They can be thicker or thinner, longer or shorter, and of course, don't forget about the very small ones, which are always in a larger distance and closer to the horizon. The upper part of the clouds is always the brightest or actually, it's absolutely white, and the lower area is always in self-shadow. Since we can't make it absolutely white again after shading, we can apply a bit of an opaque, white marker at the top of the clouds.

Now we can create the lower edges of these clouds which are also pretty illuminated so they have to be lighter than the self-shadow of the clouds. Create a tiny line all under the clouds with a sharp point of an eraser.

And now we can also lighten up the self-shadow and I want to use a kneaded eraser for this because I don't want to lighten it up too much. So gently touch this area with a kneaded eraser because it can have almost the same value as the sky in the middle. You can see that all these erasers are good for different things. So you can't remove enough graphite with a kneaded eraser and, for example, an electric eraser would remove too much. So it is a good idea to invest in a few different types of erasers to make your work easier and more enjoyable.

The next thing is to draw the sea or the ocean. So we have already determined the position of the horizon, somewhere in the middle of the paper and now we can shade right under it. We have to shade the upper part of the sea much darker then we have to make it lighter. I suggest using a ruler to place it over the sky and to shade under it. Use an HB pencil for this area. Change the pressure to create some darker and lighter areas.

As a next value, you can use a 2H and shade right after the HB area and downwards. Of course, apply only horizontal moments with your pencil. Press harder next to the HB area and then lessen the pressure as you draw downwards.

Now we can shade the sand with graphite powder just the way we did with the sky, but this time we don't have to create a smooth gradient but to make it the same everywhere. So, dip a tissue in the graphite powder and apply it over the bottom of your paper evenly as shown in the next image.

Using a blending stump, shade some hills above the horizon. Since the hills would be found in a larger distance, they should be lighter and their edges should be blurry. Of course, you can draw them with some H pencil pressing lightly, and then blend it all.

Create some darker, horizontal areas over the sea which will represent the waves using an HB and blending it.

And now we can create the foam between the sea and the sand. I want to use an electric eraser to eliminate a bit of the graphite over the upper part of the sand and the lower part of the sea. Try to make different shapes of foam; at random, just don't make it straight like the horizon.

Let's create the cast shadow under the foam, the shadow that is cast by the foam over the sand. I'm using a blending stump for this. This way we're going to make the foam more prominent and lifelike.

Next, let's create some details of the foam with a white marker or with a white ink gel pen. In the next image, you can see that I have added a lot of flying drops that are created when the waves splash to something. If you don't want these parts too bright, just tap the white marker with your finger while it's wet.

Also, draw some vertical, thick lines all over the see to indicate the foam over the coming waves that are still further from the beach.

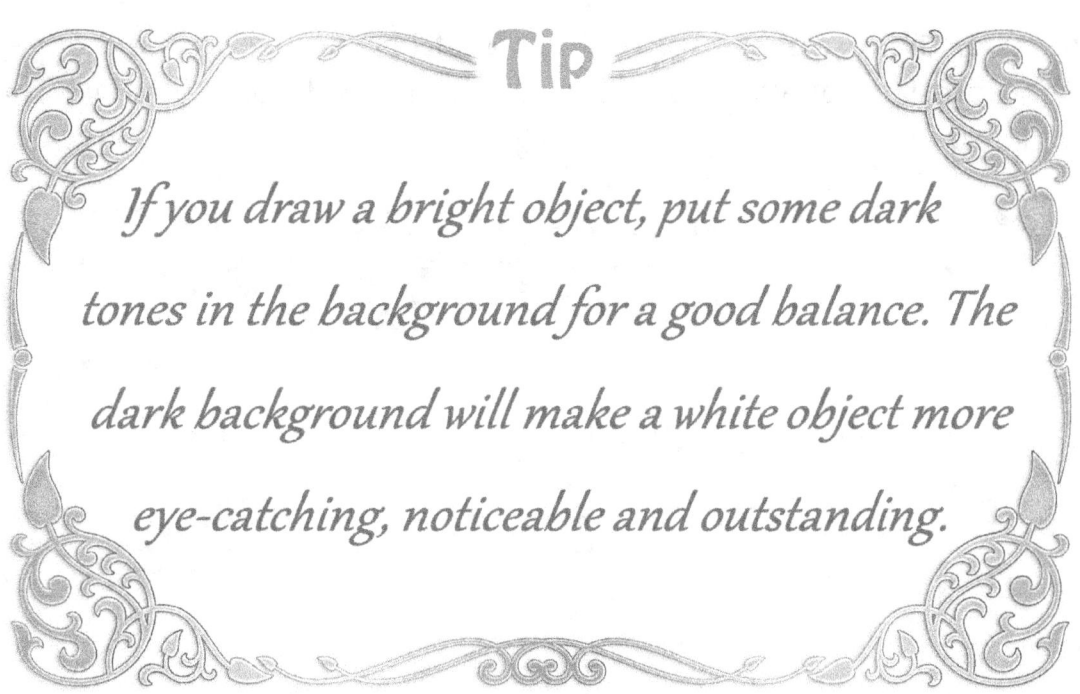

If you draw a bright object, put some dark tones in the background for a good balance. The dark background will make a white object more eye-catching, noticeable and outstanding.

Finally, let's draw a palm tree. Start with the trunk. I want to place the trunk over the sand, the foam and the see as shown in the next image. Since we have to indicate the roundness of the trunk, we have to use darker and lighter pencils to shade it. I'm using a B pencil to cover the right side of the trunk. As always, we have to imagine where our light source, or in this case the direct sunlight, we want to come from. I want my light source to come from the upper-left corner, so the right side of the trunk has to be darker. That's why I shade it with a B pencil. I have added some branches at the top of my trunk, so this is how tall I want it to be.

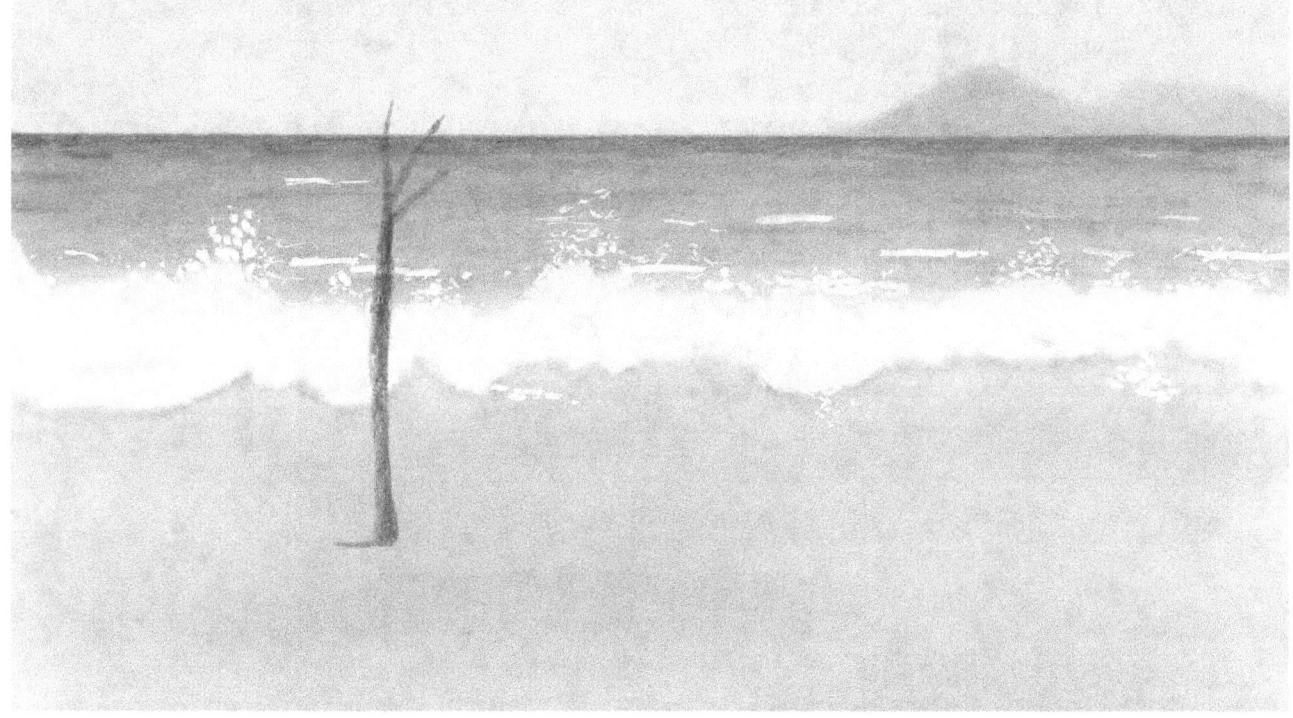

Use a 2H to cover the rest of the trunk. Press a bit harder next to the B edge, and then just lessen the pressure as you draw towards the left side of the trunk. This way the trunk will look round.

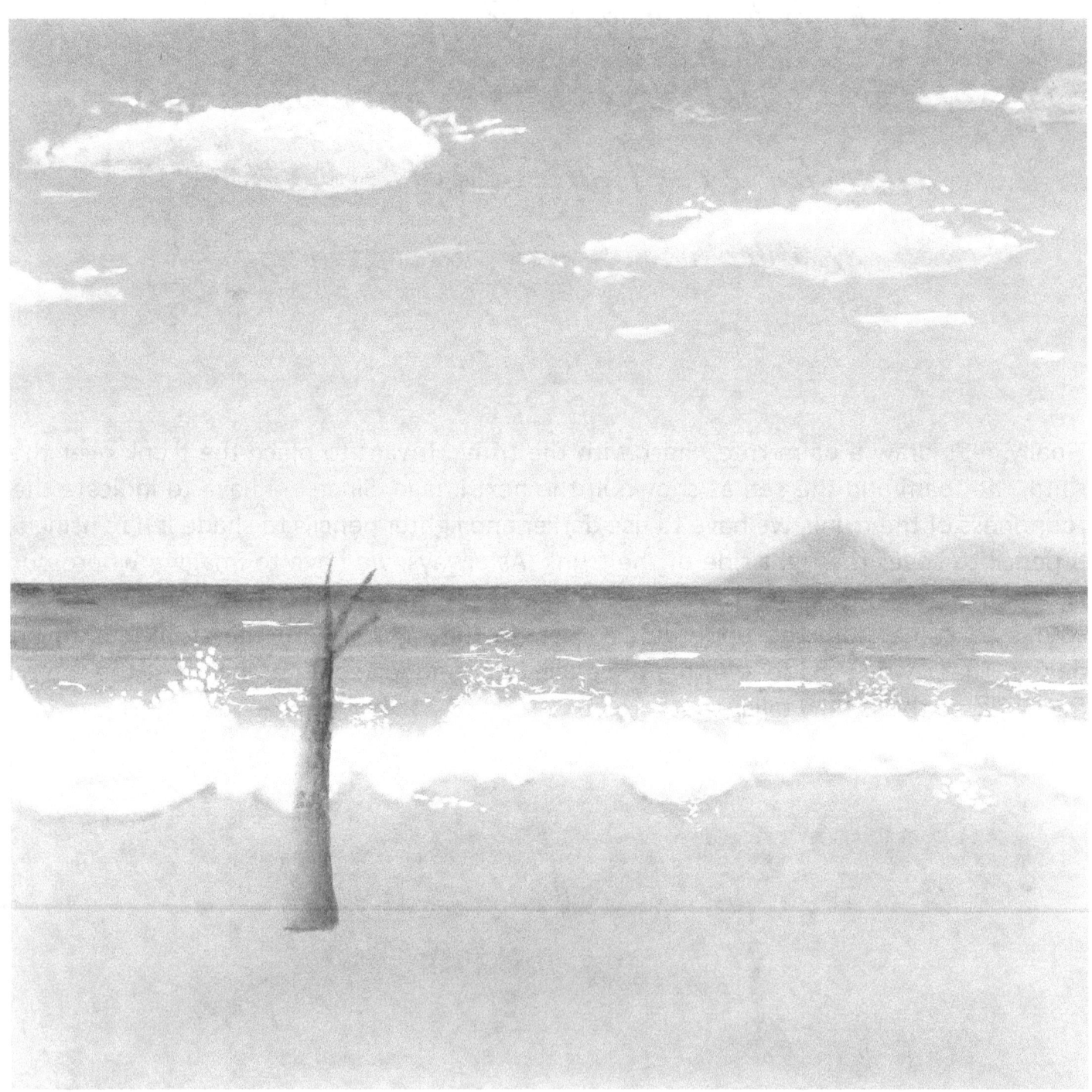

As you can see, the left side of the trunk has the same value as the sand. To separate them, we have to erase a bit of the graphite over the left side of the trunk with a pointed tip of an eraser.

Also, create some patterns over the trunk, like tiny, horizontal lines with a B pencil, at random all over the trunk. Of course, the patterns should be darker on the right side of the trunk in the shadow, and they should be lighter on the left side of the trunk. Create some branches to make it more realistic.

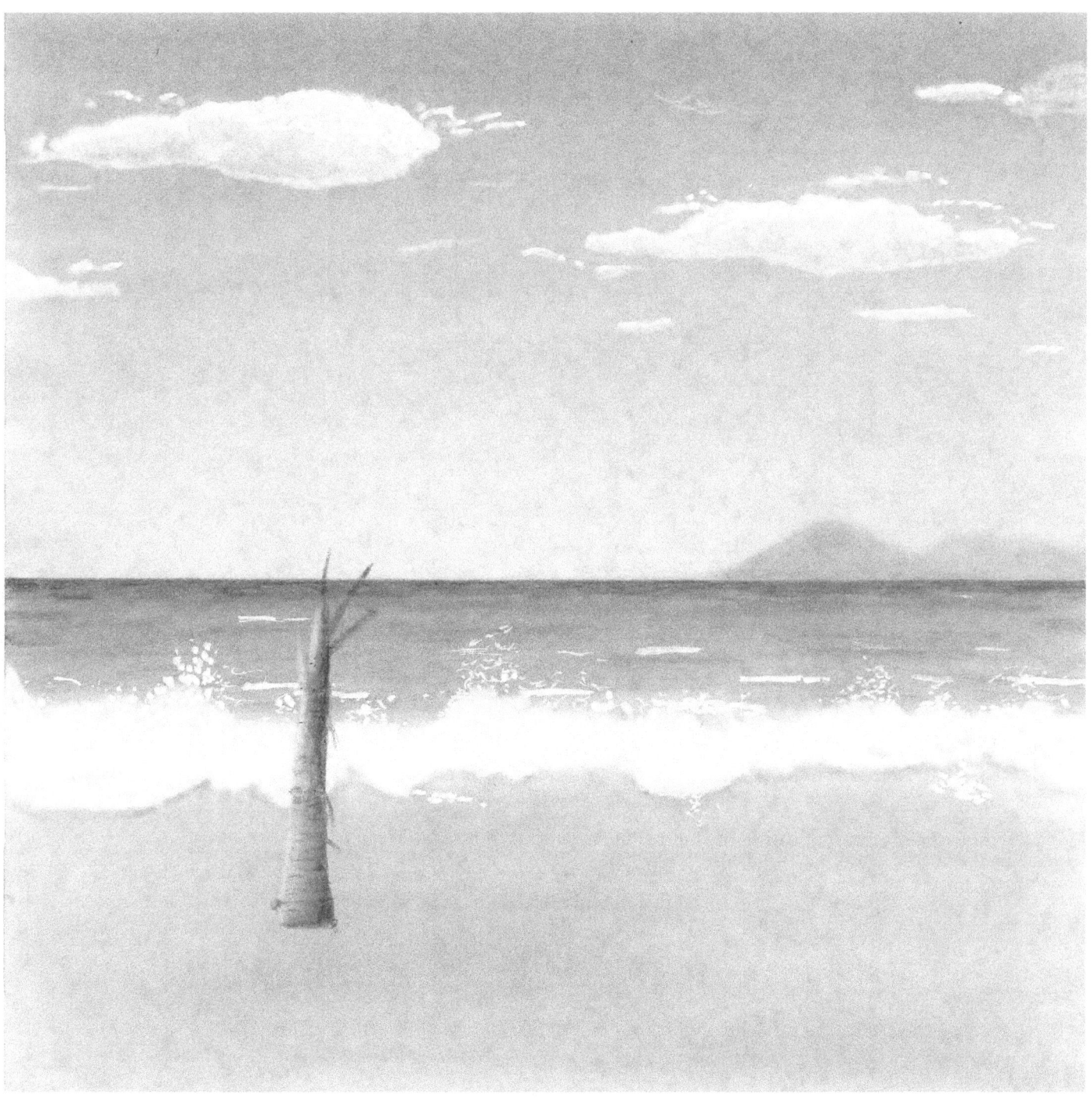

I want to make the branches as if the wind is blowing them. So, I drew all the branches in the direction towards the right side. Of course, you don't have to draw them like this, but I suggest that you always try to do something different, that you haven't seen anywhere else before or what is not usual so that you can have unique artwork.
Place a separate piece of paper over the sand because you don't want to smudge it.
In the next image, you can see the initial line for my branches and how I have sketched out their positions.

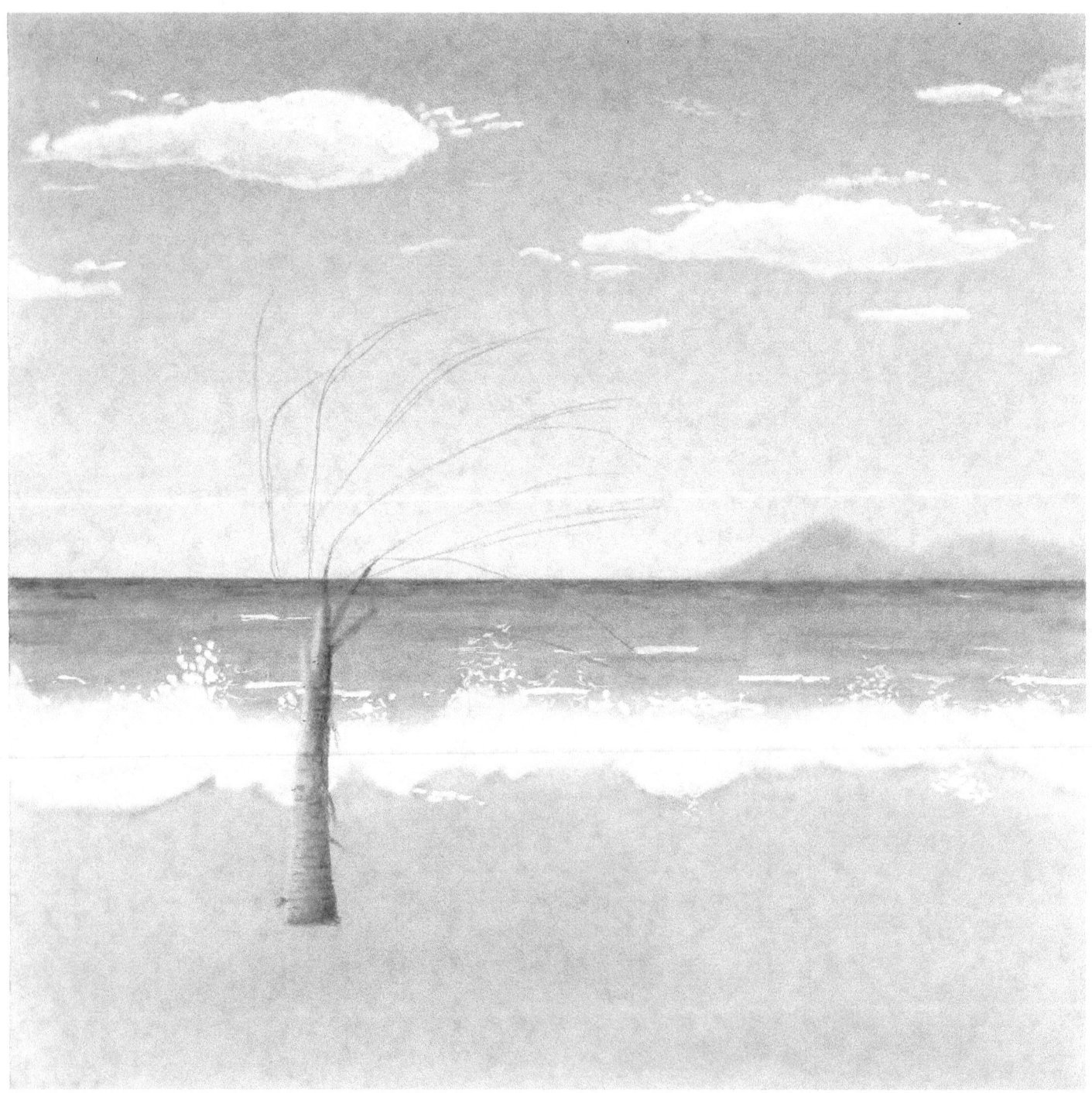

Now we can draw the details: branches and leaflets. I want to start with the mid-tone and to use an HB for it. Then we're going to create the dark leaflets behind these and to create the highlighted leaflets over them.

You can draw more or fewer branches, just the way you wish; they don't have to be the same as mine. You can also change the pressure with an HB pencil to create different values and just focus on one branch at a time.

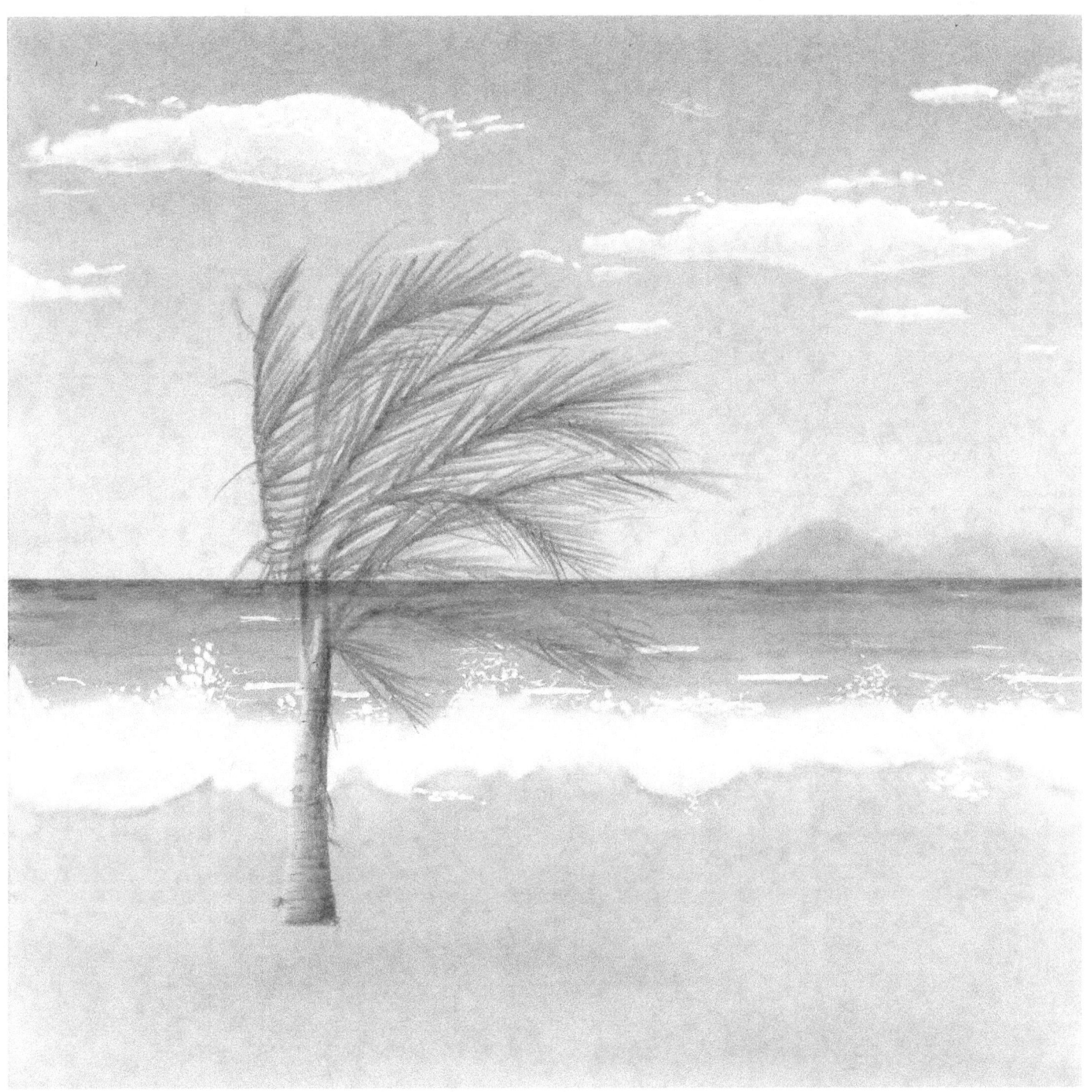

Create some darker parts, for example behind these ones that we just drew. I want to use a 6B, so use at least 3B or 4B or a darker one. Create dark leaflets in between the previously drawn leaflets, at random and press harder. The lower branches always get less light, so shade more in the lower area of the crown.

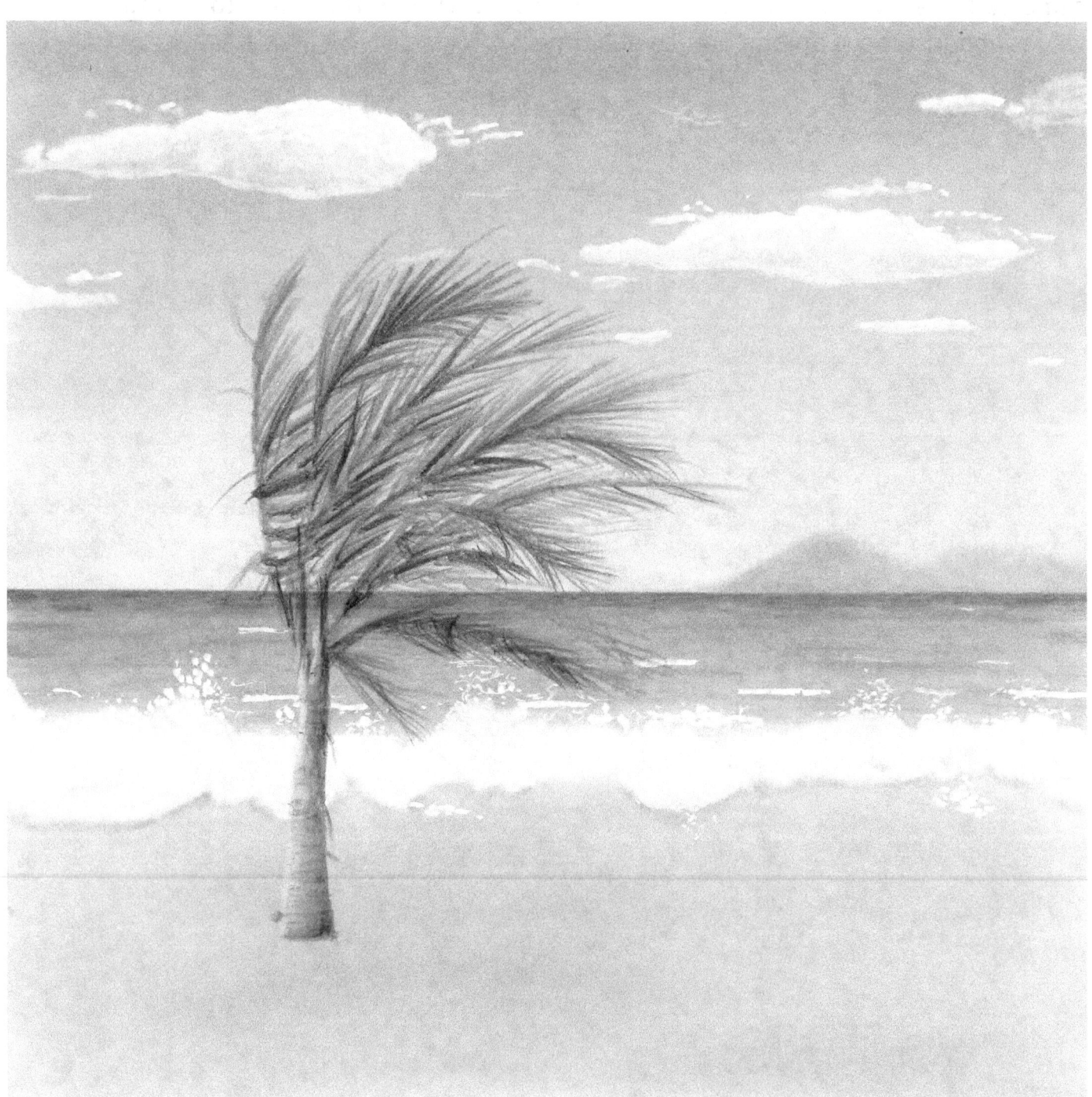

Lastly, create some highlights with an eraser over the leaflets, particularly over the sea, because in darker areas, they can be more visible. If you overdo, or make some mistake, go over with the pencil to darken the highlights.

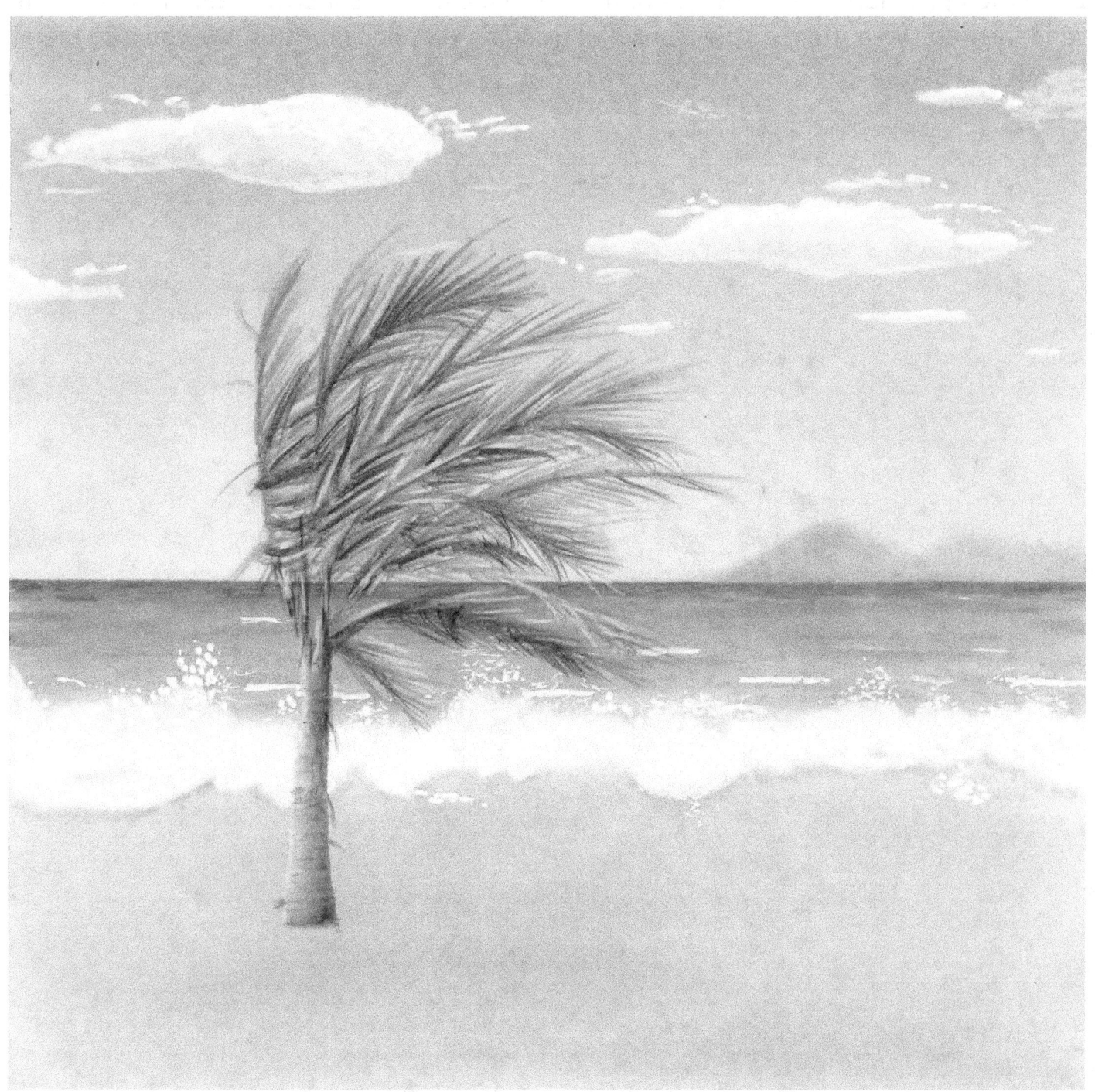

Let's create the cast shadow, the shadow that is cast over the sand by the crown. Here also, you have to imagine a light source, the direct sunlight, where it is coming from and to create the cast shadow accordingly. As I mentioned before, I want my light source to be in the upper-left corner; therefore, I have to create the shadow in the middle of the sand, next to the bottom of the trunk. I'm using an HB pencil for this. We can also blend it with a tissue.

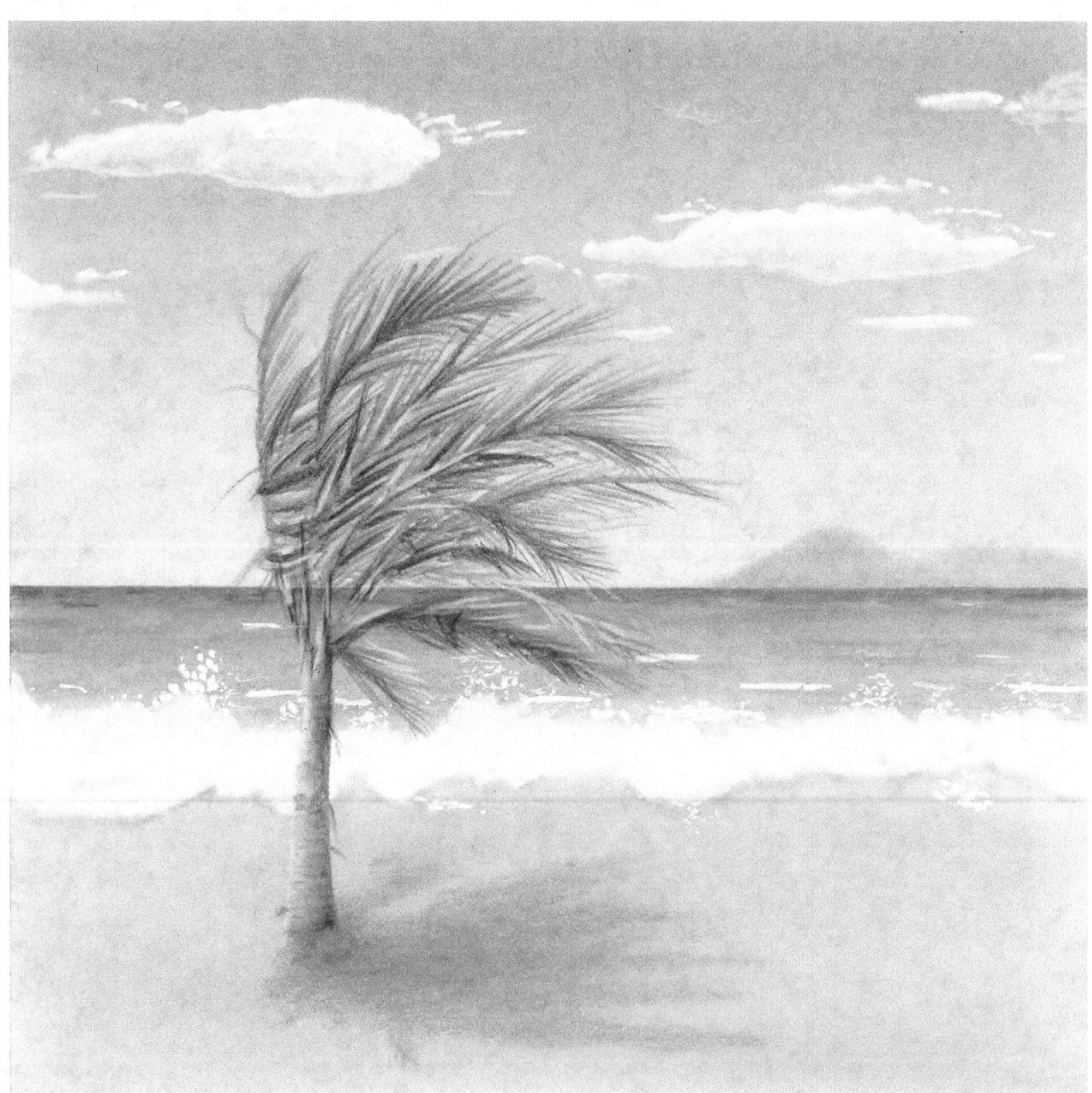

We should also add some other "imperfections" over the sand, for example, some footprints and fallen leaflets.
I use a blending stump, but you can do this with any pencil.

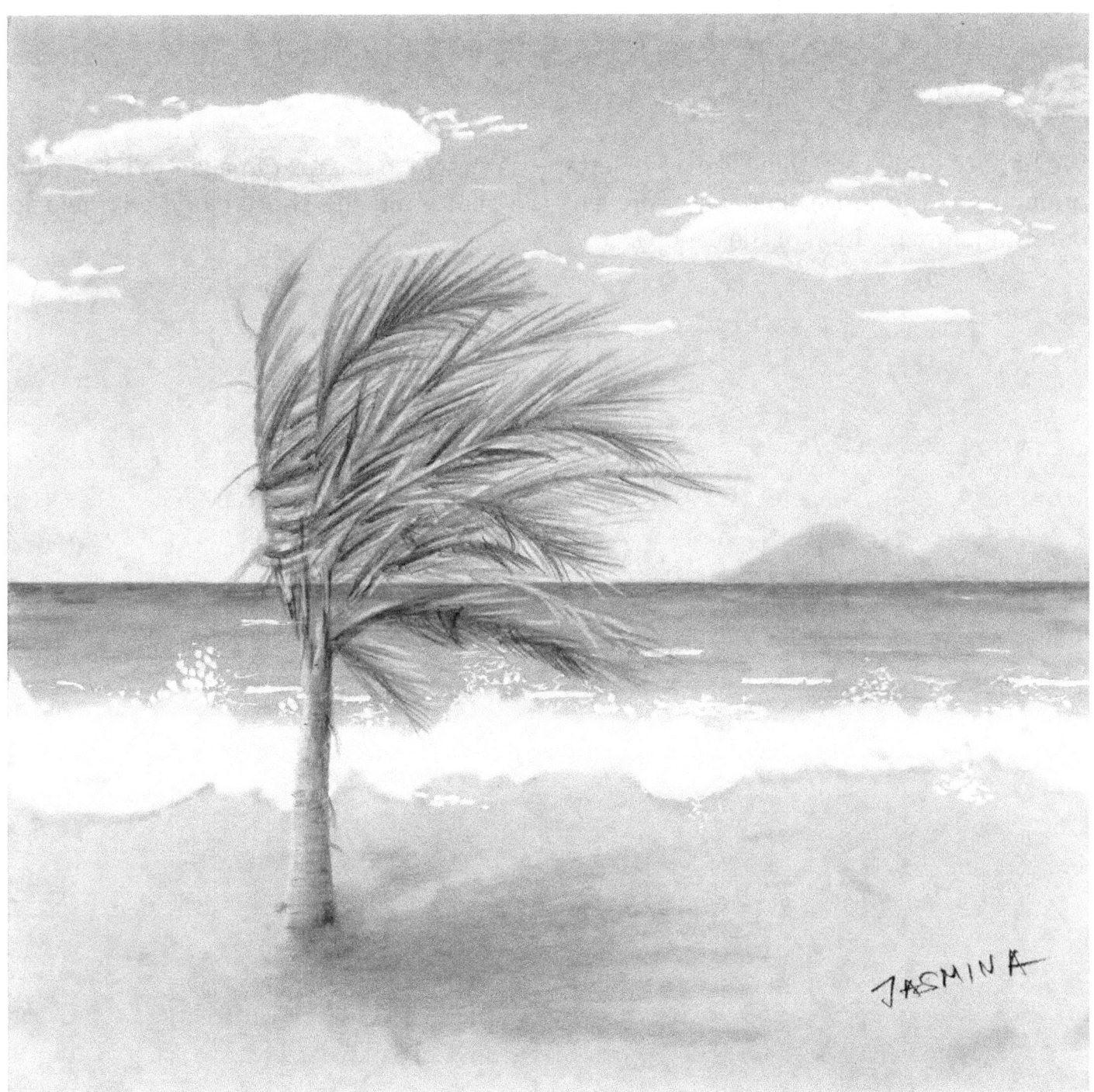

AN UMBRELLA

Next, let's draw an umbrella.

We have to draw something like a "T" letter – as shown in the next image - to have it for orientation. The longer line will represent the shaft, and the shorter one will help to determine the position of the canopy.

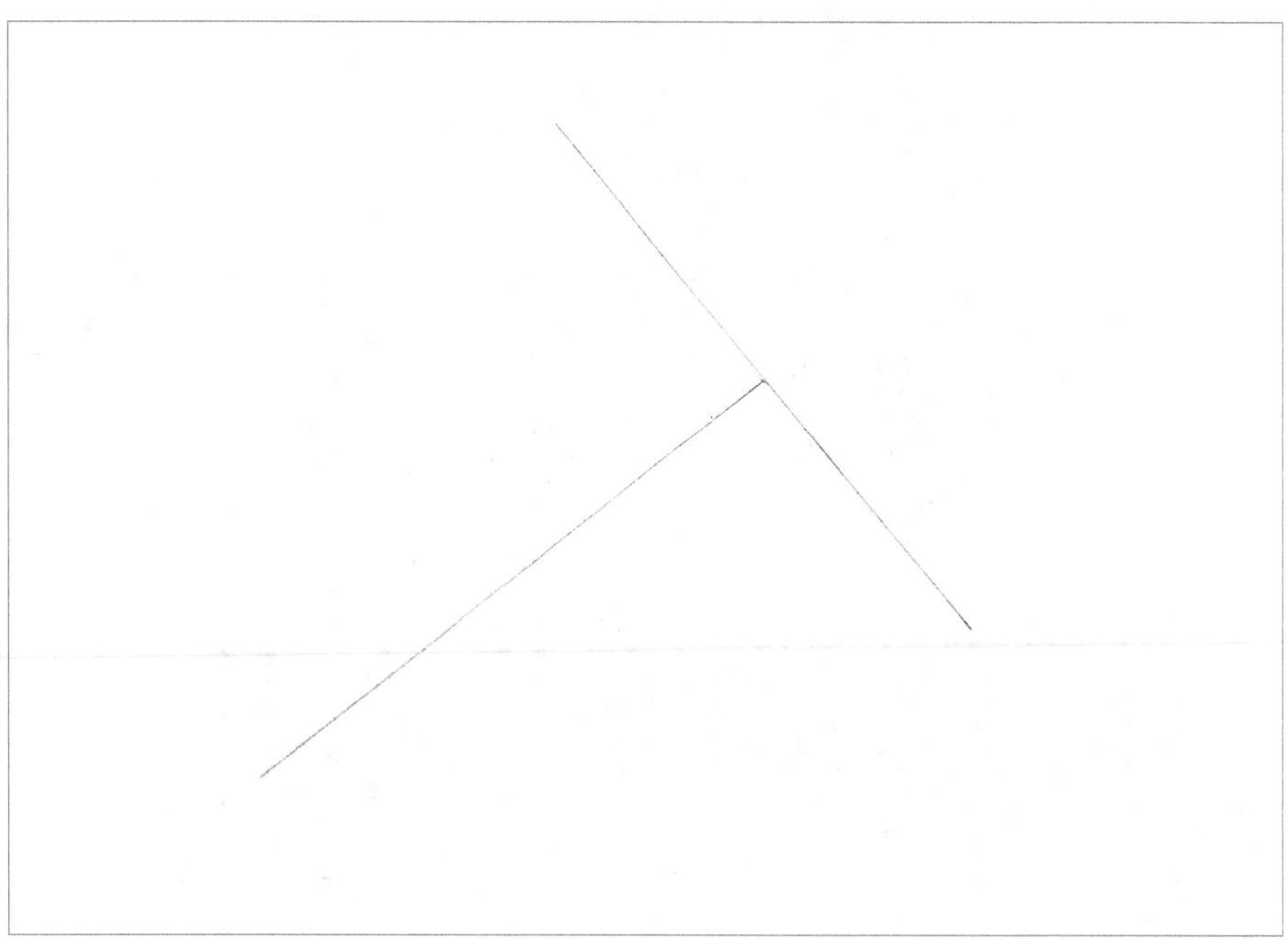

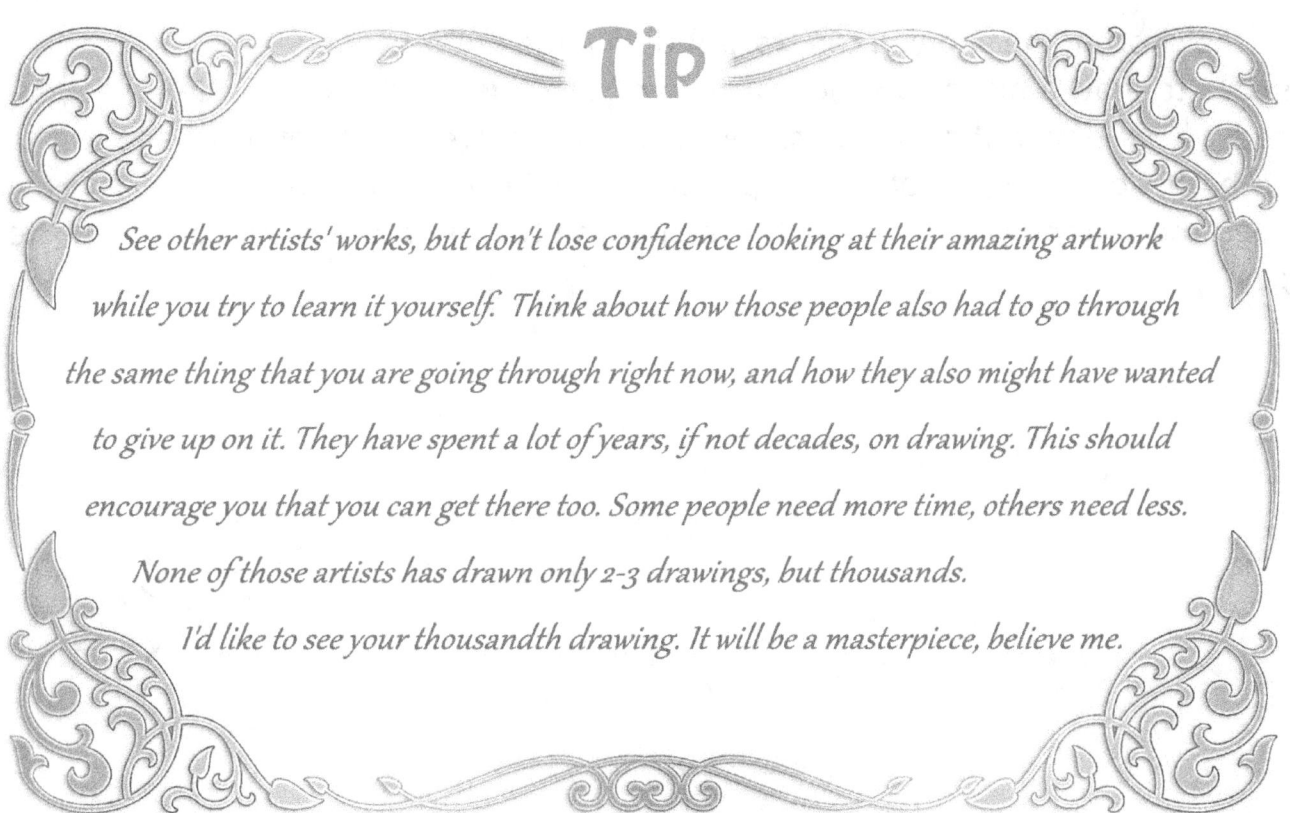

See other artists' works, but don't lose confidence looking at their amazing artwork while you try to learn it yourself. Think about how those people also had to go through the same thing that you are going through right now, and how they also might have wanted to give up on it. They have spent a lot of years, if not decades, on drawing. This should encourage you that you can get there too. Some people need more time, others need less. None of those artists has drawn only 2-3 drawings, but thousands.

I'd like to see your thousandth drawing. It will be a masterpiece, believe me.

Now we can draw two elliptic lines around the shorter line for the tip. In this step, we are actually outlining the inner canopy.

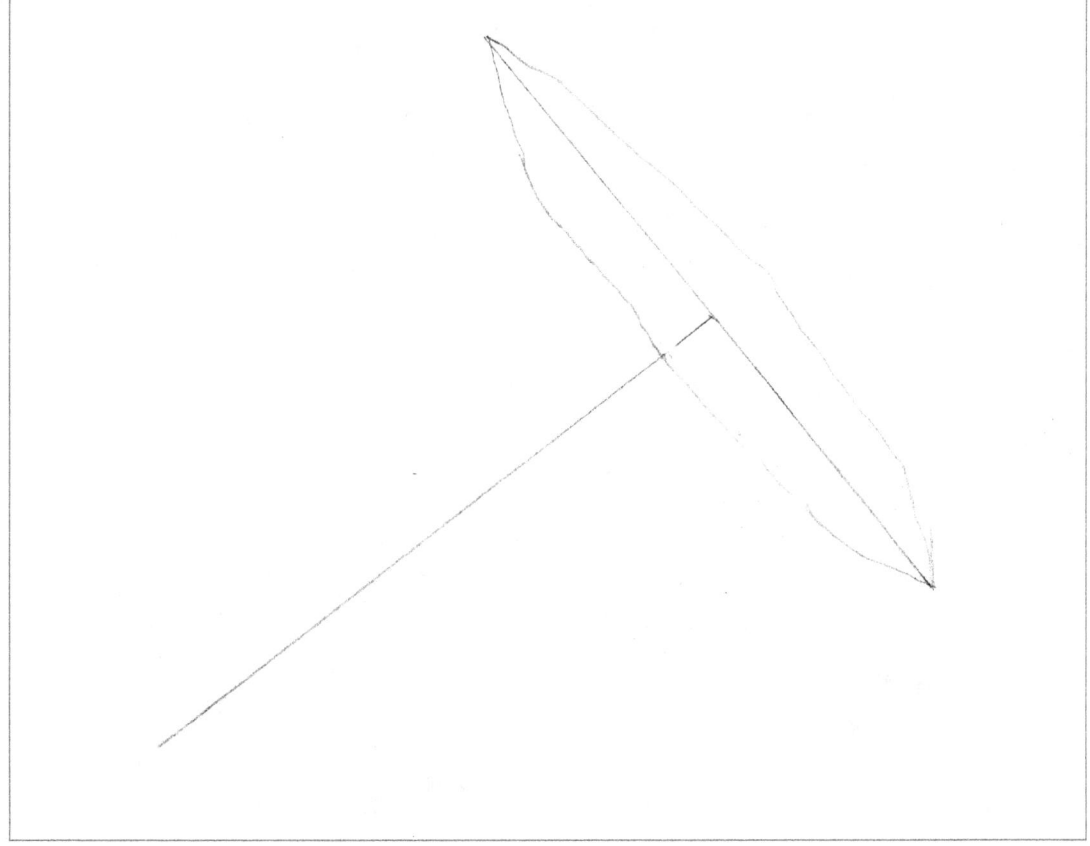

Erase the shorter line and you can start outlining the outer canopy.
You have to draw a big, curvy line starting on both sides of the shorter line that you just erased. I have drawn that typical shape, but you can create any other shape just try to make both sides as symmetrical as possible. Create the top of the shaft that is going through the canopy and often can be seen at the top of umbrellas. It can be shorter or longer.

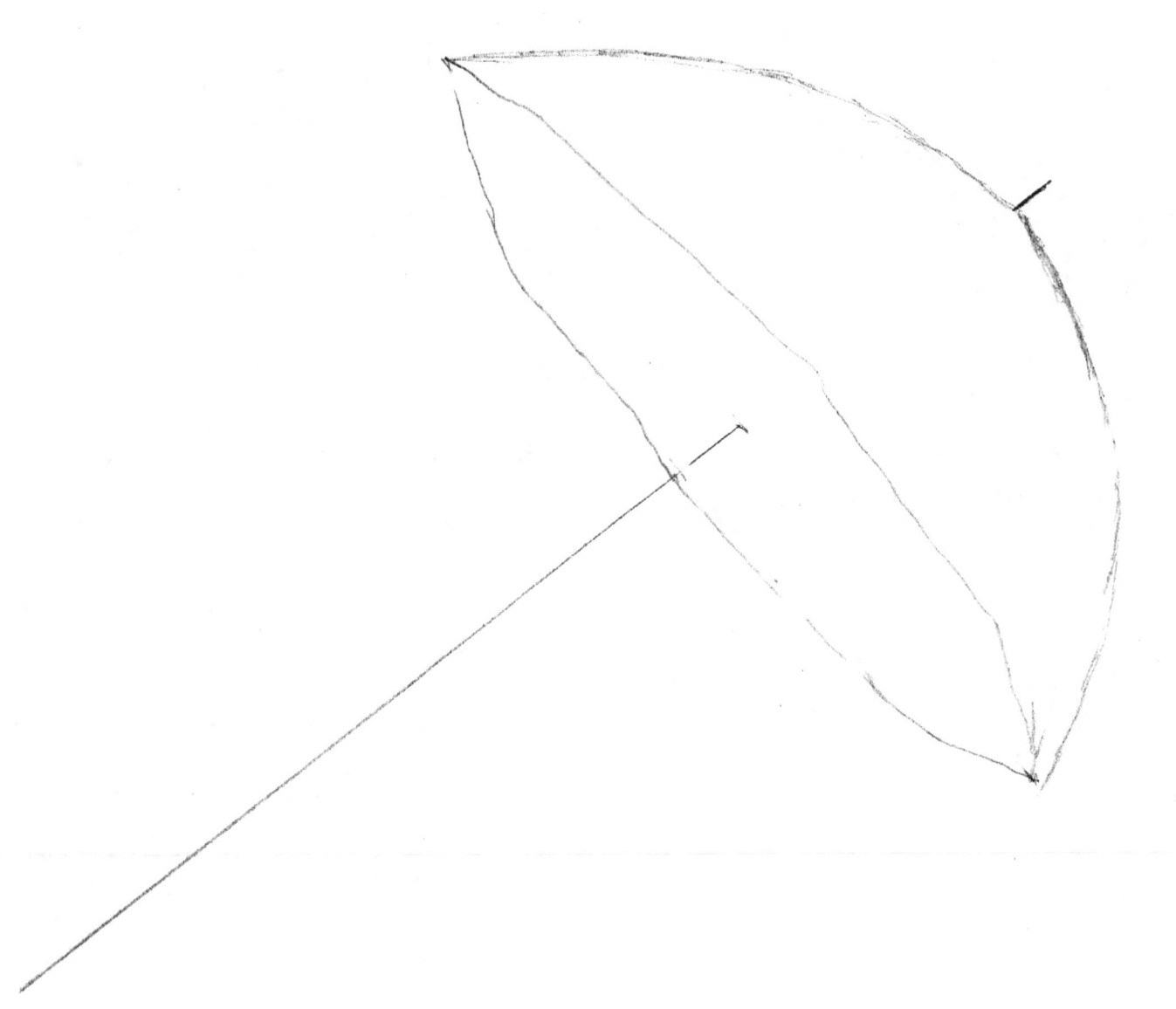

Now we can shade the shaft.
First, create lines next to the main outline and make them parallel to it. My shaft seemed to be too long so I erased a bit of it at the bottom.
I'm using an H pencil to shade the whole shaft. Do it carefully, and next to the edges because they have to stay straight. Use a B pencil over the part that is found in the inner area of the canopy because this part receives less light. I also use a B pencil for the lower area along the shaft and I press less and less as I shade upwards because I want to make it look round and this is what we can achieve by creating a smooth gradient.

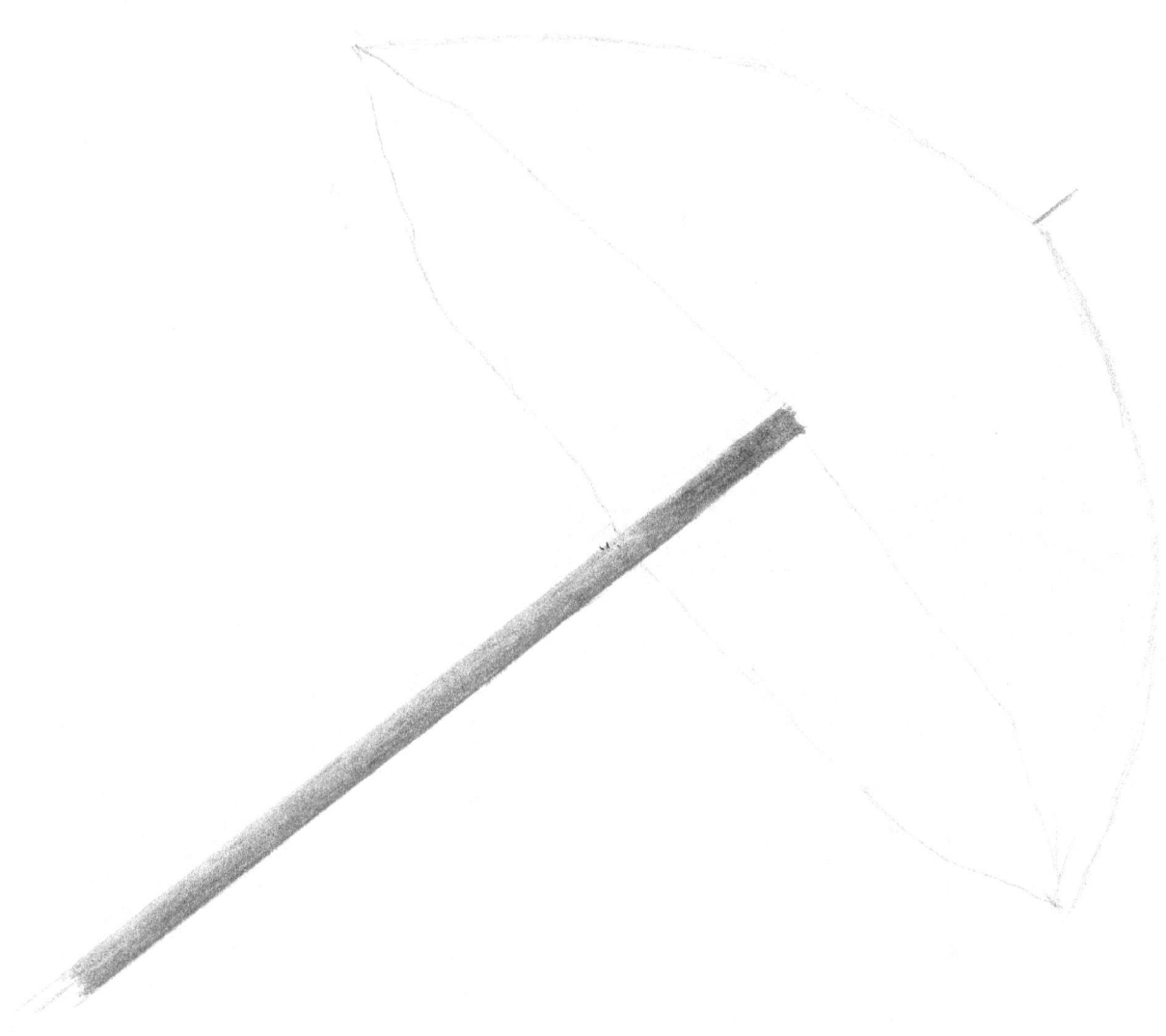

And now let's draw the handle at the bottom end of the shaft. It can have a typical, curvy shape of the handle that reminds of a "U" letter. It can be a bit thicker than the shaft. Use a B pencil for the lower area here because this area gets less light and also the other parts that are less illuminated.

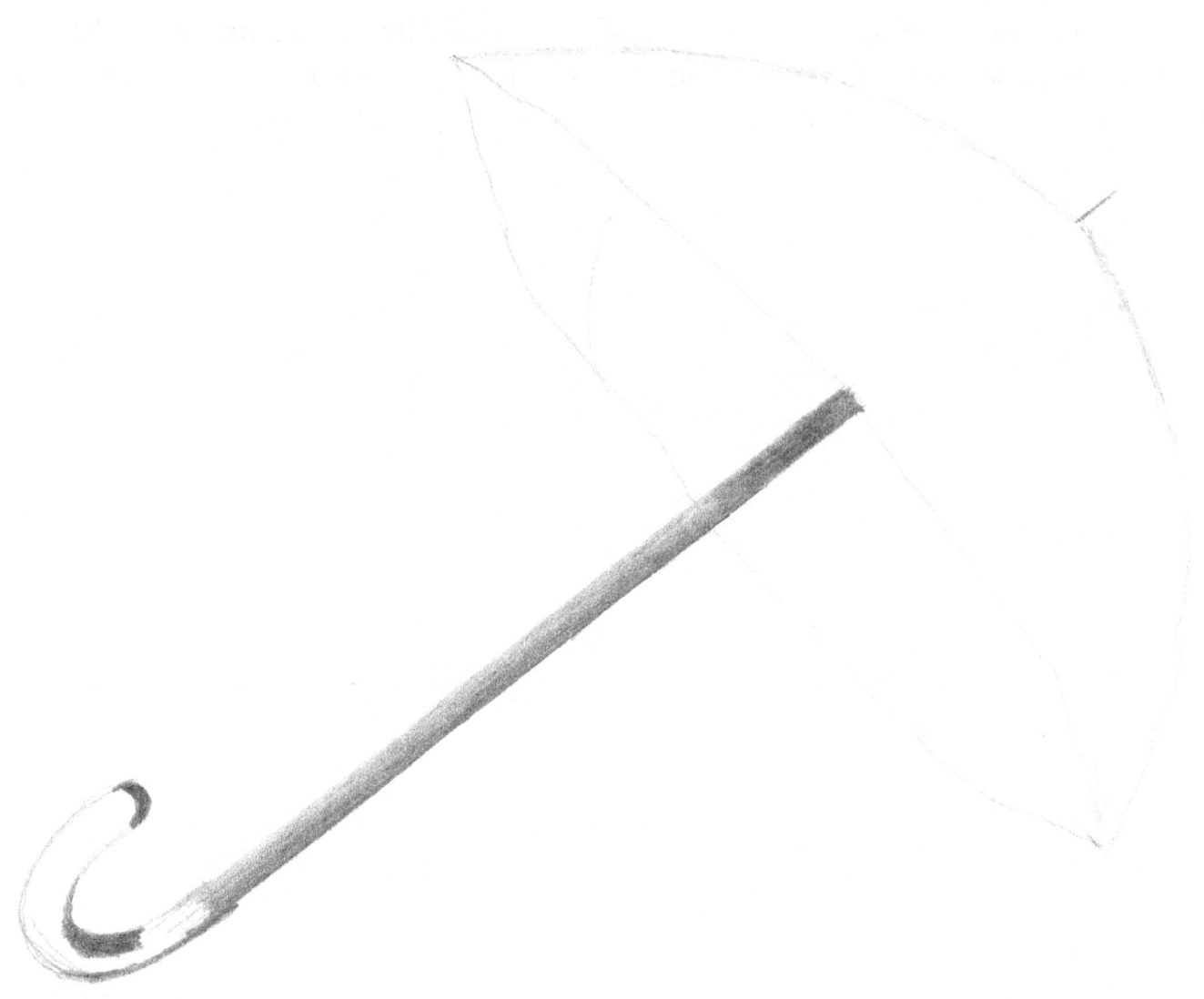

Next, we can shade the rest of the handle with an H pencil pressing lightly.

Then, shade between these two pencils with an HB because these two values should flow into each other in order to make it look round.
We can also add some highlights over the handle with an eraser, and also between the handle and the shaft.

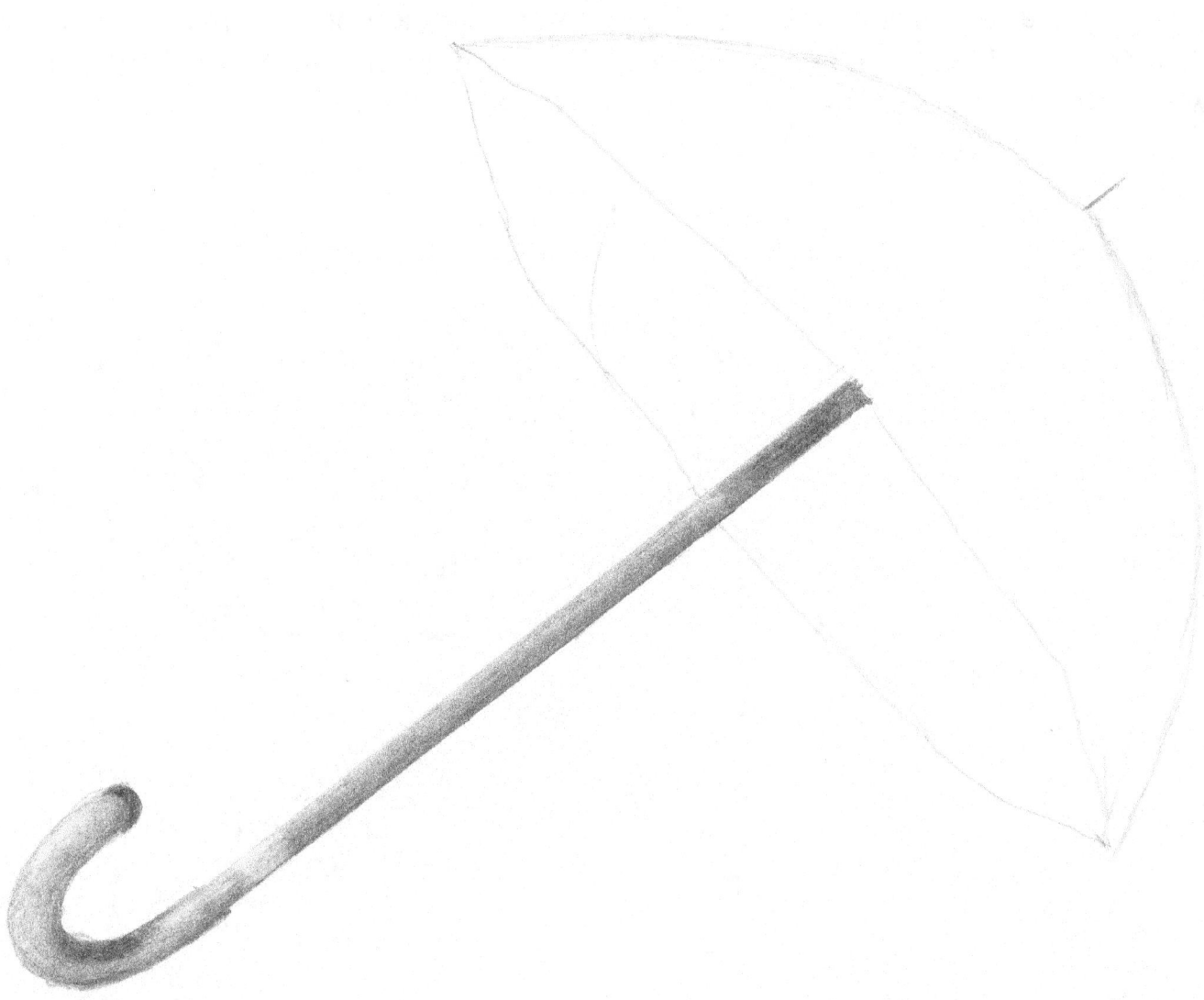

Now we can shade the canopy.
Before you start shading it, strengthen the outlines first because we're going to shade over this area and we want to see the outlines through it. Wrap a tissue around your finger, dip it into the graphite powder over the whole area of the canopy. You can also go over the background in order to shade it evenly next to the edges too. Erase it after finishing shading. Here you can see how I have damaged the paper when I was erasing that shorter initial line and it's visible now that after I have applied the graphite powder. You can see that this way of shading produces a much smoother texture than when we draw with a pencil, even when we use the Circulism method. If you don't have graphite powder you can always create it yourself with the sharpener and a pencil.

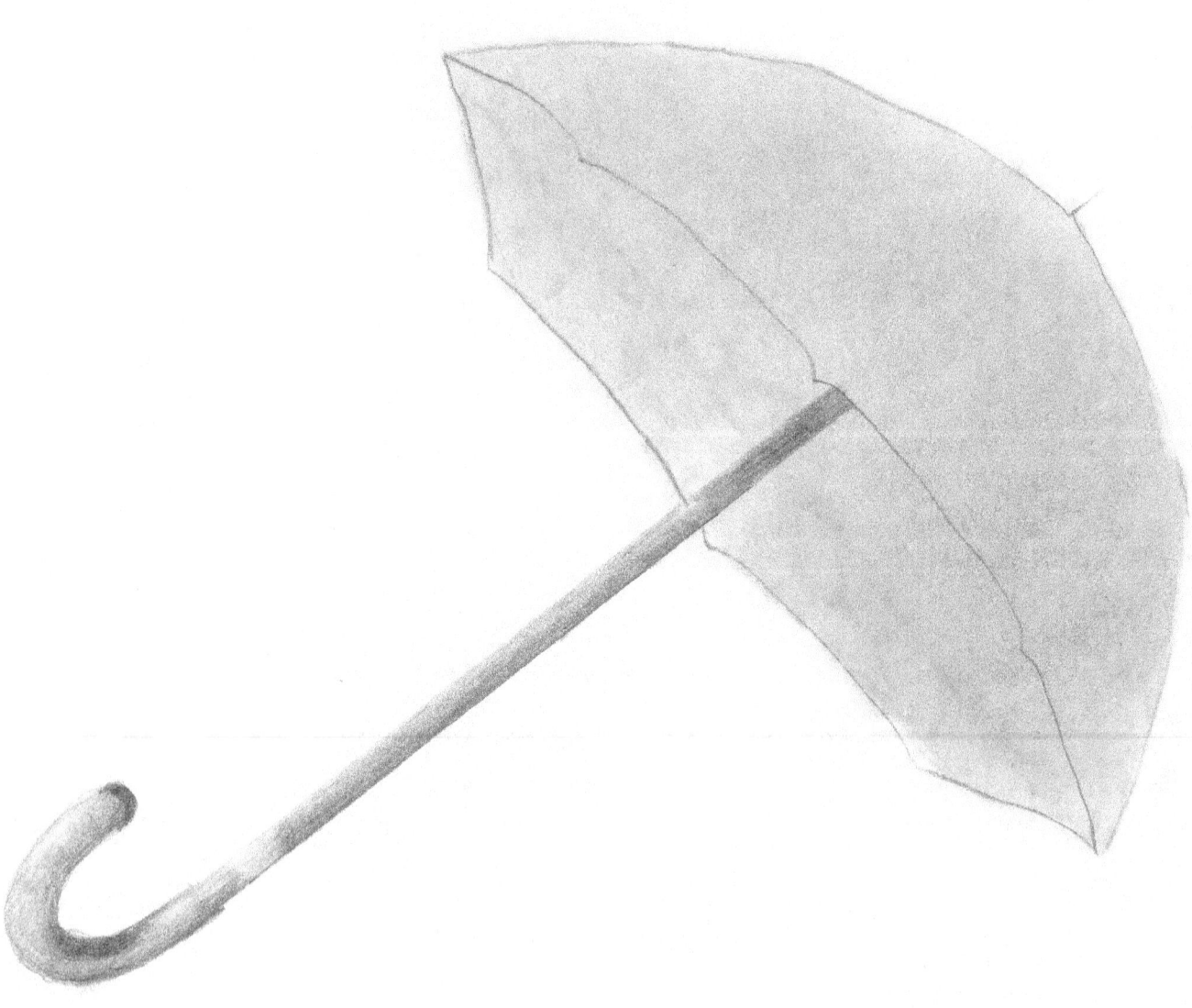

Next, shade more the inner part of the canopy because it always gets less light. I'm using a Q-tip for this and of course, I dip it into the graphite powder. So, this section has to be much darker than the outer canopy. I'm using a blending stump next to the edges and I also dip the tip of it into the graphite powder because it doesn't have enough graphite on it. Apply more over the lighter areas to create an even texture. Now it looks quite smoother.

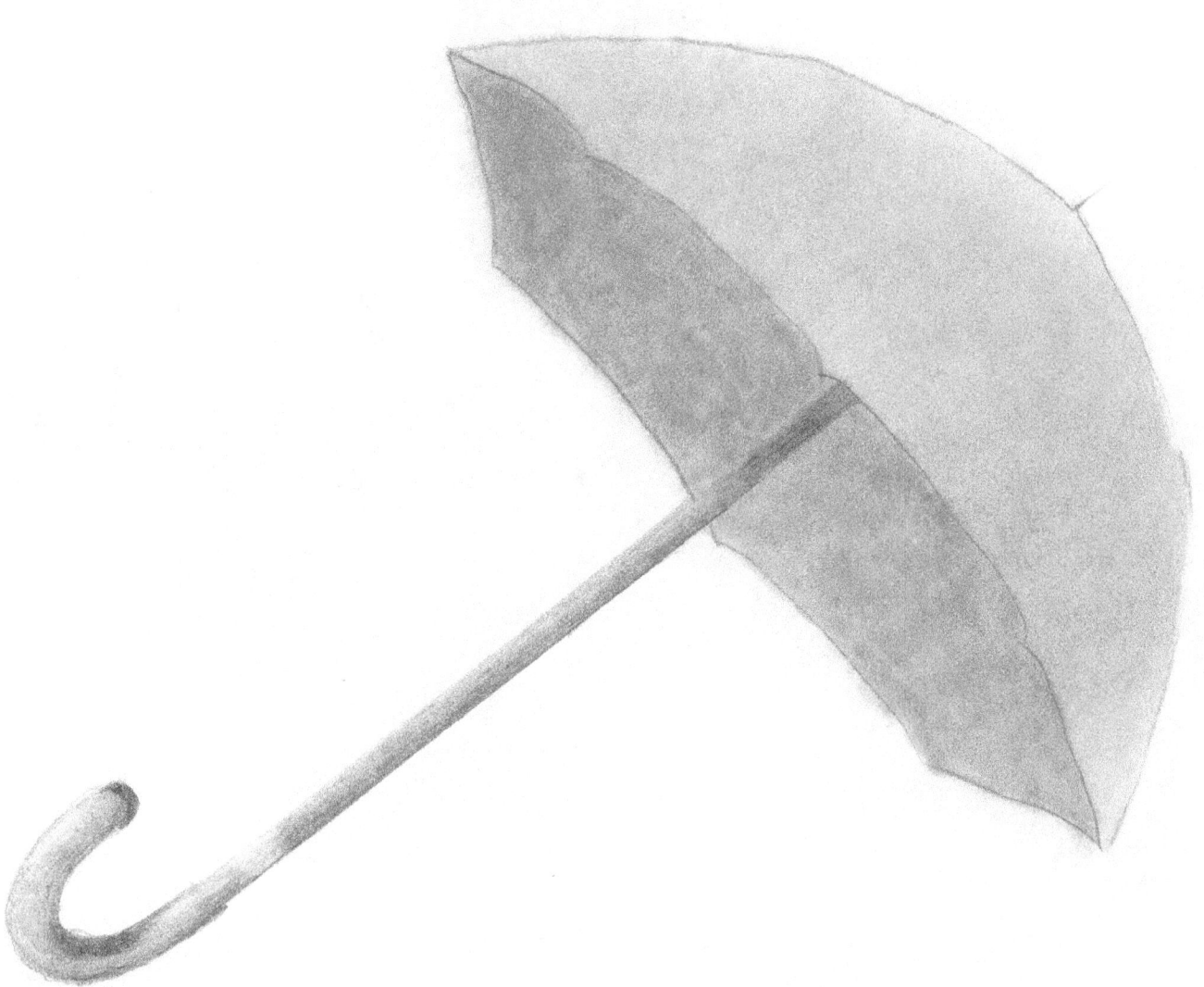

Using a 4B or darker, draw the ribs over the inner canopy, as shown in the next picture. They all should radiate from the cap on the top of the shaft. I use a 6B for this. These lines have to be a bit curvy.
Use an HB for the ribs over the outer area and press very lightly.

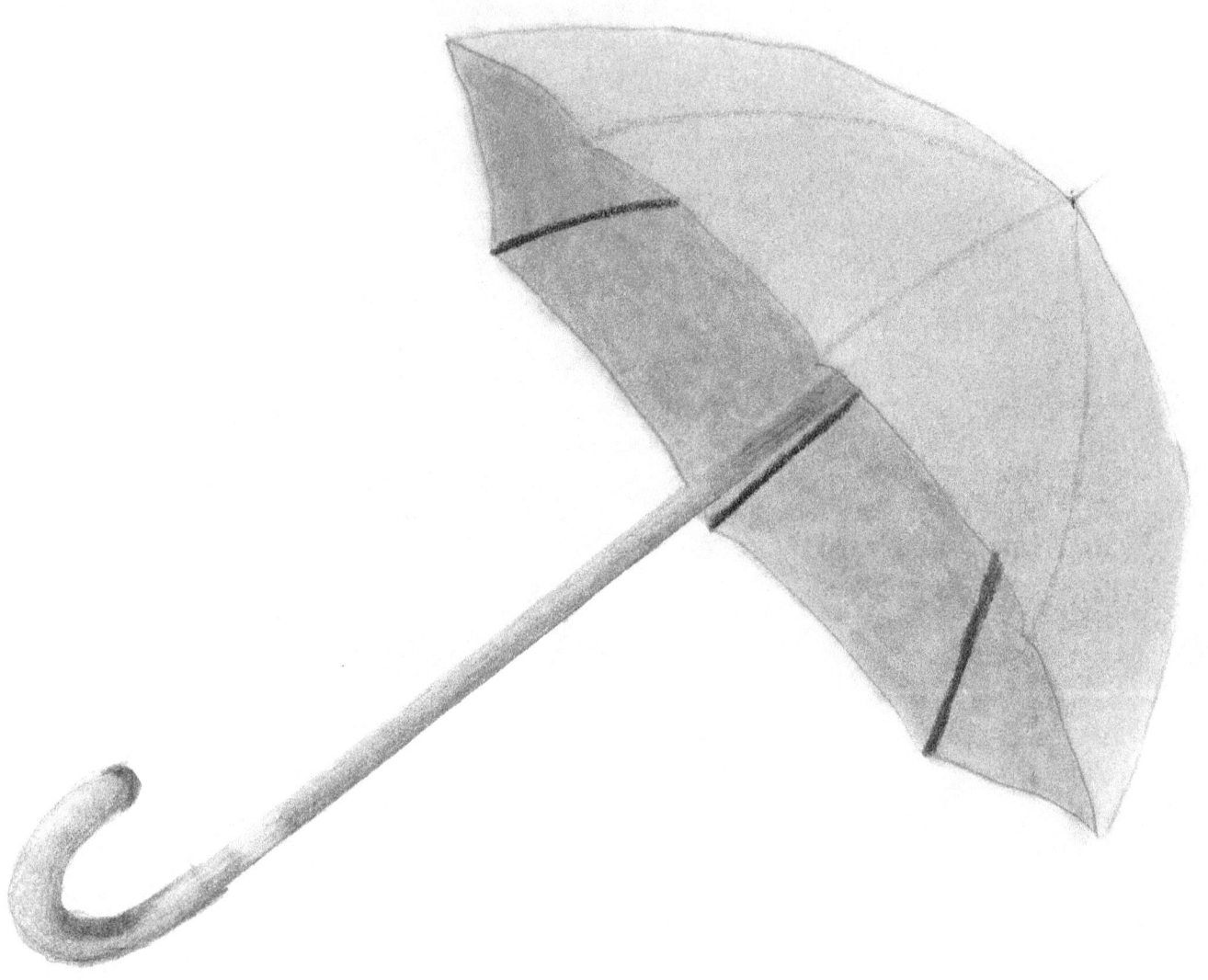

Using a Q-tip or a blending stump, shade next to the ribs over the outer canopy where it would get less light.

Lastly, create the cast shadows. Let's suppose that the umbrella is standing on the table, so shade a little bit under the handle towards the right side, using Q-tip and graphite powder. Such a thin object wouldn't cast a shadow farther from the bottom of the handle, so you can make it short, study the next image to see how I have shaded it.

Use a tissue to shade larger area under the canopy.

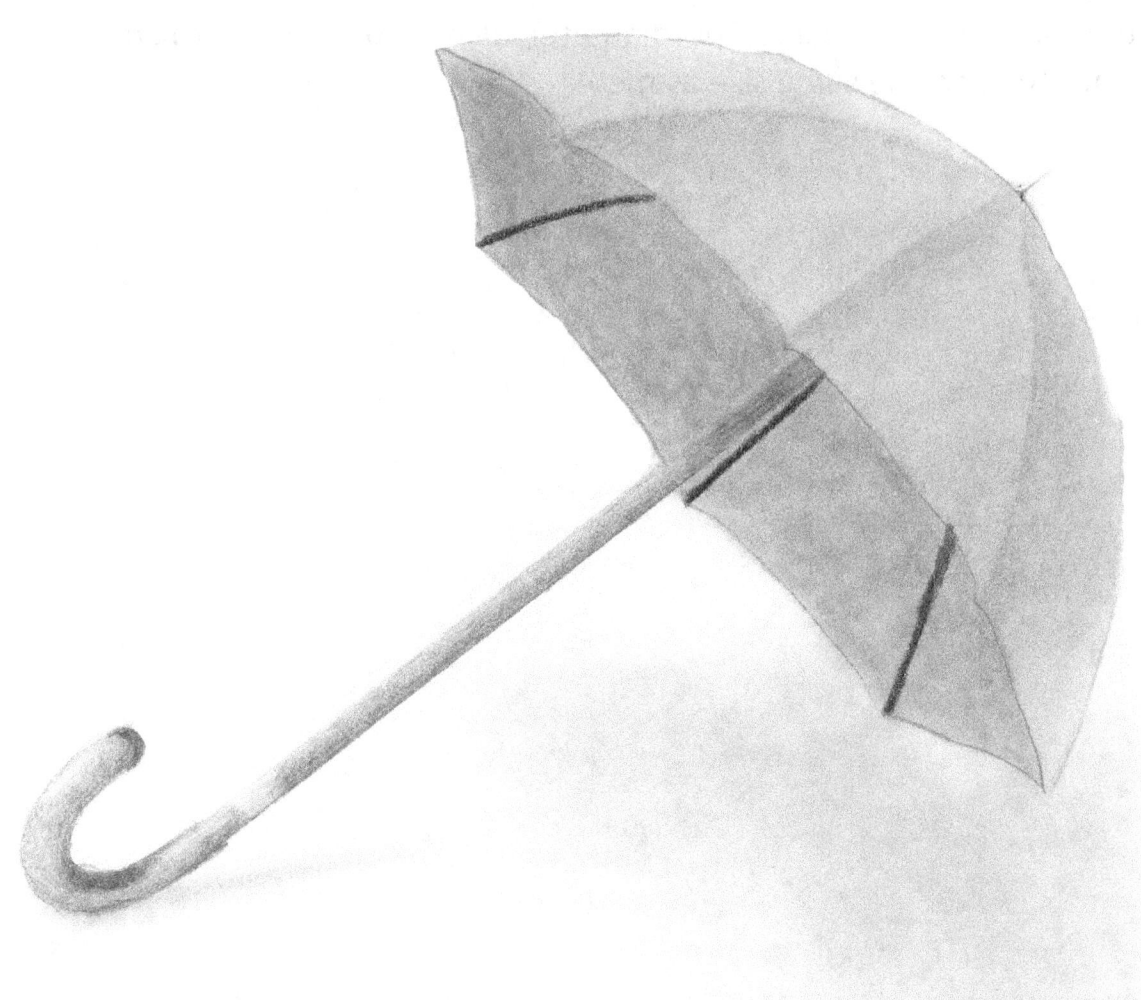

AN APPLE

Let's draw an apple. We start with a circle in the middle of the paper. We don't have to use a drawing compass, because it doesn't have to be a perfect circle—just approximately the shape of an apple. So, whatever shape you draw, it will be good.
Next, outline the sunken area where the stem is growing from. Also, draw the stem and a leaf, as shown in the next image. The diameter of my apple is approximately 8 cm (3.0") if you want to draw the same size as me.

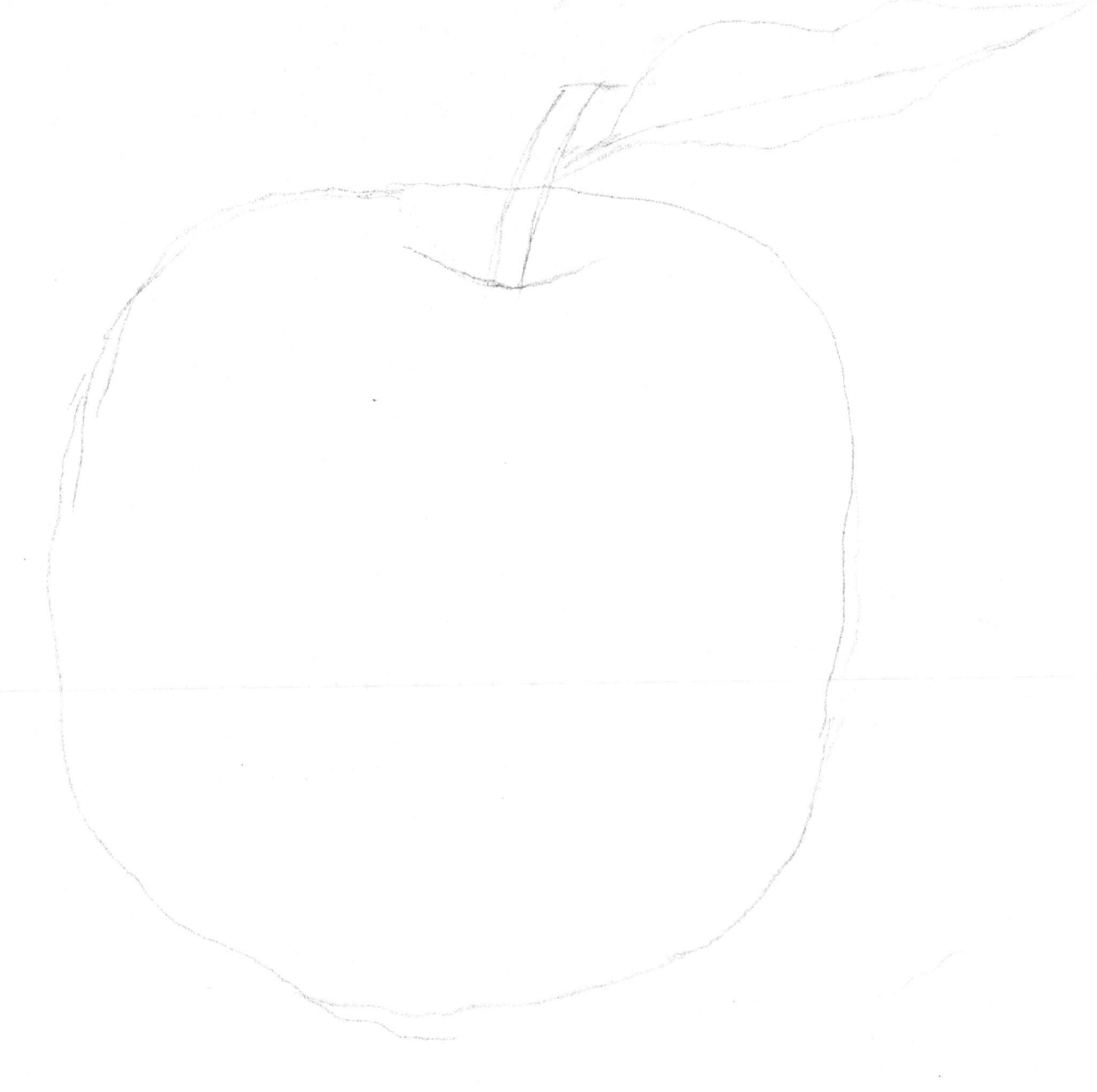

Now we can start shading. We have to imagine where our light source is coming from. I want my light source to come from our point of view, which means we must create darker shades all around, next to the edges, and create lighter shades as we shade towards the center of the apple. I will start with the 5B next to the edge, but you can use a 4B or a 3B. Here, also, we should use the circulism technique. Apply tiny, overlapping circles, pressing harder next to the edge and releasing the pressure as you shade towards the center. I skipped the upper part because it is always more illuminated, so I don't want it to be so dark.

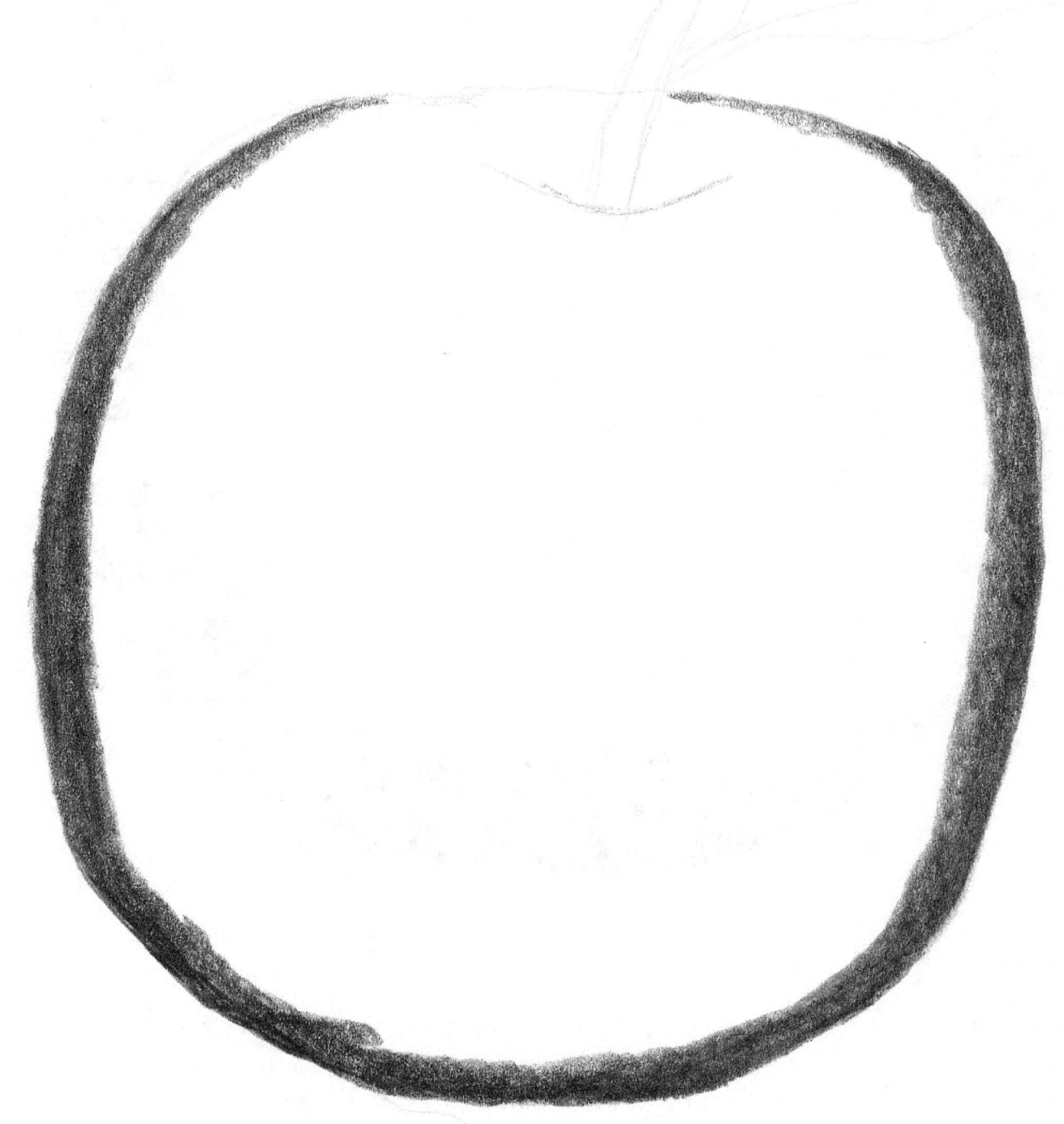

Let's continue with a 2B. Go over the 5B area a bit, then lighten the pressure on your pencil as you work towards the center of the apple.

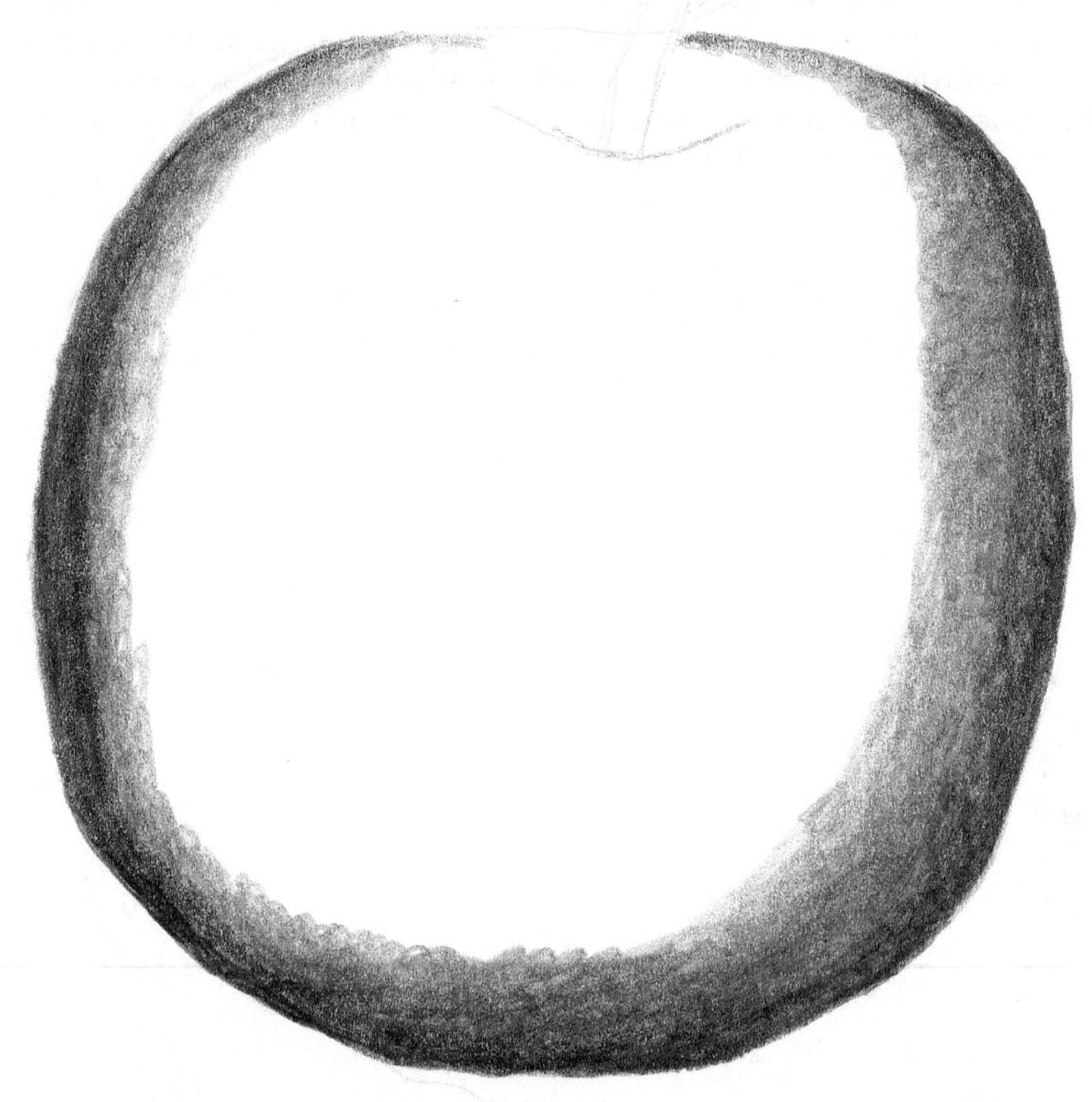

Next, use a lighter pencil, such as a 2H pencil, and do the same. Go over the 2H area a bit and then lessen the pressure as you shade towards the center. Here we can also shade the edge between the upper edge and the sunken area where the stem is growing from. Press harder over the edge; less and less as you draw downwards. This way, you will create a smooth gradient which will suggest the roundness of the apple. Shade the outer edge of the upper part, the area that we didn't shade with a 5B in the first step.

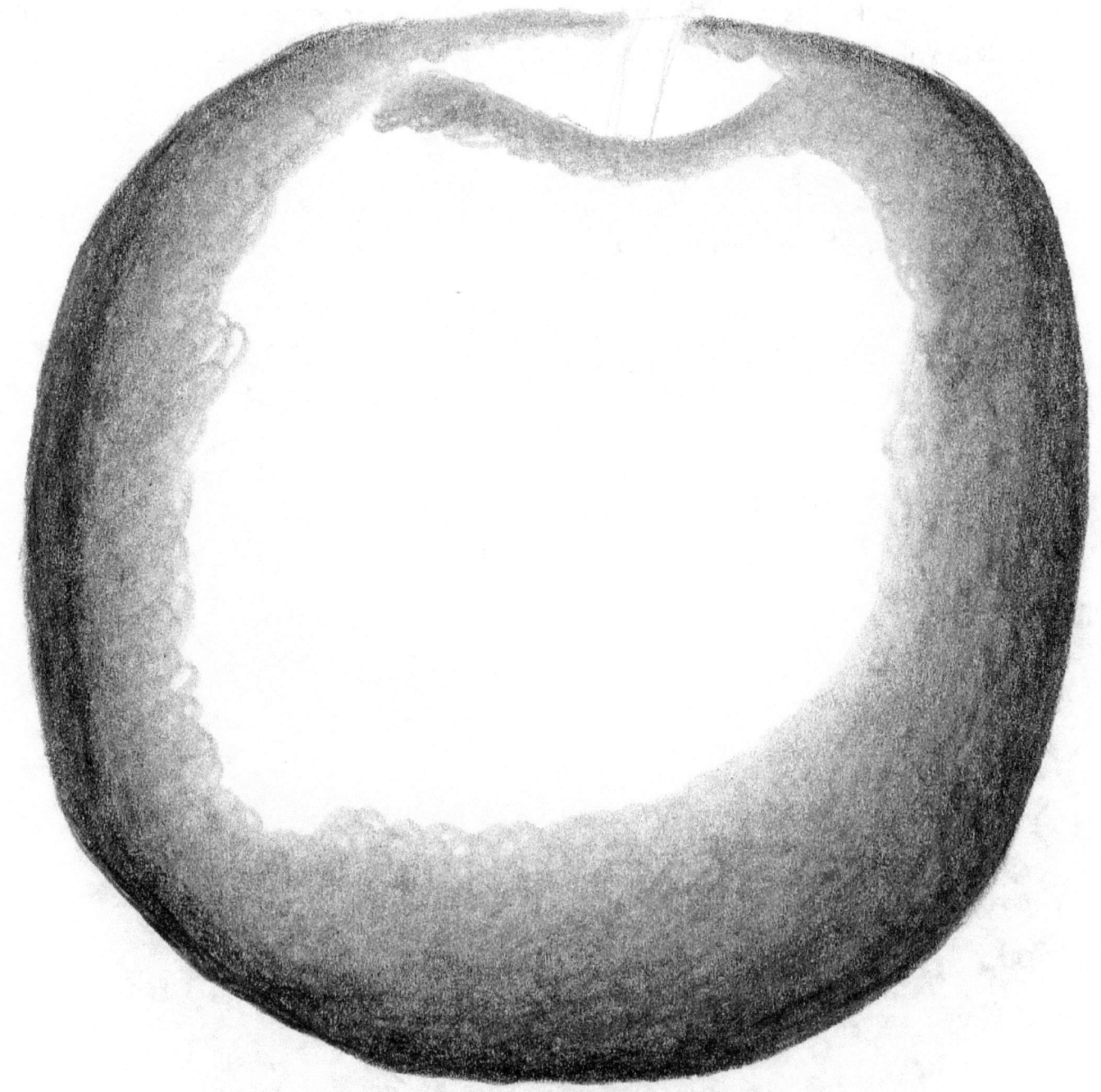

In the following image, you can see that I have outlined the highlight, somewhere in the middle of the apple, that must stay white or be significantly brighter than the rest.
Then, I used a 2H to shade more towards this highlight in the same manner as with the previously used pencils.

Work more in the sunken area next to the stem. Specifically, skip the stem and shade a bit over the upper edge, lessening the pressure as you work downwards. Notice how I have resolved this and now even the upper area (behind the stem) seems to be round. The deepest part can stay highlighted, while the upper edge in the front of the stem should stay very dark. This way, these two areas will appear separated, as they should. Also, the stem will add more to the impression after we have shaded it later.

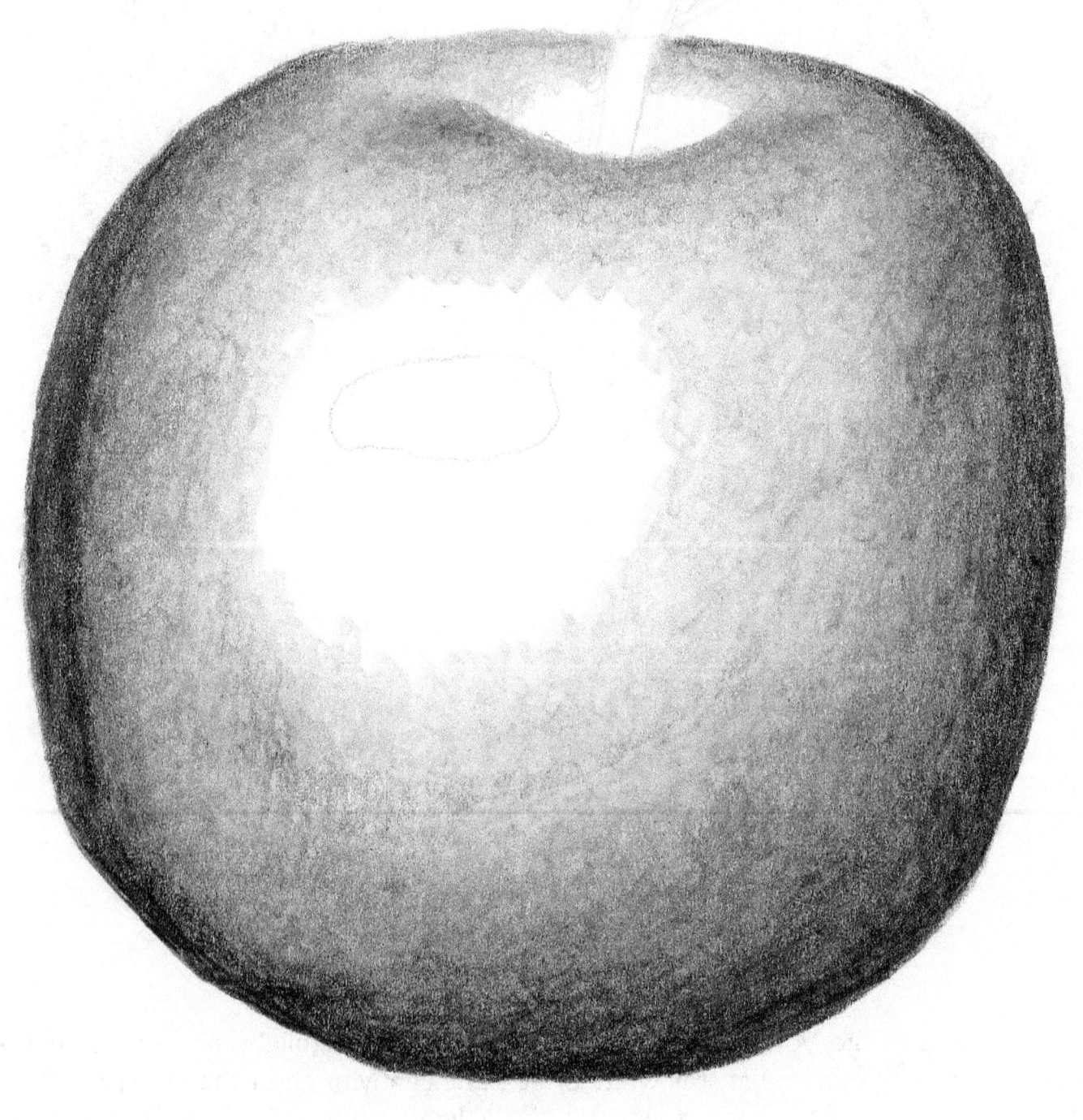

Now, we can use a 4H for the rest of the apple, except for the outlined highlight. Same here: go over the 4H area and then press less and less as you shade towards the highlight. Also, shade the sunken area where the stem is growing from, pressing lightly because this area has to stay very bright.

Create the shadow that is cast by the stem and falling over the right area behind it. Make this cast shadow curvy so that it can also indicate the round shape of that part of the apple. Check the next image to see the position of it before you draw it.

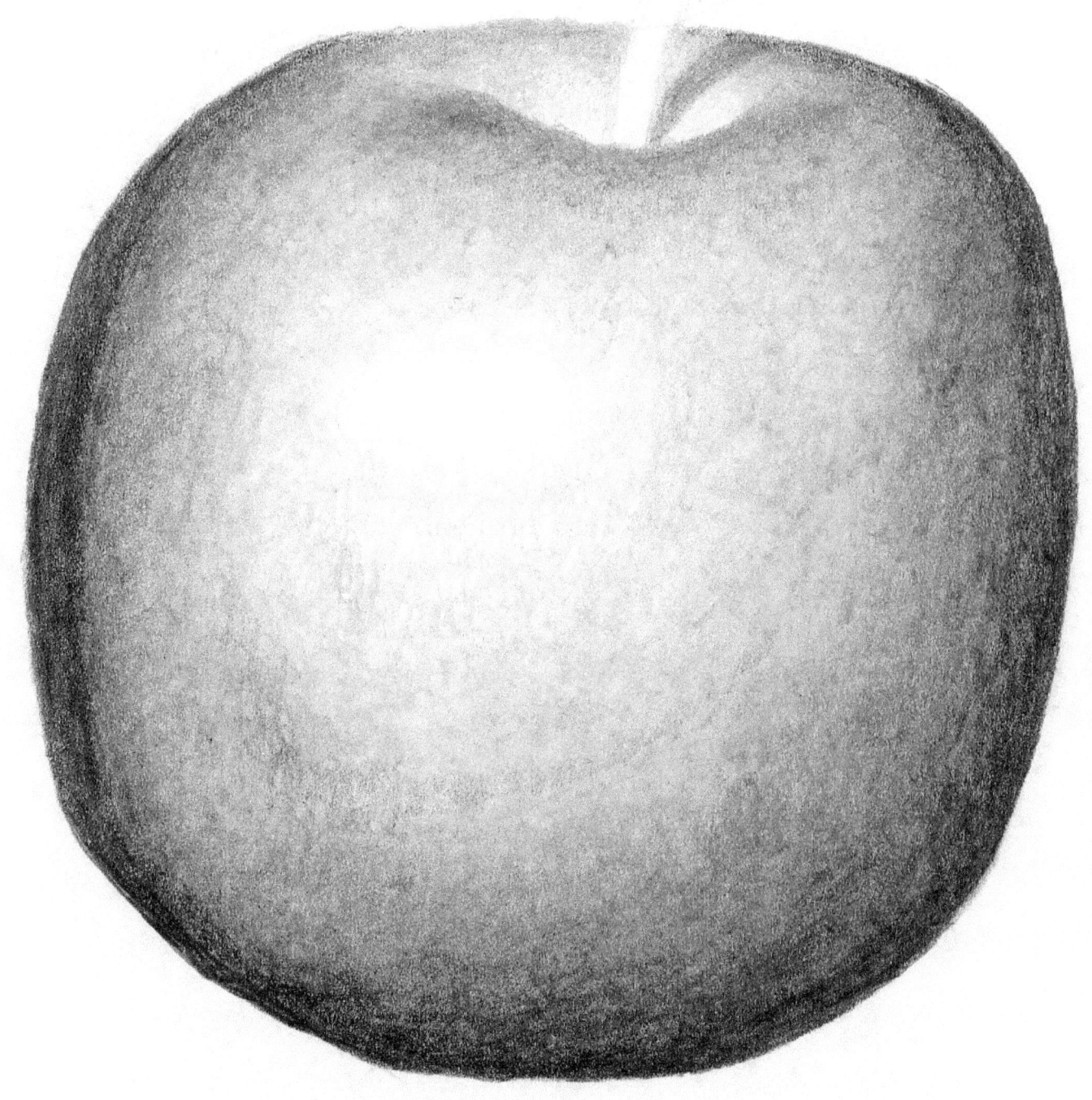

Next, blend it all with a tissue. Again, skip the highlight in the middle, and carefully blend around it. We can see whether we need to shade more because, after blending, some areas become lighter. We need to shade those lighter areas more. Use a blending stump or a Q-tip to blend the upper area, around the stem, because your finger with a tissue wrapped around it is too big for this area and you don't want to smudge it all and darken the highlight.

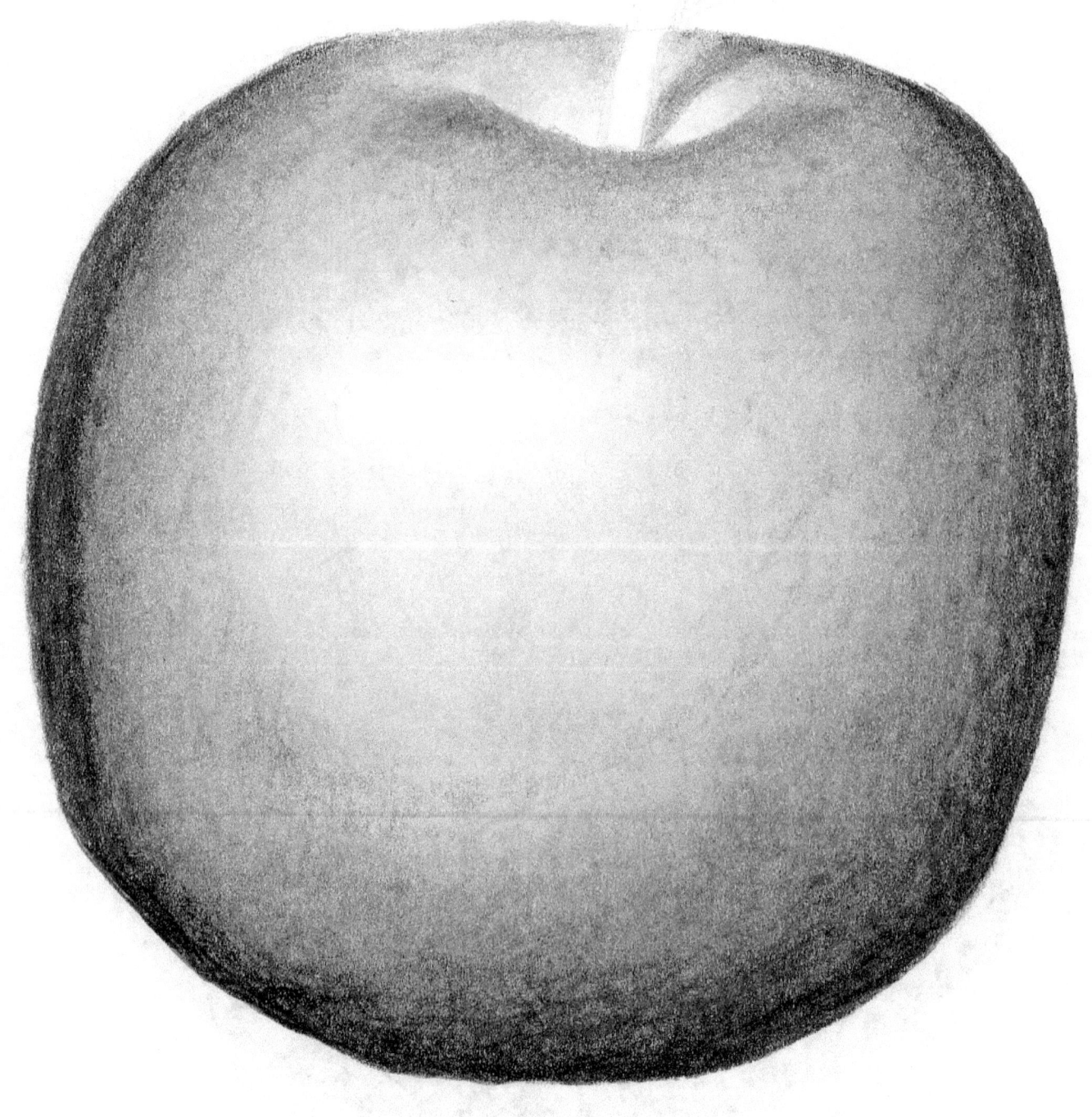

Since I have lightened up these areas, I have to go over it again a bit, wherever necessary because there is a clear edge between the dark and light values. I'm using a 2B again. When we shade with a 2B over a 2H, we are not able to make it too dark; we can make it just the appropriate value. I also want to shade a bit more over the highlight to make it more prominent and brighter.

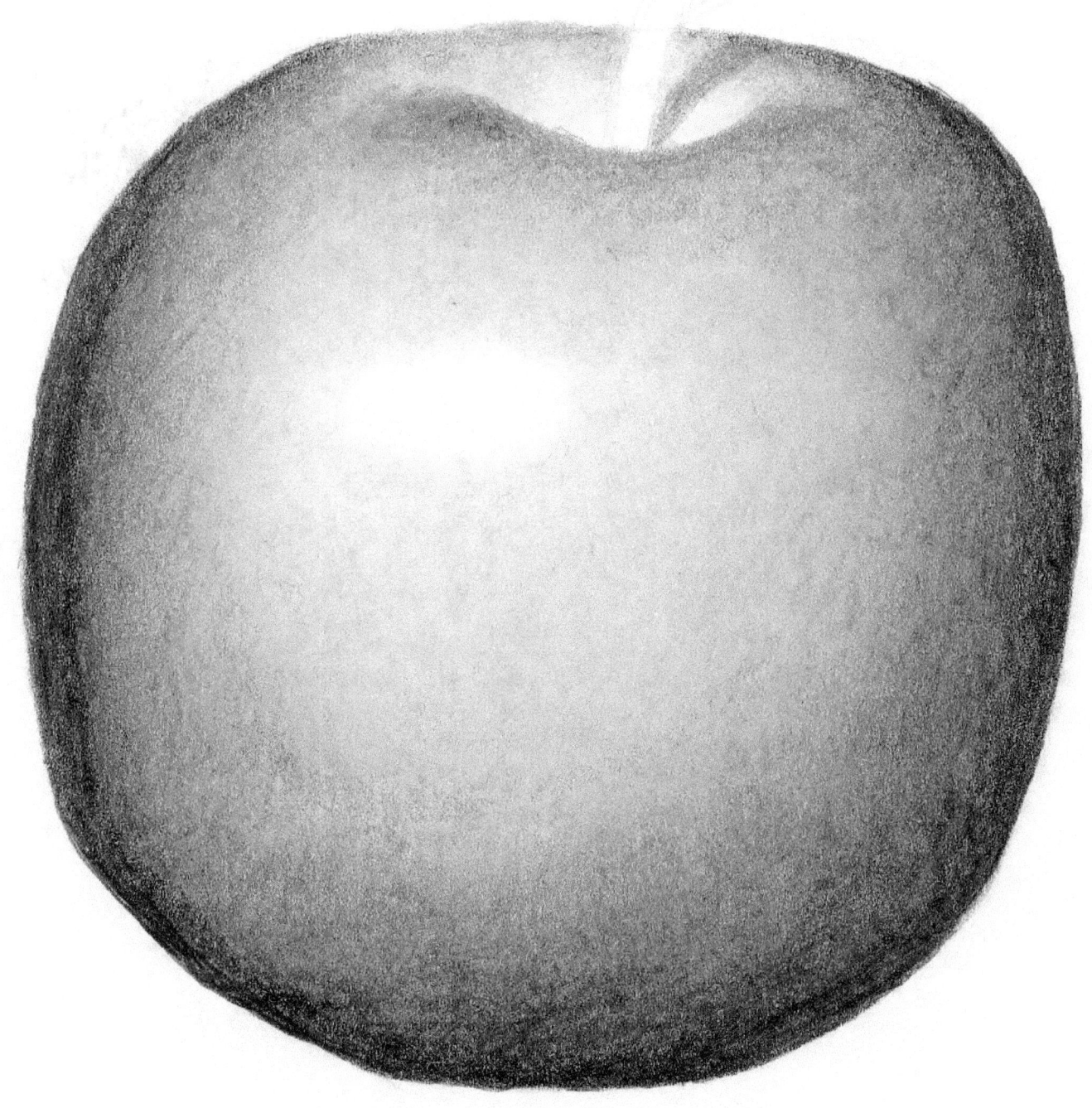

I feel that the shape of my apple should be a bit wider in the upper area, so I have created a new edge around it and filled it with a 5B that I used for the edge at the beginning of the shading process. We can always change its shape and enlarge it, but we can't make it smaller.

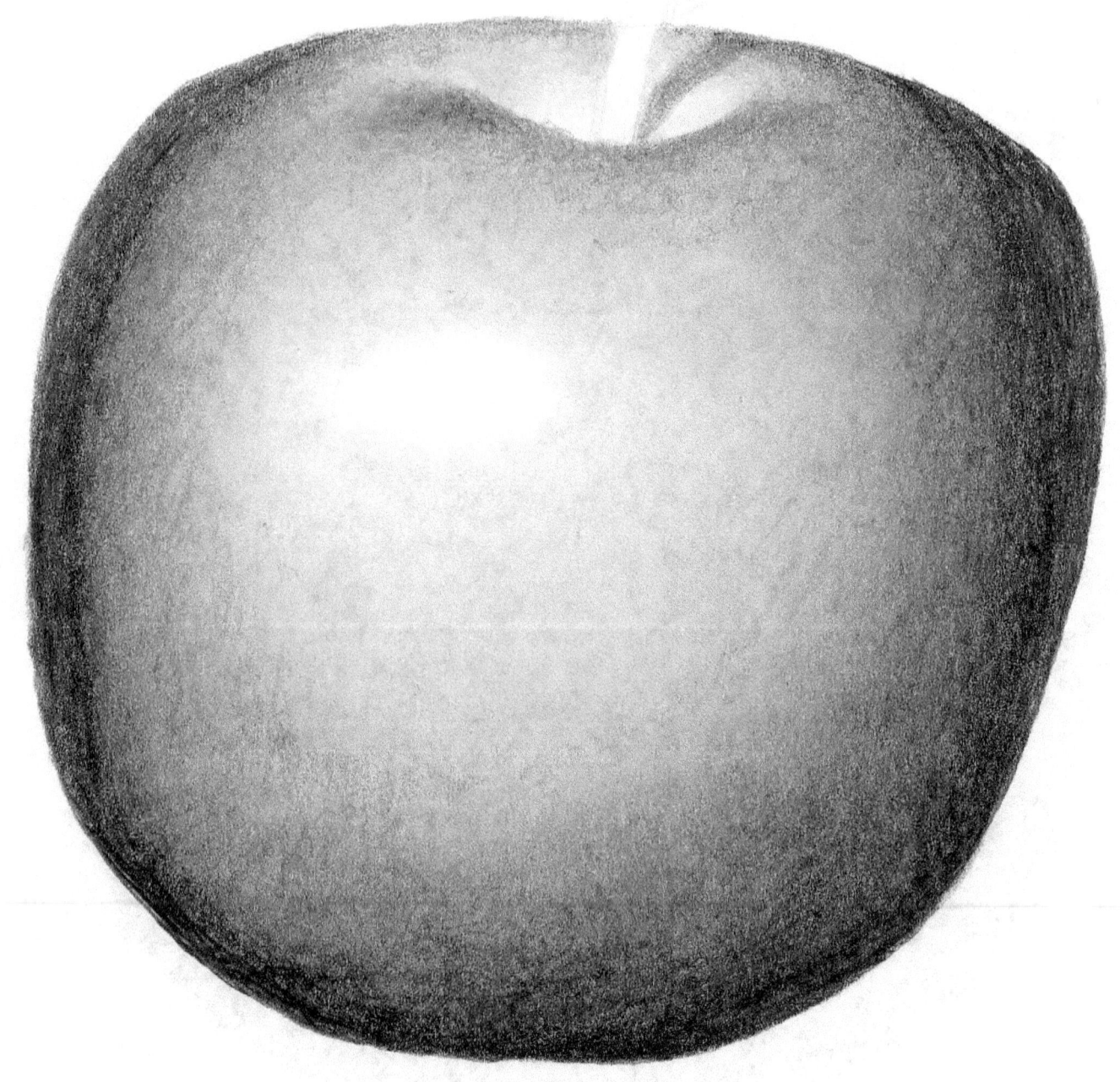

Now, we can create some patterns that apples usually have - some vertical stripes. I'm using a 5B for these, but I don't press too hard. We should draw the straight stripes in the middle of the apple, which must become curvier as we draw them towards the edges on the left and the right sides. Positioning the stripes like this will also suggest the roundness of the apple. Do not draw them over the highlight in the middle that we have left unshaded. The highlight is so bright that we wouldn't be able to see any patterns over it because apples are shiny. Make the stripes different, at random. And, of course, these stripes should be lighter over the lighter areas and they should be darker in the shadowed parts of the apple.

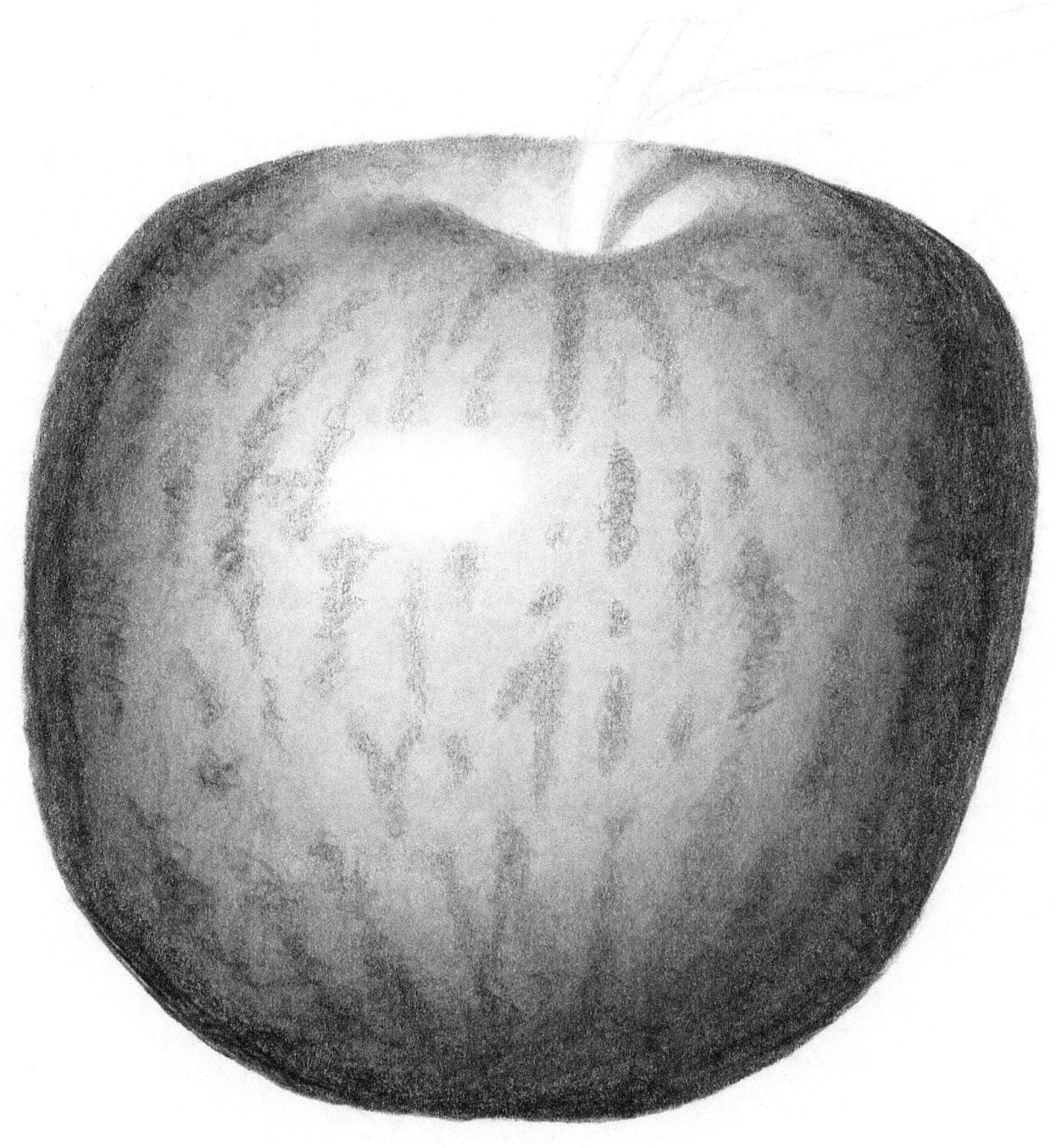

And now we can blend these stripes and shade the area around the highlight to enhance the highlight even more. I'm using an HB in this step because, besides blending the stripes, I also want to slightly darken the whole area in the middle. If you make it too dark, just tap it with a kneaded eraser and you can eliminate a bit of the graphite. Then, blend it with a Q-tip. After the blending, the stripes look less prominent, which is good because we don't want it to look like a watermelon. Yet, we want to have some stripes to make the apple look less flat and more interesting.

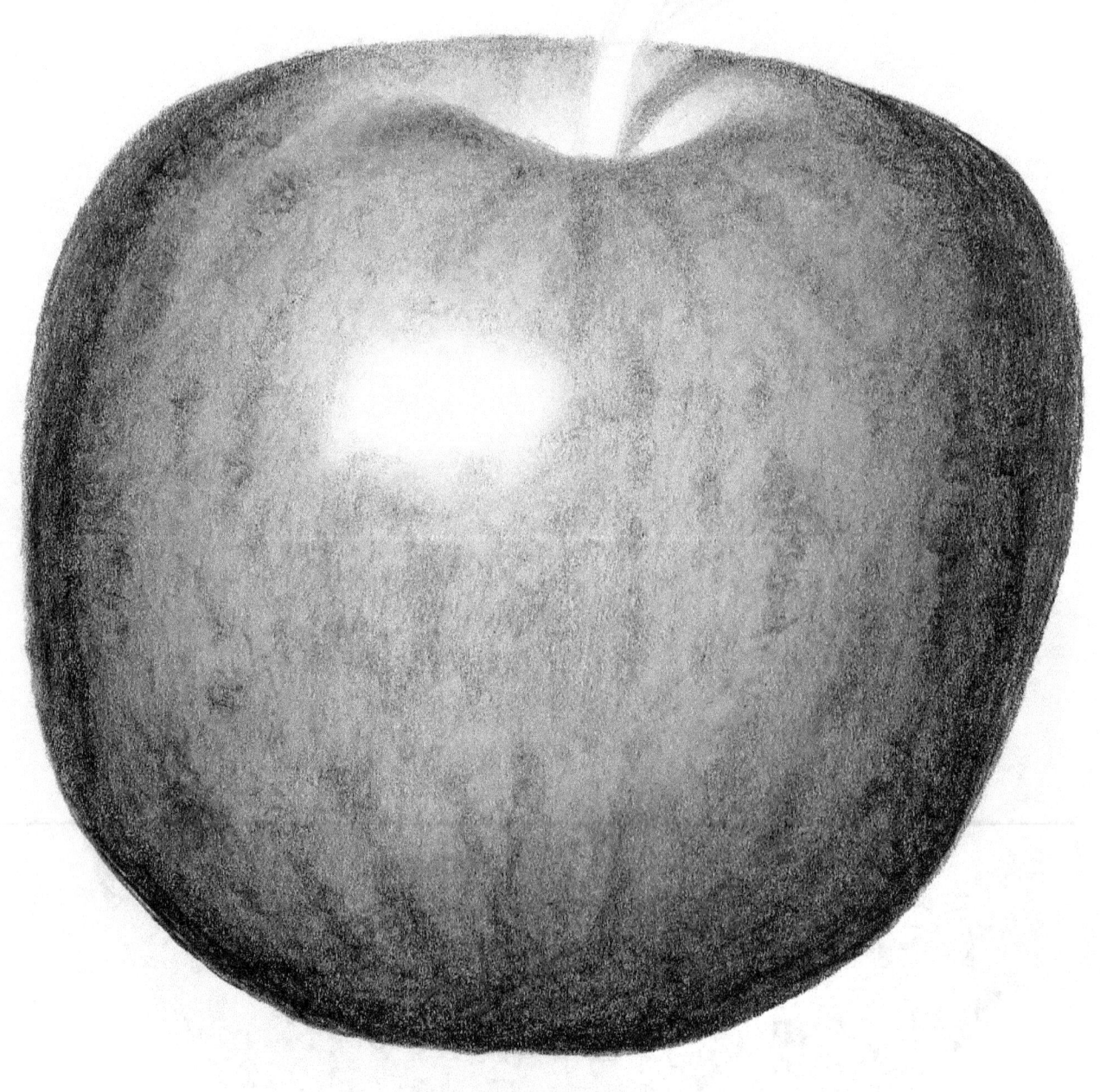

Now, let's create those tiny specks that apples usually have. For this, I want to use an electric eraser. I have created a pointed tip of my eraser by brushing it over the sandpaper while running the eraser, so I can create tiny, tiny dots over the apple. Create them at random all over the apple. If you find some of them to be too bright, just go over them with a blending stump and they will become darker. Or, if you want to eliminate them, just draw over them with a pencil.

If you don't have an electric eraser, you can use a white ink gel pen or a white marker. Create a dot and tap it with your finger while it's wet. These dots are pretty difficult to make with a kneaded eraser; that's why I always recommend getting different types of erasers because, as you can see, you will need them all for different actions and they will make your job easier and more enjoyable.

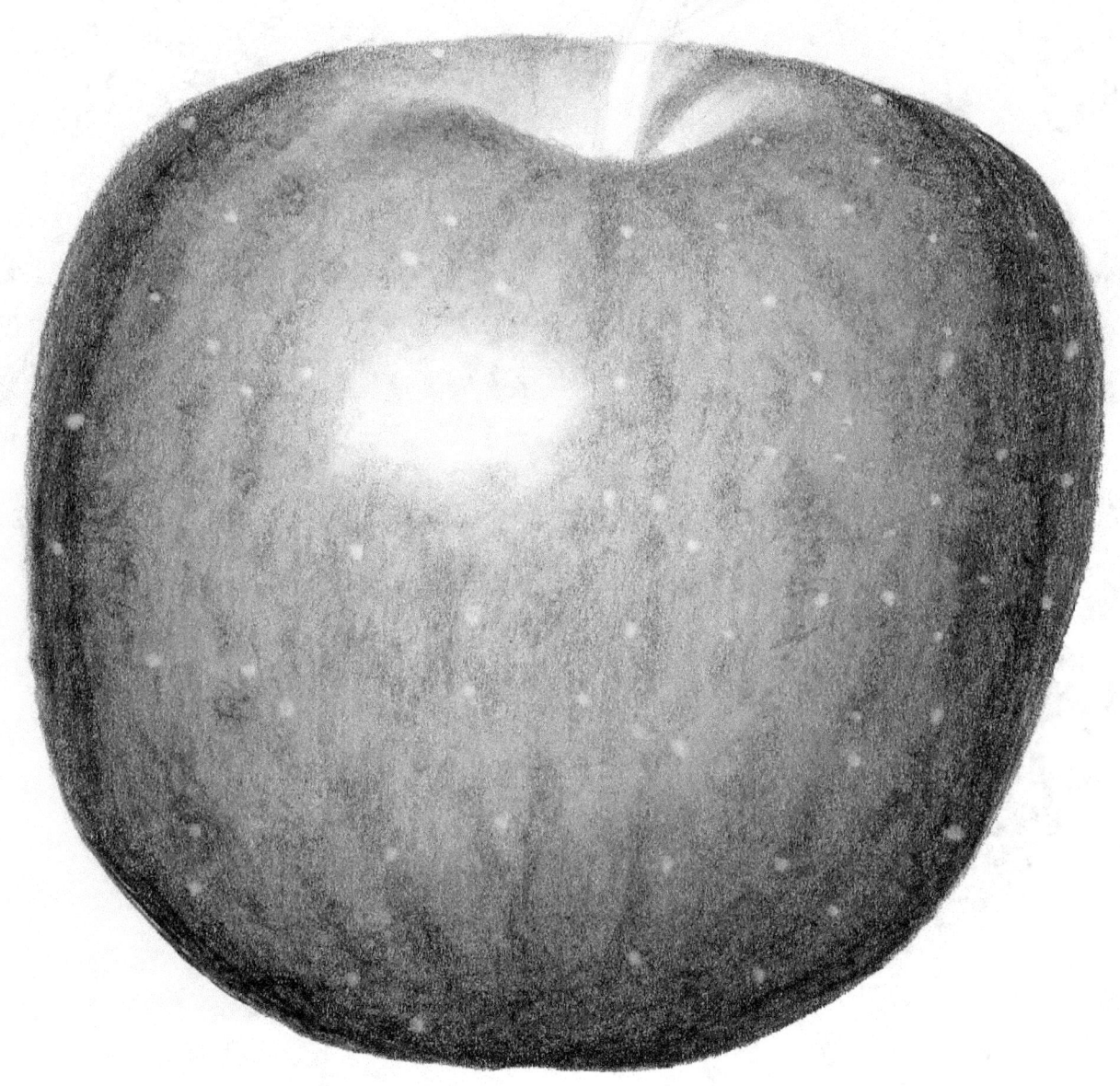

If you're satisfied with your apple, you can draw the stem. I want to use an HB for it. We have to make the stem darker on both right and left sides, so press harder. It has to be lighter in the middle so it can show its round shape. So, press less in the middle or use a lighter pencil.

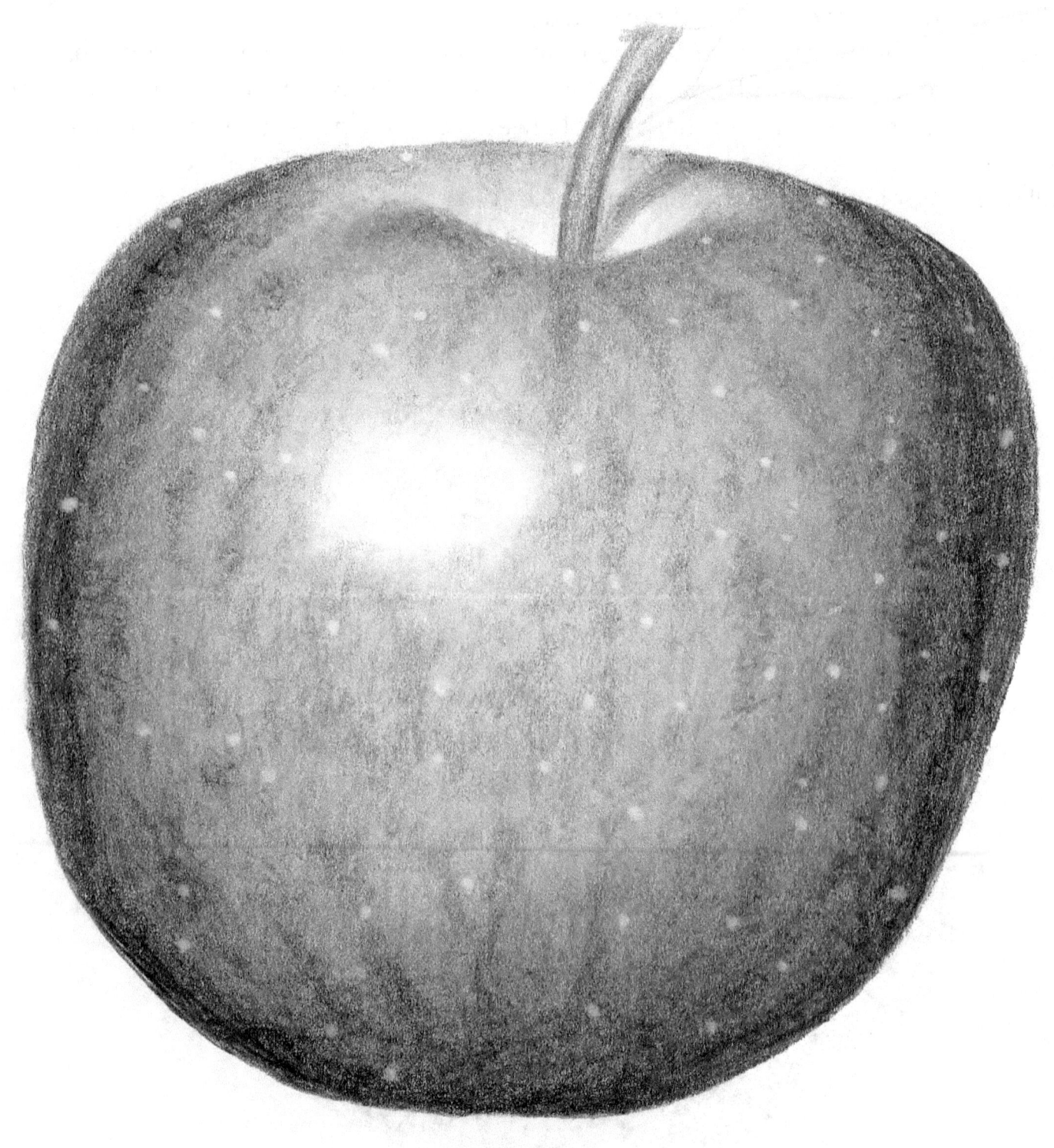

Next, shade the leaf. You can either shade the whole leaf, and then create the veins with an eraser, or you can skip the veins and shade around them—as I do, using a 2H pencil. We have one main, thicker vein in the middle, along with tinier ones, growing from the main one. In the left image, you can see how I have shaded it, and in the image on the right side, you can see how it looks after I have blended it with a blending stump.

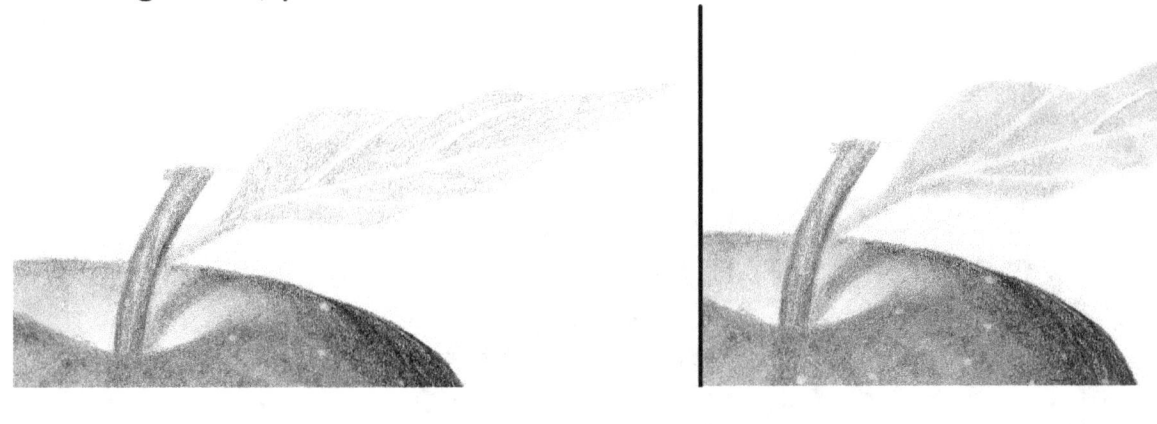

Tip

Always try to create even surfaces with a chisel-shaped tip of the graphite pencils. Be careful not to rotate your pencil during shading as it will draw sharp strokes. It's best to scrub one side of your pencil tip on the sandpaper and shade with it. It makes shading the larger surface easier and faster.

Lastly, create the cast shadow. So, if our light source is coming from our point of view, we'll have our cast shadow behind the apple. I suggest using the graphite powder for shading it. Shade behind and under the apple. Use a blending stump right next to the apple and create a bit darker tone for the cast shadow.

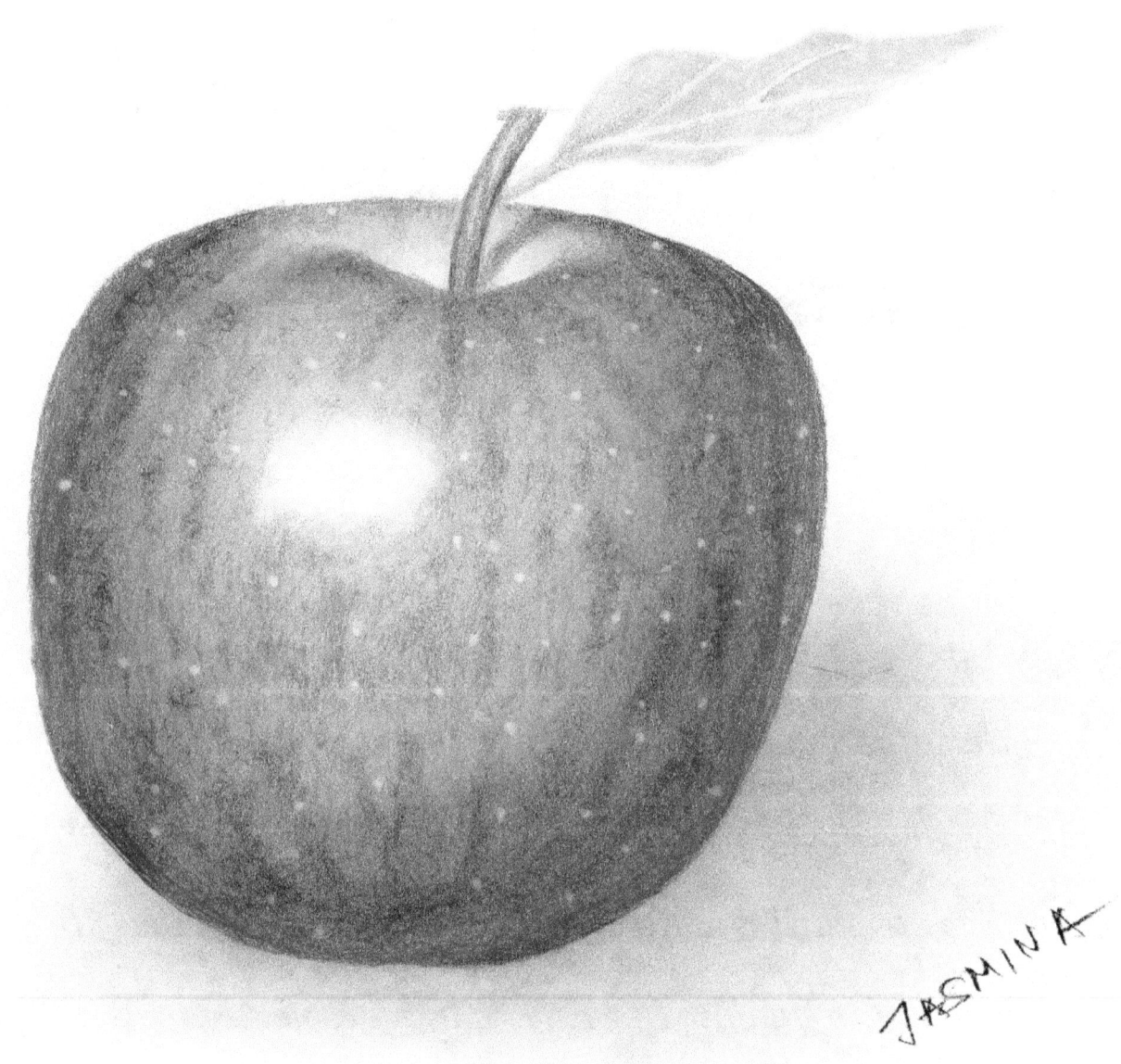

A TEASPOON

In this tutorial, I want to show you how to draw a teaspoon from photo reference. I have taken a picture of my teaspoon and printed it out on the left side of my drawing paper so that I can see it the whole time while I draw the spoon on the right side. So, these are the shadows and the highlights that I caught with my camera. They will always depend on the direction of the light source. You can also take your own pictures after practicing this drawing. Take any object that you want to draw, place it next to the window, make sure that it casts a nice shadow for a good 3D effect, and do *not* use flash. As always, let's start with outlining. So, we have to create a shape similar to this spoon as much as possible. Of course, it can differ a bit, but the spoon should be symmetrical. Check out your outline in the mirror and if it looks symmetrical there too, then you can start shading. I sketch the outline with a dashed line so that I can easily correct it and change it while outlining. Once I make sure that everything looks fine, I just go over it with a full line. I'm using a 3H for sketching.

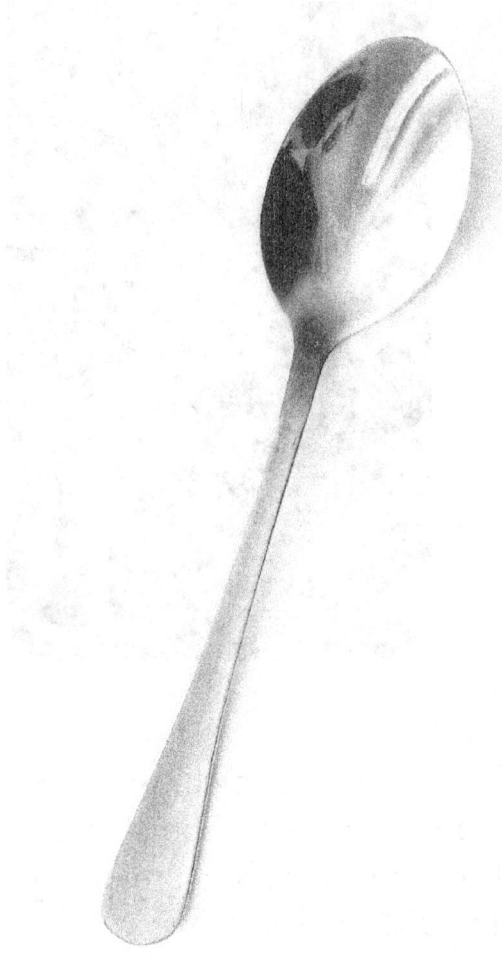

We can start shading our teaspoon.

If you often draw from reference photos, you might have often wondered which pencil to use for a particular area. I have developed mobile and desktop applications for that purpose where users upload their own pictures, select any point of an image, and the app suggests the pencil for that particular part. If you want to know more about it and to buy it for yourself, you can find more info and links on the website www.pen-pick.com
The apps have two panels: one for graphite and one for colored pencils. It is a huge help in choosing the right pencils, particularly for beginners.

In the next image, you can see that it shows a 2H for the area where the target is placed (clicked) and I will definitely be using a 2H for the handle.

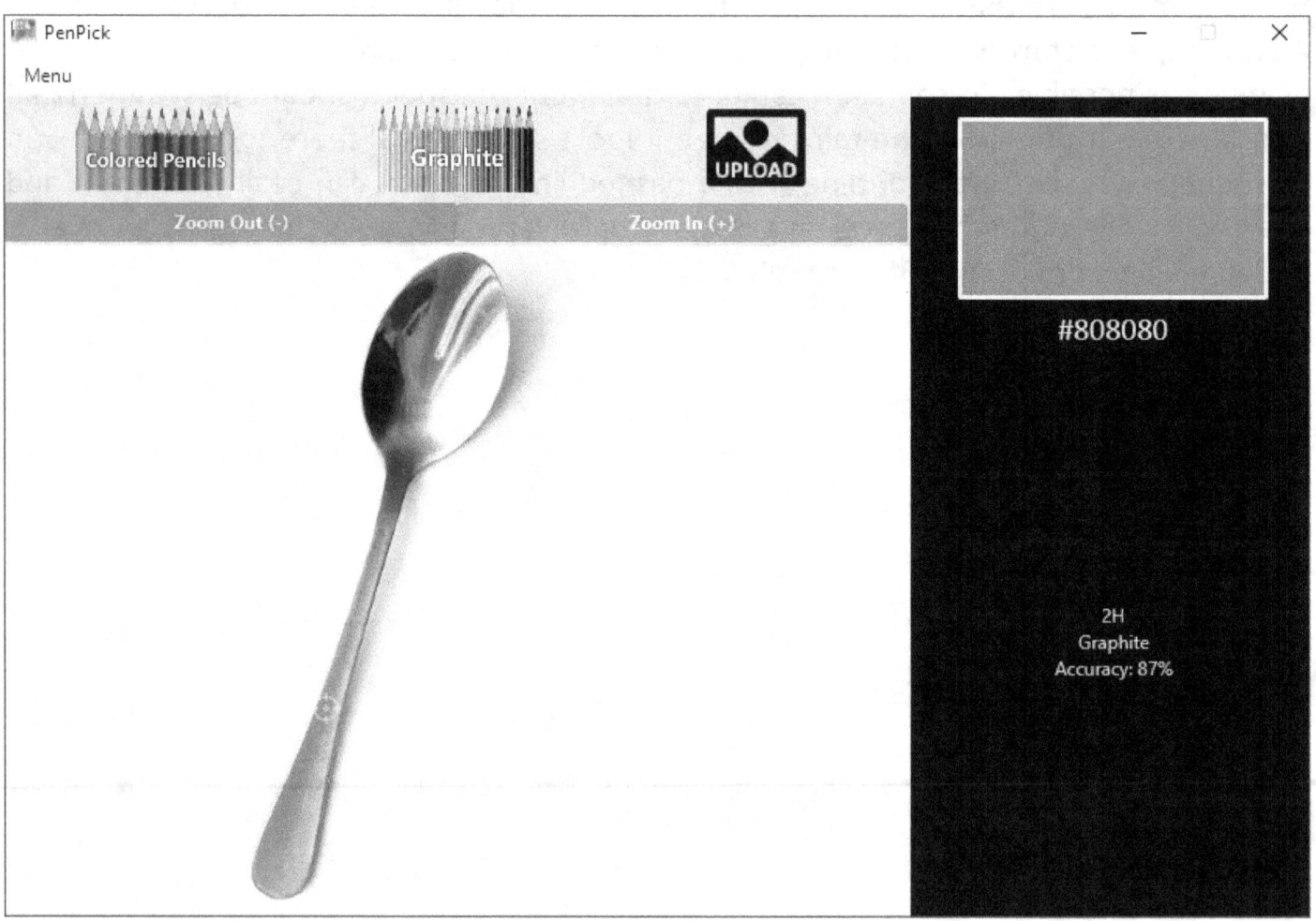

However, I want to start with the darkest parts of the right side of the bowl, using a 5B pencil. Just to make it simple, I will be doing exactly the same. So, I won't be changing anything. Usually, when I draw from reference photos, I try to change something, but this time I will just draw what I see to make it easy for you to understand.

Shade very carefully next to the other edge. Press very hard to fill the tooth of the paper so that you won't have those white dots of the paper visible. Here also, use the circulism method because we want to create smooth textures.

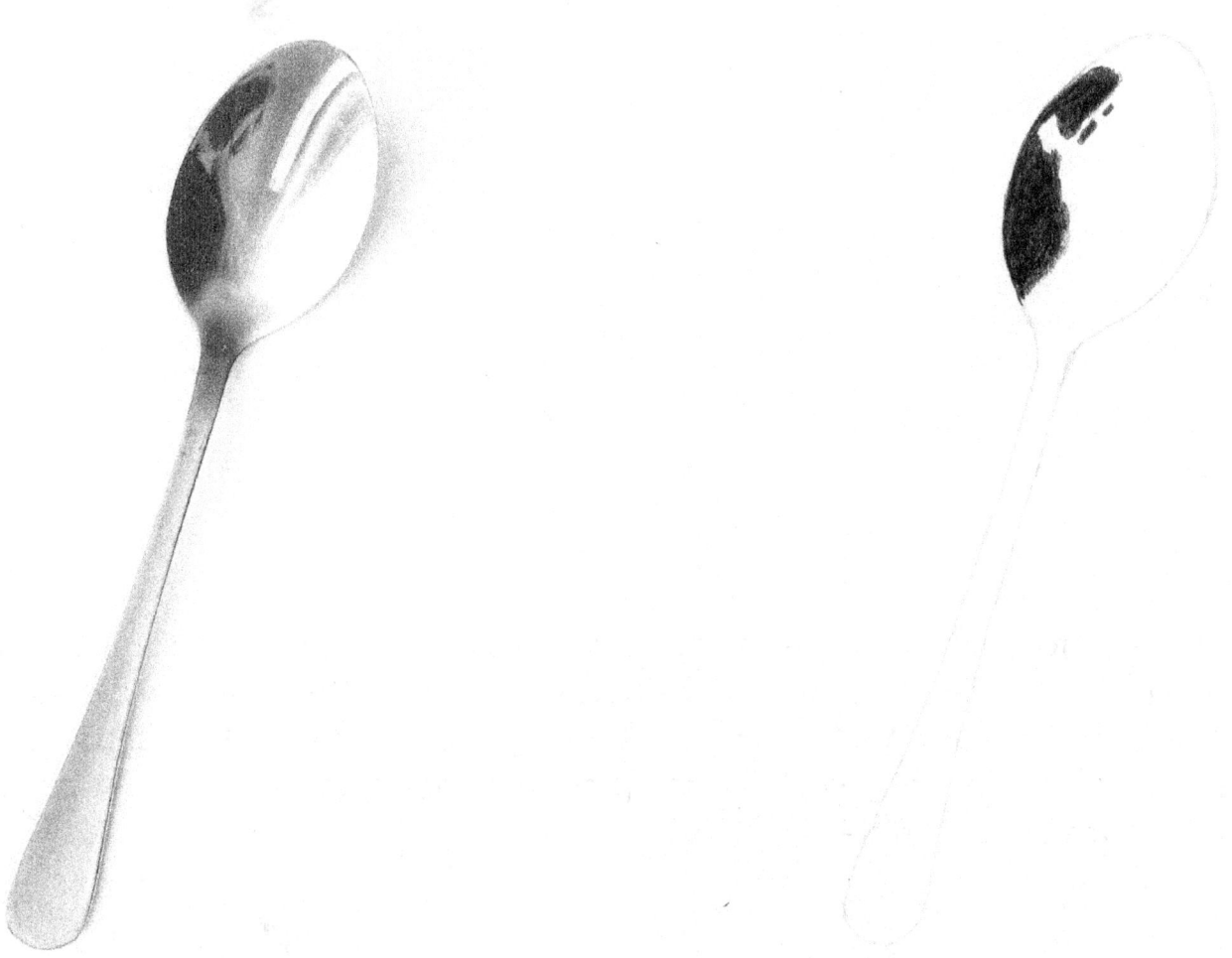

Since we don't have such dark areas anywhere else, we can start using lighter pencils. I want to continue the area next to it and to use an HB for it. I have drawn around the highlight because it has to stay white. Study the next image to see what I have shaded in this step.

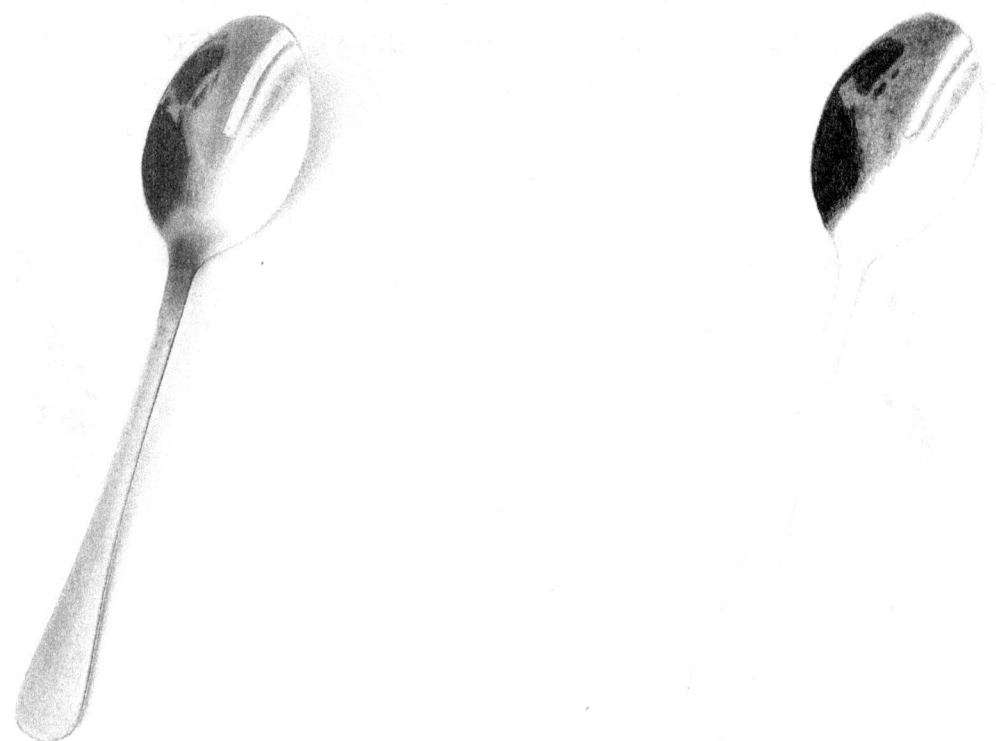

Let's use a 2B for the area between the bowl and the handle. Use the same pencil and outline the edge on the right side and the bottom of the handle. Do it very carefully with a well-sharpened pencil. You can even use a magnifier, if you want, to see the details better; it can often be very helpful. Don't press too hard because you won't be able to erase if you make some mistakes.

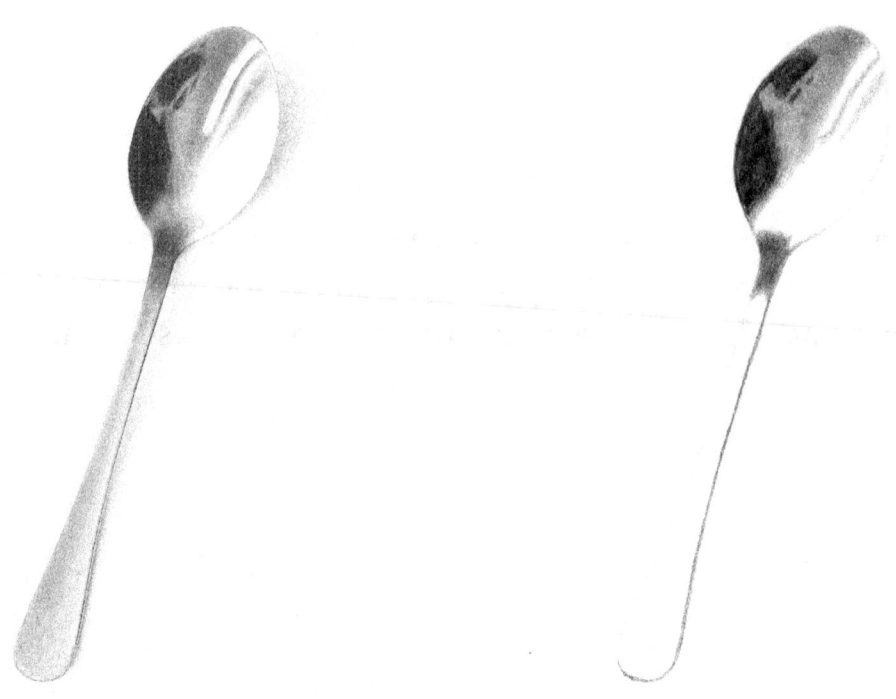

Continue shading the bowl with a lighter pencil, between the previously shaded darker areas and the white highlight on the right side. Of course, it should stay untouched. Use an H pencil, starting over the edges of the darker areas, then pressing less and less as you shade towards the highlight.

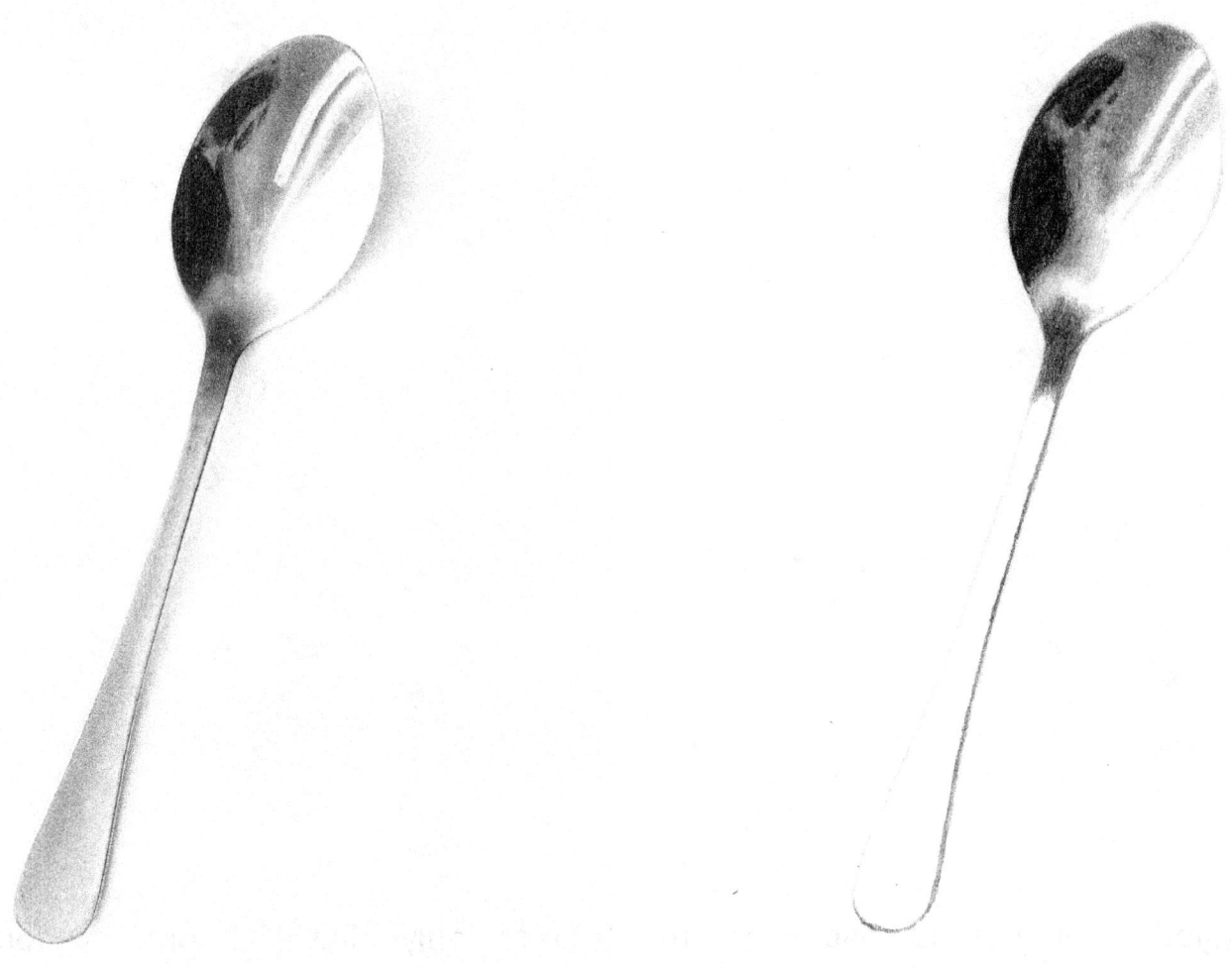

Now, we can use a 2H for the lighter shadows on the bowl, the ones next to the white areas, and we are done with the bowl. In the end, blend it all carefully with a blending stump.

Still using a 2H, move to the handle and shade it. You can see in the reference photo that we have to create a smooth gradient over the handle. That's why we should press normally next to the edge on the left side. Then, either lessen the pressure as you shade towards the edge on the right side or start using a lighter pencil, such as 3H or 4H.

Don't press too hard. Instead, go over multiple times until you create the desired tone.

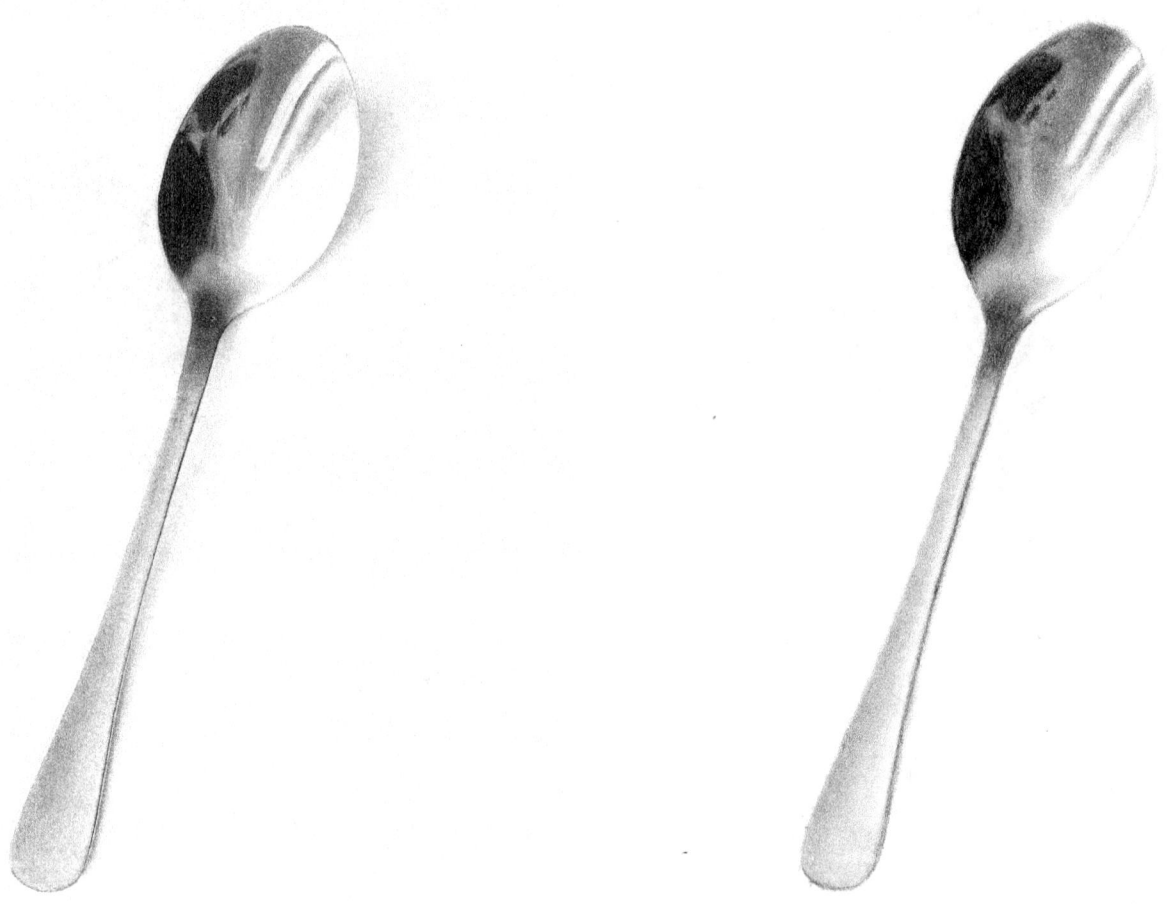

Lastly, let's create the cast shadow because this is the only thing left to do. It is enough if we use a blending stump that has some graphite on its tip, but not too much. To prevent overdoing shading, just wipe its tip a bit with a tissue.

Create the cast shadow that is cast by the upper part of the handle. Shade a thin line just a little bit farther from the spoon. The upper part of this cast shadow should be connected to the part between the bowl and the handle, and the lower part should also be gradually disappearing under the lower part of the handle. You can see that the cast shadow will suggest that this part is higher from the surface and it will indicate the shape of the spoon.

Then, create the shadow cast by the bowl and shade carefully next to the white part of the spoon because it has to stay white. The cast shadow, as in every case, should be darker next to the objects that cast it, and it should gradually disappear into the paper. The cast shadow should be as smooth as possible.

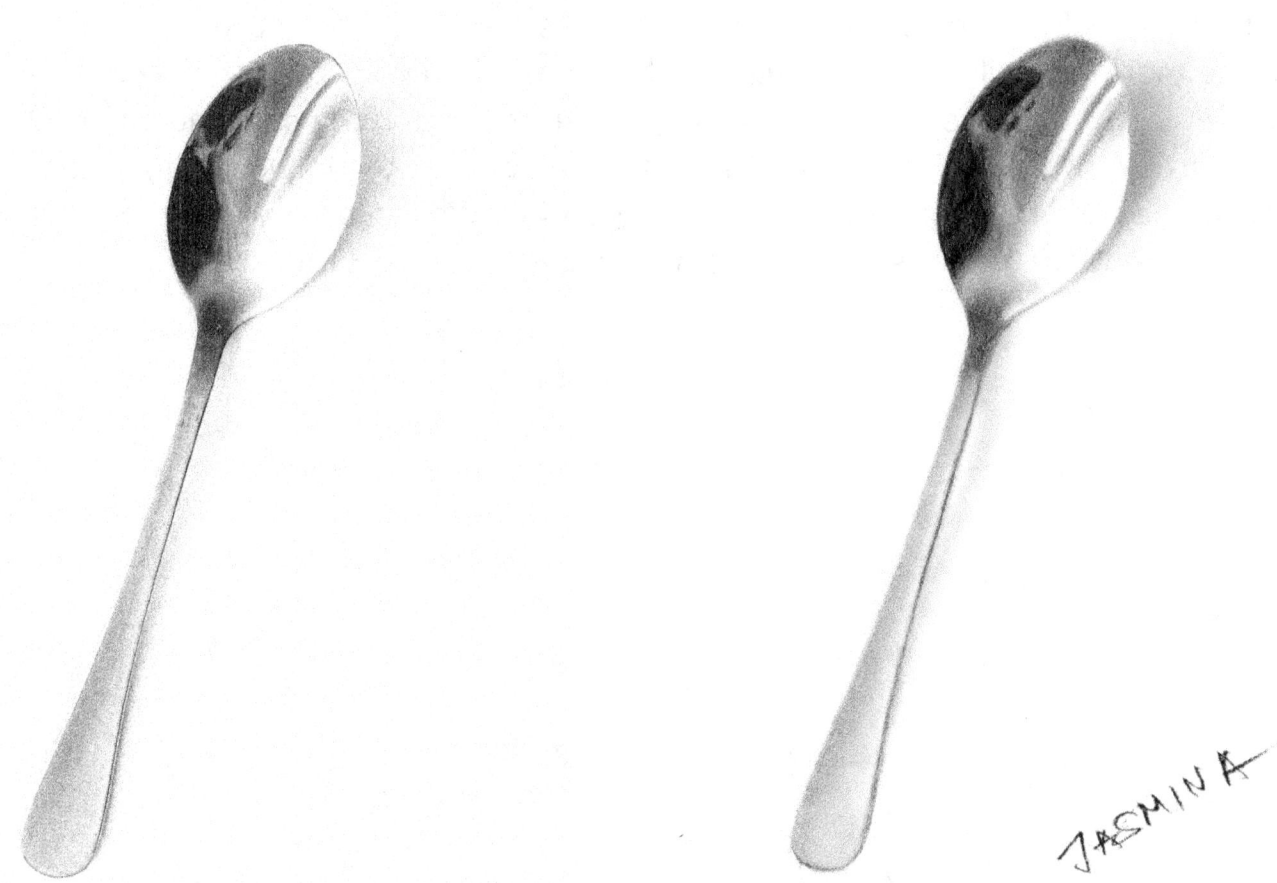

AN EAR

In this tutorial, I want to show you how to draw and shade an ear. I want to show you a different kind of shading so that you can try this way too. The more methods you try out, the more you will learn. You will also be able to find your own style and what suits you the most. Not to mention, it is always good to try something new and different.
Let's start with an outline. In this case, we don't have to draw the lines too much because the ear, like a nose, requires mostly shading. We can draw just the outline and a few lines inside the ear, as shown in the next image. I use a 3H for sketching.

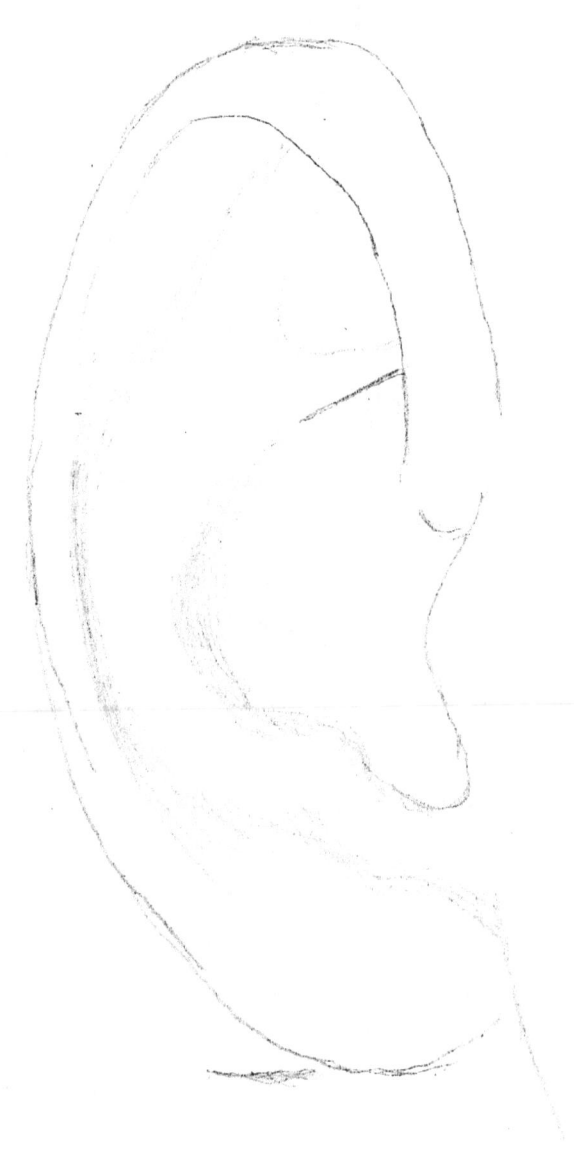

Now, let's shade the whole area with a tissue and graphite powder. Strengthen your outlines so you can see them through the layer of the graphite. Apply circular motions all the time and evenly spread the graphite, even out of the edges because you want to shade the edges too. As you can see, the texture is very smooth when we shade this way.

Before you move forward, just erase the graphite all around the ear, next to its edge. And now we have a basic tone of the skin, so we can start creating highlights and shadows.

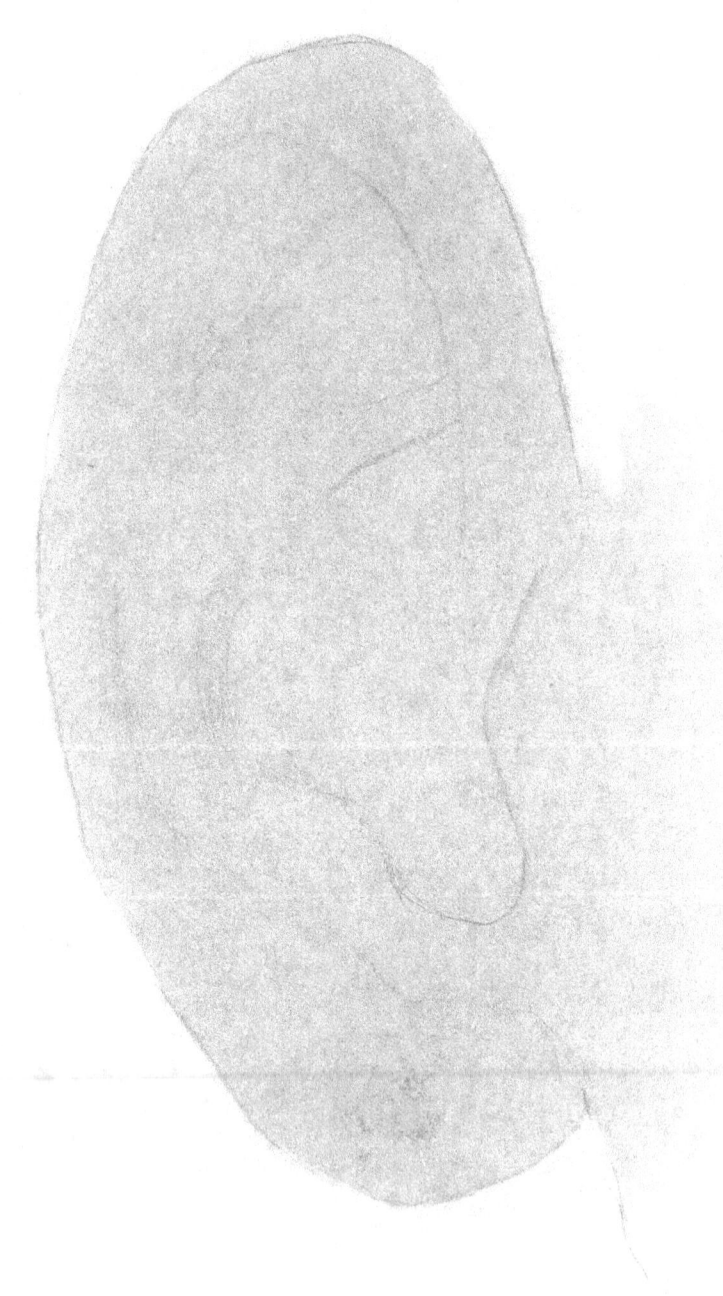

We can start with the highlights, we can start with shadows, and we can do them both—a little bit of this and a little bit of that.

I want to start with the shadow that is cast by the top part of the ear, over and under the inner area. I'm using a 2B for this. Study the next image to see where I have drawn the cast shadows. You can see that the cast shadows will make the areas above them appear as if they are closer to the viewer's eye and the drawing has depth. Blend them a bit with a blending stump.

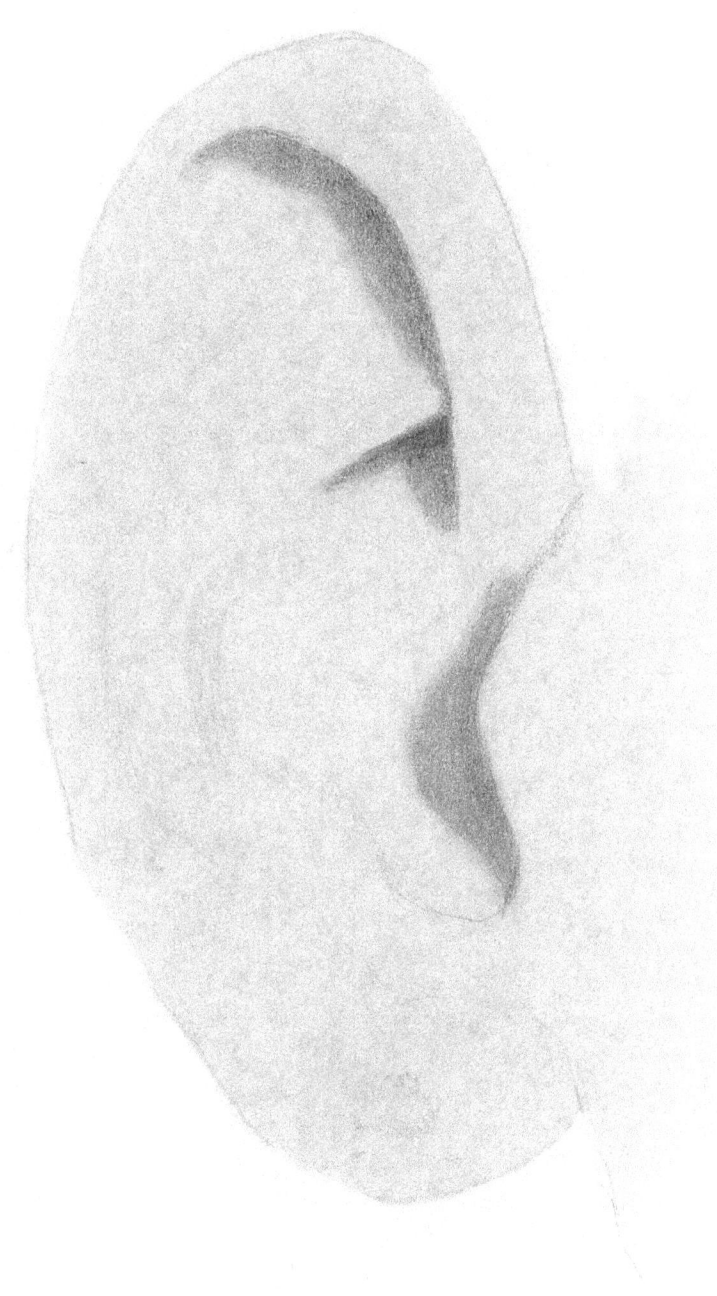

Next, we can create the brightest highlights over the protruding areas, as shown in the image below. I use a plastic eraser for these because I want to remove a lot of graphite and make these areas almost white again. Before I started drawing this ear, I studied some reference photos of ears and my own ears in the mirror. You should do the same, no matter what you draw, to check for the shapes, shadows, and highlights so that you can draw realistic drawings.

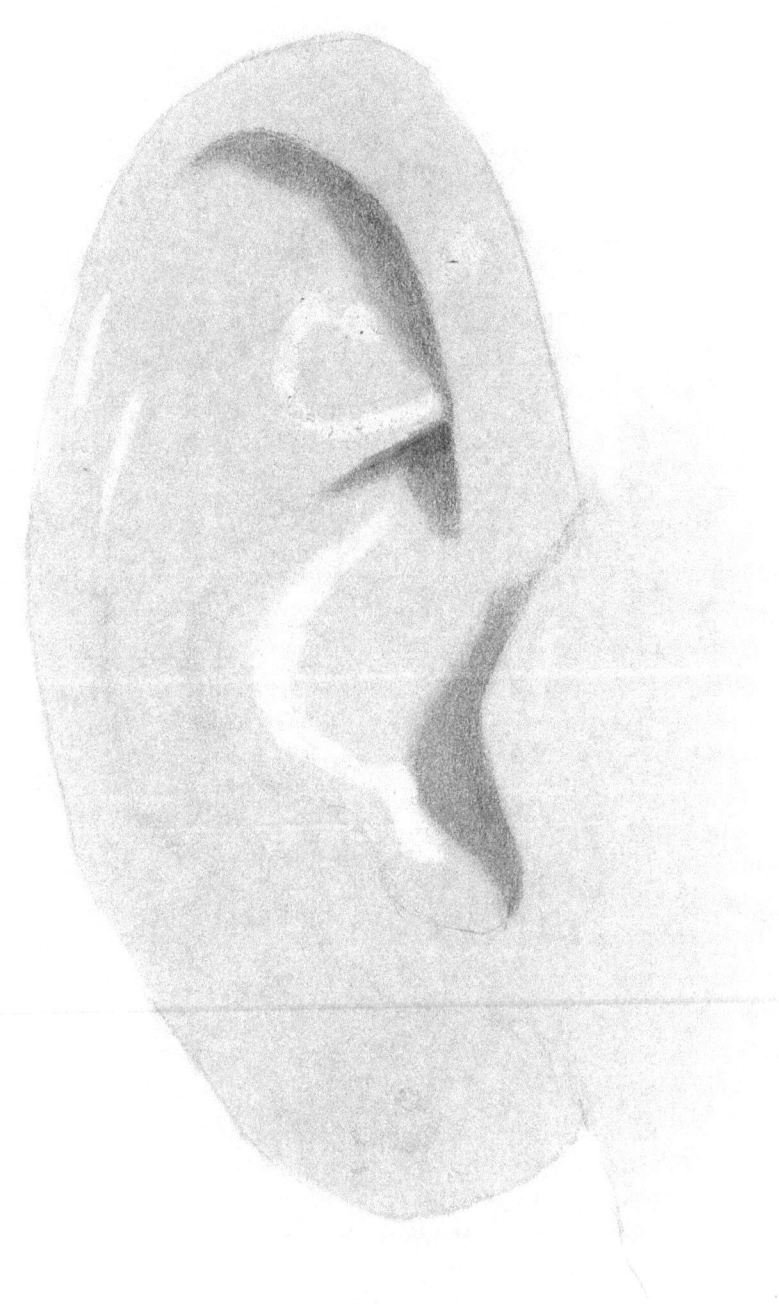

Now, we can create slightly lighter shadows than the cast shadow. For this, it is enough if we use a blending stump. Shade in the sunken areas and don't press too hard. Instead, press lightly and go over again and again. We have to press less and less as we shade towards the highlighted areas to create a smooth gradient in order to make the parts appear round.

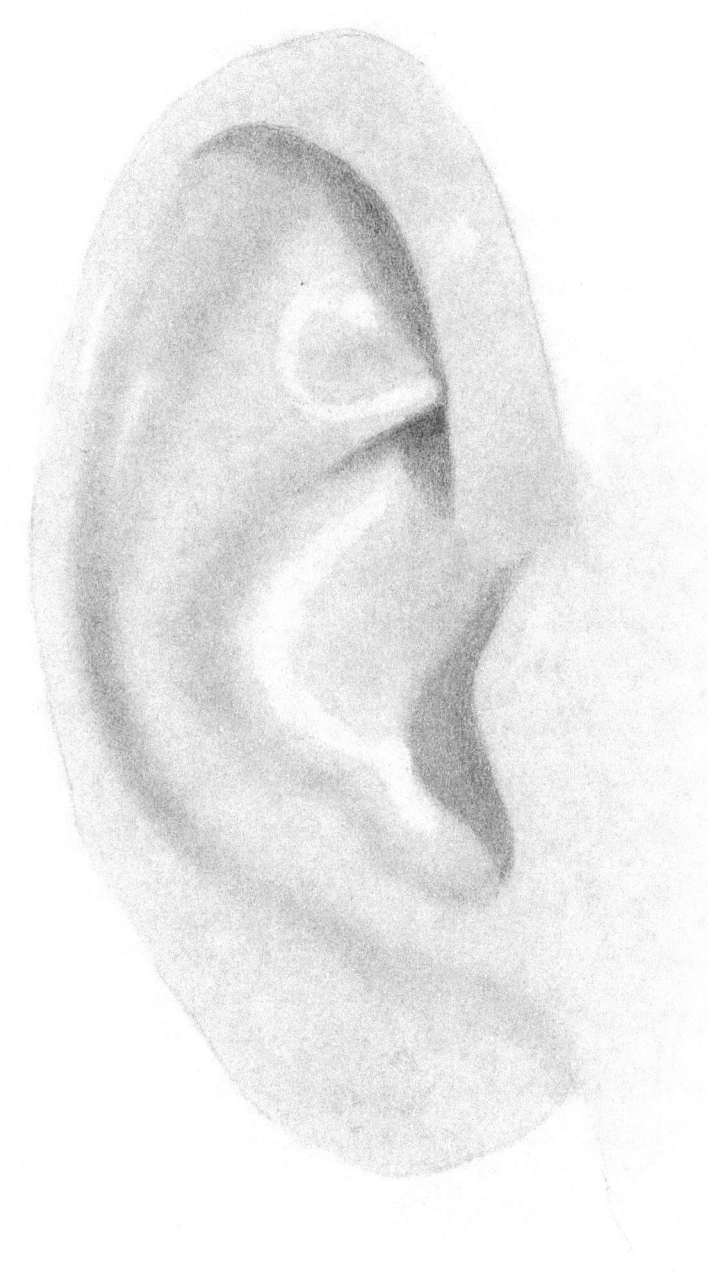

Next, still using a blending stump, shade the edge all around because we have to make the edge look round. And the same here: press harder over the edge and lessen the pressure on your blending stump as you work away from the edge.

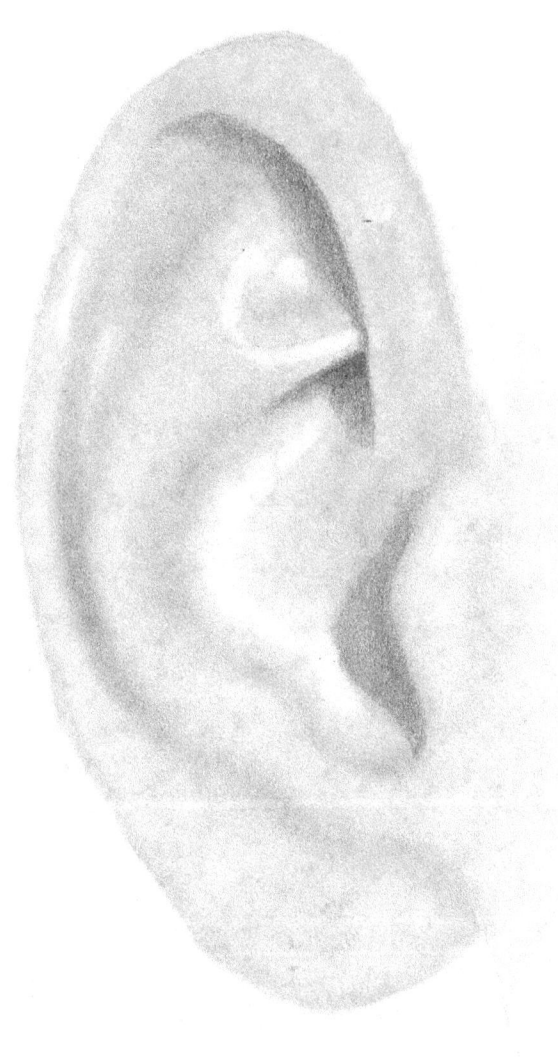

Let's create the less bright highlights, next to the highlights that are almost white (the ones that we created with a plastic eraser). I want to use a kneaded eraser to create highlights between these very bright highlights and the basic skin tone because the edge between them shouldn't stay clear. These two values should flow into each other. We have to just tap next to it and we can remove just enough of the graphite. Do it carefully because you don't want to remove a lot of graphite.

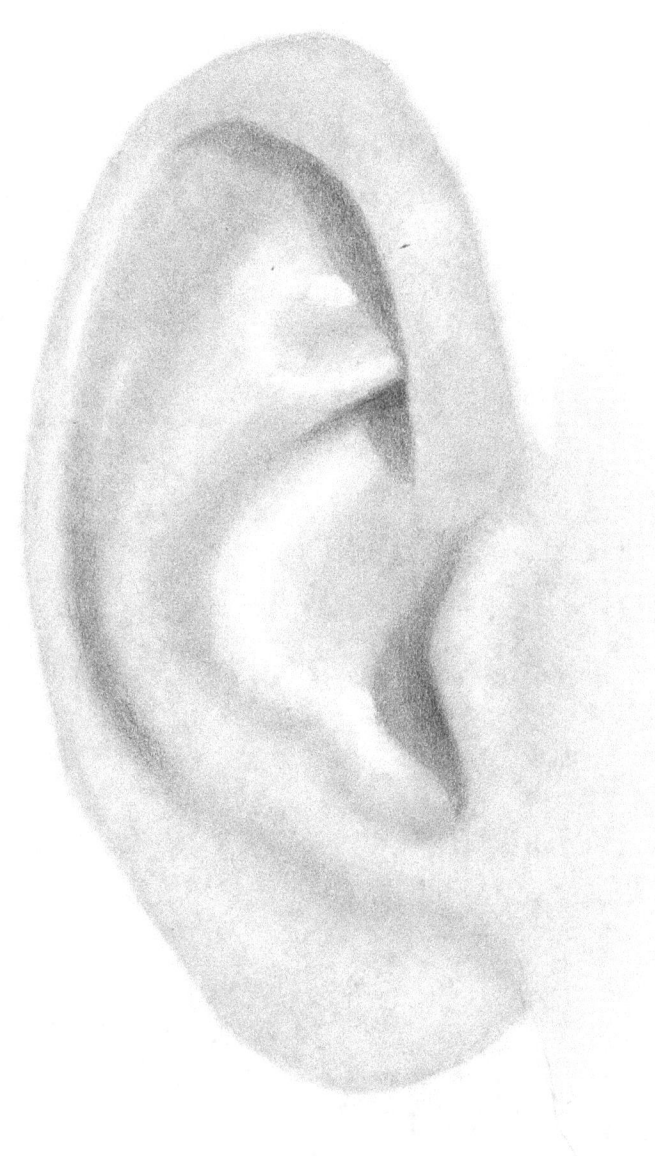

Now, let's draw a bit of the hair that goes behind the ear. I'm using an HB for the hair. Of course, avoid drawing over the ear, but create some flyaways. Draw curvy hair next to the temple. We can also blend it a bit with a tissue to make it look soft.

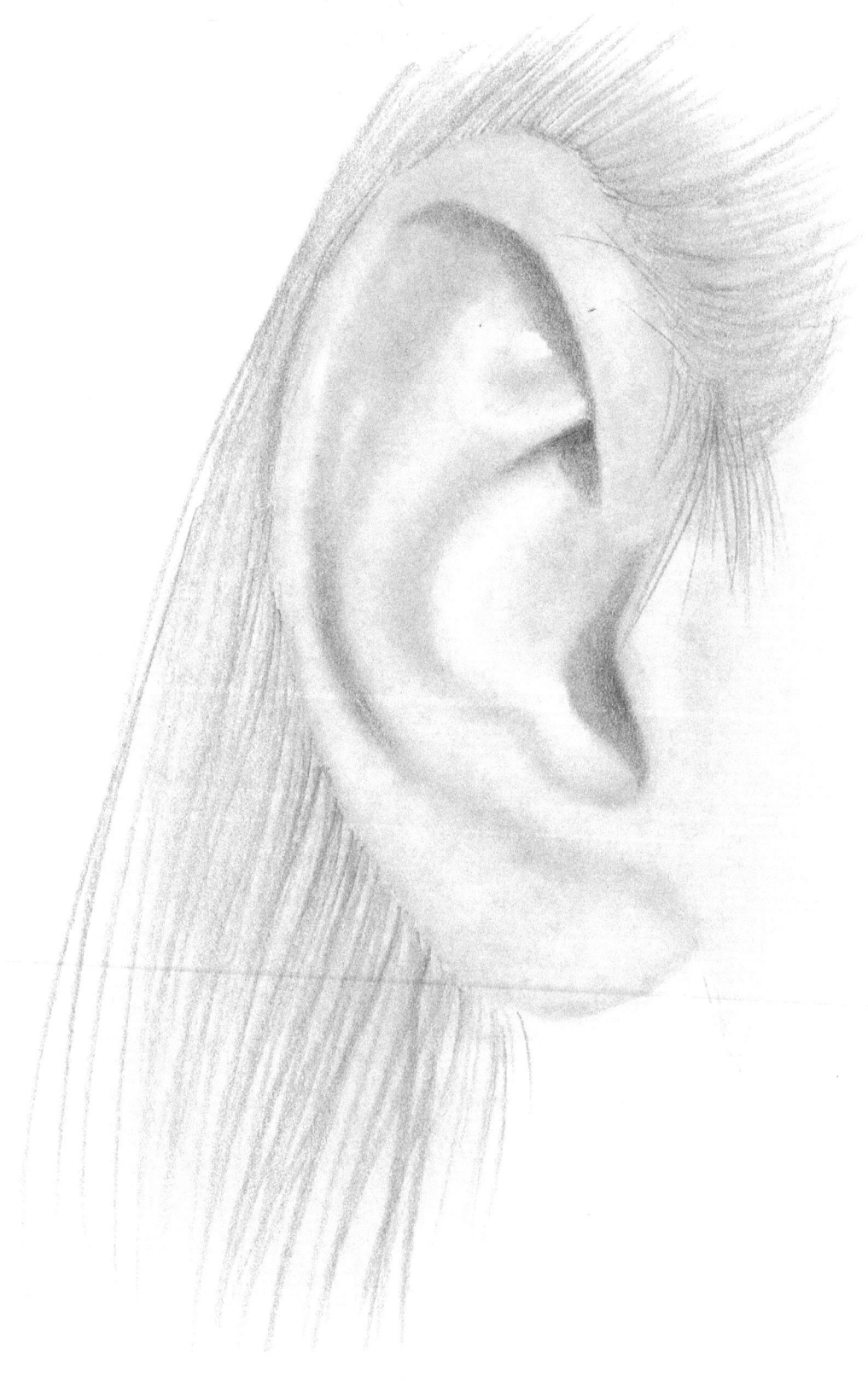

Draw some highlighted flyaways with an eraser. Also, darken the area under the ear to create the shadow cast by the ear over the hair. I'm using a 5B for this.

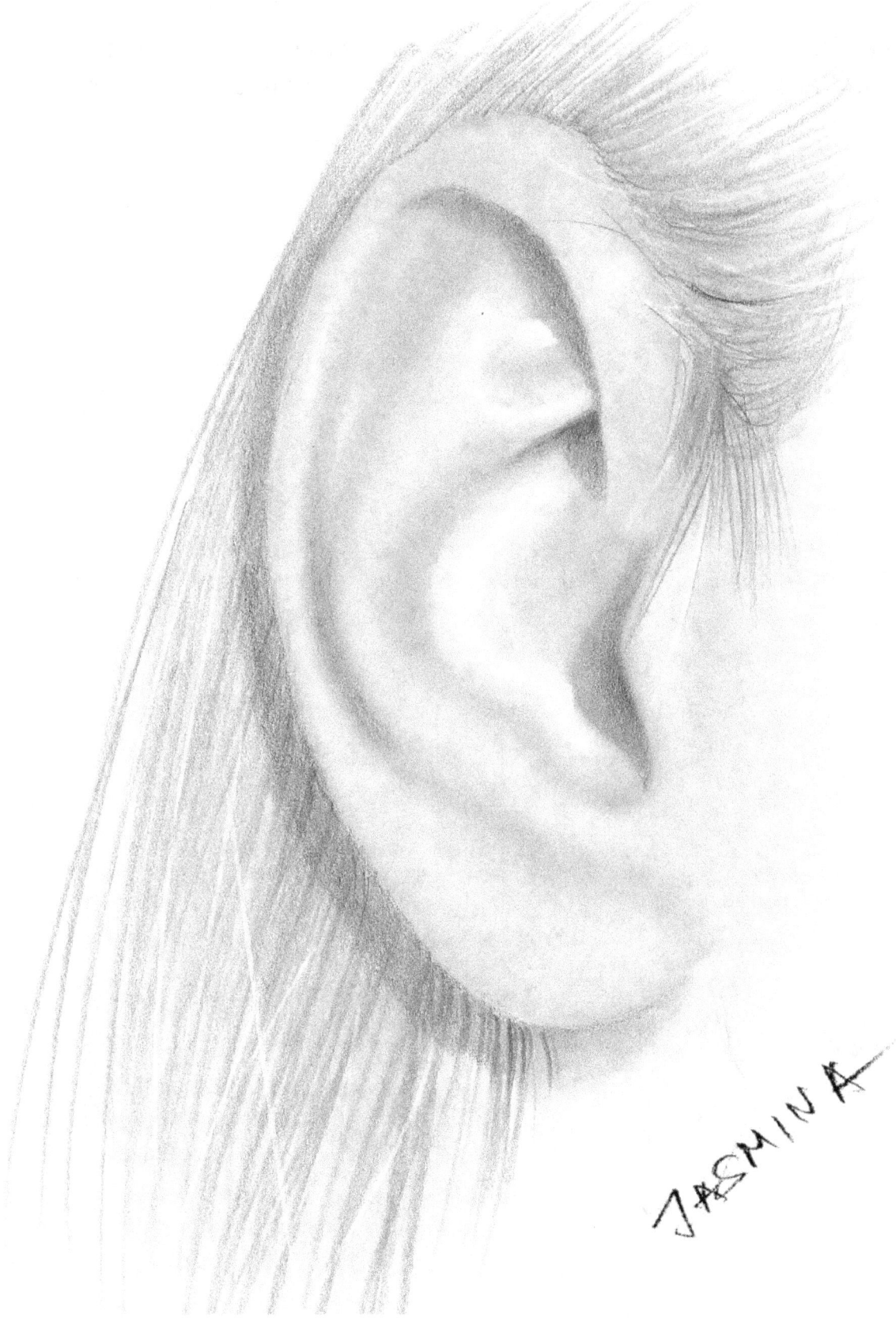

A HALF-CUT ORANGE

Start with a circle and use a drawing compass if necessary. I have also added some tiny leaves around and details inside the orange. In the next image, you can see my main lines.

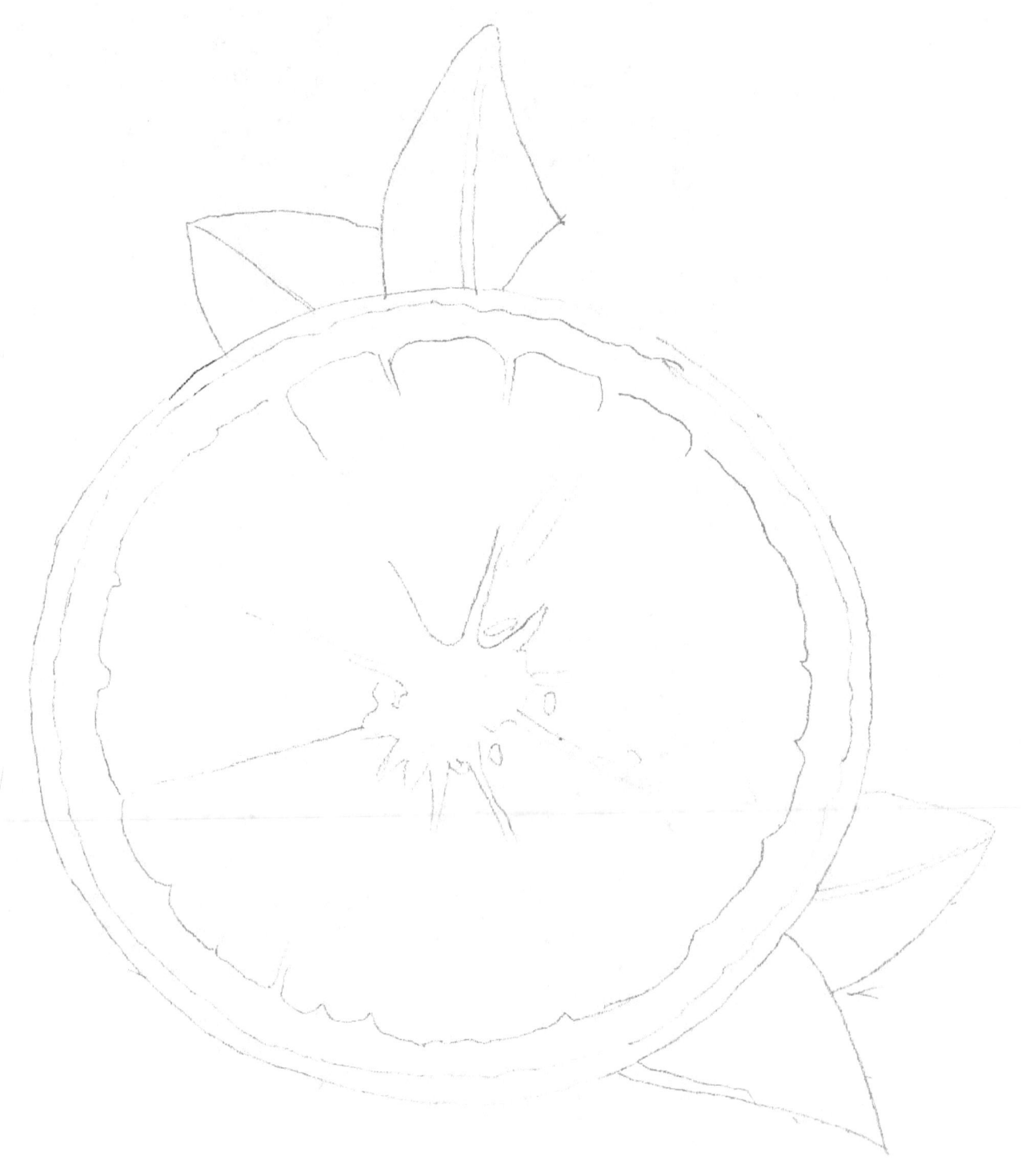

Let's start with shading the leaves. I use an HB to create the basic tone. So, fill the leaves, making small circular motions to spread the graphite evenly. Use the flat surface of the chisel-shaped tip of your pencil to create a smooth texture faster. Then, blend it all with a blending stump.

Now, create the darker areas of the leaves, using a B pencil over the previously drawn areas. When drawing the edges between two leaves, try to make a strong contrast, to make the edge of the leaf which is closer to the viewer's eye much brighter, and to shade the leaf behind it. This way you will create a more realistic drawing and give more depth to it. So, in this step, focus only on the shadowed areas. Analyze the next image to see how to shade and where.

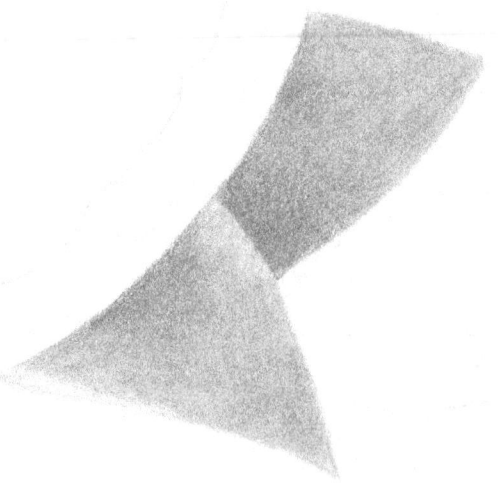

Add the highlights, and this is the last step for the leaves. Firstly, erase a bit over the highlighted areas using a kneaded eraser and try to create a subtle gradation between these bright parts and the shadowed areas. Also, create the veins over the leaves using the pointed tip of an eraser. Erase the thicker vein in the middle and the thinner ones from the thicker vein to the edge of the leaves.

If you are done with the leaves, you can move on to the orange.
As a first step, shade the ring around the cut piece using a 2H. Create a sharp outer edge. The inner one should be blurry, so blend it with a blending stump.
The peel basically has two parts: the so-called "flavedo" and the so-called "albedo," which is white, and these two tones (colors) gradually flow into each other.

Continue with a 2H to fill the whole area of the pulp. Leave the central column and some walls white, drawing around them. Here, you shouldn't fill the area with circular motions, but rather with lines, starting from the center and going out towards the peel. Try to make this texture as smooth as possible and blend it all with a tissue. If you accidentally apply some graphite over the white areas, just erase it. Study the next image to see where I have shaded.

Add the darker parts of the juicy pulp - in the outer area, closer to the peel - using an HB pencil over the previously drawn tone. Create the juice sac as shown in the following picture. Draw them randomly, focusing on the pressure on the pencil. The majority of these lines should radiate from the center of the orange. Press harder into the outer edge and lighter as you go toward the center. You can also use an H pencil to create lighter lines.

Using an eraser, create highlights over the pulp and juice sac. Don't go over the shadowed, darkest areas that you created in the previous step—only in the middle. Press harder and highlight more next to the central column, which is the brightest area. This step will make the pulp shiny. Also, add a few brighter highlights with an opaque white marker and it will make the pulp in those places appear even wetter and shinier.

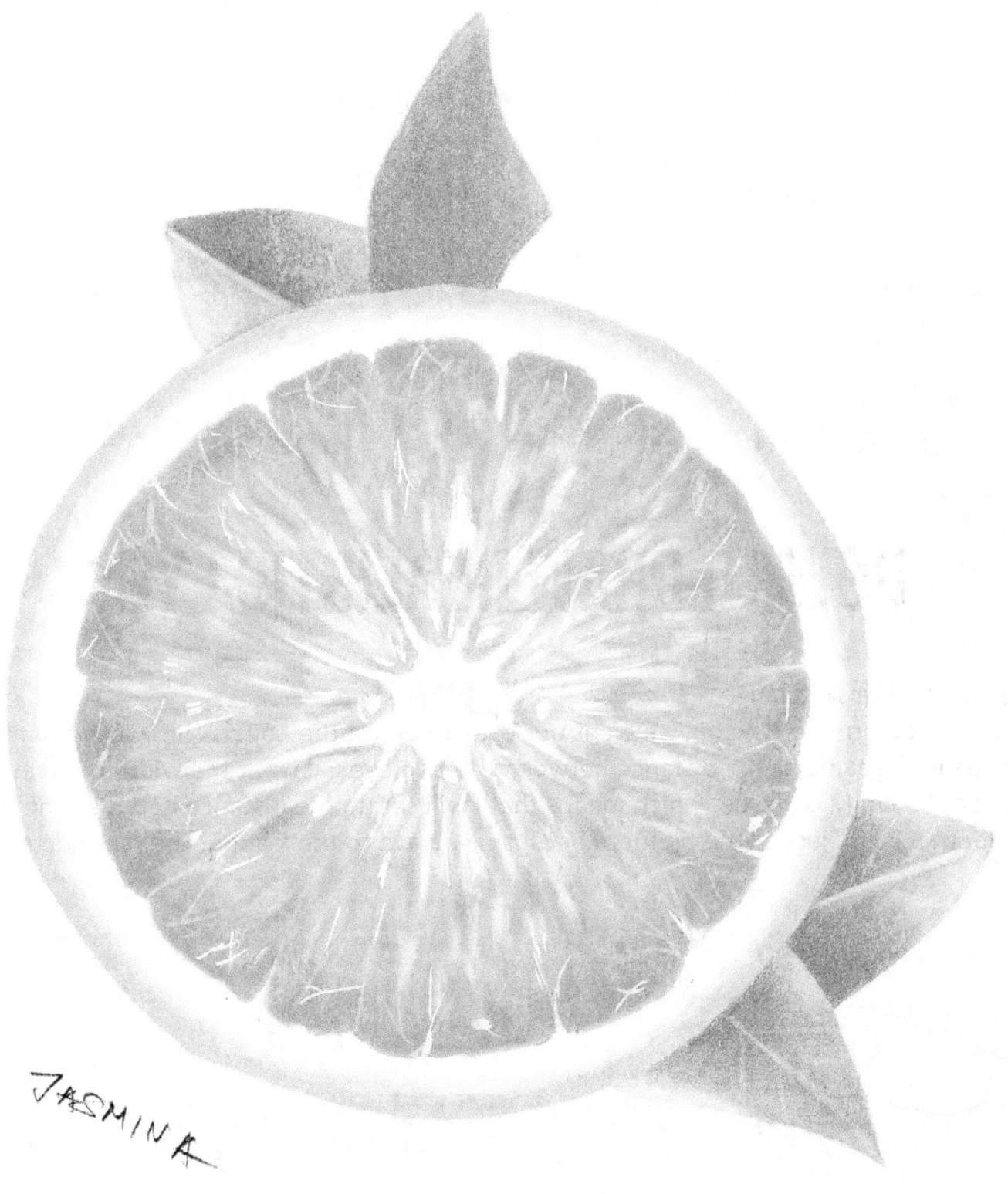

Tip

If you hold your pencil closer to its tip, you will have more control and accuracy, but darker stroke. Gripping the pencil further from its tip will result in less control and accuracy, but with lighter marks.

HOW TO DRAW REALISTIC EYES

Let's start with sketching.
We must determine how big we want our eyes to be on the paper. The width of an eye is usually the same as the distance between the two eyes. I want the width of an eye to be about 5 cm (2.0") wide, which means that I will set up the distance between the eyes to about 5.2 cm, just a little bit more because we have to think about the tear ducts too.

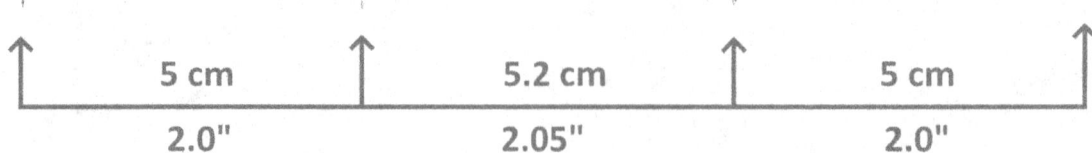

Next, draw the pupils with a drawing compass. I want to place the center of the pupil somewhere in the middle of the width of an eye. So, if the eye is 5.0 cm (2.0") wide, the center of the pupil should be found at 2.5 cm (1.0") measuring from both ends.

For the pupil, I set up the distance between the needle and my pencil lead to be about 3 mm (0.11"). Place the needle in the previously marked place and draw the pupil boundary for both eyes.

Next, draw the iris boundary, keeping the needle in the same place and enlarging the distance between the needle and the pencil lead. In my case, it's about 1.0 cm (0.4"). I want to let you know about my measurements, in the case you want to draw the same size as me.

Now, let's outline the eyes, namely, to draw the upper and the lower eyelids. I use a 3H for sketching. The upper eyelid should cover the upper area of the iris, so start drawing a horizontal line between the iris boundary and the pupil boundary. Start horizontally and then start curving the line towards the points that you marked in the first step. You can create a dashed line first, to see where the line will connect. When everything looks fine, just go over with a full line. Also, determine the position of the tear duct in the inner corners of the eyes.

Then, outline the lower eyelid. Start right over the lower line of the iris boundary and draw it horizontally over that. Then start separating it from the iris boundary and head towards the outer corners and towards the tear ducts.
The lower eyelid is usually less curvy than the upper eyelid but, of course, it varies from person to person.

Erase the upper part of the iris boundary that is now found above the upper eyelid.
Then, draw the eyelid fold. It should be a line above the upper eyelid that is parallel to it. It can be closer to the eyes or farther from the eyes.

Also, draw the thickness of the skin under the eye. Go over the previously sketched line of the lower eyelid and create a dashed line, pressing lightly because this area will be highlighted later - just mark the position of it. Outline the space for the eyelashes next to the outer corners as shown in the next image.

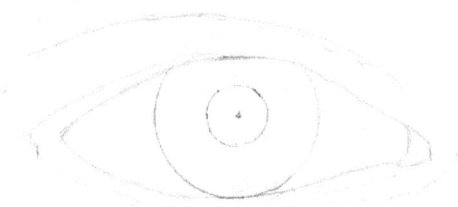 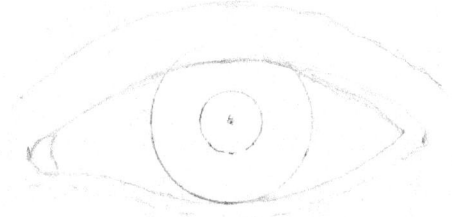

Let's also draw the outline of the eyebrows. Of course, you don't have to draw eyebrows, but I think the drawing of the eyes looks more complete with eyebrows.
They can be thicker or thinner, just outline them with tiny dashed lines and create hairs of the eyebrow instead of a full line.

Since we have touched this paper a lot and also erased some parts during the sketching progress, we should transfer the sketch on a new piece of paper and avoid touching it with our fingers. Put some tissue under your hand because after applying the graphite, the fingerprints will be visible.

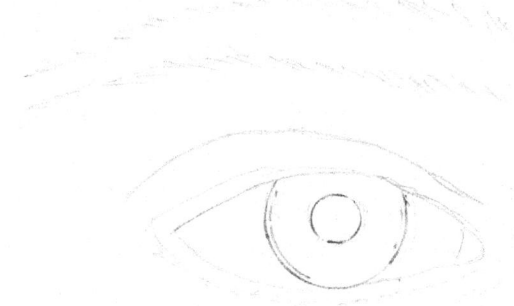 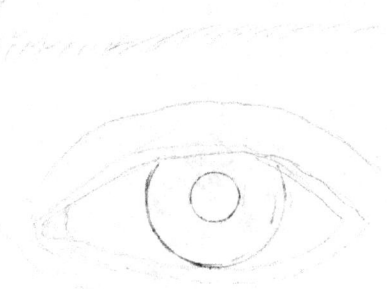

Let's start with the pupils. I want to use an 8B to fill the two circles. So, use at least 4B or darker and press very hard because here we have to create an absolutely black color. Do it very carefully next to the pupil boundary to preserve the perfectly round shape.

The next thing is to shade the iris boundary. I'm using an HB for it. Go over the initial outline, about 1 mm deep, and press harder in the upper area. Everything found in the upper area, right under the upper eyelid should be darker because the upper eyelid blocks light and casts a shadow over the upper part of the eye.

Here also, try to preserve the perfectly round shape between the iris and the whites of the eyes, which is also called sclera.

Blend the edge between the iris boundary and whites of the eye with a blending stump because it should be blurry.

Next, let's draw the iris. I want to use a 3H for it, but you can use any other pencil. It just depends on the color that you want your eyes to be. Here we have to draw the spokes that radiate from the very center of the pupil. I have created a few spokes over the iris to show you the direction in which you have to draw.

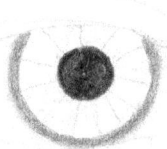 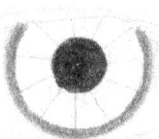

Now that we have established their direction, we can draw the spokes and fill in the whole area for the irises.
If you don't have a white ink gel pen, white marker, gouache or anything like that on hand, you can leave out the parts for the reflected light as white dots or a similar shape then draw around it. You can also change the pressure on a pencil to create spokes of different values.

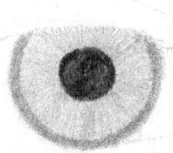 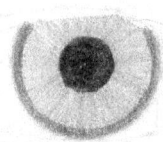

Since we have the edge between the spokes and iris boundary, and the edge between the spokes and pupil clean, we have to make them blurry. I want to use a B pencil to make both ends of the spokes gradually disappear into the pupil and into the iris boundary. Begin over the pupil and iris boundary, drawing tiny spokes inwards to the iris. Lessen the pressure as you finish each stroke. Then, blend it all with a blending stump.

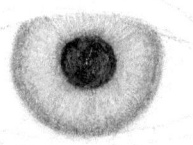 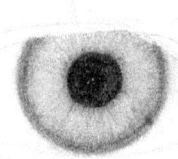

Draw some darker spokes to create the patterns of the iris, as shown in the next image. I'm using a 3B pencil for it. Make them at random, in an unpredictable order. Some of them shouldn't go over the whole iris, so you can stop drawing them somewhere in the middle. They can also be thicker and thinner.

In the upper area, right under the upper eyelid, we have to make the iris absolutely dark, to create the cast shadow from the upper eyelid. I use a 6B for this.

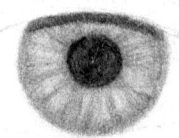 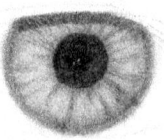

Create some highlighted spokes or patterns in between the dark spokes that you just created, using a sharp point of an eraser.

Then create the reflected lights over the iris and pupil with a white marker. Here we can think already about the eyelashes and how they would block the light. So, we can create the reflected light as if the light is going through the eyelashes. Analyze the next image to see how I have drawn it. Also, draw a white dot at the bottom of the iris boundaries. These highlights will also indicate the wetness of the eye. Try to make everything the same on both eyes.

As you can see, now the eyes look shiny and more lifelike. If you want to enhance these highlights even more, just shade next to them with a very dark pencil and they will look brighter.

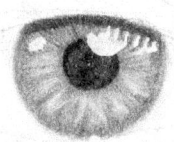 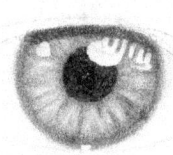

Now, let's shade the sclera or the white of the eye. Here we have to imagine a sphere. In the same way that we shade a sphere, we have to shade the eyeballs. The eyeballs must be darker in the corners and become lighter as we shade towards the iris boundary. So, we have to create a subtle gradient from dark grey to light grey.

I want to start with an HB in the corners, next to the tear duct. I recommend using the circulism technique, which means applying tiny overlapping circles, to create a smooth texture. We have to press harder right under the upper eyelid because it casts the shadow over the sclera.

As we shade towards the iris boundary, we have to lessen the pressure and of course, we're going to use lighter pencils in the following steps.

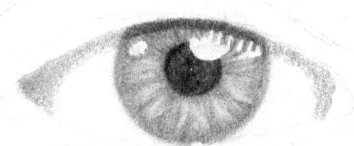 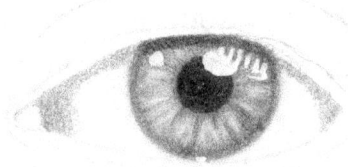

And now we can continue with a 2H next to the HB area. Go a bit over the HB area, then continue shading towards the iris boundary, lessening the pressure on your pencil. Keep working with the circulism technique. It might seem scary when you shade it like this because the sclera is actually white, but it has to be shaded completely. The only white spot should be the reflected light; everything else has to be shaded.

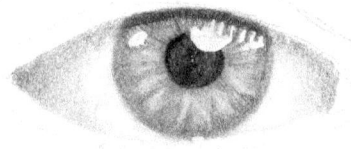 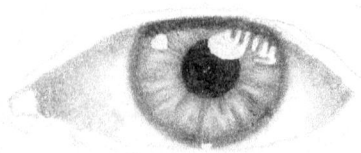

As you can see I have left the space for the next, lighter pencil, so let's continue with the 6H. You can use a 5H or 7H, it doesn't have to be a 6H. Shade the rest of the sclera using circular motions. Go over the previously shaded areas with a 6H to blend the edge between the values. Blend it all carefully with a Q-tip, starting over the lighter areas towards the dark ones.

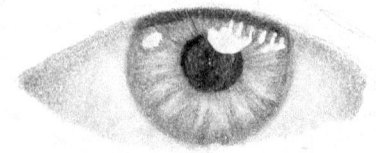 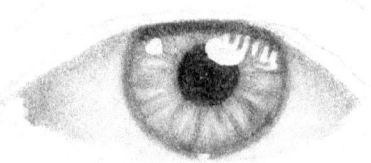

Shade both tear ducts with an HB and leave out the areas for the reflected lights. You can also apply them with a white marker after you have shaded the whole tear ducts.

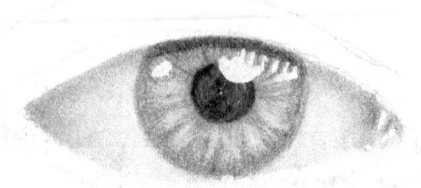 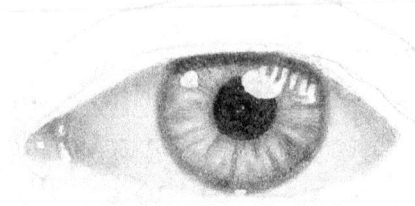

Next, draw a thick line over the upper eyelid, between the sclera and the skin, as shown in the next picture. If you want to draw female eyes, you can make it thicker to indicate the eyeliner. I'm using an 8B for this. These are actually the roots of the eyelashes, but we will draw the eyelashes over the skin because that's easier and better to do when the skin is completely shaded and done.

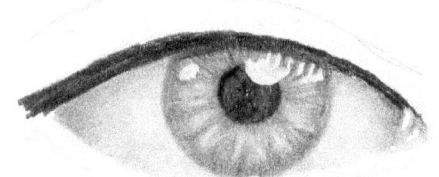 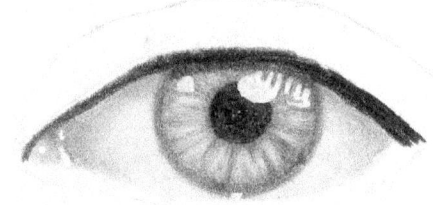

Now let's shade the skin above the eyes, and let's split this task into two phases: shading under the eyelid fold and shading above the eyelid fold.
First, strengthen the line for the eyelid folds. I'm using an HB for this.
Still using an HB and the circulism method, shade the skin above the sclera of both, the left and right eye. We will use a lighter pencil for the skin above the iris so that even the skin will suggest the roundness of the eyeball. Make the texture as smooth as possible. Press harder next to the eyelid fold and next to the eyeliner.

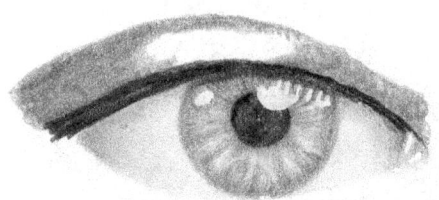 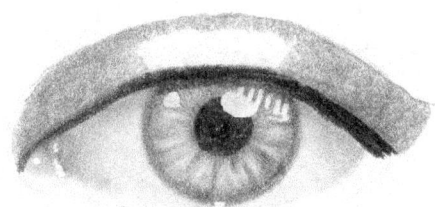

Shade the area in the middle with a 2H. Press harder next to the HB areas, then release the pressure as you shade towards the center of this highlight. Strengthen the eyelid folds again if necessary.

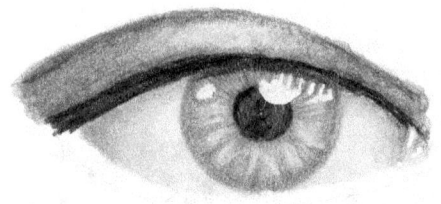 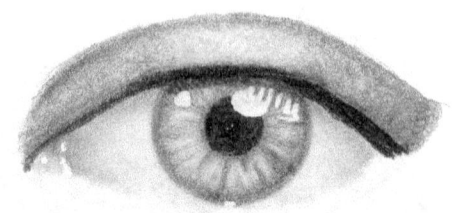

Next, shade the skin above the eyelid folds, between the eyebrows and the eyelid folds. Strengthen the eyebrows so that you can see the outlines when the shade is applied. The sunken areas next to the nose are always more in shadow, so here we have to press harder. I use a 2H and also circular movements. Press harder next to the eyelid fold and then just lessen the pressure as you shade towards the highlight, or upwards.

Also, shade a bit right under the eyebrow because the brow ridge would block light and create a self-shadow. In the next image, you can see the areas that I have shaded and left untouched.

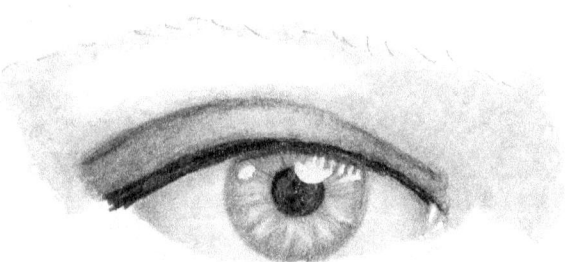 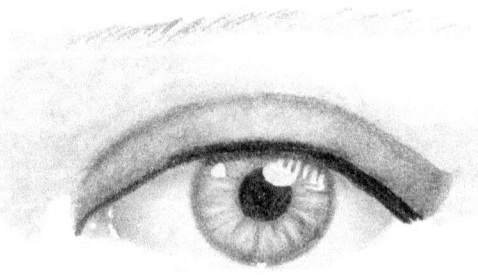

The next thing is to shade the highlighted parts that we left unshaded. I use a 6H for this. Then blend it all with a tissue and you will see how it'll become smoother.

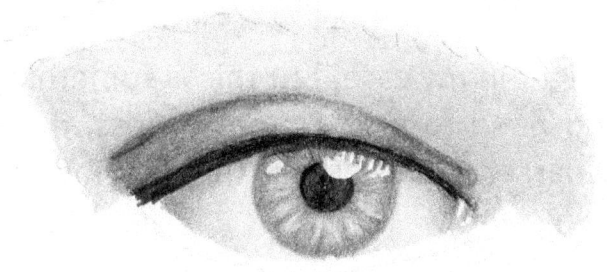 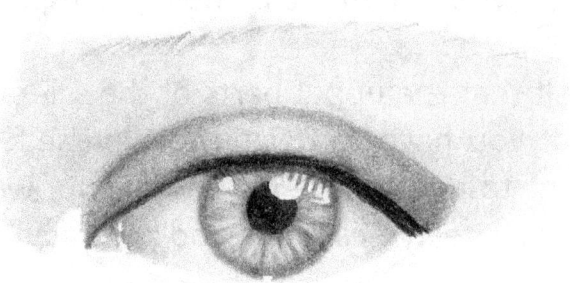

Since the areas in self-shadow are still too bright like this, we can shade more. But of course, you can make the skin more pale. For this, I'm using a 2B. When you have drawn a bit, you can blend it with a blending stump or a Q-tip and then you can see whether you need to shade more.

I have also shaded more right above the eyelid folds. As you can see, it is always better if we create darker shades, but don't start with the strong shadows because it's difficult to erase. Just shade layer by layer and start with a light pencil and then, you can always add more shade if necessary. And if we're shading with a 2B over the 2H areas, we can't make it too dark. This is good because you won't accidentally overdo shading.

The shadowed areas will also depend on the light source. I have imagined my light source somewhere in the mid-top area.
Blend it all with a Q-tip.

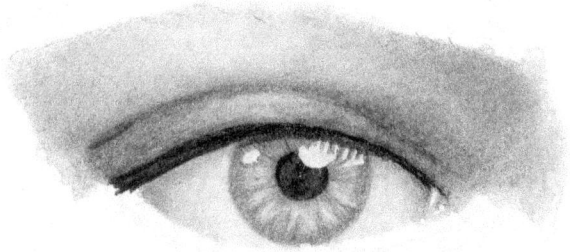 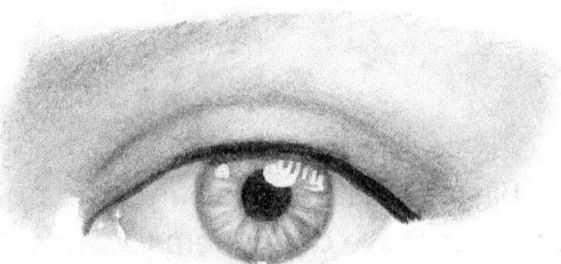

If you are satisfied with the skin above the eyes, you can finally draw the eyelashes. But before that, shade around the thick, dark line that we drew over the thickness of the upper eyelid. Create some eyelashes over the sclera that grow downwards. Also, if necessary, shade more between the eyeliner and the sclera. The edge seemed to be too sharp between these two values, which is why I shade it with a 2B. These are actually the tiny shadows cast by the eyelashes, or the groups of the eyelashes, over the sclera.

Then, blend it with a blending stump.

I felt that the upper parts of the sclera were too bright in my case, but this is something that you have to decide for yourself, whether you need to shade more or less. If we want to add a little bit of makeup, we can apply darker values. Then, the drawing will look more eye-catching and spectacular.

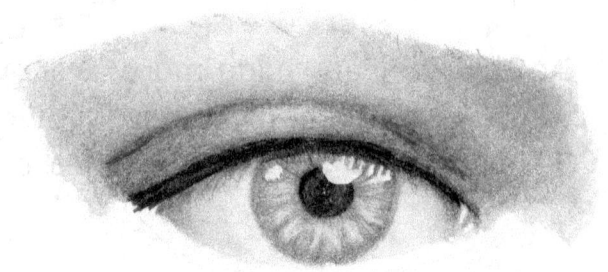 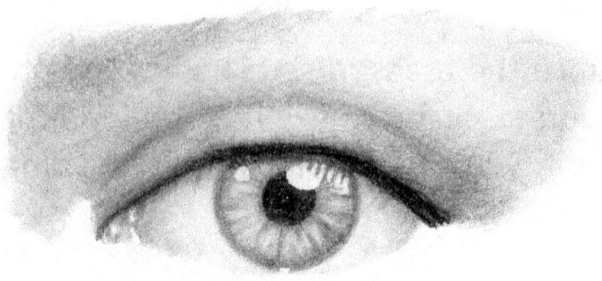

We can finally draw the eyelashes.
Start with the vertical ones in the middle, above the iris. I use a 7B for the eyelashes.

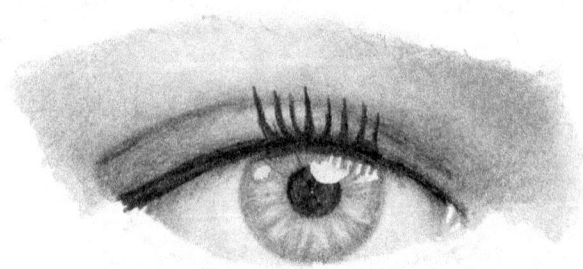 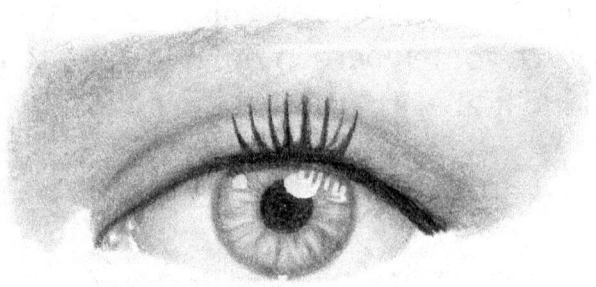

Draw bigger eyelashes towards the outer corners. They also have to be curvier, thicker and denser as we draw them towards the outer corners.

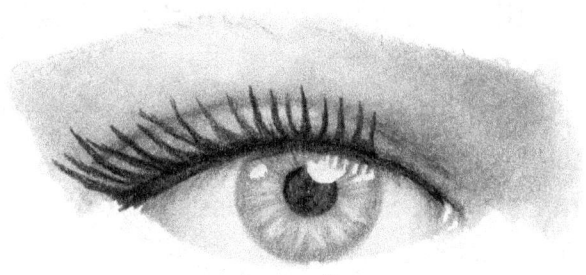 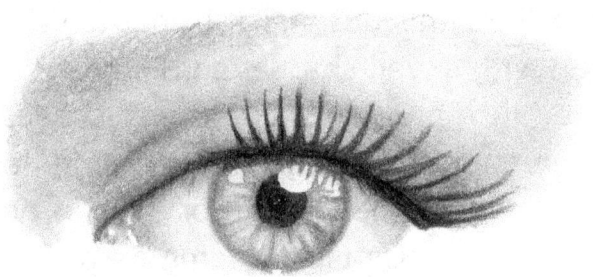

Now, I can see that the cast shadow is not long enough over the upper part of the iris, so I have to shade it more with a dark pencil such as a B. When the upper eyelid casts a shorter shadow, a person usually looks like they're staring. You may notice that it looks less like a stare with added shade when you compare the previous and next image. So many things will become clear after we have drawn the surrounding areas. Of course, it's easier when we draw from reference photos—we can see the values and copy them—and when we draw from scratch, like this, we don't know how the things will turn out. However, we can always go back and change something.

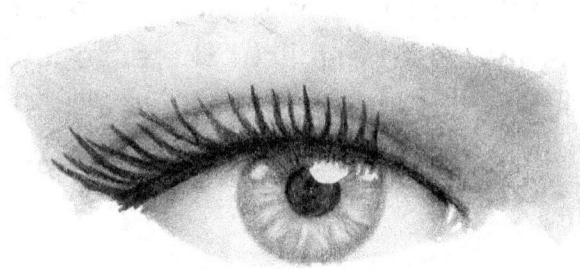 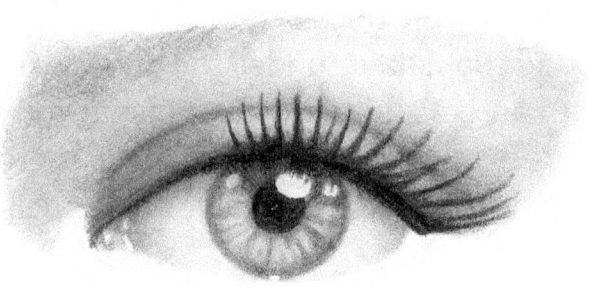

Now, we draw eyelashes towards the tear duct. Here, we have to make them shorter, less dense, thinner and curvier as we draw towards the tear ducts.

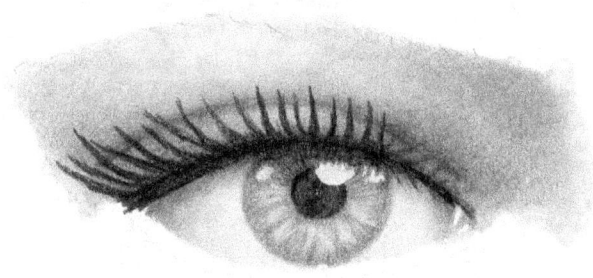 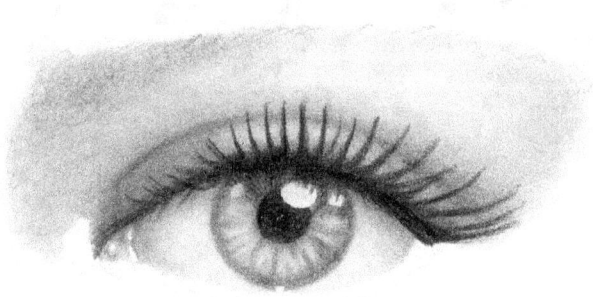

Next, shade the thickness of the skin of the lower eyelid. We have to use a very light pencil for this but, first, strengthen the line between the sclera and the thickness of the skin with a well-sharpened H pencil.

Then, use a 6H to shade the thickness of the skin. It should be a bit darker next to the corners and lighter in the very middle, right under the iris. Blend it a bit. For this, you should use a clean Q-tip or a clean tip of a blending stump. So, don't use the one that you already used for shading because you might darken it.

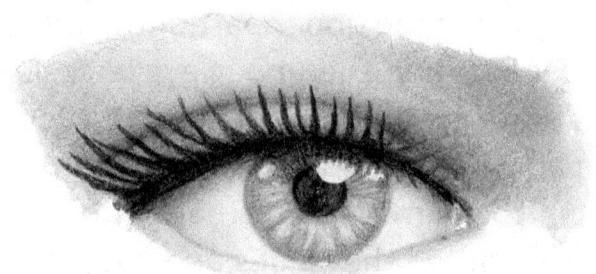 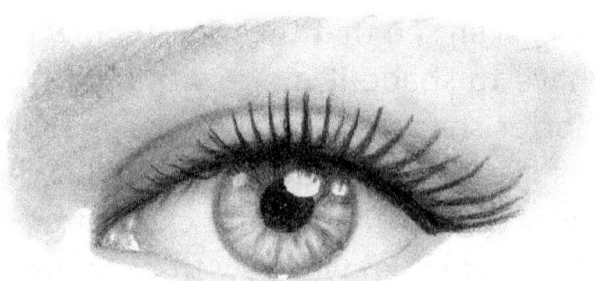

Before we draw the lower eyelashes, let's shade the skin under the eyes. I'm using an H pencil and, of course, the circulism technique. We have to create the highlighted edge between the thickness of the skin and the skin where the roots of the eyelashes are found. So, shade under the thickness of the skin, and you can highlight the edge later with an eraser. In the next image, you can see that I have left a thin, untouched area for the edge. Press harder under the protruding muscle to create the core shadow. Just increase the pressure on your H pencil or use a darker pencil such as an HB, or even a 2B for this.

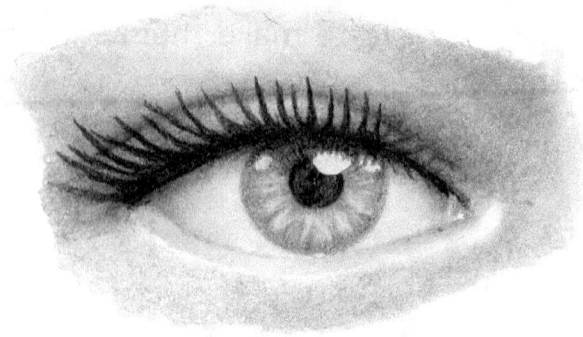 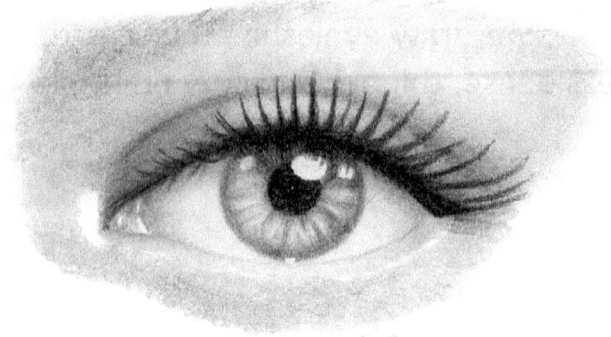

Tip

You need to change the technique to create different textures. You do not want to draw the human skin in the same way as metals or fur. Each has unique properties that need to be shaded differently. It is a good starting point to consider whether the texture is coarse or smooth and whether it absorbs or repels light. Reflective and smooth textures, such as metal, have higher contrast, while absorbent and coarse textures, such as cotton and many other fabrics, have low contrast and have little or no highlights.

Now, we can blend it all with a Q-tip. As you can see, the skin became much smoother after blending.

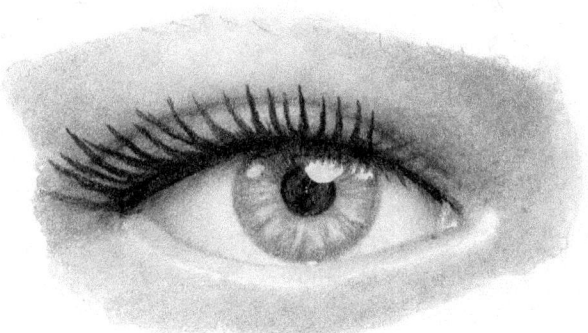 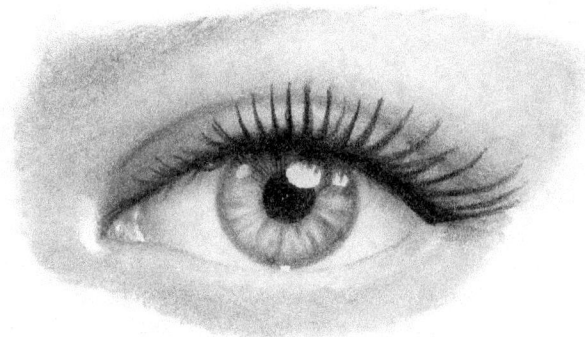

Now, let's shade a little bit more of the skin. I want to use a 3H to shade under the previously shaded area because it has to be much lighter. Also, shade a bit of the nose. I suggest shading the part of the nose between the eyes so that the drawing can look more complete and, of course, to practice shading. We have the highlight in the middle of the bridge of the nose, so we have to create a smooth gradient between the dark shade next to the tear ducts and the highlight on the nose.

The highlights can be very narrow or wide—it depends on the shape of the nose. Of course, it also depends on the light source. If we have a light source coming from, for example, the right side, then the left side of the nose should be shaded much more and the right side of the nose should be more illuminated.

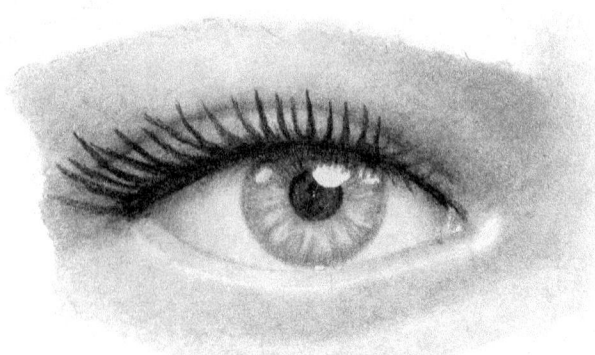 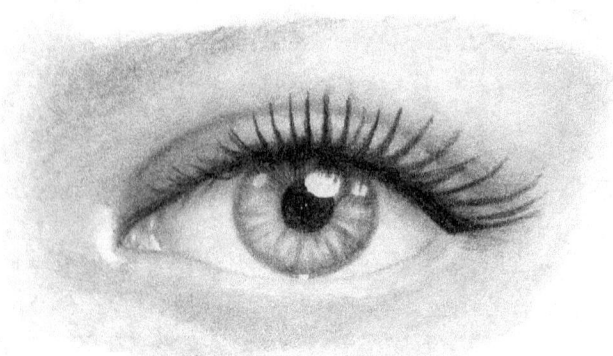

Next, shade the rest of the nose using a 6H. Start next to the 3H area and lessen the pressure as you shade towards the center of the nose. Press harder over the area between the two eyebrows to shade the self-shadow of the frontal bone. It has to be darker than the bridge of the nose.
Lastly, blend it all with a tissue and then you will see whether you need to shade more.

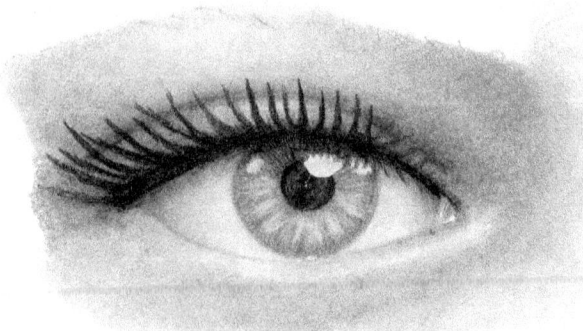 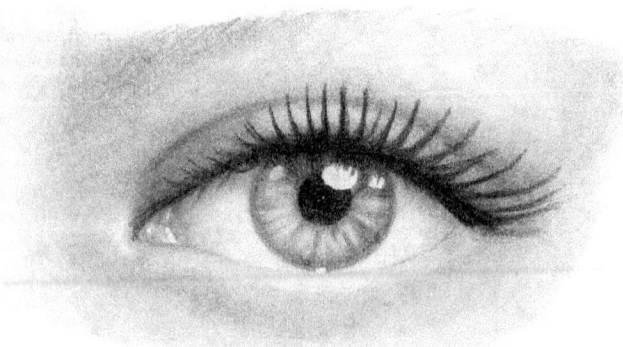

Draw the lower eyelashes next. It's enough if you use a B pencil. I used a 7B for the upper eyelashes, but lower eyelashes are always thinner so they can be drawn with a lighter pencil. Place the tip of your pencil over the edge between the thickness of the eyelid and the skin, and create quick, confident strokes in the direction of the hair's growth. The lower ends of some neighboring eyelashes should be stuck together.

Draw longer eyelashes as you work towards the outer corners, and of course, make them thicker and denser.

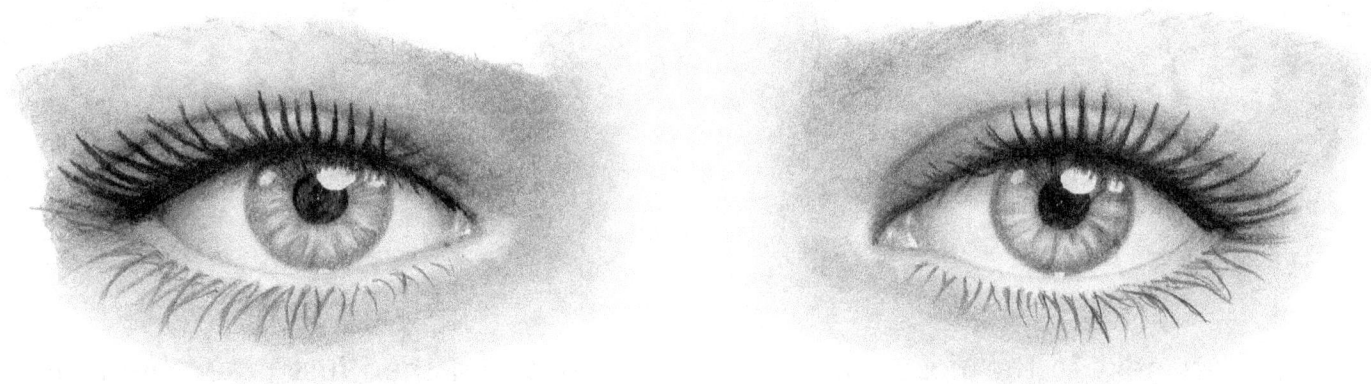

Now, we can draw the eyebrows.
First, shade the areas for the eyebrows with a blending stump that you already used for shading because you have some graphite on its tip. See the next image to see how I have shaded these areas. It's not a good idea to draw the hairs over the white paper because when we shade the areas prior to drawing the eyebrows, we are creating the shadows that are cast by the eyelashes. You can see that my initial lines of the eyebrows are still visible, so I know where I wanted to place them.

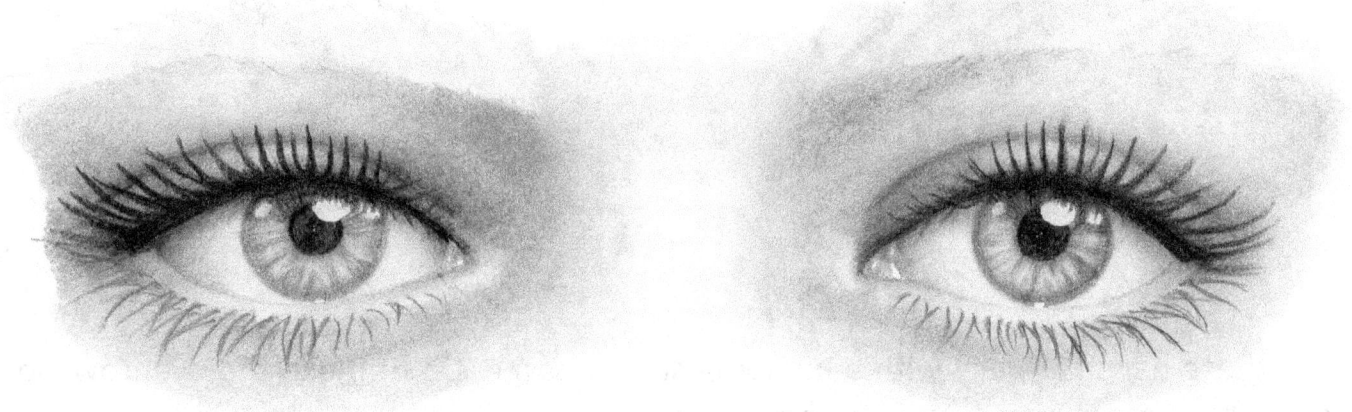

Let's draw the eyebrows in the direction of their growth. In the following diagram, you can see the digitally placed arrows to show you the directions in which you should draw the eyebrows. Of course, you can also check out your own eyebrows in the mirror or look at some reference photos.

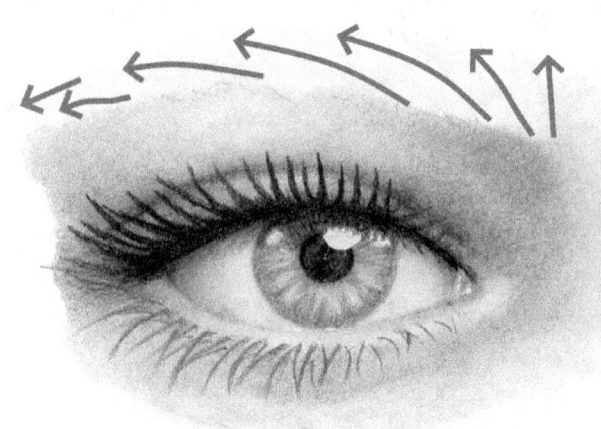 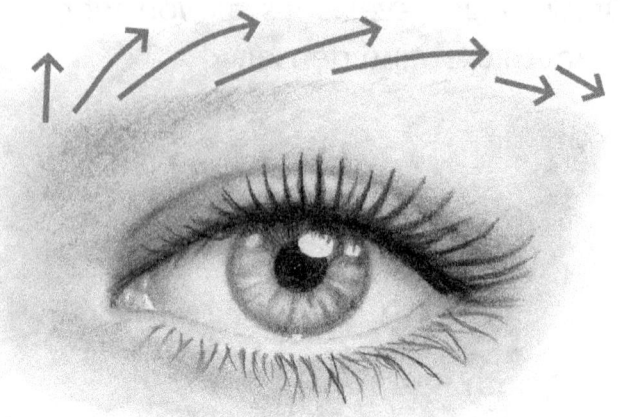

You can start next to the nose with the vertical ones and then just draw them more horizontally as you work towards the temple.

I'm using an HB pencil, but I change the pressure to make the hairs have different values.

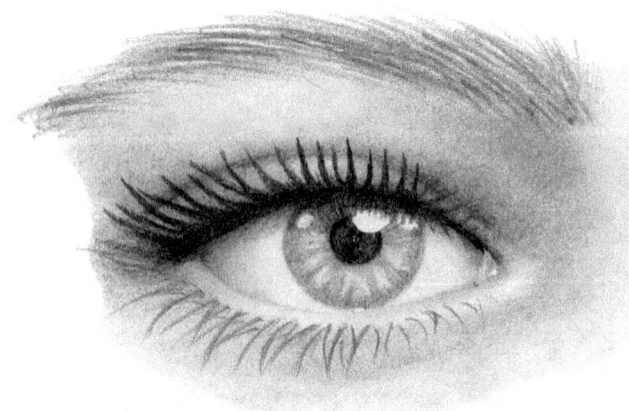 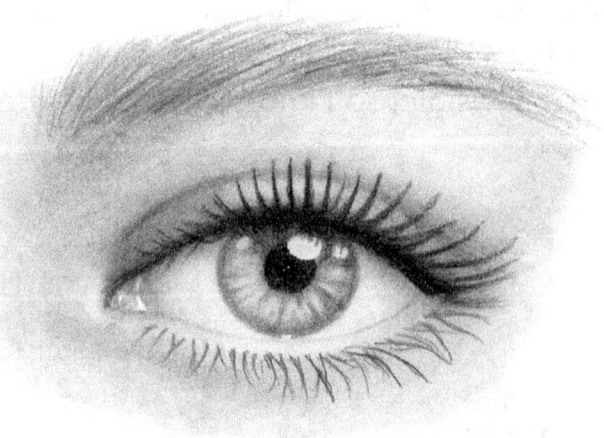

Blend these hairs carefully with a blending stump or a Q-tip to make the eyebrows look soft and to press the graphite into the paper.

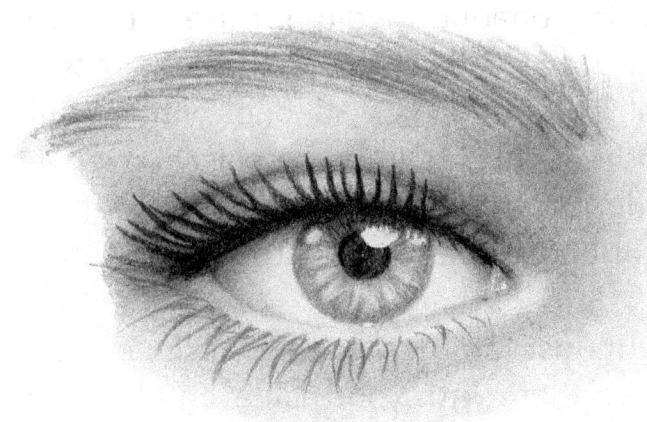 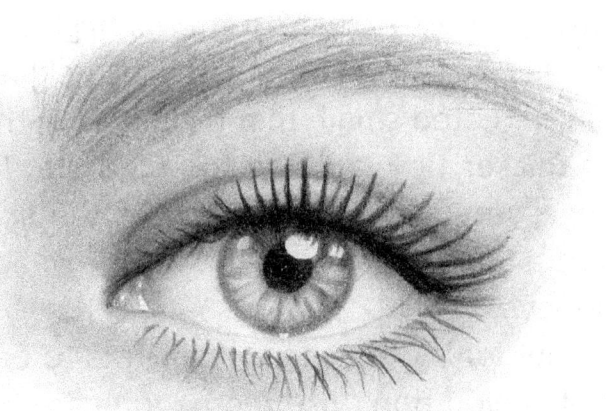

Then, add some darker hairs, at random, using a 3B in the same direction of those arrowed lines. Draw more darker hairs in the lower area, under the brow ridge where these hairs get less light. If the eyebrows are plucked, they can stay like this, but we can add some tiny hairs all around to make them look more natural. Notice where I have drawn these lines and try doing the same. Seems to me that my pair of eyes look somehow genderless - they could belong to a woman, a man, or even a teenager. So, this is how they turned out, which is ok.

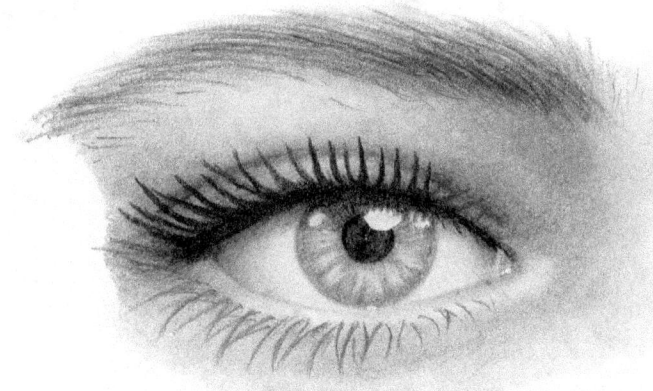 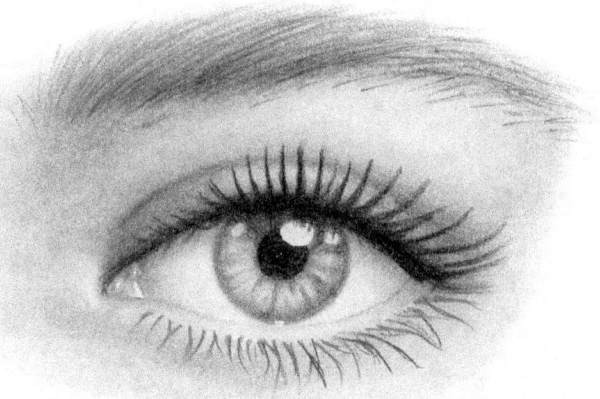

Now that the eyes are basically completely drawn, we can see whether we need to shade more, to change what we want, or to add some finishing touches.
I feel that the skin on the nose still looks pale, so I have added one more layer of a 3H, pressing lightly.
I have also darkened the iris a bit, but this is arbitrary. You can choose not to shade more. You can even lighten them up with an eraser.
I have added some tiny wrinkles under the lower eyelashes, the ones that even young people have. Those are visible only from close-up view, but it is also good to practice going much more into detail.

Lastly, we can create some highlights with a white, opaque medium. I use a pin-type marker by Uni Posca, but any ink gel pen will also do. As you can see in the next image, I have created small, thin highlights with the small tip of a marker. So, ones with a 1 mm or thicker tip would be too big here. I created the highlights in these places: over the edge between the thickness of the skin and skin under it, the tiny lines between the sclera and thickness of the lower eyelid, and right above the wrinkles that I drew under the eyes.

If you don't want these highlights to be too bright, just tap them with your finger while wet. If you don't like them, you can easily remove them with your nail even after they dry up.

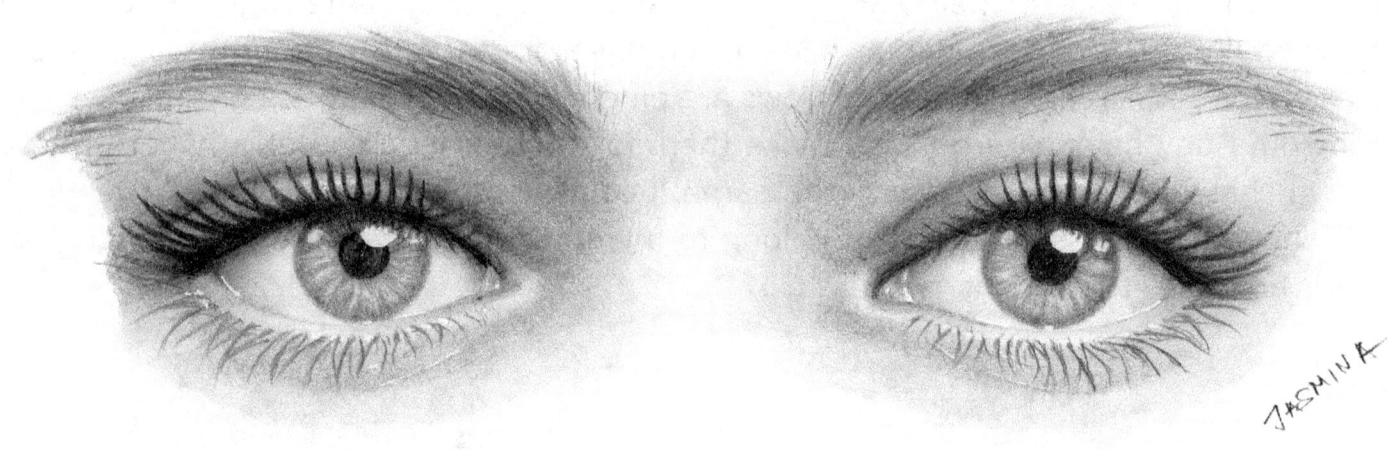

Tip

It is normal when you work on a drawing and it makes no sense, you don't like it and you want to give up on it. But don't. Just keep working and changing whatever you feel needs to be changed. You might end up having one of your best drawings ever created.

BLACK HAIR

Now I will show you how to draw black hair with graphite pencils. In order to be able to erase over the black hair and create highlighted flyaways, we should apply a 5H or 6H as a first layer. So, wherever you want your hair to be drawn, just go with 5H, but you don't have to draw hair by hair, just cover the area that you want your hair to be and don't press too hard. In the following picture, you can see how it looks in my case.

Now we can apply a 6B or darker. I'm using an 8B. Start at top of the area you covered in the previous step and draw hair-like strokes to midway. Then do the same from the bottom to midway. This way, you will create the highlight in the middle as shown in the next image. Lift off the pencil slightly as you finish each line so they can gradually disappear into the paper and have a gradient transition from an 8B to the white color of the paper.

Some of the hairs can be longer and go over the highlight, too. When you draw the hair, you can do it lock by lock, longer or shorter locks, the same way as you do in this tutorial. So, once you acquire this method, you will be able to draw any hair. And you can see, my lock already looks curvy and shiny. It looks like it bends in the very middle of its length.

Since this highlight seems to be too bright for the black hair, we can go over with an HB not pressing too hard, but changing the pressure to create highlighted hairs of different values. Since we have applied a 5H as a first layer, we won't be able to create too dark areas over it, so it does matter which pencil we apply first.

I show a quick example of this in the next image. On the left lock, I have applied a 5H first, and I created the layer of an 8B over that (just the way I did with the lock from this tutorial).

For the right lock, I used an 8B as a first layer and I tried to create the highlighted flyaways with an eraser over both locks. Notice how my highlights aren't even visible on the right lock because it was impossible to erase an 8B when it was applied first. I had a quite easier job with the lock on the left side because the 5H layer didn't allow an 8B pencil to color the fiber of the paper and I just revealed the 5H layer with an eraser.

Now, let's create the highlighted flyaways over our lock. I always cut the top of my mechanical eraser because I want to create a very sharp edge. If you use a kneaded eraser, it won't work because these erasers are too soft to be erase such tiny lines when pressed harder. So, it is essential to invest in different kinds of erasers because they all are good for different things.

We can now create some highlighted flyways by erasing lines all over the lock, at random. You'll see, it's quite easier to do over the highlighted hair in the middle of the lock, but it's much more difficult to do over the darker areas. However, it's still possible with this eraser due to the order in which we have applied the pencils.

Cut the top of an eraser to get a clean edge before you use it.

Lastly, darken some areas at the top and the bottom if you want and create the dark flyaways. Place the tip of an HB or darker pencil over the hair and use quick, confident strokes to create hairs that are not stuck to the lock. Create them around the hair to break the clear edge between the background and the lock. Draw these lines at random, without following any patterns. These flyways are important and create both dark flyaways and highlighted flyaways.

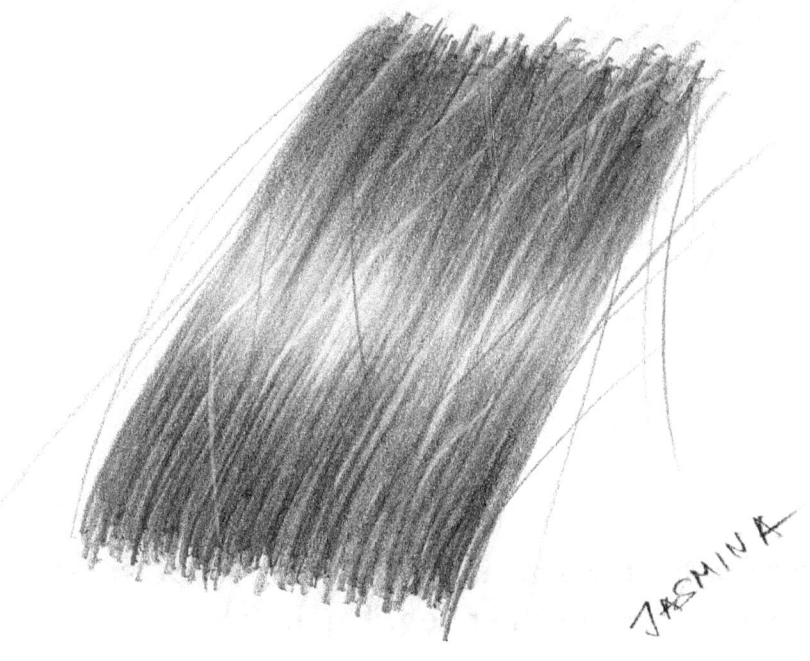

BROWN HAIR

Now let's draw brown hair. We will apply the first layer with a 5H, 6H, or 7H. Cover the entire area you want your hair to be. I will make just a single lock again. Draw the lines in the direction of the hair's flow as shown in the following picture.

Now we can go over with an HB for the brown hair. If you want to draw blonde or light brown hair, you can use a 2H or lighter pencil in this step.

Start on the top and draw the hairs towards the middle area and don't press.
Some of the hairs can be longer and go over the whole length but most of these hairs should end before the highlight which we want to create in the middle of the lock. Lift off the pencil slightly to create a smooth gradient at the end of each stroke because they should gradually disappear into this basic tone. Change the pressure on your pencil to create different tones. Do the same from the bottom to midway.

Study the next image to see how it should look after applying these kinds of strokes.

Next, blend it with a blending stump and then add the highlighted and the mid-tone flyaways.

I used an HB for the mid-tone flyaways and my mechanical eraser for the highlighted ones, just as I did in the previous tutorial.

Here you can add some darker tones to make the hair brown or darker brown, and you can create more of the light flyaways to make the hair blond or light brown.

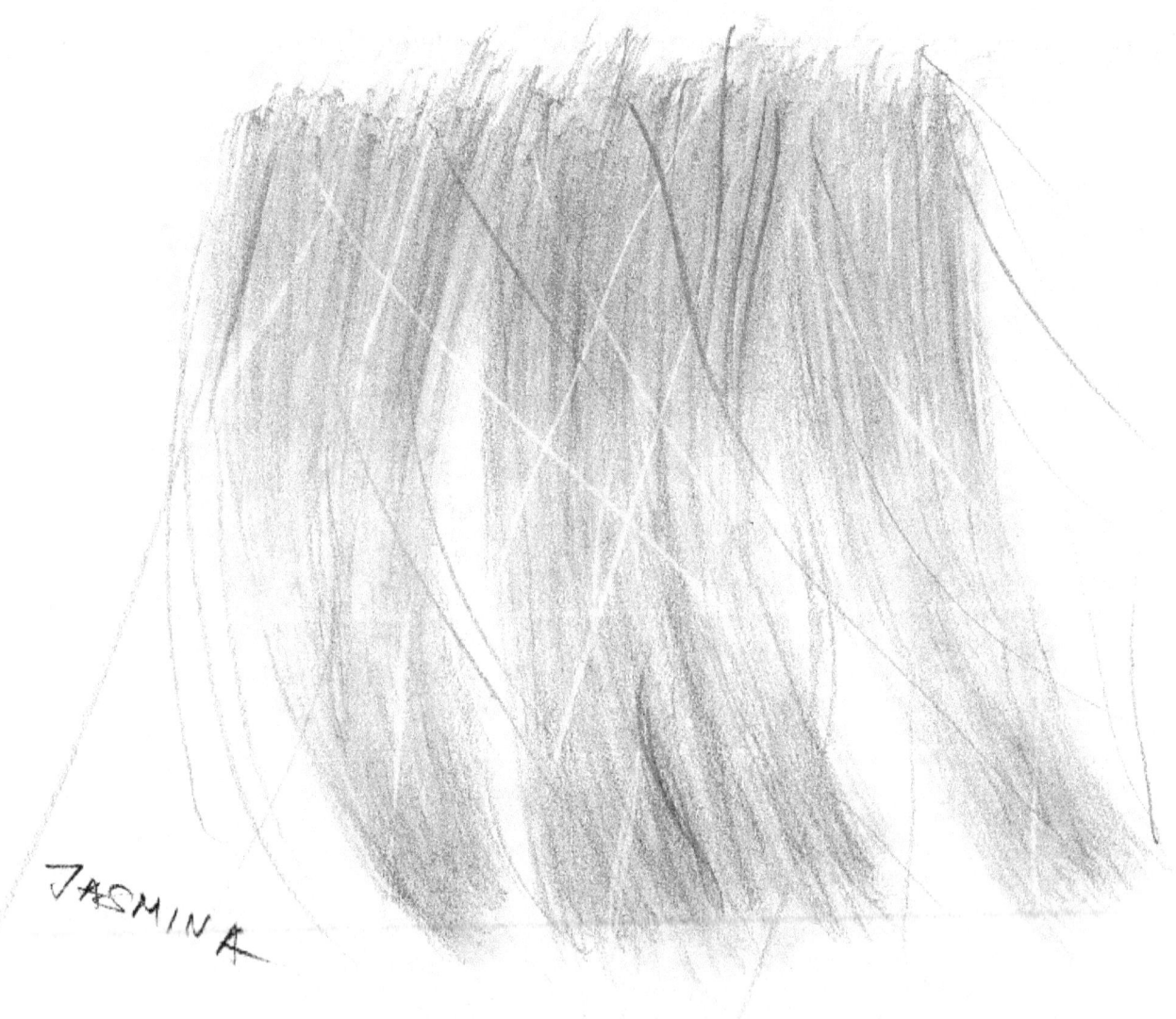

HYPER-REALISTIC LIPS

Hyperrealism is a much more detailed drawing style than realistic drawing. Once you acquire the techniques of creating realistic drawings, you might want to create more details for a hyper-realistic appearance.

Artists usually create hyper-realistic drawings from a photo reference, which can be achieved by anyone who's been practicing for years or decades. But we will create one from scratch.

The steps to making a drawing hyper-realistic are to do the same as when you draw realistic drawings. Therefore, the steps are:

1. Sketching
2. Basic coloring
3. Highlights and shadow

When these three steps are done, we add the two kinds of details: the ones that are visible when observed from a further distance, and the ones that can be seen only when we zoom into the photo.

4. Two kinds of details.

These are the four phases we will to go through in creating our hyper-realistic drawings.

The first step is sketching. To make a proportional outline for our drawing so the ratio of the dimensions reflects real life.

The second step is a basic coloring when we apply the basic color over the areas to be colored. Of course, we can use the different values within an object, but in the case of these lips, I used one value to cover the whole area.

The third phase is to create highlights and shadows so objects can get their shapes and be recognizable from a farther distance. In the next image, you can see the drawn lips with only shadows and highlights, before I added the details.

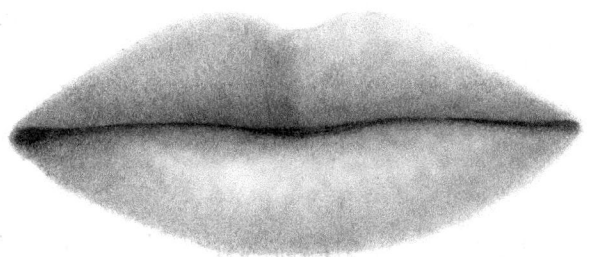

Finally, the fourth phase is adding the details over the realistic drawing that are visible only when we take a closer look at the picture.

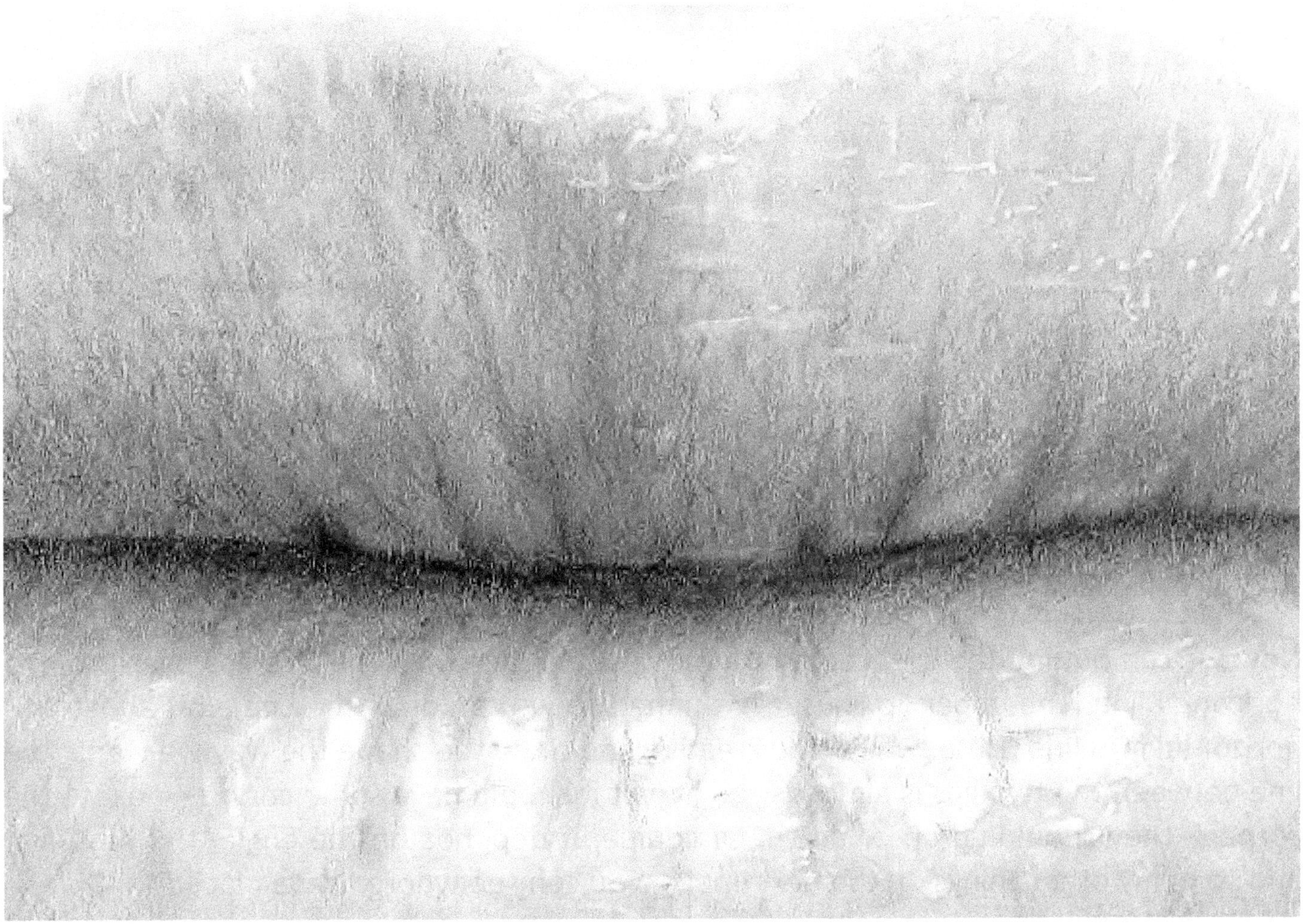

So, the third phase will make the drawing realistic or photorealistic, and the fourth phase is when we make our drawing hyper-realistic.

Let's get started at the beginning.

Start by creating a simple grid that is very good for orientation and to know where to start creating the outlines.

I start with the outer lines of the grid at 12 centimeters wide (almost 5 inches) and 5 centimeters high (2.5 inches).

Next, create a horizontal line almost in the middle. If the height is 5 centimeters (5"), we want to mark the dot 2.5 centimeters (2.5") from the top or from the bottom, on the left and the right sides of the vertical grid lines. Then, we connect them and get the horizontal line in the middle, as shown in the following picture.

Now we can outline the lips. Let's start with the line between the two lips over the mid horizontal line. The upper lip is usually thinner, so we can draw the line a bit above this horizontal grid line. Here, we can be creative and draw the shape the way we want. The line between the two lips is almost straight, yet it should have some curves—next to the corners, they should go up or down. Of course, it depends on the angle, the gestures, and so many other things. In the next image, you can see where I have placed this line.

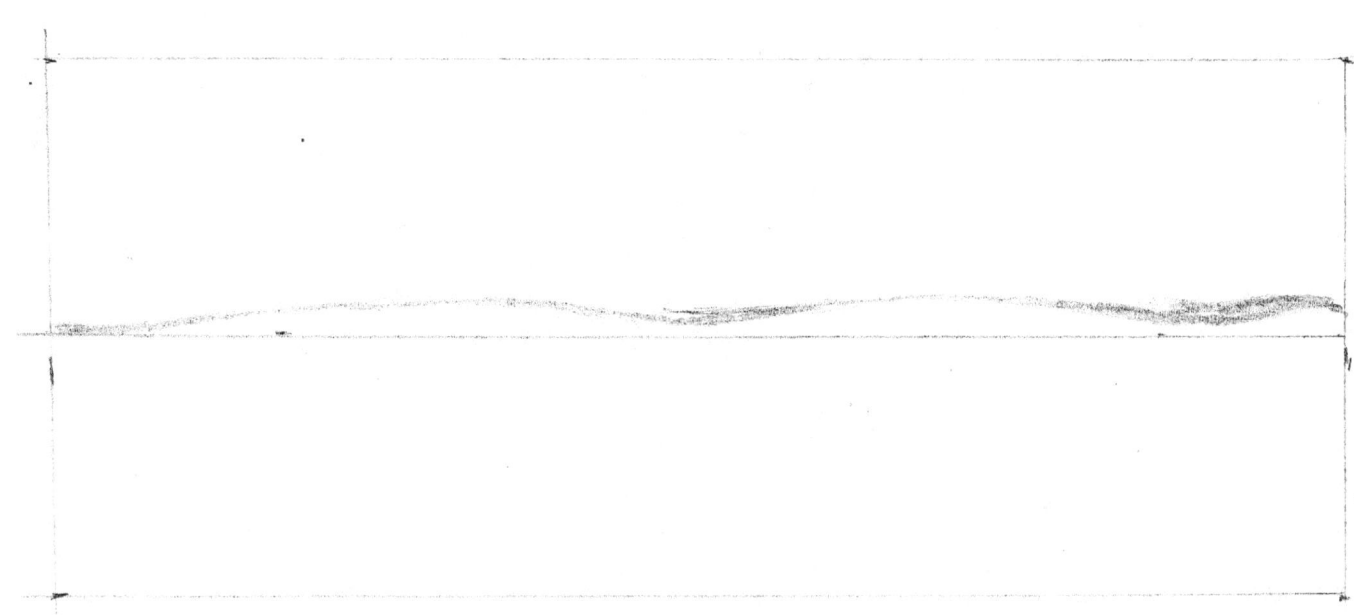

Next, let's outline the outer edge of both lips.

The lower lip is usually less complicated, so you can start with it. Start over the lower horizontal grid line, draw a horizontal line over it a bit and then start to separate it from the grid line and draw both sides upwards and towards the corners. Try to make the two sides as symmetrical as possible.

For the upper lip, we must determine the center point of the upper horizontal grid line and draw the Cupid's bow in the middle, connecting it to the corners of the lips.

Now let's erase the grid lines because we don't need them anymore.

The next thing is to "color" the lips following the direction of the lines you can see in the following diagram. These lines represent the wrinkles.

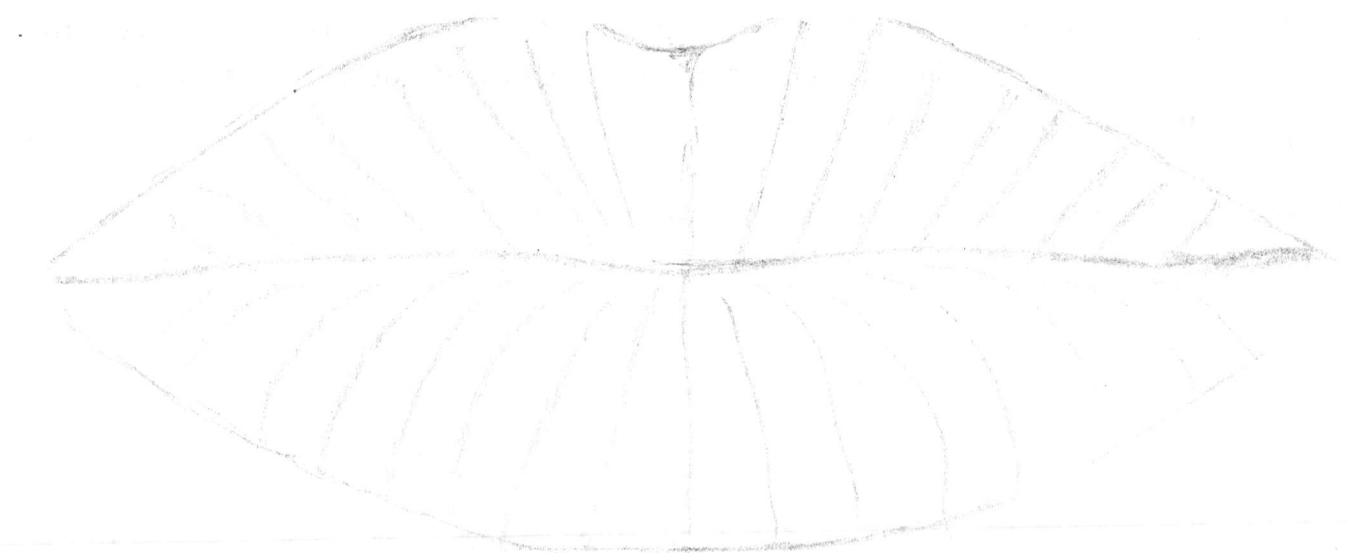

I'm using an HB pencil, but you can use any other pencil.

In this step, cover the entire area of both lips, applying the same pressure everywhere to create the basic tone of the lips. If you want to see the line in between the two lips, darken it by pressing harder with an HB or use a 2B or darker to strengthen this outline because you will want to have it visible later.
Here, we don't have to create a smooth texture, so don't worry about it now because

we're going to blend it. You can use the chisel-shaped tip of your pencil to cover the areas faster than with a well-sharpened pencil.

Now, we blend it all with a Q-tip. Press very hard to impress the graphite into the fiber of the paper and you will see how the texture becomes smooth. You will also see it looks darker after blending due to the smeared graphite.
We have our basic tone, and now we can create shadows, highlights, and details.

I suggest starting with shadows. I use a 4B pencil to darken the areas that get less light, so usually the corners and, of course, between the two lips.

If you're afraid of using a very dark pencil, I suggest going lightly first and once you make sure that everything looks good and in the right place, go over it again, pressing harder. This is particularly important when drawing from scratch, as in this situation, because we never know how it will turn out. Therefore, we make slow progress and not overdo the shading.

Here, we have to create a cast shadow, the shadow cast by the upper lip over the lower lip, particularly in the corners. The area in the middle of the lips is highly illuminated because it is exposed to the light more than the corners so the corners should be darker. For this, you don't have to use a 4B as I did, you can use a 9B or any other dark pencil, or even an HB and press very hard. However, working with an HB and lighter value will not make it dark enough.

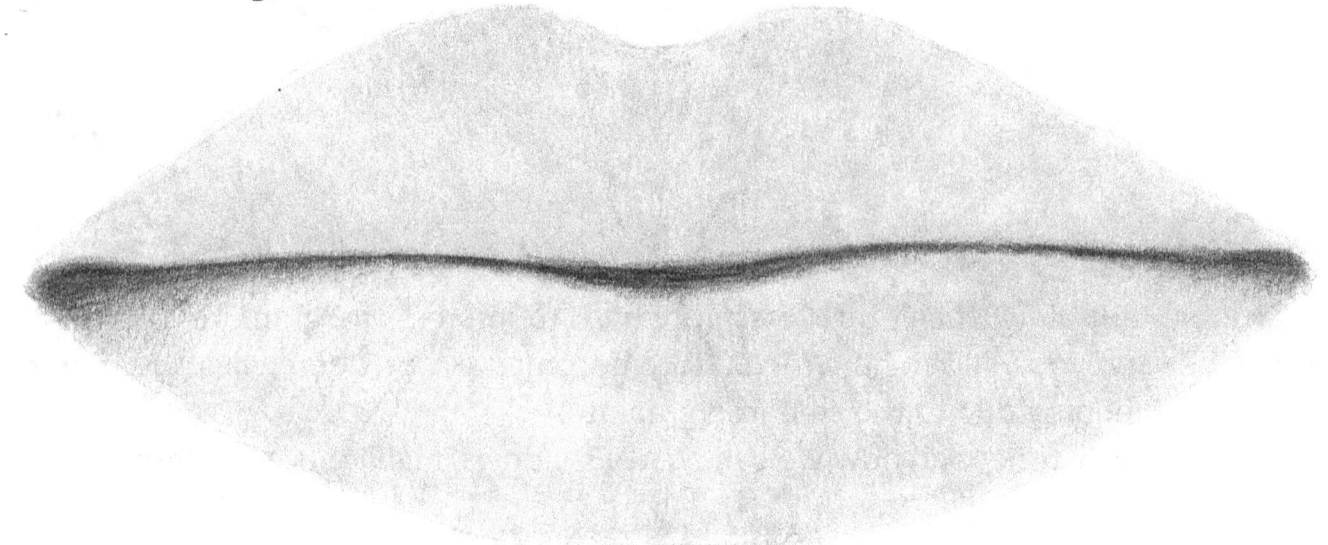

Now we will create the values between this very black area and the basic tone of the lips that we created with an HB. After that, we can add the highlights. We should use a shade much brighter than 4B. I'm going to use an HB and this time I want to press harder over the upper lip to make it darker. You can use a B or an F pencil for this, as well as an H and press harder or a B and press lightly.

I like to work with an HB because it allows me to create a lot of shades by changing the pressure and I don't have to change pencils as often. The lower horizontal part of the upper lip always receives less light so we can shade it in this step. This area is called a self-shadow.

Following the direction of the wrinkles, press very lightly in the upper area of the upper lip and press harder in the lower area. Press less somewhere in the middle to create a gradient transition between the dark tone and the bright tone which will make the lip appear round.

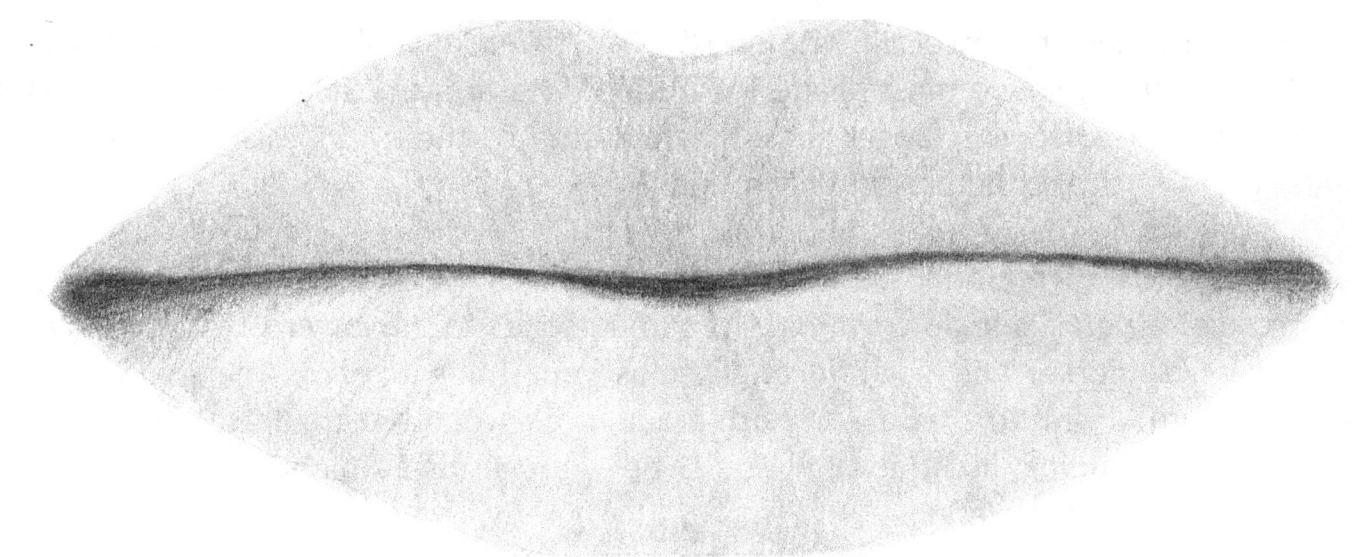

Since the lips are placed on a round plane, we must make both lips horizontally and vertically round. So, still using an HB, go over the upper lip again, pressing harder in the two corners and in the lower horizontal half of the upper lip. Then, gradually release the pressure on your pencil as you shade towards the Cupid's Bow. This way you will create a smooth gradient between the self-shadows and the highlighted areas.

Next, start using a B or a 2B pencil and go over these areas again to darken them slowly, particularly next to the black line between the lips. Press very lightly and shade patiently.
After having shaded a bit, blend the area with a Q-tip, a tissue, or a blending stump.

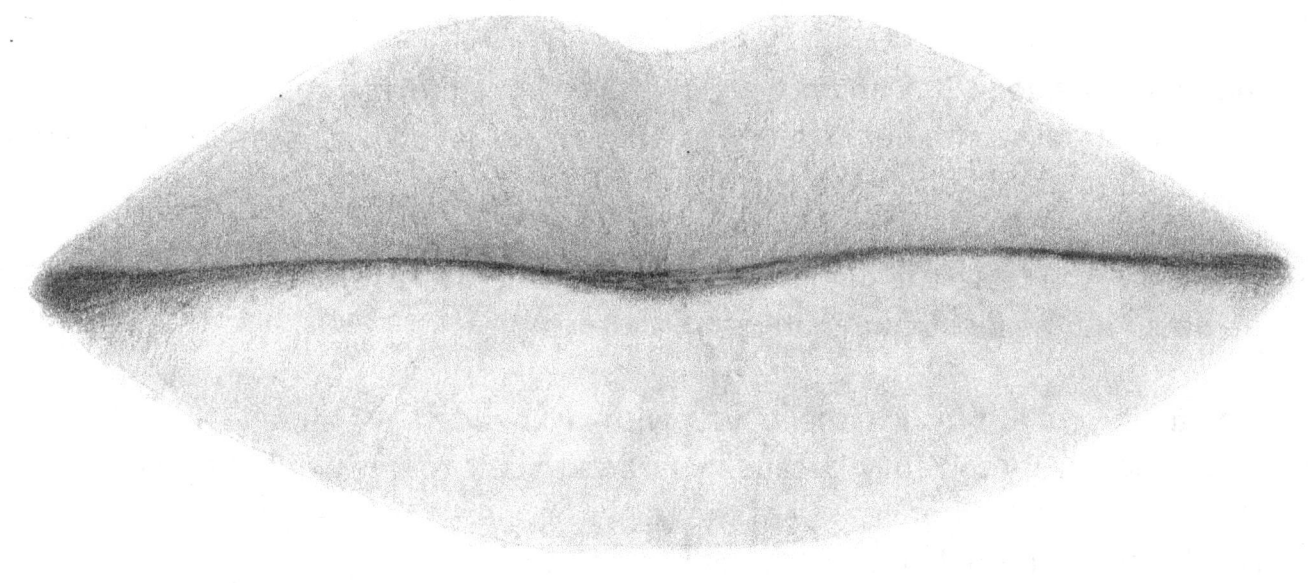

Now we can shade the lower lip with an HB. The lower lip is always more illuminated then the upper lip, so we must shade it carefully. The areas next to the left and right corners must be shaded stronger than the mid-area of the lip as this lip also has to appear to be vertically and horizontally round.

Also, press harder right under the black line we've drawn between the lips. Then lessen the pressure as you shade downwards. The same applies to the lower edge of the lower lip. It must be darker and become brighter as you shade towards the mid-area. As always, it is important to create a smooth gradient between the shades. When you are done with the shading, blend it all with a Q-tip; you can use a blending stump on the edges for more precise blending.

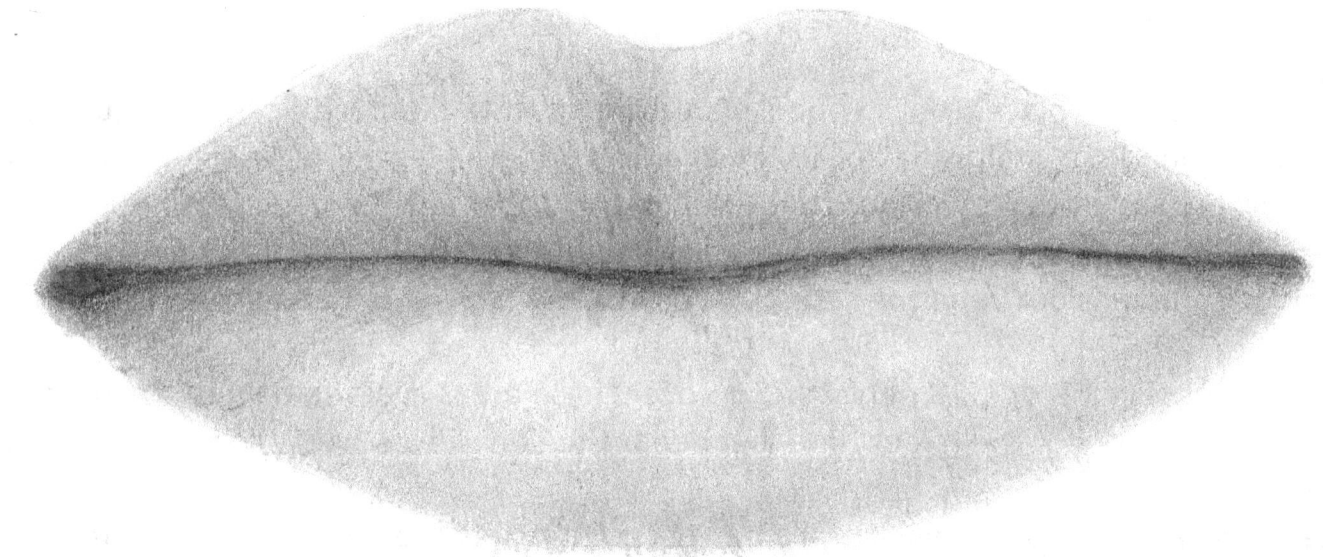

Now the lips don't look flat anymore. But we haven't created any details yet. We're going to go much more into detail later. For now, we must focus on creating the shape of the lips by adding the shadows and the highlights.

The next step is to create the highlights by erasing the basic tone over the parts of the lips that would be the most illuminated.

It is enough if you just touch the paper with a kneaded eraser and it will become brighter. So, do it very carefully because you don't want to overdo highlighting. Erase a bit of the graphite in the upper area of the upper lip, next to the edge because the edge is bent and receives more light, and in the middle of the lower lip.

If you accidentally overdo highlights, just go over that area with a Q-tip and you can darken it again.

When creating the highlights in the middle of the lower lip, press a bit harder in the middle of the highlight with a kneaded eraser and press less and less as you work away from the center of the highlight. The edge between the highlight and the basic value of the lip should be blurry.

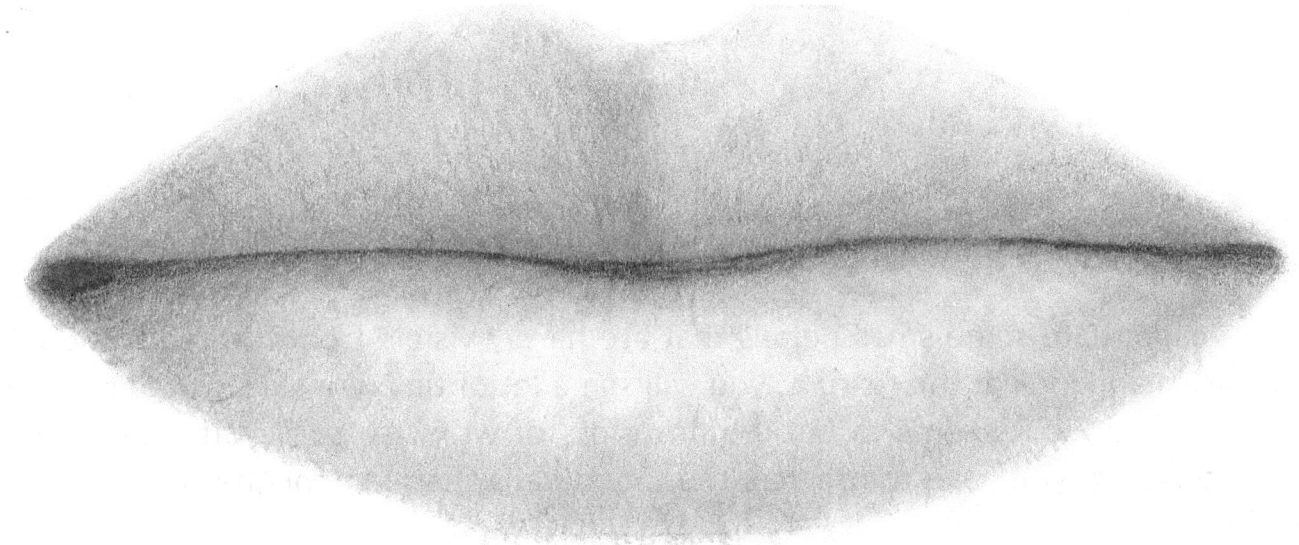

Now that we have created less bright highlights, we can create very bright highlights which means that we must create absolutely white areas over the lips, particularly in the middle of the lower lip. Since no matter how hard we press with an eraser, we can't get that white color of the paper anymore, I suggest using something like a white ink gel pen, gelly rolls, or a white marker—anything that is opaque to create the highlights over the graphite.

In the next image, you can see which areas I have colored with a white marker. With such bright areas, the lips will appear drier, which is also something you can go with. When you add white highlights, the lips will appear glossy, shiny, and wet. The highlights will be shown over the protruding parts between the wrinkles. The next photo demonstrates my explanation.

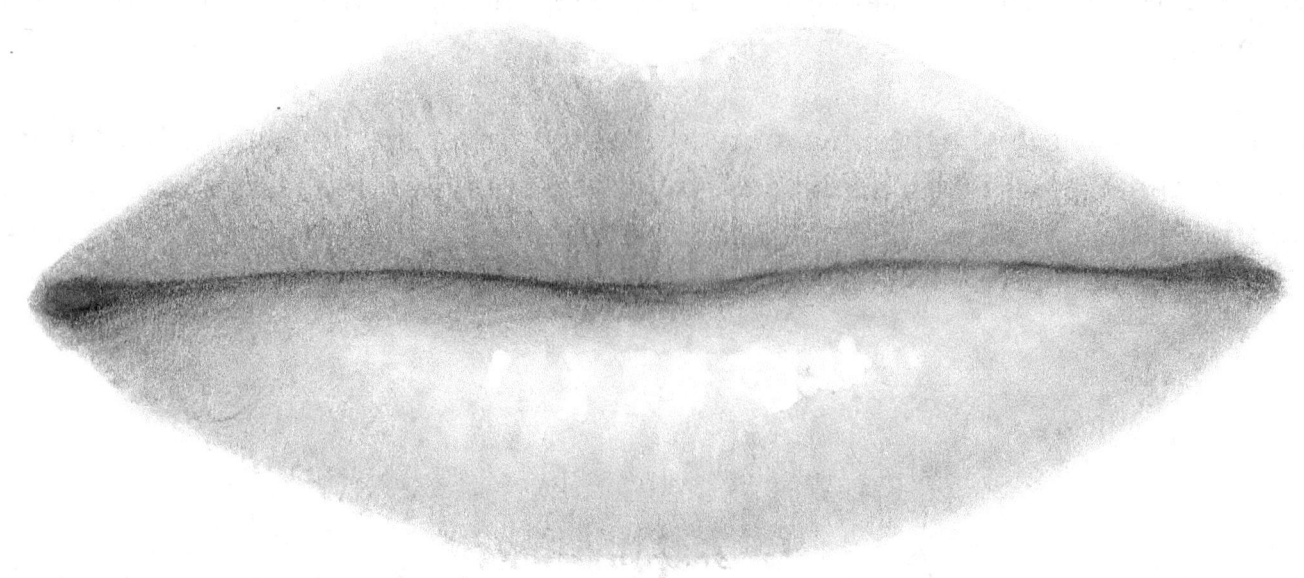

Now we can create some small details that are hardly visible from further away. When you zoom in and look at the texture, you will see a lot of tiny wrinkles, so the skin is not actually smooth as it seems to be. We have lots of wrinkles, so if you want a hyper-realistic drawing, you have to draw all the tiny details that can only be seen when you zoom in.

Start with the upper lip and draw the wrinkles using a 4B. We need to create wrinkles in their natural direction. In the lower area of the upper lip, they should be quite darker than in the upper area, so either lessen the pressure as you draw over this area with a 4B or use a lighter shade. Just draw them at random wherever you want, they don't have to be drawn in order. If we draw them in some order, the drawing can look less realistic.

I suggest starting in the middle of the lips, because here we have very simple, vertical wrinkles, and as you draw them towards the corners, just make them curvier and curvier. Some of them should go over the whole lip and some of them can be shorter. When you have drawn some wrinkles, blend them with a blending stump. There are no wrinkles found in the corners, so we draw them mostly in the middle. Anyway, you can add more shade to the corners in this step.
Continue creating all sorts of tiny wrinkles, even the horizontal ones, particularly in the middle of the upper lip, as shown in the following image.
Use an H2H or lighter grade for the lower lip because the wrinkles over the lower lip are not deep and they are more illuminated.

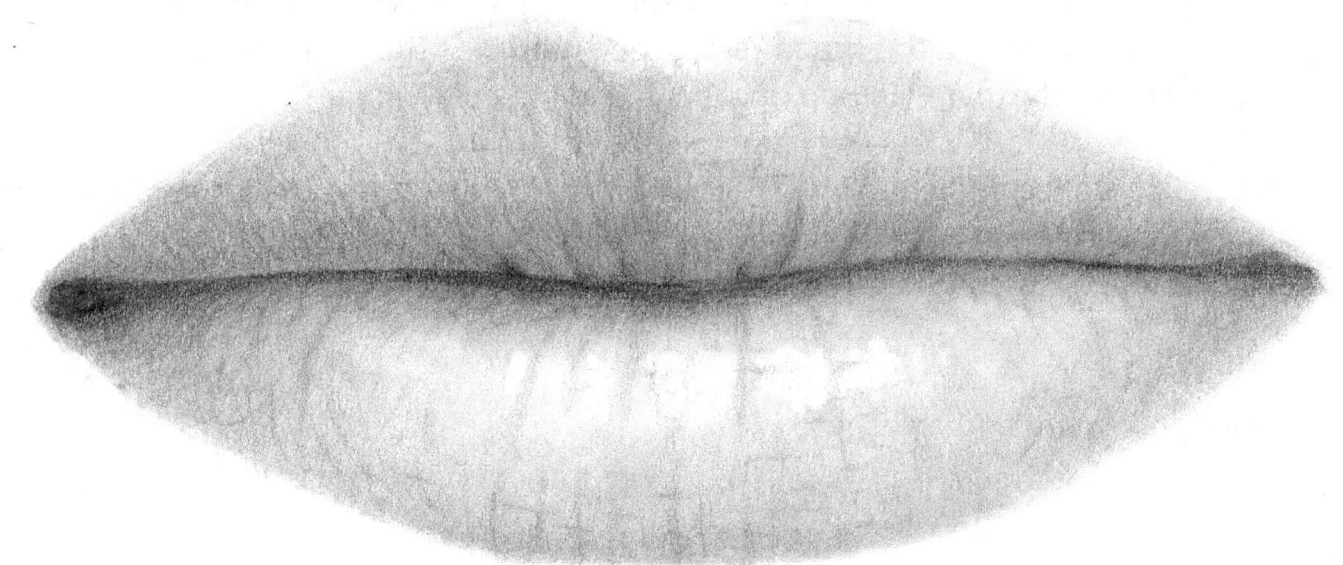

Now we can create tiny highlights which are not too bright, formed over the edges of the wrinkles. I'm using a kneaded eraser to create these tiny highlights next to each wrinkle that I just created. So, the horizontal and vertical wrinkles are both highlighted. In the shadowed areas, these highlights should be quite darker, and we create them by gently touching the paper with the tip of an eraser to eliminate a bit of the graphite, but not too much.

You can even use a white ink gel pen or a white marker for these. If you don't like the highlighted wrinkles you create, just go over them with a blending stump or any pencil.

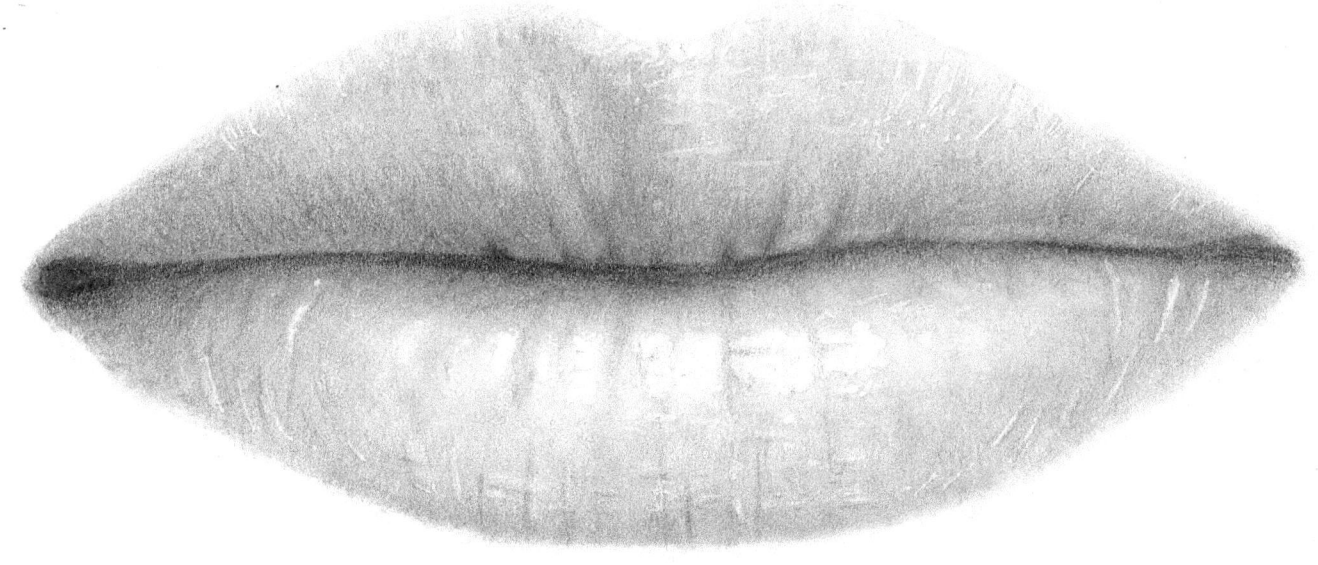

If you're satisfied with the lips, you can add some cast shadows, for example right under the lower lip. I'm applying the graphite powder with a Q-tip. The shadow cast by the lower lip will make the lower lip pop on a page and make it appear round.

Also, create the reflected light over the edge of the lower lip by eliminating a bit of the graphite with an eraser. The cast shadow should be the darkest in the middle and gradually disappear towards the left and right sides.

We can also shade the sunken areas above the Cupid's bow to make the Cupid's bow even more prominent and highlighted.

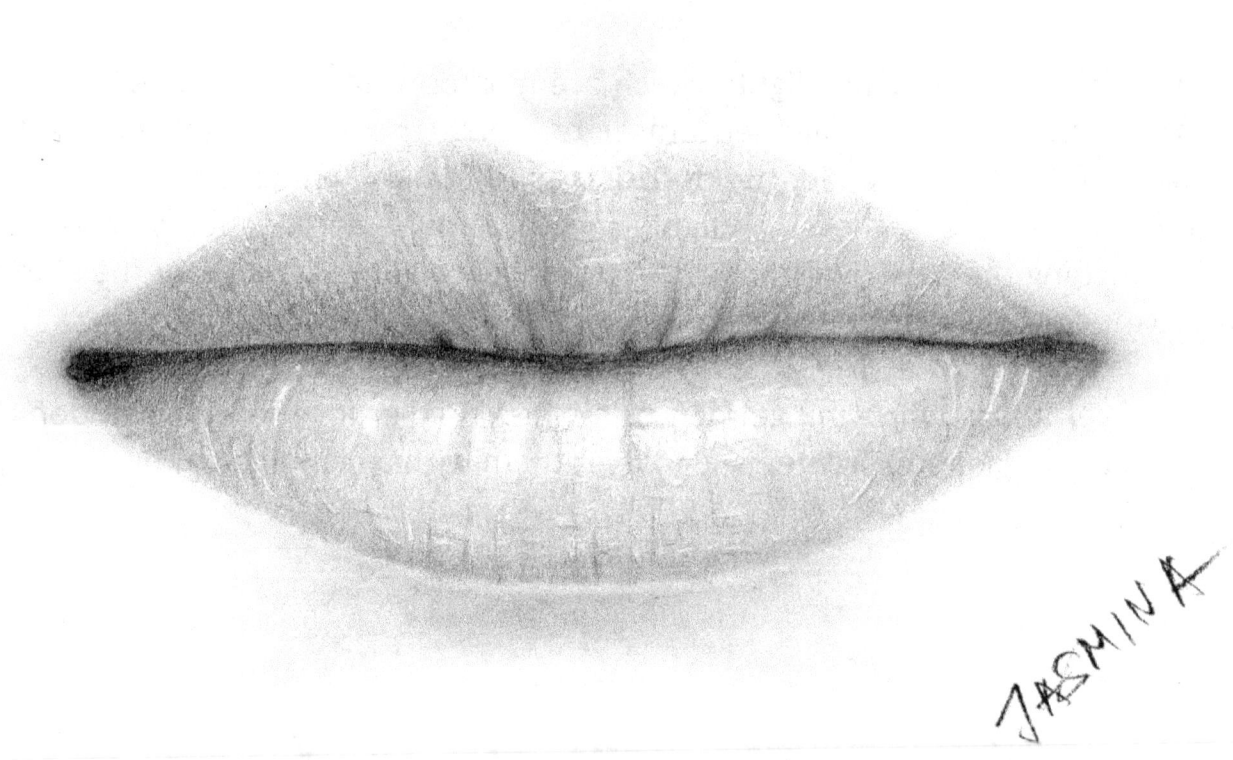

KISSING LIPS

Let's draw kissing lips next.

We will start with a circle. I want the diameter of the kissing lips to be about 6 centimeters (2.5") just to let you know the size of my drawing area if you want to draw the same size.
Draw a circle with a drawing compass in the middle of your paper. The circle doesn't even have to be perfectly round, we need it just for orientation.

Since the shape of kissing lips is not usually in the shape of a circle, we have to prolong it on the left and the right sides, as shown in the next image. Just to go over the circle and as a continuation, start separating from the circle and create the corners of the lips which should be placed just a little bit farther from the circle.

Erase the parts of the circle that don't belong to the outlines of the lips.
Next, create an edge between the two lips. You can start in the middle, right under the hole of the needle of your drawing compass, and create a wavy line towards the corners.

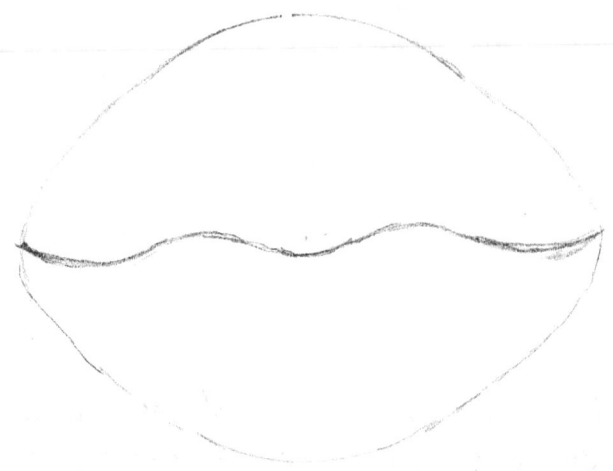

Outline the Cupid's bow by creating a tiny, curvy line at the top, within the circle.

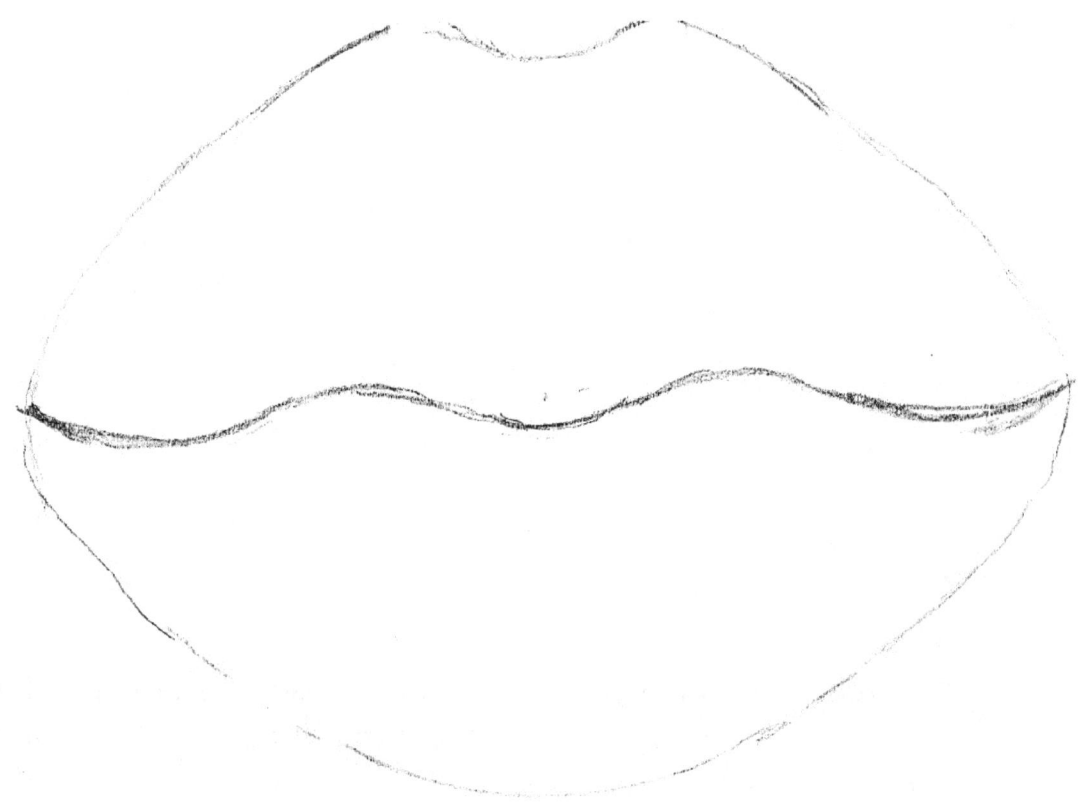

Now we can color the lips in the direction of the wrinkles, just the way we did in the two previous tutorials. But first, let's determine the position of the wrinkles. They are vertical in the middle and they should become curvy as we draw them towards the corners. In the very corners, we don't have any wrinkles.

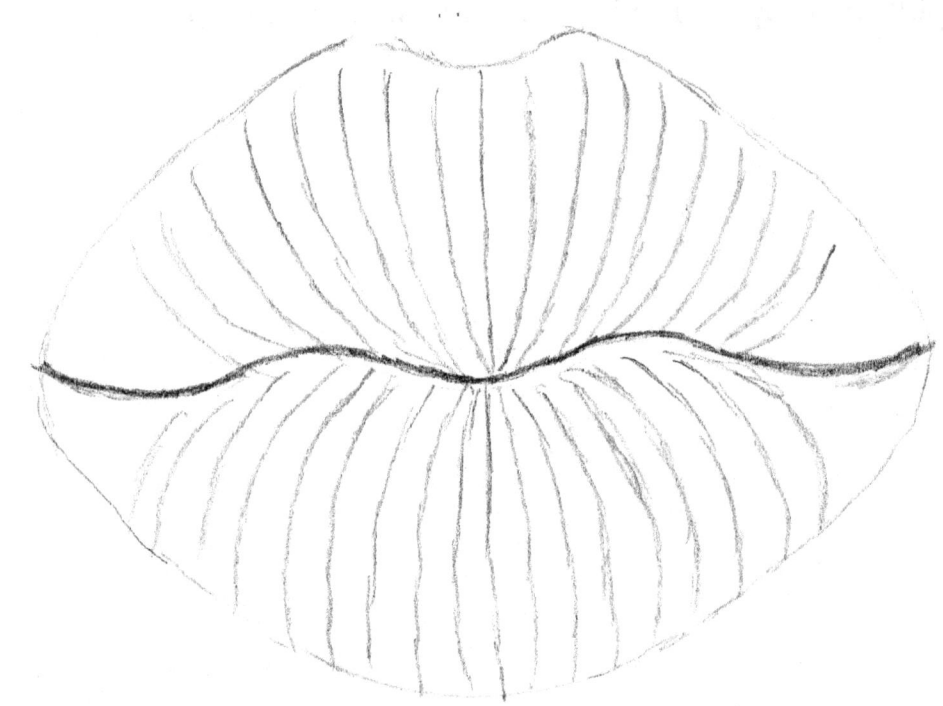

Next, color the entire area of both lips. I'm using an HB chiseled-shape graphite pencil, which allows me to color the areas faster. Just follow the direction of the wrinkles and cover both lips with the pencil of your choice.

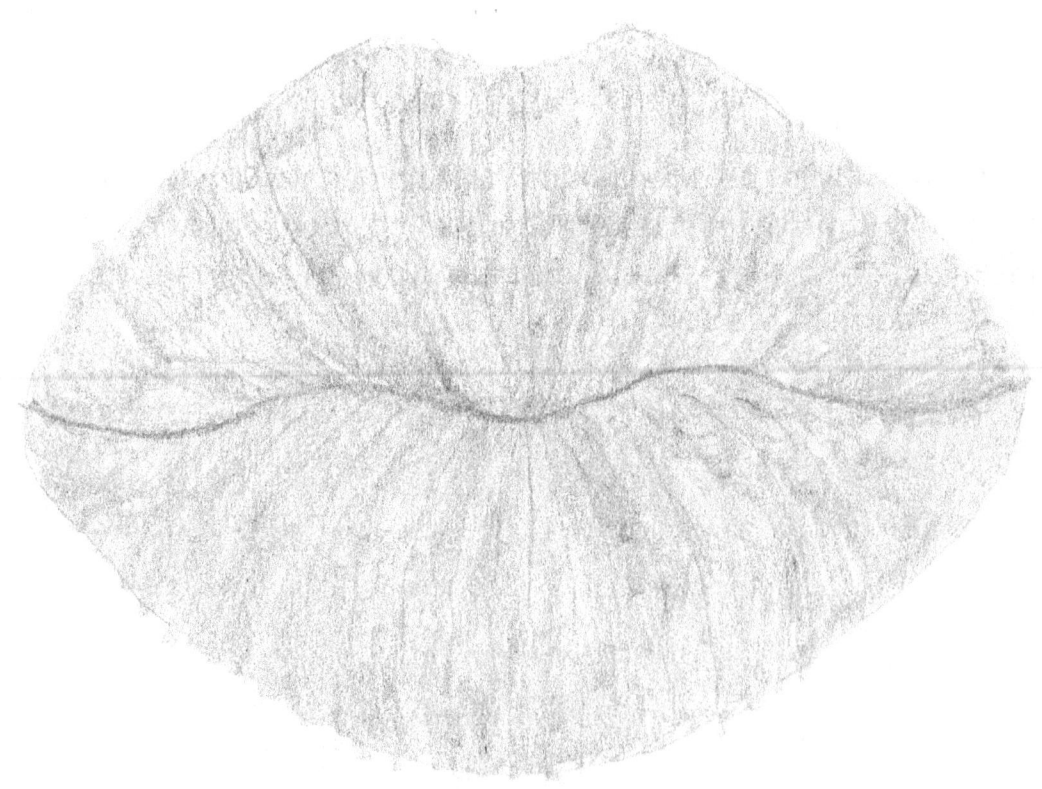

Blend it all with a Q-tip, using circular motions and pressing very hard to impress the graphite into the tooth of the paper. Now the lips look much smoother.

Next, let's create the shadowed parts, starting with the lower part of the upper lip, to create the self-shadow, next to the edge between the two lips because it receives less light. I'm using a 2B pencil, pressing harder next to the edge between the two lips and I release the pressure on my pencil as I shade upwards because we have to create a smooth gradient between the shadows and the basic tone of the lips. I stop somewhere in the middle because the upper part should stay brighter.

After we have shaded a little bit, we can blend that area with a Q-tip or with a blending stump and then can go over it again until we achieve the value we need.

Between the two lips, we don't have to create too strong of a shadow because both lips are flattened in the kissing position and their inner parts also receive light, which is not the case in their normal position.

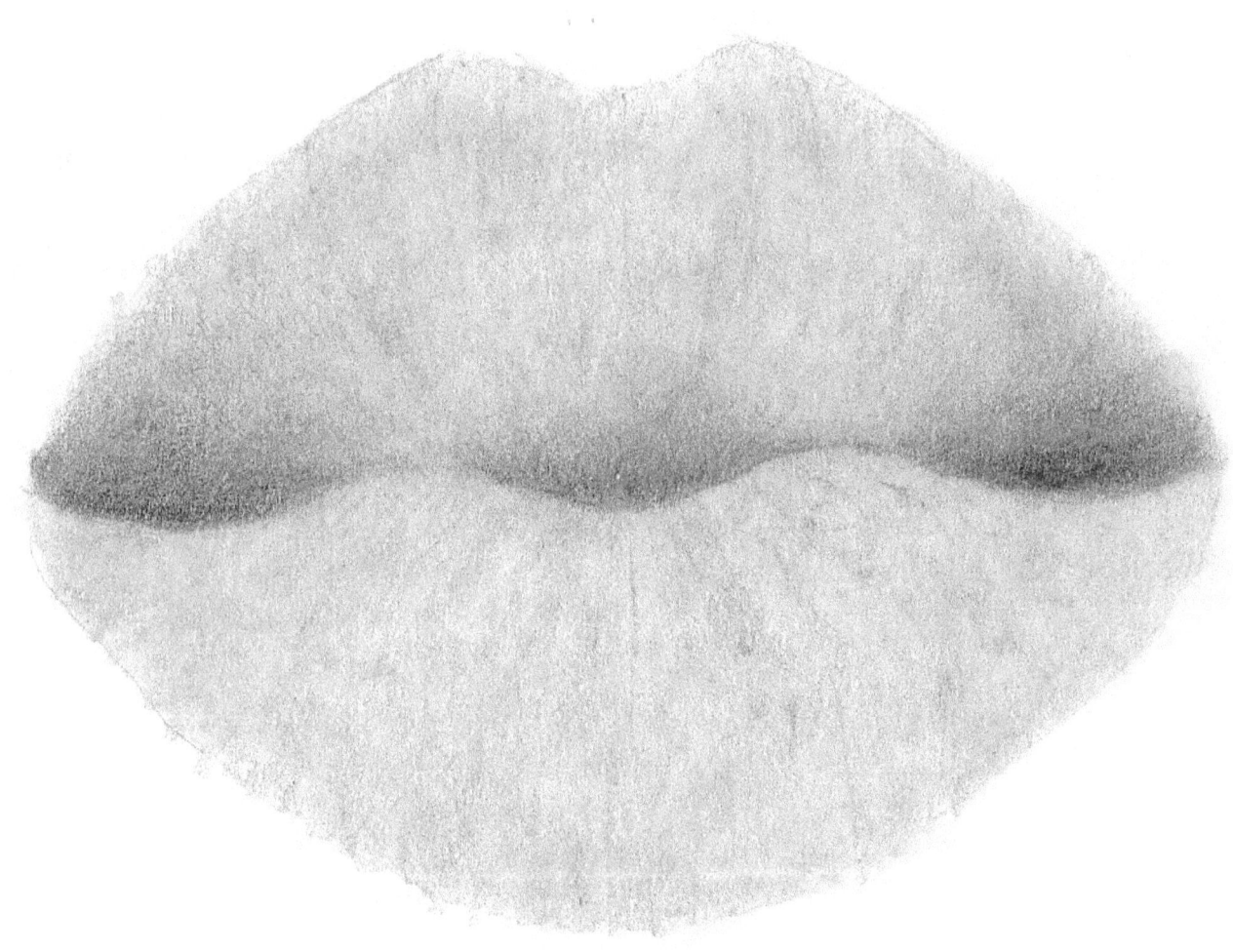

It is important to create the shadows and the highlights in general, and then to create details, wrinkles, and so on.

Create the shadowed areas that are not as dark as the areas we just created but quite brighter and yet darker than the basic value of the lips. It's usually found in the lower area of the lower lip where the lip receives less light. Shade these areas with an HB.

When shading the upper part of the upper lip, leave out the upper edge that has to be highlighted because it's bent and it gets more light. Shade right under this edge and leave it untouched.

Also, shade a bit in the corners right under the upper lip because there are no protruding muscles found.

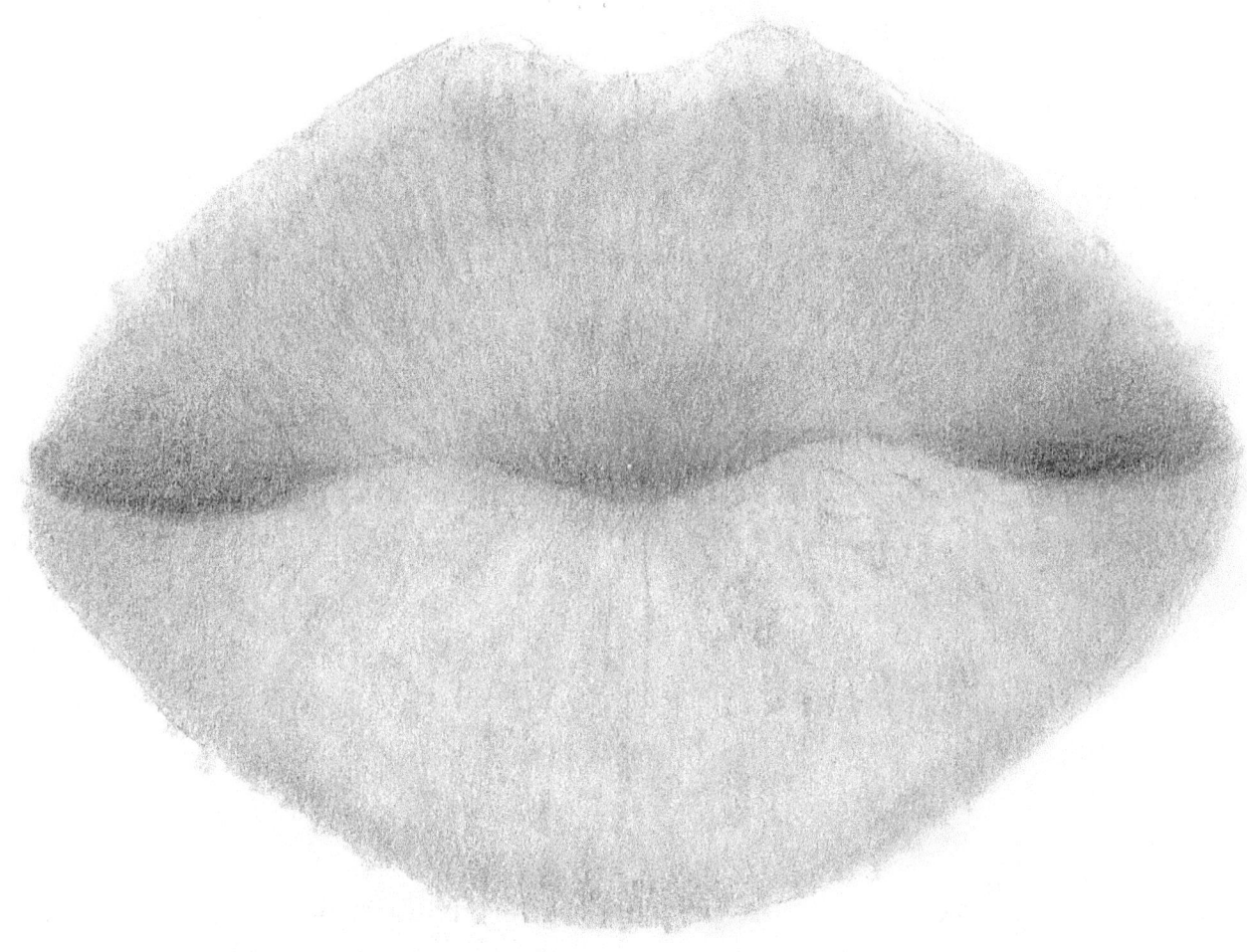

And now let's create the highlights by erasing the graphite. As I already mentioned in the previous tutorials on lips, we have to create two kinds of highlights: the highlights in general and highlights that we have to apply with a white ink gel pen which will make the lips appear wet or glossy.

To create the first kind of highlights, erase a bit of the graphite in the upper area of the lower lip. Gently touch the paper with an eraser because you don't want to brighten it too much. Just a little bit to make it brighter than the rest of the lips.

Do the same over the upper edge of the upper lip to make it look even more bent.

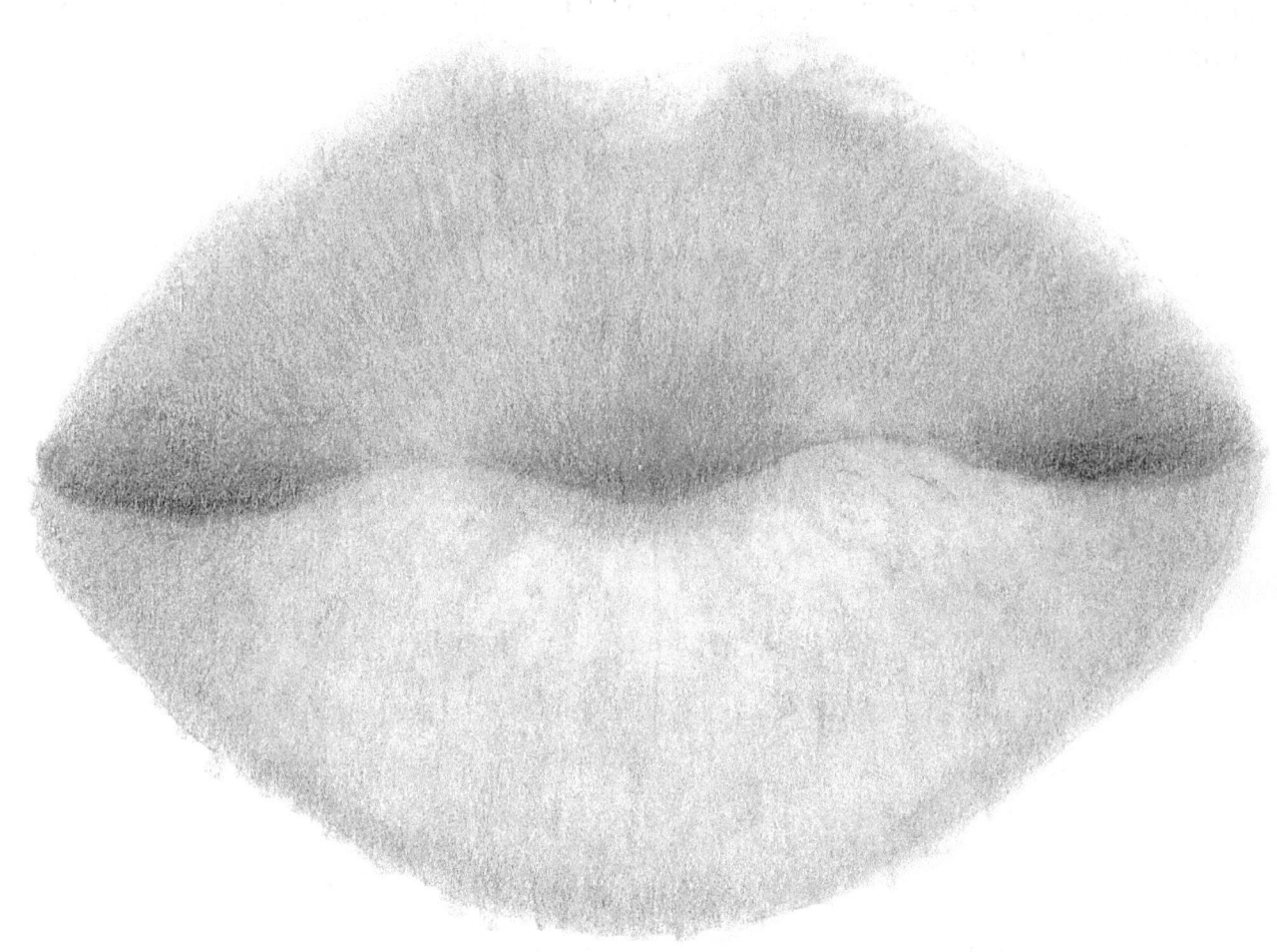

Next, create some wrinkles because they are highly visible when lips are in a kissing position. I'm using an HB for this and I want to draw them in the direction of the wrinkles that I drew at the very beginning. The wrinkles should be the darkest in the very middle and each one of them has to have the gradient transition between the darkest part and the basic tone of the lips, so just press hard in the very middle of the wrinkle and then press less and less as you shade away from the wrinkle.

Create different wrinkles as shown in the next image. They shouldn't be placed in any order. Some of them should go over the whole lip, others should go over only half the upper half of the lip. As I mentioned, in the very corners we don't have any wrinkles.

In the next image, you can see that I have drawn some tiny horizontal wrinkles too. After having drawn all the wrinkles you want, blend them with a blending stump.

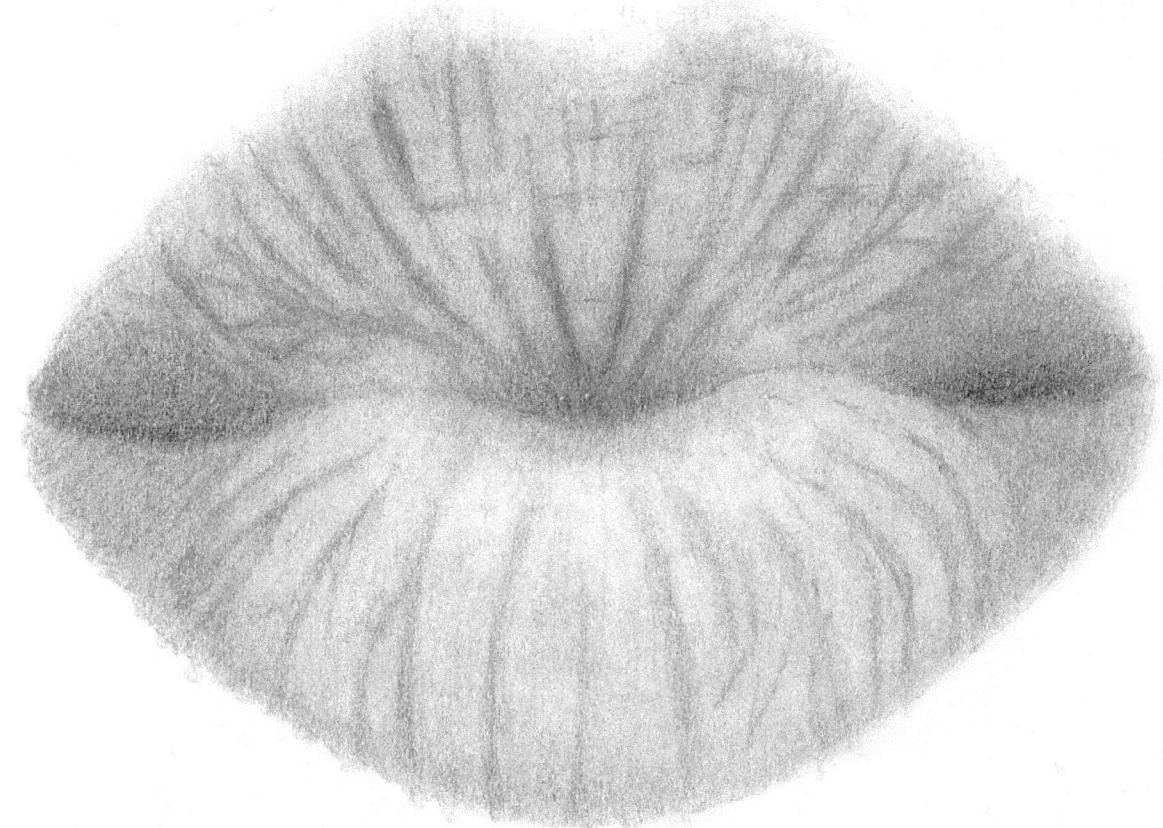

But, as you can see, now these wrinkles look nothing like wrinkles, but like a bunch of lines without the highlights. So, let's create the highlights among the wrinkles to indicate the protruding skin among them. Use a sharp tip of an eraser and eliminate a bit of the graphite in between the wrinkles. These are the first highlights that I mentioned, the highlights of the skin that will suggest the round shape of the skin between the wrinkles.

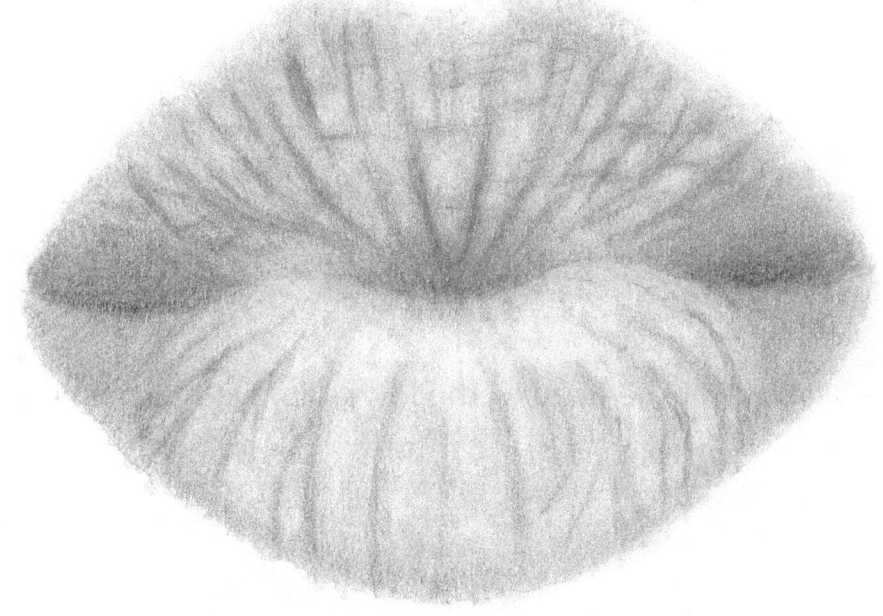

Last, we create highlights with a white ink gel pen or a white opaque marker that will make the lips appear wet.

Draw longer and shorter lines and dots between the two lips, and over the highlighted, protruding areas. Analyze the next image to see where I have drawn the highlights with my white marker by Uni Posca 0.7 mm.

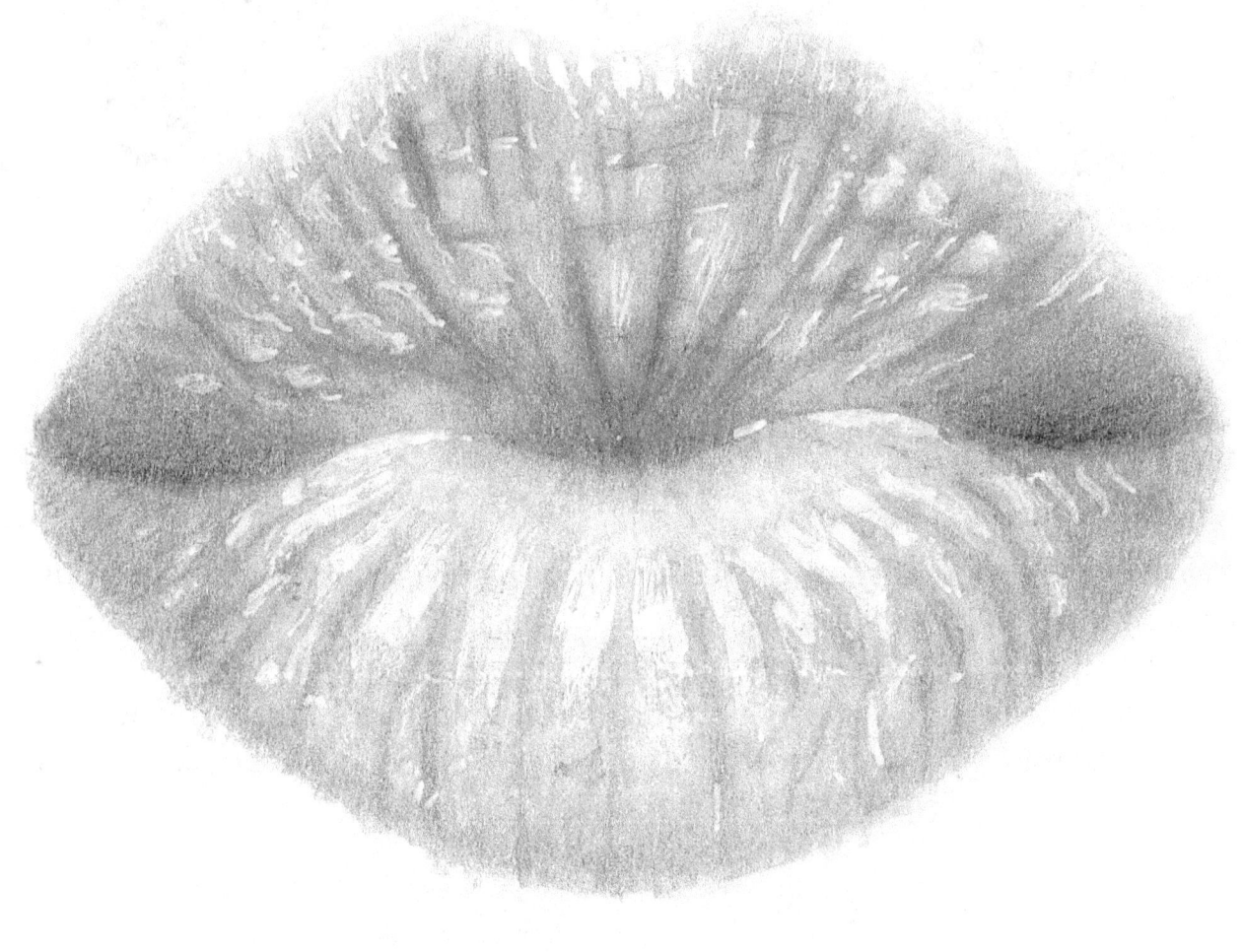

We can also create the cast shadow under the lower lip with the Q-tip and graphite powder, and in the corners and above the Cupid's bow.

Create the reflected light over the edge of the lower lip, next to the cast shadow with an eraser.

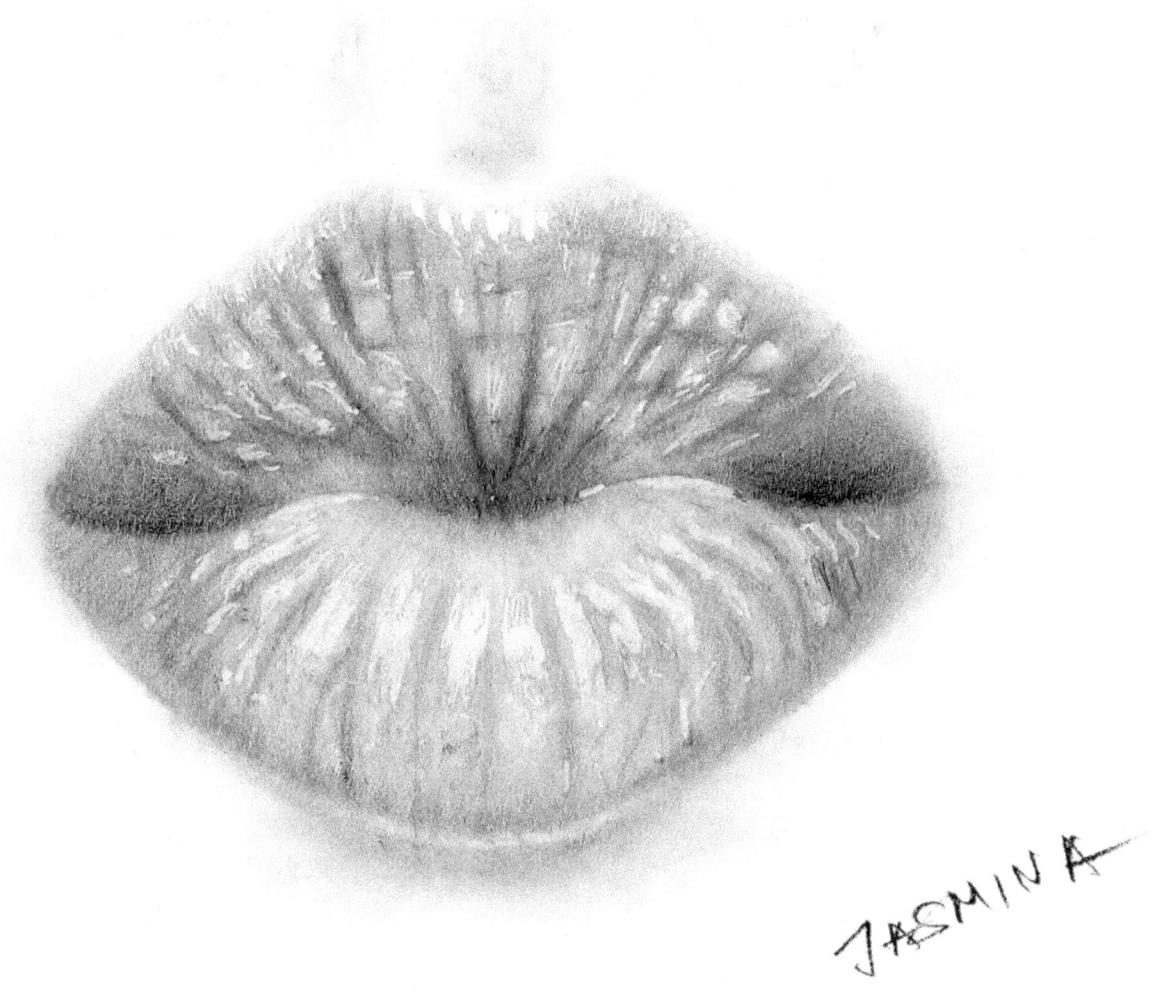

GLITTER LIPS AND TEETH

Now let's draw a slightly open mouth with visible teeth so you can practice drawing the teeth too. I want to draw the lips with heavy lipstick, and I want to make them glitter, so not as natural as the lips from the previous tutorial.

The first thing is to draw a circle to have some points for orientation. The diameter of my circle is about 6 centimeters (about 2.5"), if you want to draw the same size as me.

This is the height of the open mouth with both lips, but we want to make it a bit wider so that the distance between the two corners can be about 10-11 centimeters (4,5").

Mark these points and draw the outlines of the lips.

I start with the upper lip where we will create the Cupid's bow in the very middle, just over the upper part of the circle, create a tiny, curvy line inside of the circle and continue drawing the lines outwards and then a bit horizontally, then connect it to the corners of the lips. Analyze the next image to see where to place the lines around the circle.

You can create a dashed line first to see how it will connect and then you can draw a full line over it. The corners also should have some height since the mouth is slightly open. Try to stay the same on the left and the right side to make the mouth vertically symmetric. The lower outline can be less curvy and should follow the outline of the circle in the middle. Then just draw upwards, towards the corners.

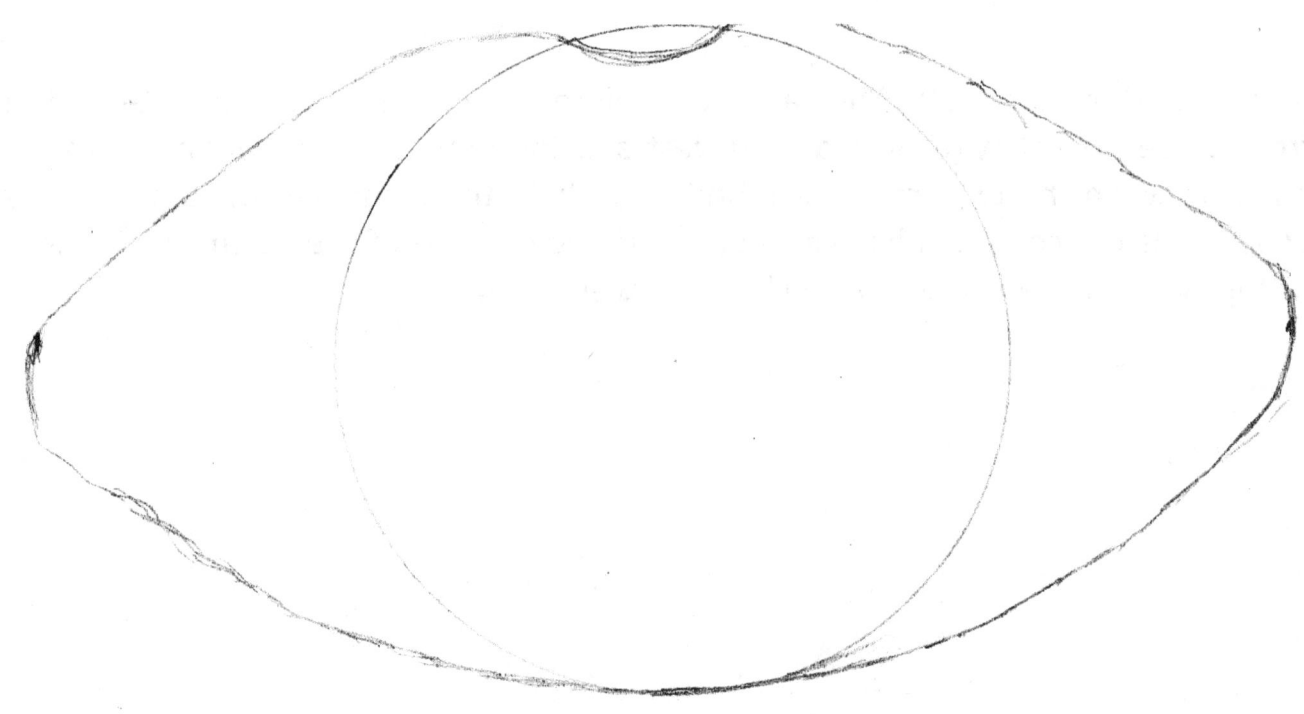

Now you can erase the circle.

Next, sketch the inner edges of the lips and leave as much space for the teeth as you want. The lower lip is usually a bit thicker than the upper lip, but it doesn't mean that it always has to be like that. You can create any shape, since there are many shapes of lips. You can see in the following image how I have outlined them.

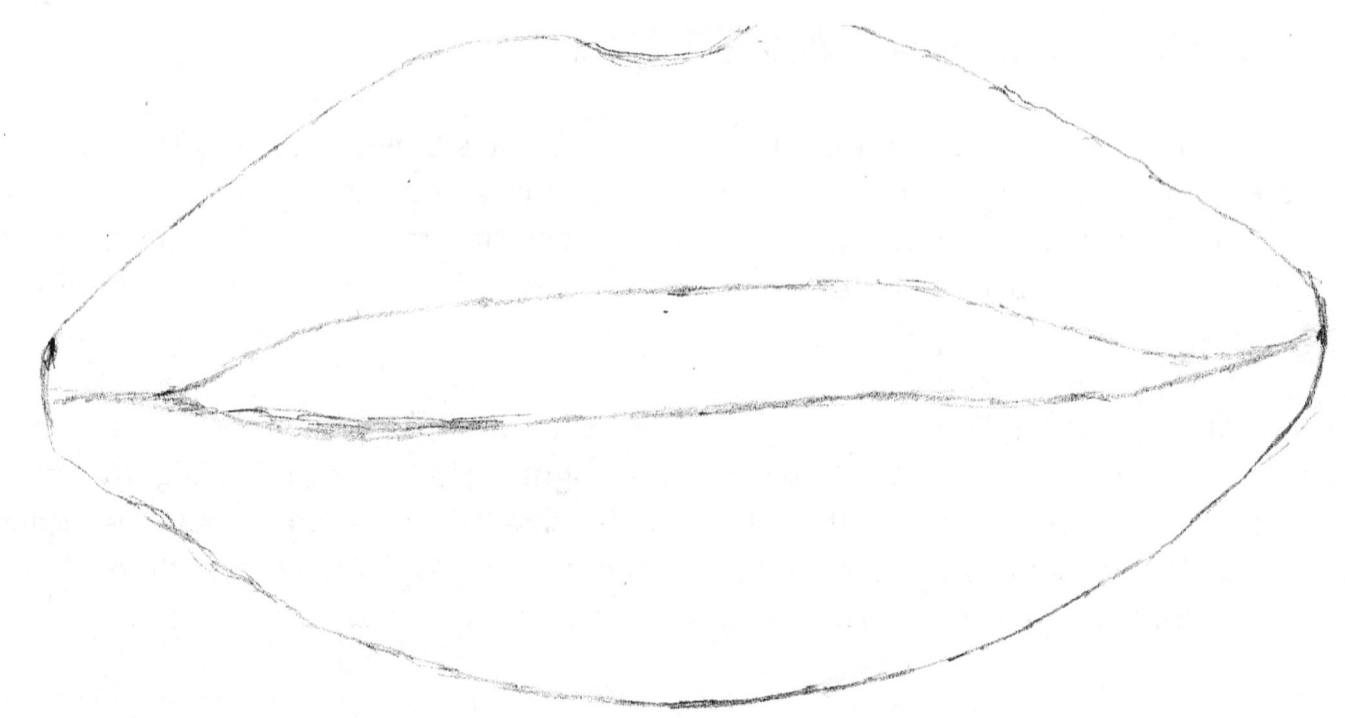

Now we can draw the teeth. You can check reference photos or your own teeth in the mirror to see how they're placed. I suggest starting with the vertical line in the very middle, between the two front teeth and then draw them smaller and smaller as you draw towards the corners. I have also drawn the lower row of the teeth which has only their tops visible. The rest is covered by the lower lip.

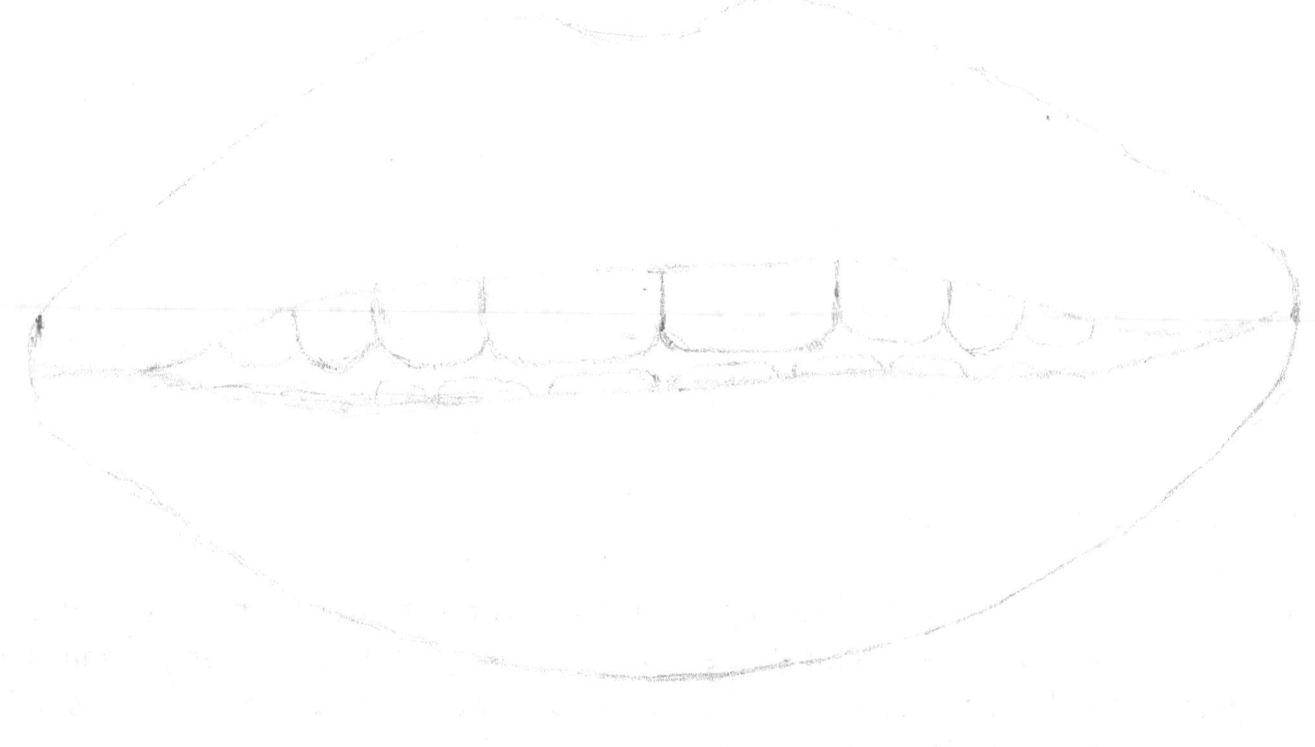

Now let's shade! I suggest starting with the teeth. The teeth are white, but we have to shade them too, particularly those found deeper in the mouth and shadowed by the lips. I'm using a 6H in a circular motion because I want to create a smooth texture. Press lightly over the front teeth and press a bit harder as you shade the teeth towards the corners of the lips. Then start using a 4H for the inner teeth, and finish with a 2H for the teeth next to the corners. Shade the lower teeth with a 2H as well.

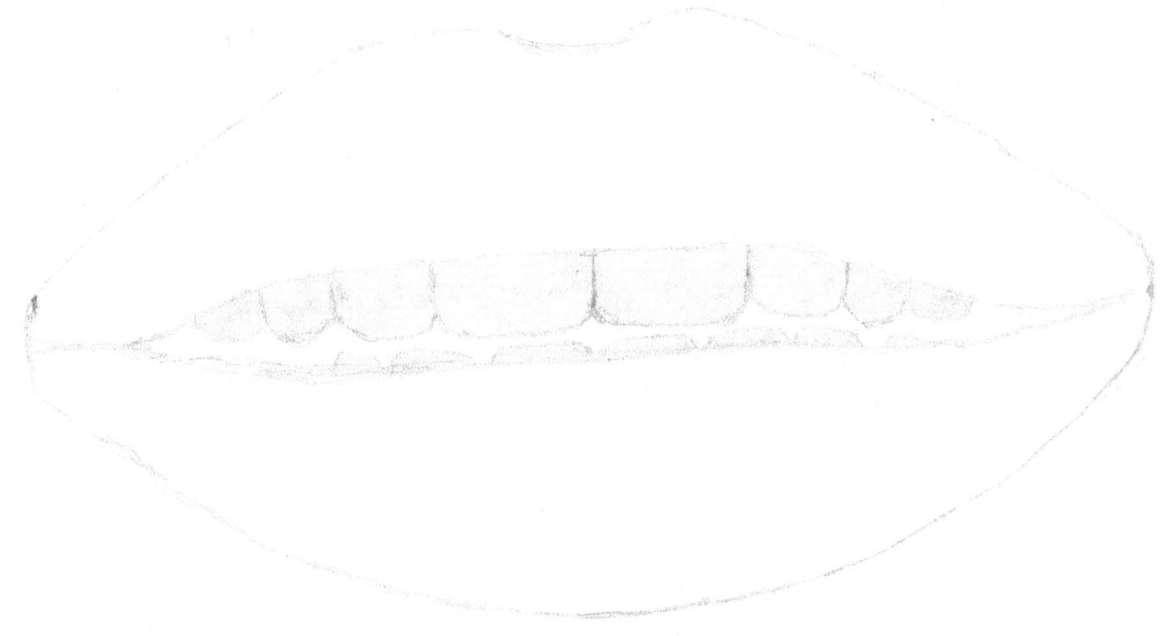

Blend it all with a clean piece of a Q-tip to make the texture of the teeth smooth.

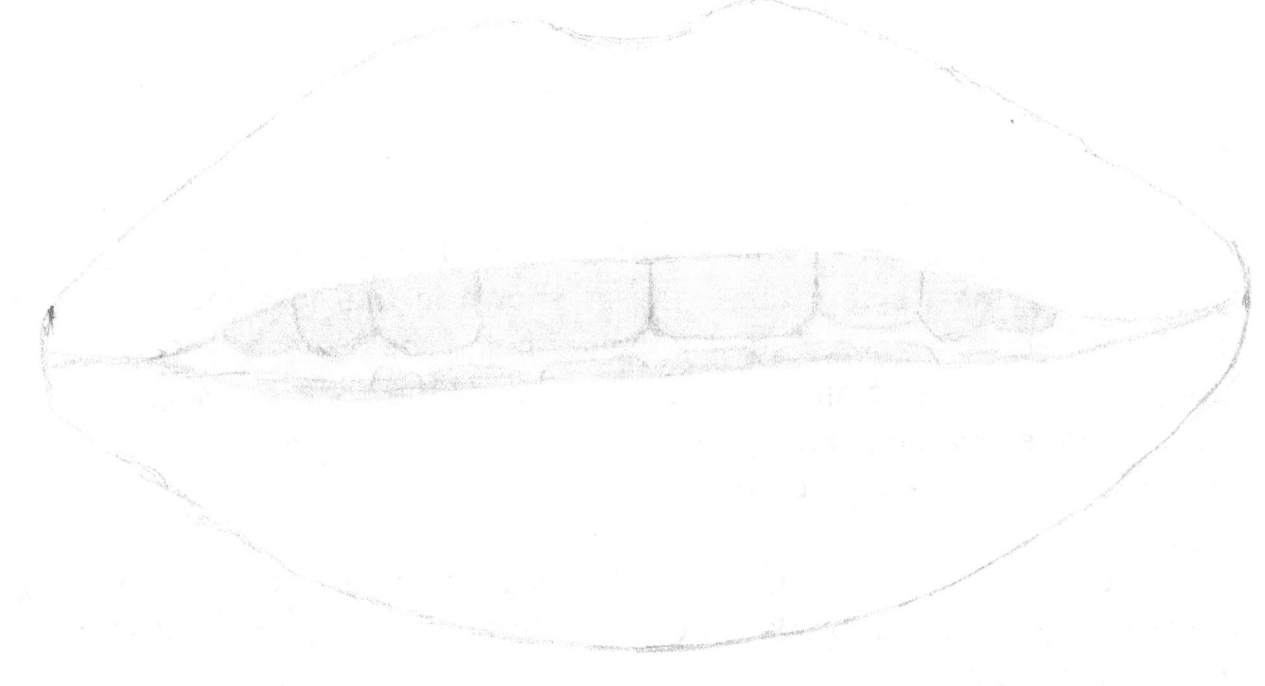

The next thing is to create a shadow cast by the upper lip over the upper row of teeth. For this you can use a 2H or an H, pressing hard, or an HB, pressing lightly. Study the next image to see where I have shaded the cast shadow.

You should cover the inner teeth completely because the upper lip casts a bigger shadow over them since they are found deeper in the mouth are receive less light. This will make the upper lip appear closer to the viewer's eye and give a third dimension to the drawing. That is why the cast shadow is always important. Also, shade between the teeth with an H pencil.

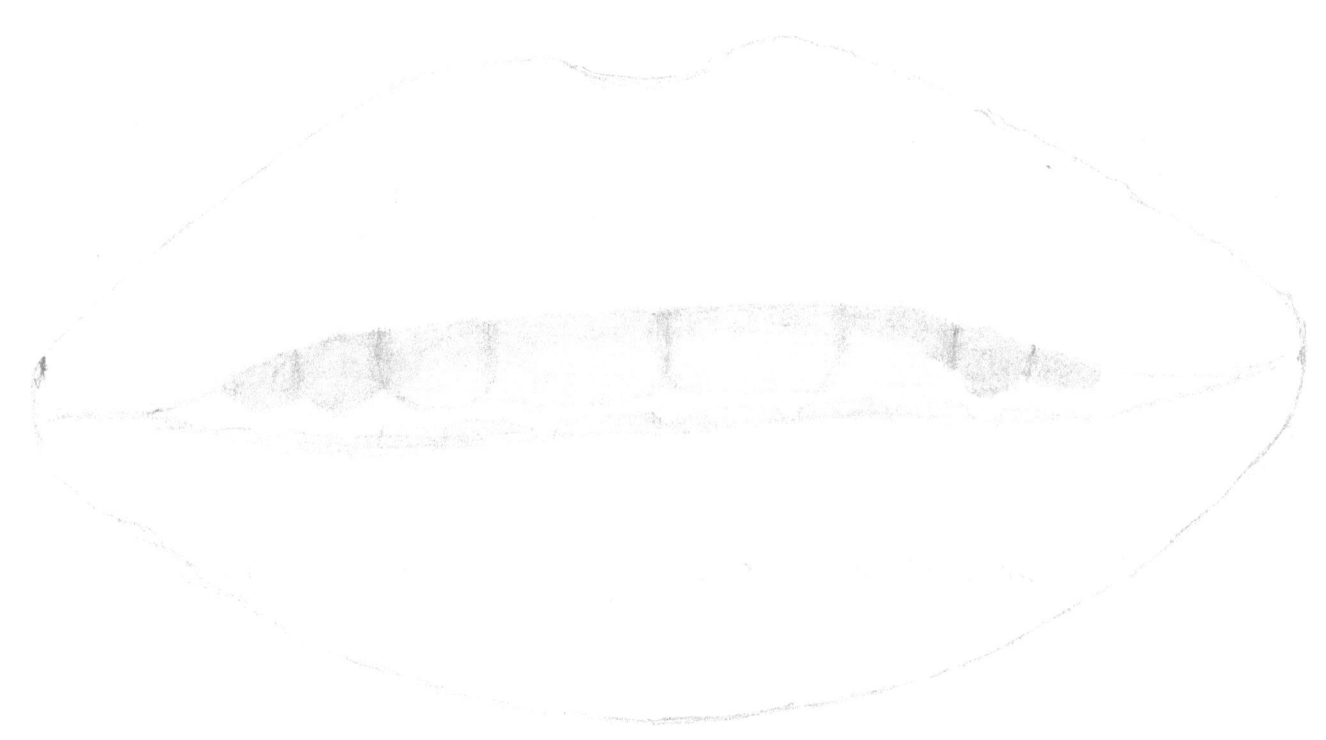

Now let's color in the inner area of the mouth with a 4B or darker. I am using a 4B. In this step, color everything except the teeth, as shown in the next image. Be careful around the teeth because you are outlining the teeth and could change their shape, and these dark pencils can't be completely erased. Go over the area, pressing lightly, and when you are sure everything looks good and just the way you want, go over it once again with an 8B or other dark pencil, pressing hard.

This area is actually the inner part of the mouth, including maybe tongue or some gum that receives no light so it can black. Now the teeth don't look dark because we have drawn the surrounding area.

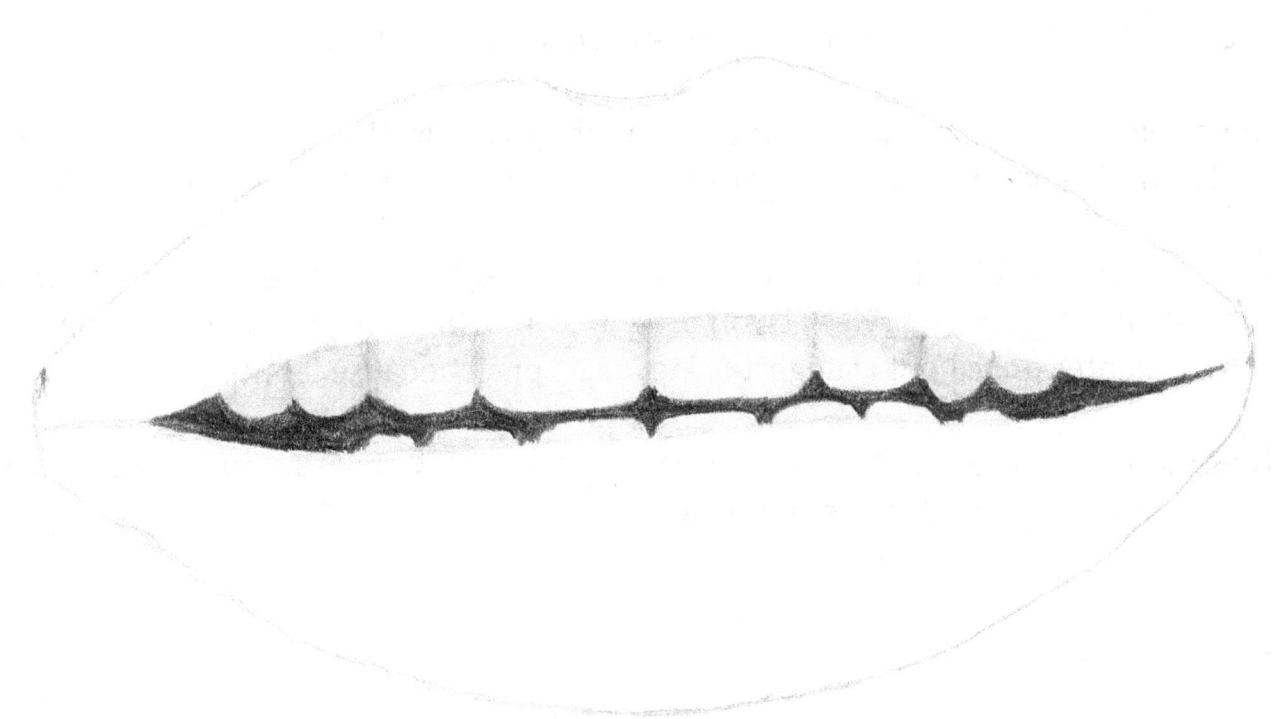

As you can see, there is a sharp edge between the teeth and the background or cavity of the mouth, so we have to soften it a bit with a blending stump. Use a blending stump that you haven't used before and go over the edge between the teeth and the background. Q-tips are too large for blending this, so that's why we should use a blending stump. Also, go in between the teeth to blend the edge between them because it shouldn't stay sharp and clean. Do the same with the lower teeth.

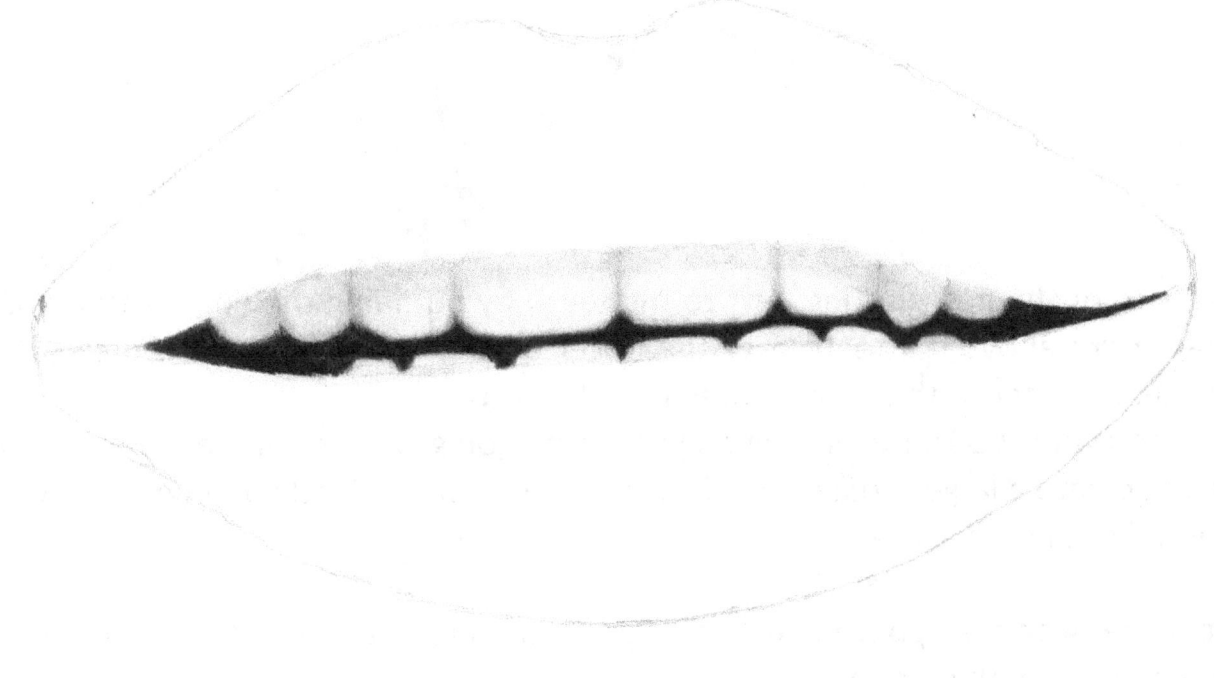

If you are satisfied with the teeth, you can start coloring the lips.

As I mentioned before, I want to draw lips with glossy lipstick, so I will color both lips with a 2B and follow the direction of the wrinkles. Let's create the wrinkles first, though.

Start in the very middle of the both lips, where the wrinkles are vertical and then start making them curvier and curvier as you draw them towards the corners. You can use an HB or even lighter pencil but I suggest using a 2B pencil because it's still not too dark.

Analyze the next image to see where I have drawn the wrinkles and notice how they already indicate the round shape of the lips.

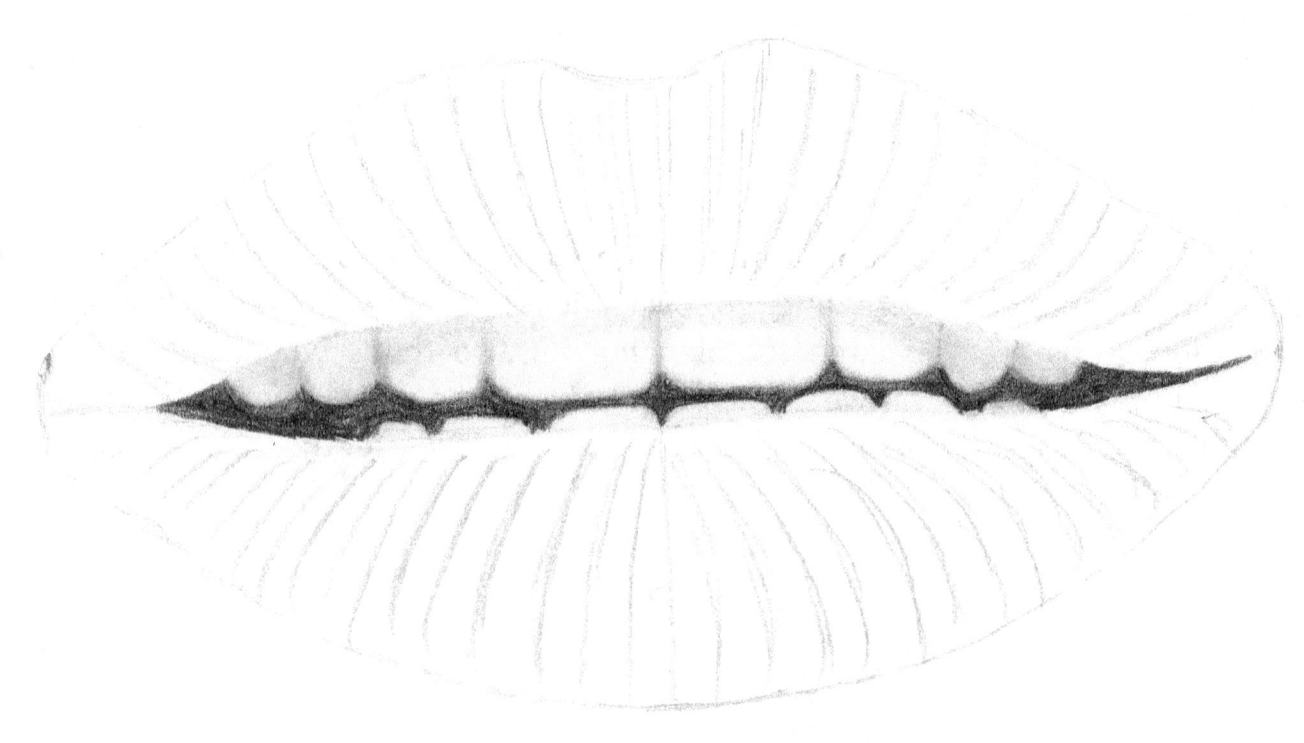

Now let's color the lips, starting next to the teeth by outlining the edge with a 2B. Press very hard right above the teeth over the lower edge of the upper lip. You can see that the lips and the teeth that I have drawn so far look rather like a smile than a slightly open mouth, but we can always change that by going over the inner teeth with a 2B pencil and create a larger area of the lips. I want to draw a slightly open mouth with only the frontal teeth visible.

Do the same over the upper edge of the lower lip and carefully outline it. Now we can shade the inner teeth more if necessary, using an HB pencil.

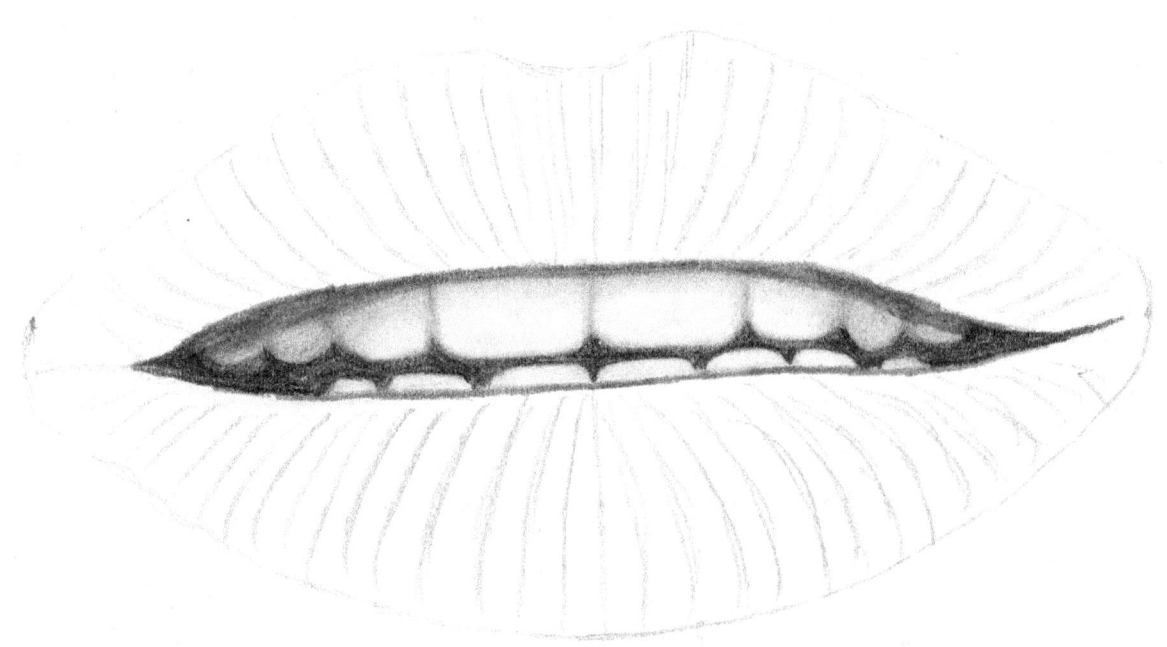

Color both lips by following the direction of the wrinkles with a 2B pencil. You can use a darker or a lighter value for this. Cover the entire area of both lips, being very careful next to the outer edges. You don't have to press very hard. As you can see in the next image, the texture doesn't look smooth yet and there are visible lines, but it's okay because we are going to blend it. I recommend using the chisel-shaped tip of a pencil so you can cover the areas faster and it will make the texture smoother even before blending. In this step, we're just applying the basic value (color) of the lips wearing lipstick. Focus on a single action before you move forward.

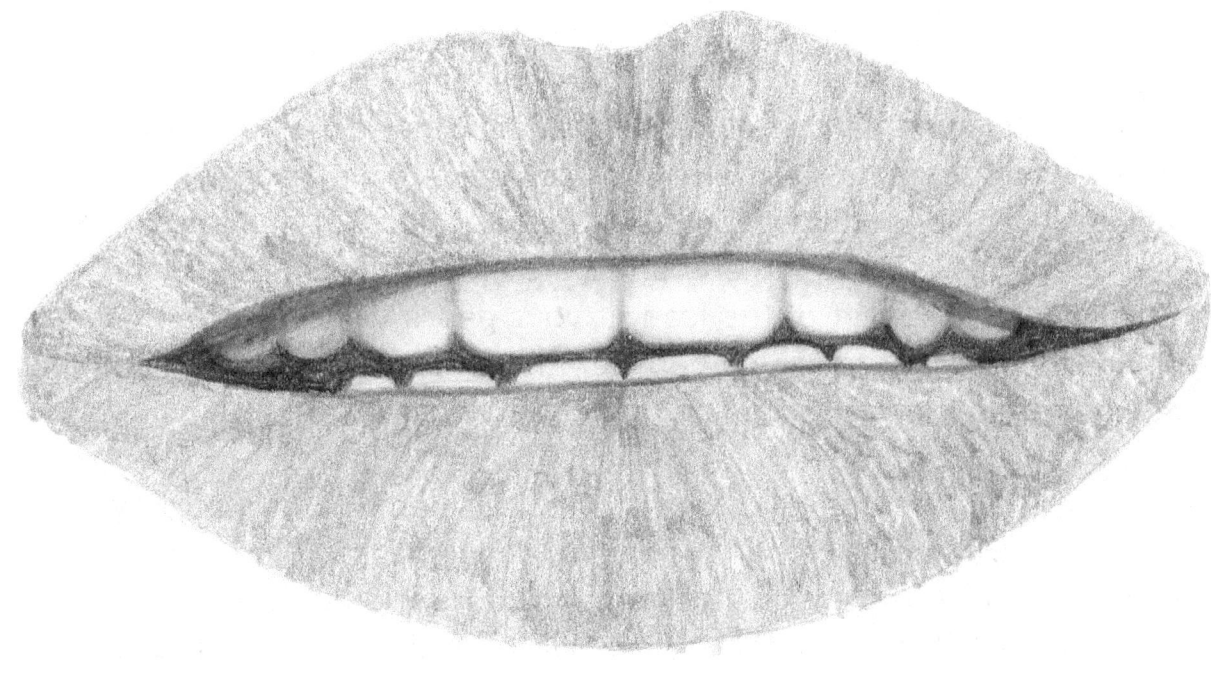

Next, let's blend it all with a Q-tip. Just go all around over the area you just drew and press very hard and blend it all. I use a circular motion to spread the graphite evenly over the paper. Now you can still see some of the wrinkles and lines that I initially created when I was showing you the direction of the wrinkles, but it's okay because this is just how they look, so it's fine if you have them visible on your drawing.

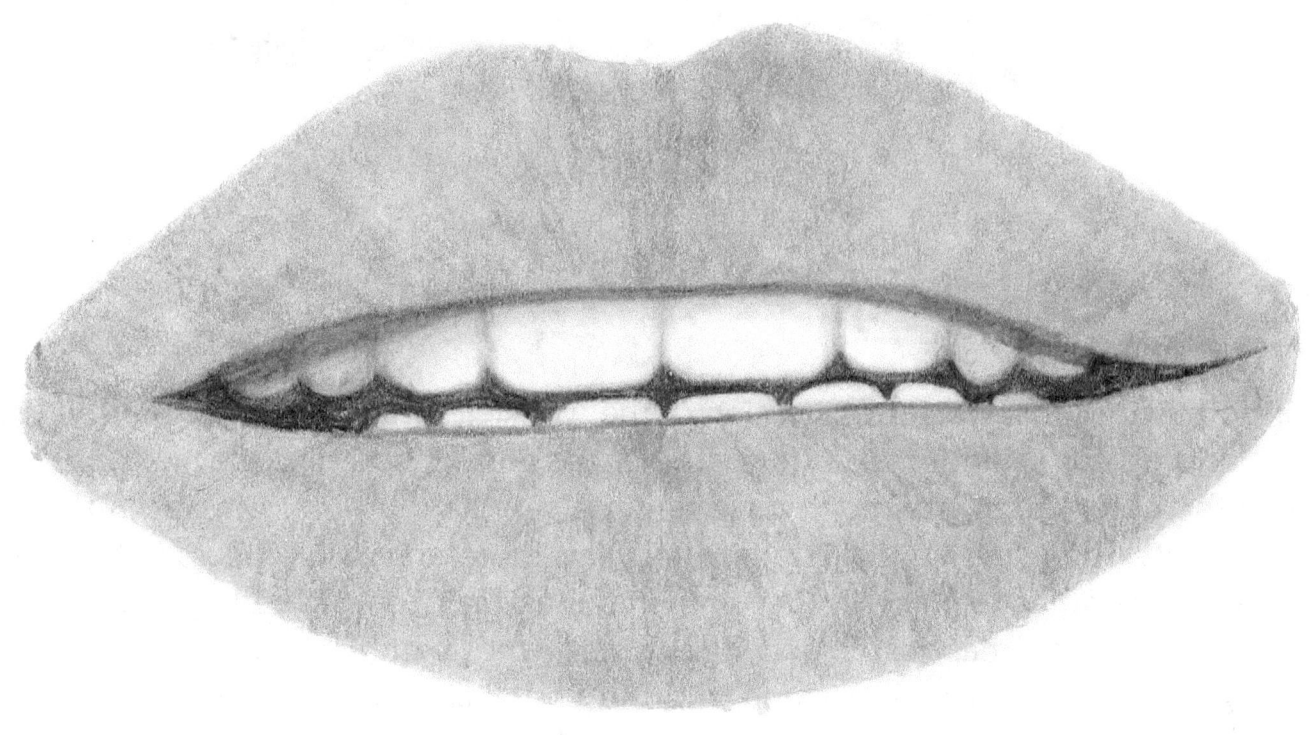

Now we can create some darker values next to the inner edges of the lips and in the corners. Here we must create the gradient transition between the dark outline that we created between the lips and the teeth, and the basic color of the lips we just made in the previous step. Use a 2B for this and place the tip of your pencil over the dark edge, draw away from it and lift off of the lead of your pencil when you finish the stroke in order to make the gradient transition between these values. Draw some longer lines, at random, to indicate the wrinkles. Blend it all with a blending stump.

Since the corners always receive less light, they can be quite darker, so we can press harder when shading the two corners. There are no wrinkles in the corners of the lips or they're very tiny, so we can make a smoother texture there. We must create a lot of values to give shape to the lips so that they can look proportional and round.

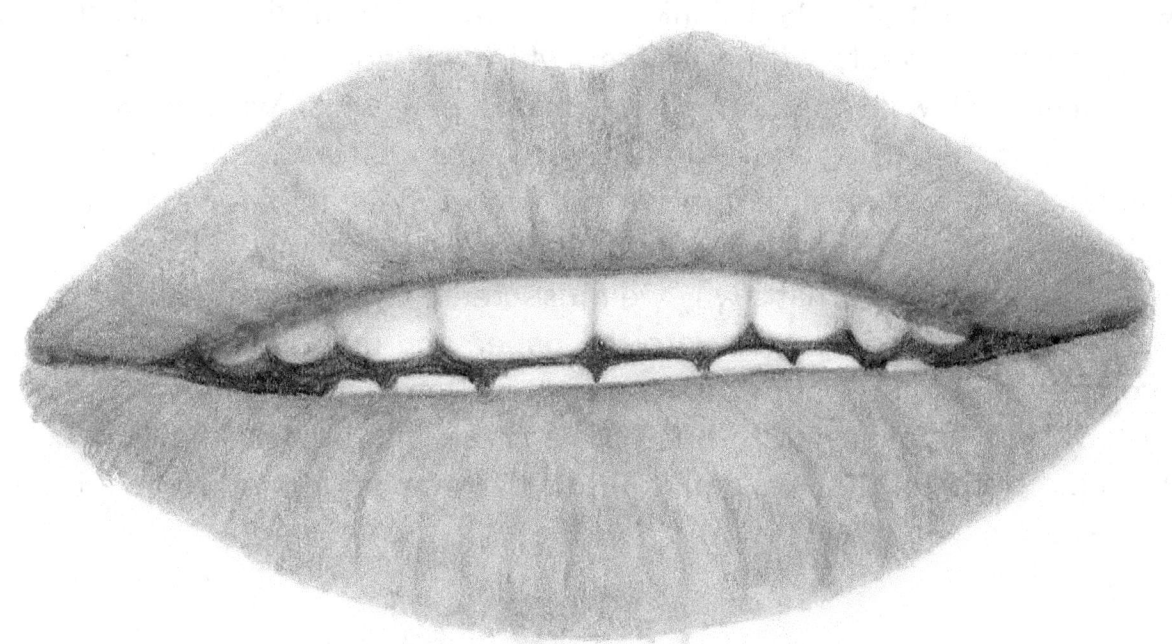

Now we can do the same but next to the outer edge. On the lower lip, we have a kind of bent edge. In my case, it's like two millimeters which should be shaded with a darker value. You can use a 2B and press harder or even introduce a 3B or a 4B. When shading the upper area of the upper lip, leave out the edge (also about 2 millimeters) because that edge is bent inwards and it receives more light. Just shade under it as shown in the following image. Press very hard under the edge, and then release the pressure with each stroke and, of course, we can draw the wrinkles, but in the upper area we shouldn't have many wrinkles. We only have tiny wrinkles. The deep wrinkles are found in the lower area. Always press less in the middle of the lip because the mid-area should appear closer to the viewer's eye and we can do this by making it lighter.

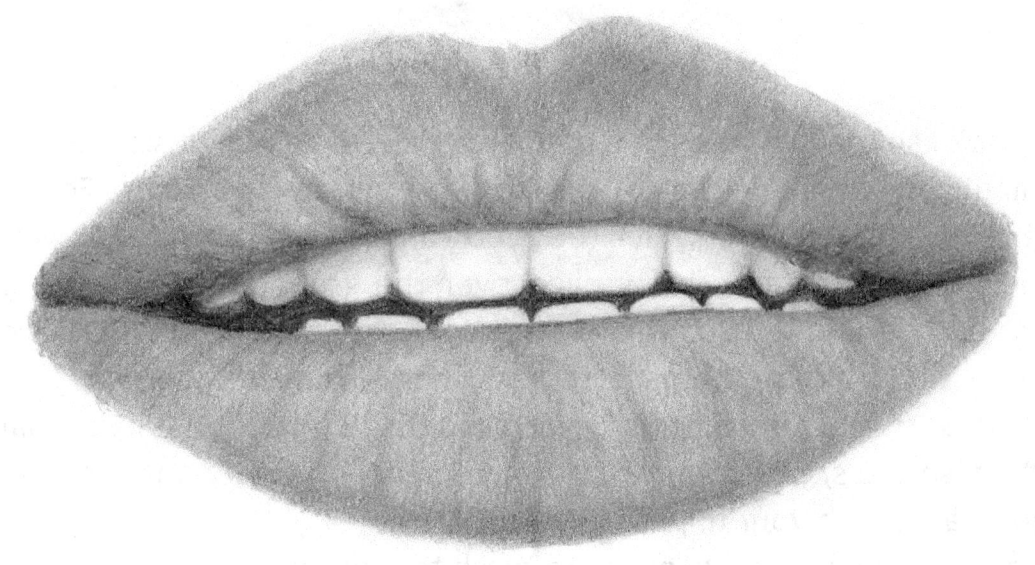

Next, let's create the highlights. I think of two kinds of highlights in this situation: the highlights we have to create with an eraser, which will add the round shape to the lip, and the highlights we will apply with a white ink gel pen, which will add the glossiness to the lips. As a first step, using a kneaded eraser, erase a bit of the graphite in the upper horizontal half of the lower lip. Here we have a highly illuminated part, but since we want to draw the lips wearing lipstick, it won't be white enough, yet it has to be brighter than the surrounding area. That's why we must create two kinds of highlights. Place the tip of your kneaded eraser, press it into the paper, and quickly lift off. You will see the area becomes a bit brighter but not too bright, just enough to give it a round shape. If you overdo it, just go over it with a Q-tip. To create the arched highlight, we have to erase the middle area of the lips, and it has to become darker and to go a bit upwards, towards the corners.

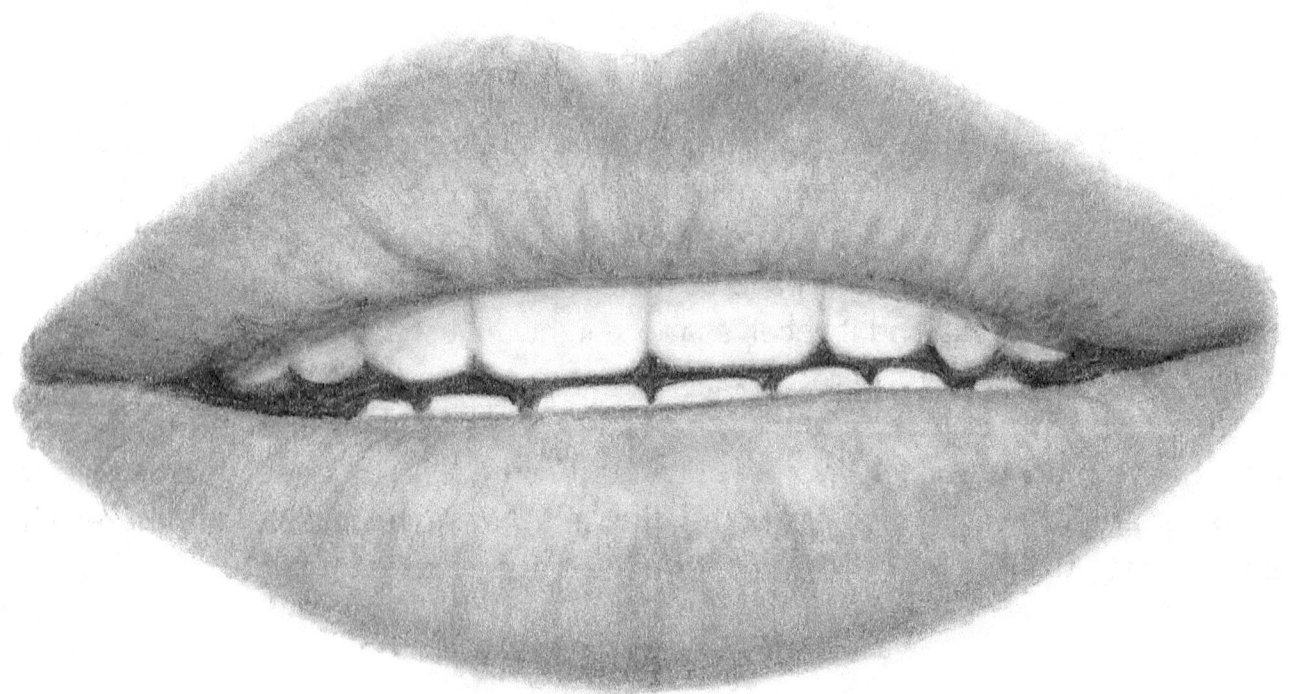

Now the lips look like they're wearing a matte lipstick—it can even stay like this, but let's create the highlights which will make the lips very glossy and shiny. For that, I use a white marker by Uni Posca, 1mm thick, but you can also use a white ink gel pen or any other opaque medium that can be applied over the graphite. Create the glossy parts where they would be found, usually over the bent areas, but of course, it depends on the light source. Study the next image to see where I have drawn with this tool. Also, draw lines and dots all over the place, at random. If you don't like what you have created with these tools, just remove it with your nail. If you want the highlight to be less bright, just tap it with your finger.
We can also apply some highlights over the teeth to make them look shiny and wet.

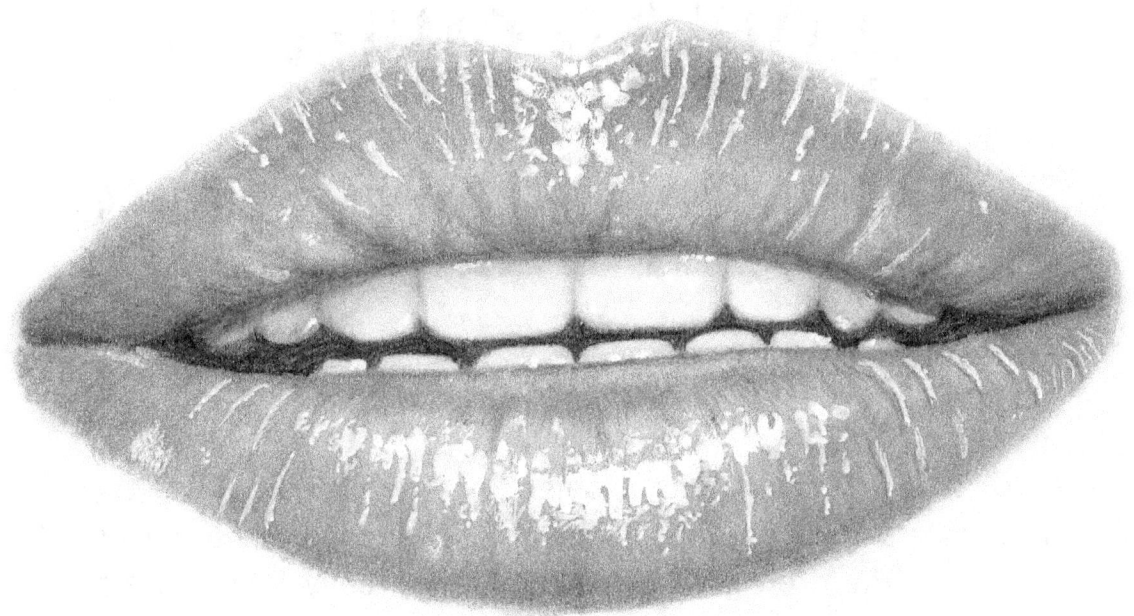

As a final step, let's add some cast shadow under the lower lip. Dip your Q-tip into the graphite powder and apply it right under the lower lip as shown in the next picture. Apply more in the very middle and then less and less as you shade towards the right and the left sides. This cast shadow will make the lower lip pop on the page and appear even more round. Also, shade next to the corners of the lips (because this skin is bent inwards here), and the sunken area above the Cupid's bow.

The last thing is to create the reflected light over the edge of the lower lip, the light that reflects off the chin, by erasing a bit of the graphite with a pointed tip of an eraser.

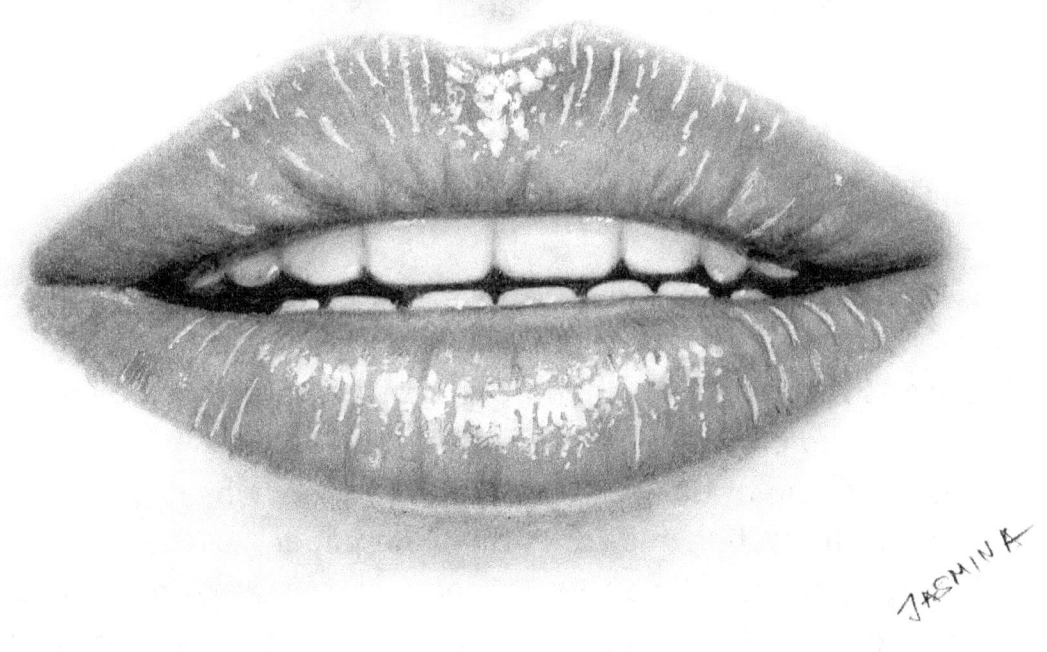

HOW TO DRAW A SMOKEY GLITTER EYE

Sometimes when I draw white objects or white animals, they don't look noticeable and eye-catching on white paper unless I color the background too. This is why I choose to draw them on grey paper, and they really look more prominent and three-dimensional.

So, if you haven't drawn on grey paper before, I would like to convince you to try it out because it's really fun and enjoyable after drawing only on white paper.

Drawing on toned paper is a fun way to step outside the box and try something different. You can expand your drawing skills by drawing on grey paper because it will help you to discover opportunities and ideas that wouldn't otherwise be possible if you only drew on white paper. Drawing white objects or animals on white paper is especially tricky as they would look far less noticeable. To make such a drawing more prominent, we would have to color the background, and this is quite difficult and tedious, which may discourage you from drawing.

Reasons to Draw on Toned Paper:

- You can start with white, which is pretty interesting.
- Your work will seem more complete and won't look pale.
- Your highlights will appear much more spectacular and three-dimensional.
- Drawings on toned paper look more realistic and lifelike.
- You can use the tone of the paper as your mid-tone, which is particularly helpful if you struggle with creating mid-tones on white paper.
- Working on grey paper will help you to see and evaluate tonal values more easily.
- The experience and skills gained by working with toned paper is something that

you can apply to your white paper in the future.
- Working on grey paper will boost your creativity.

In this tutorial, I want to show you how to draw a smokey, glitter eye on grey paper. I used the Clay grey paper by Fabriano. I also used a white colored pencil, but you can use a white charcoal or pastel.

I want to draw an eye in three-quarters point of view, when an eye is shifted over to one side a bit. Therefore, the upper eyelid should be curvier than it appears from the front view, and the lower eyelid can be almost straight. I'm using an 8B pencil all through because I want to draw an eye with heavy makeup: the so-called smokey eye with glitter eyeshadow.

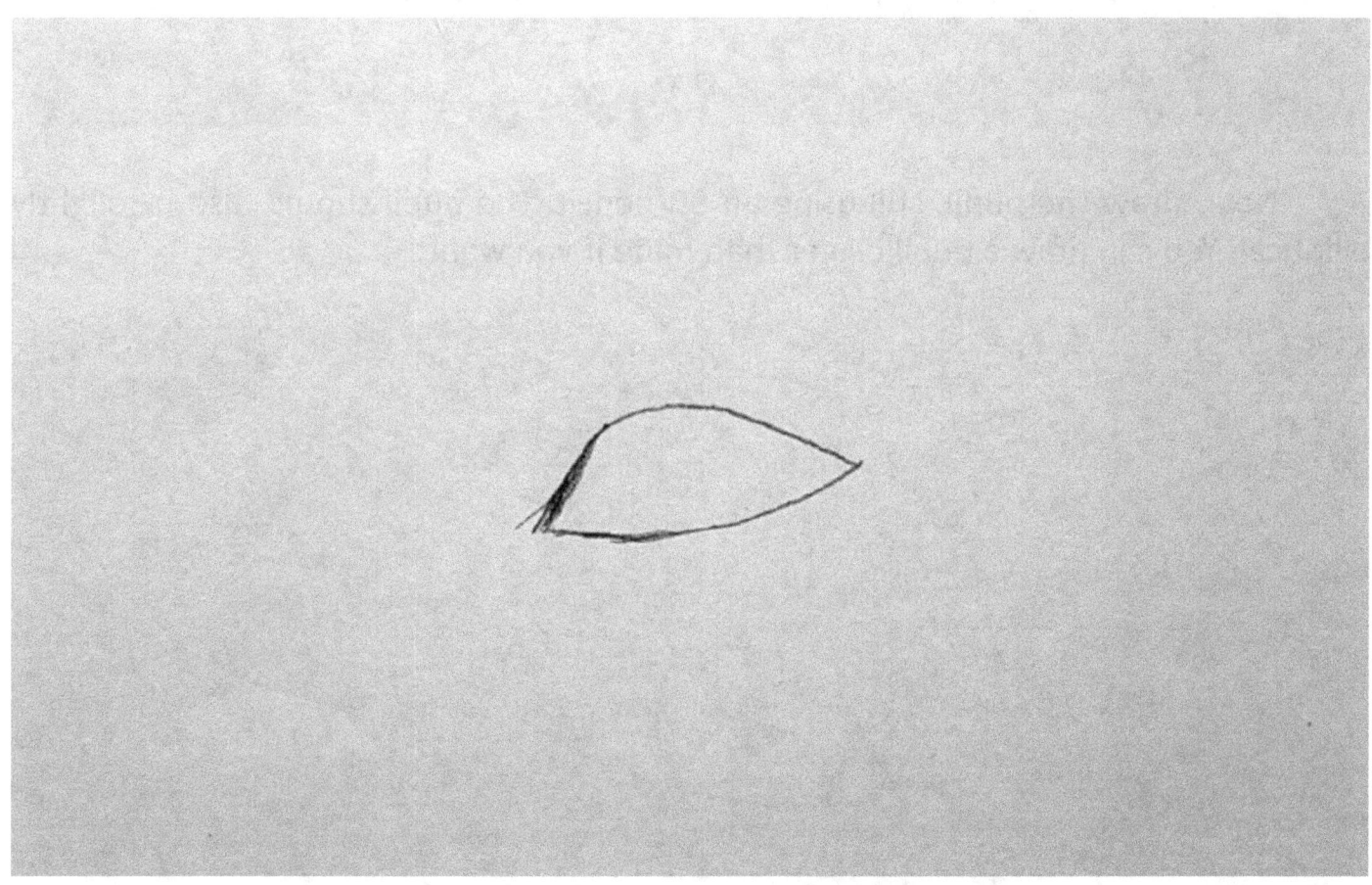

Let's draw the iris boundary, which shouldn't be perfectly round from this point of view but elliptic. The upper part of the iris should be covered with an upper eyelid, and the lower part of the iris should be covered with a lower eyelid.

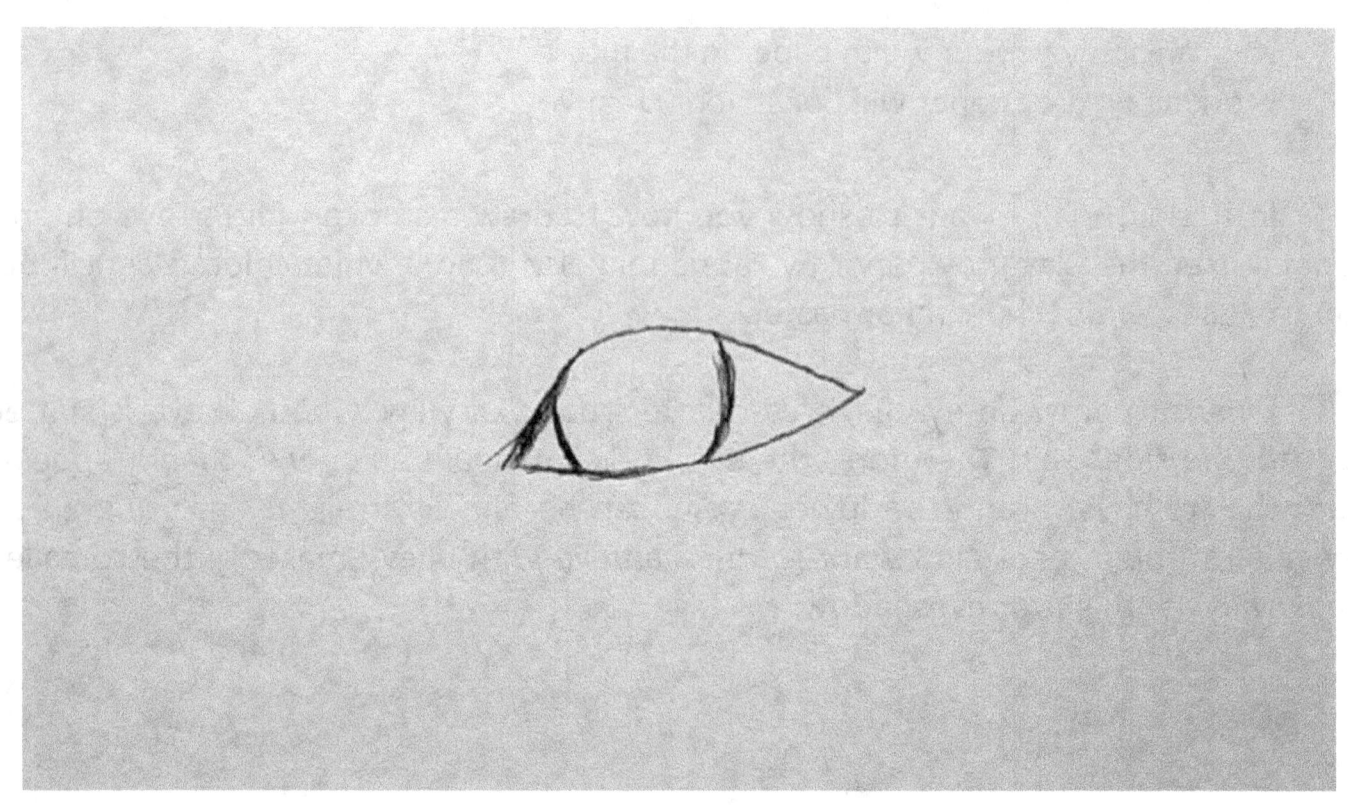

Next, draw the pupil, still using an 8B pencil. The pupil should also be slightly elliptical. You can draw a pupil bigger than mine if you want.

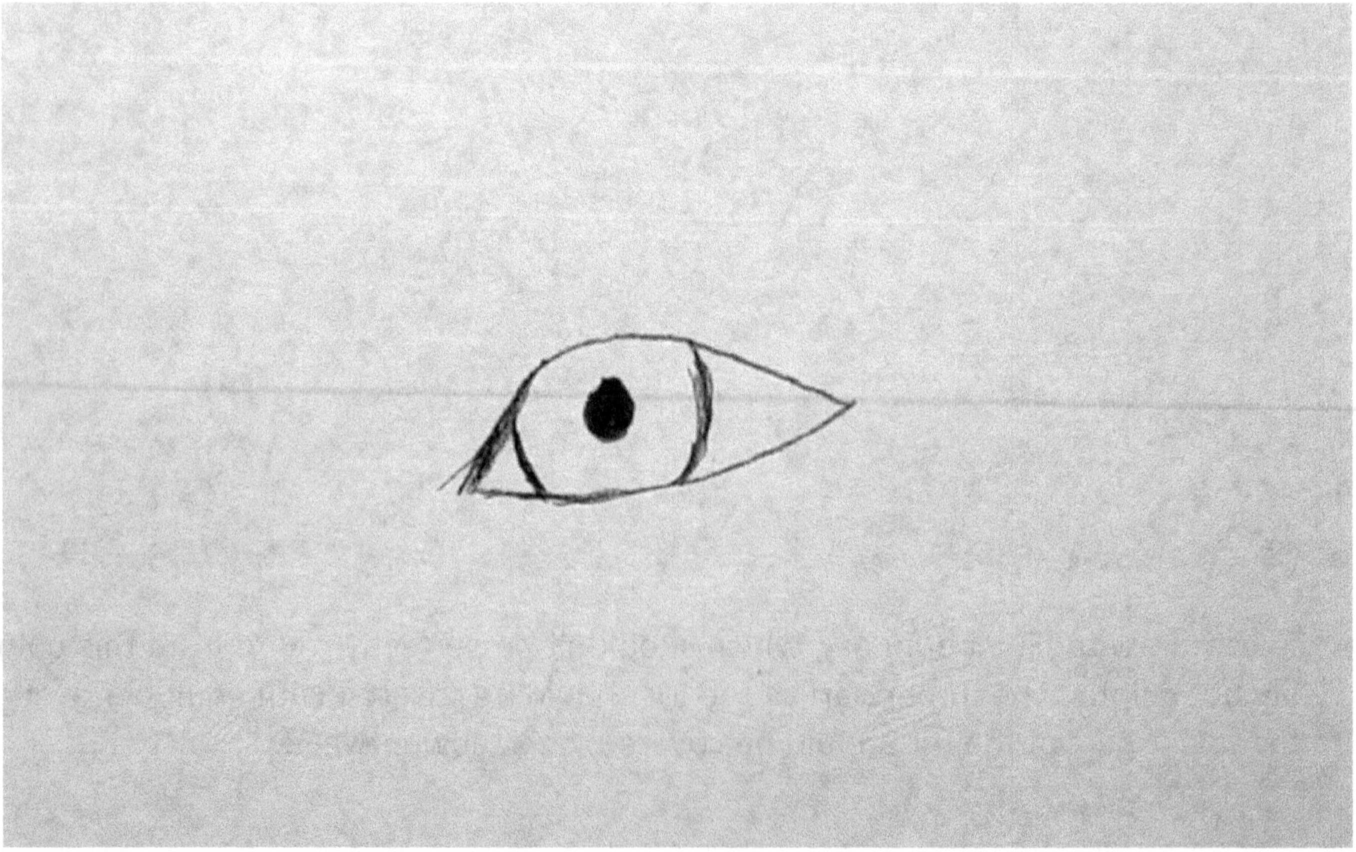

Now that we have determined the position of the iris boundary, we can improve on the outline of the upper and the lower eyelids.

In the following image, you can see that I have darkened the eyelids all around and drawn them a bit deeper than my initial outline.

Also, create the shadow that the upper eyelid casts over the iris, as shown in the next picture.

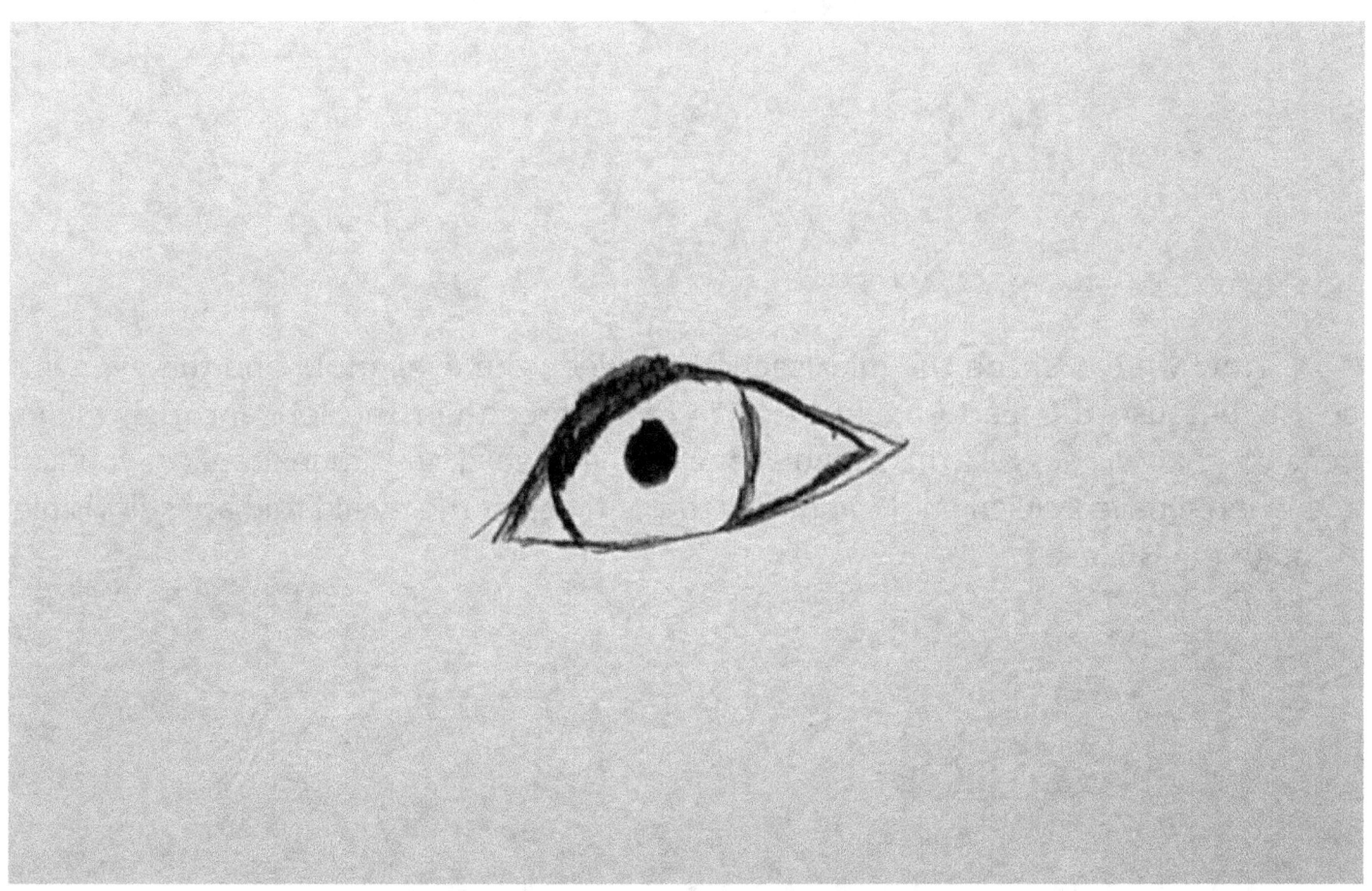

Here we can draw the eyelid fold, using an 8B. Just draw a curvy line parallel to the upper eyelid, and you can even draw a tinier one in between as I did.

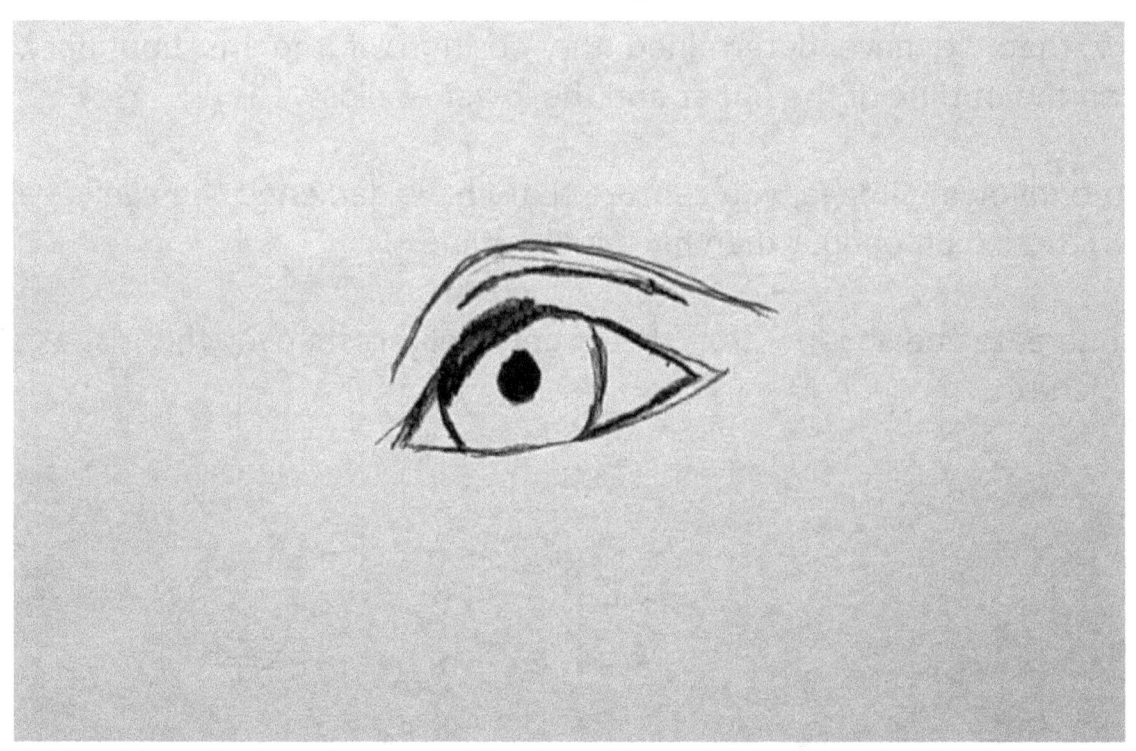

Now we can shade the mid- section between the eyelid fold and the eye with an HB because this part should be slightly brighter than the left and right sides because that will suggest the round shape of the eyeball. In the next image, you can see where I have applied an HB and how the outlines of the eyelid fold are still visible through the HB layer.

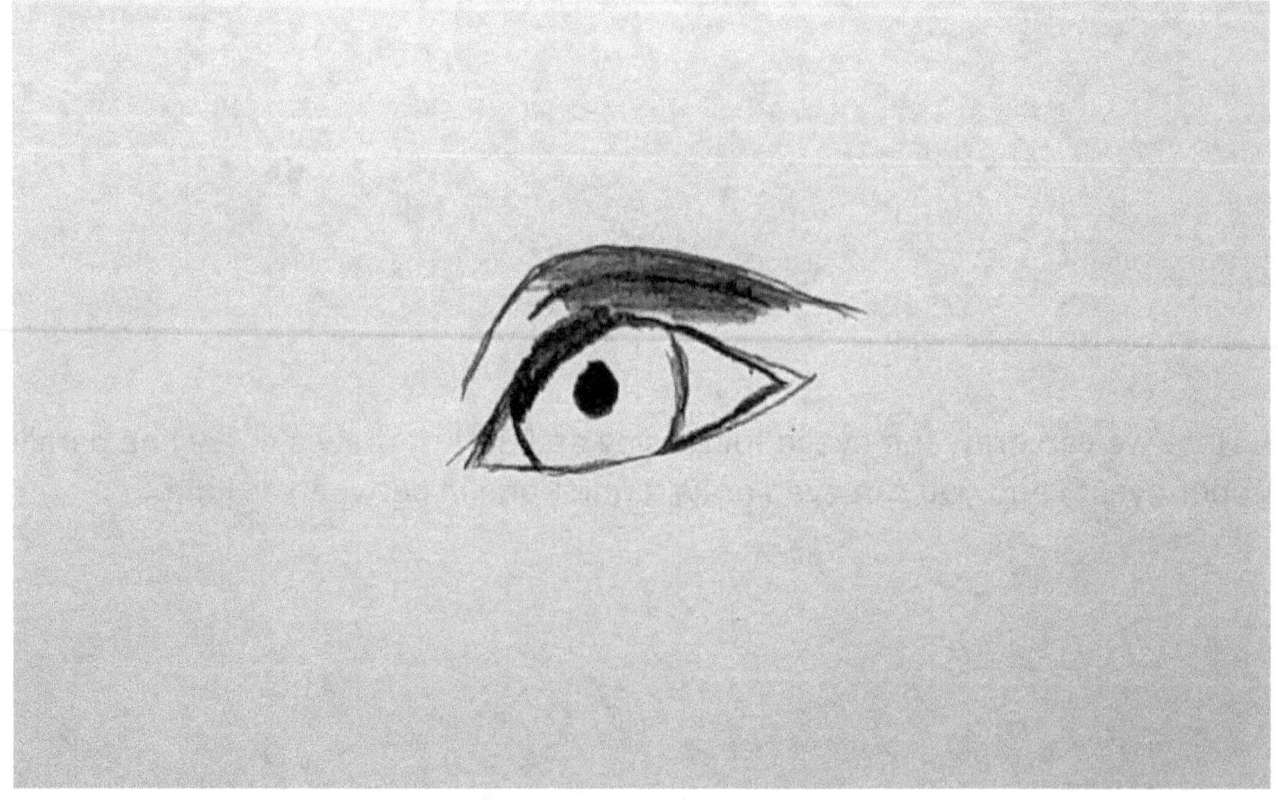

Let's use an 8B again to cover the skin between the eyelid fold and the eye on the left and right sides. They have to be much darker than the mid-area so that the skin over the eyelid ball can appear round.

I have imagined my light source coming from the top, and that's why I want the eyeball to be the brightest in the middle.

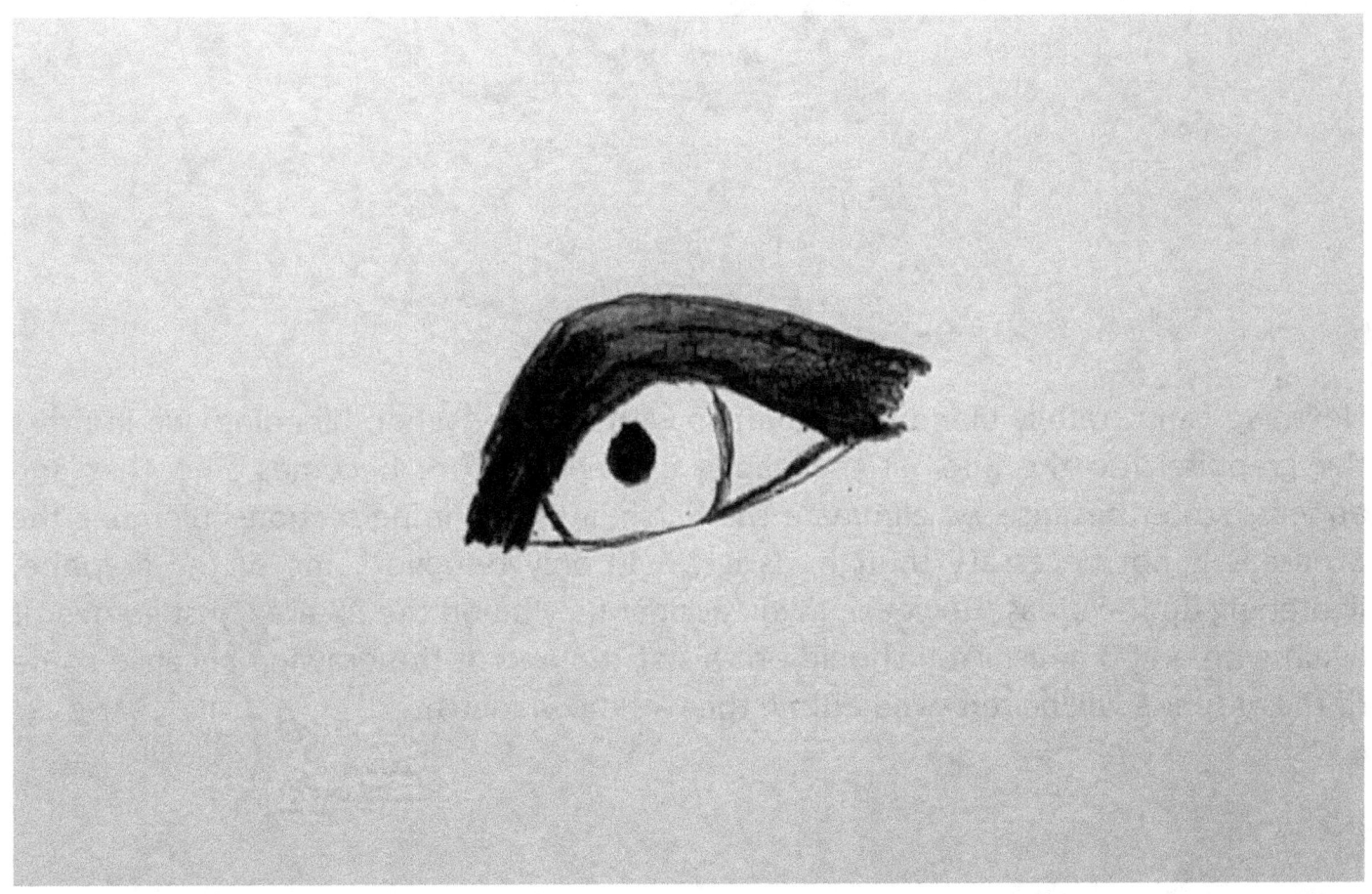

Using an HB, cover the large area under the eye, as shown in the following picture. Here also, under the left and the right side of the eye, the lower eyelid should be a bit darker than in the middle.

Then darken the thickness of the lower eyelid with an 8B, and cover the tear duct completely, using the same pencil, or any other very dark pencil.

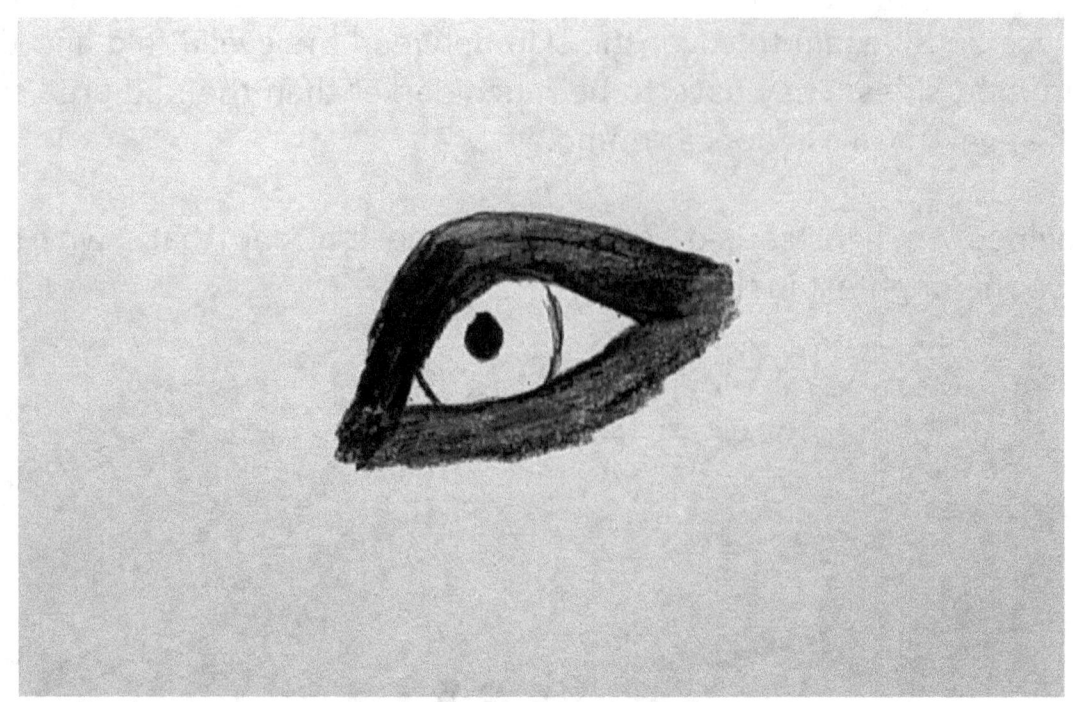

Next, we can carefully blend the HB areas with a Q-tip. When blending, we impress the graphite into the fiber of the paper, and the texture becomes smoother and appears softer because we eliminate the harsh lines and imperfections. Blending the 8B areas is not necessary though, as it would only remove some of the graphite, lightening up the areas. However, if you accidentally blend the 8B area, just go over it again with an 8B pencil. You should do this at the end of the drawing because some of the graphite will be removed during the workflow anyway.

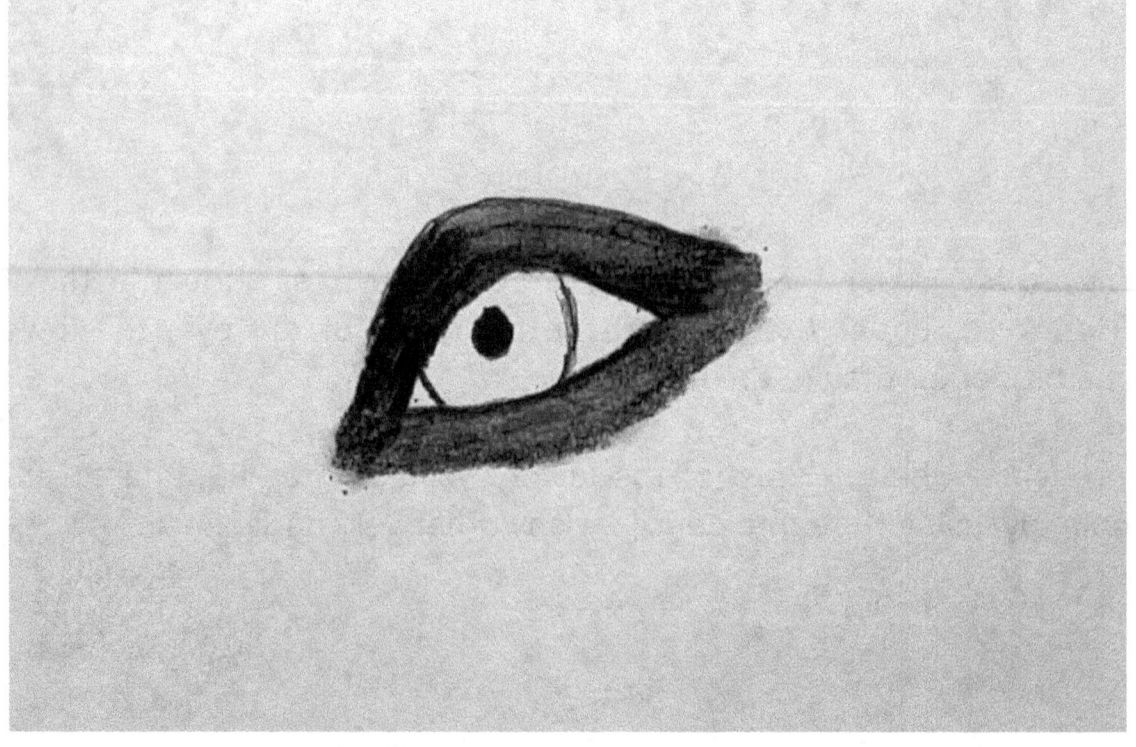

Now we can draw the iris. I use a 5H for the iris and I draw the spokes that radiate from the very center of the pupil. You can change the pressure on your 5H pencil to create some patterns.

Draw the spokes between the pupil and the iris boundary and, of course, the iris should be much brighter in the lower area, much darker in the upper area, and absolutely dark under the upper eyelid. That's why I'm using an 8B in the upper area of the iris, and an HB in between these two shades, keeping the strokes light as I draw from the center of the pupil.

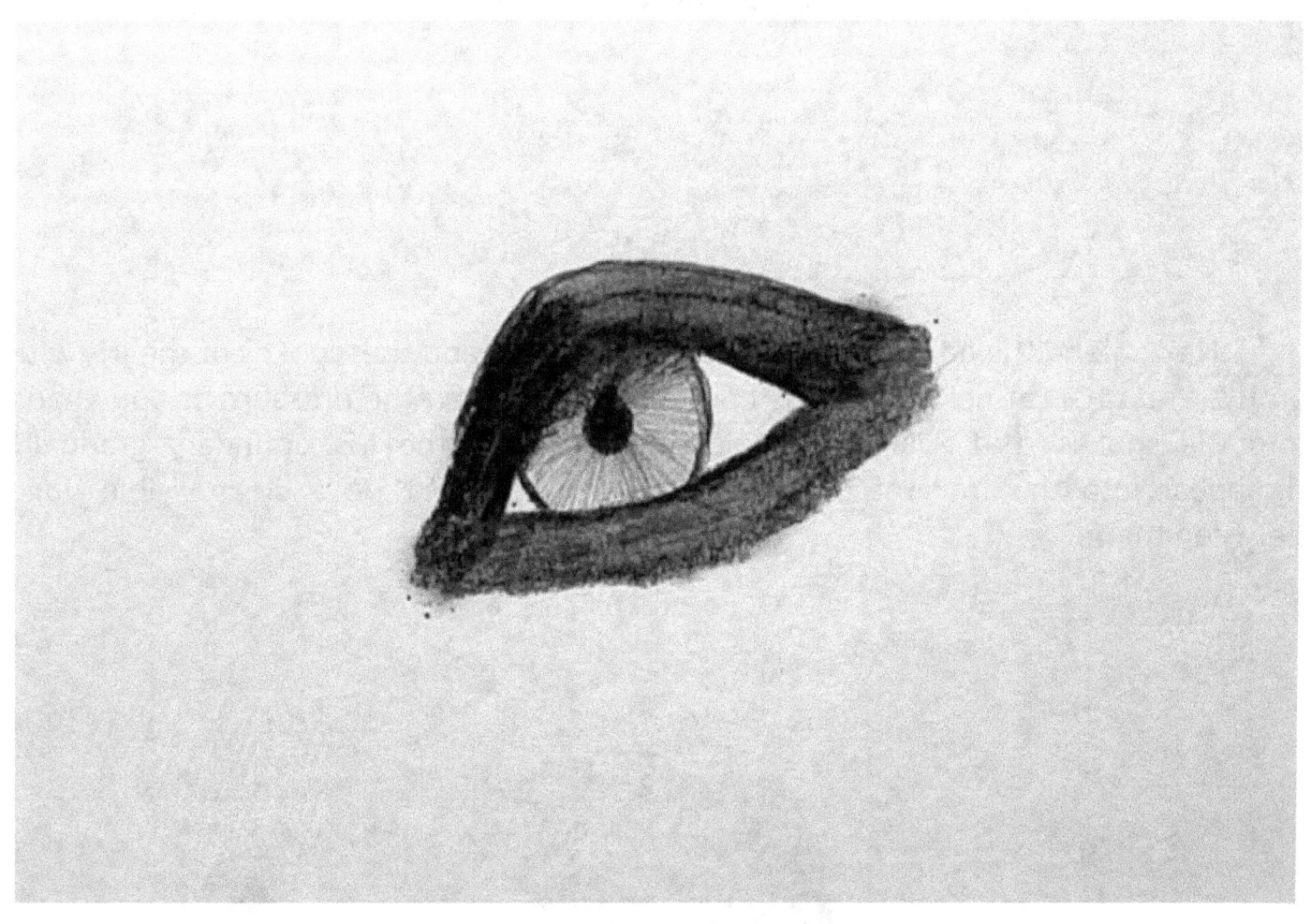

Carefully blend the iris with a Q-tip. Try not to go over the sclera or over the pupil.

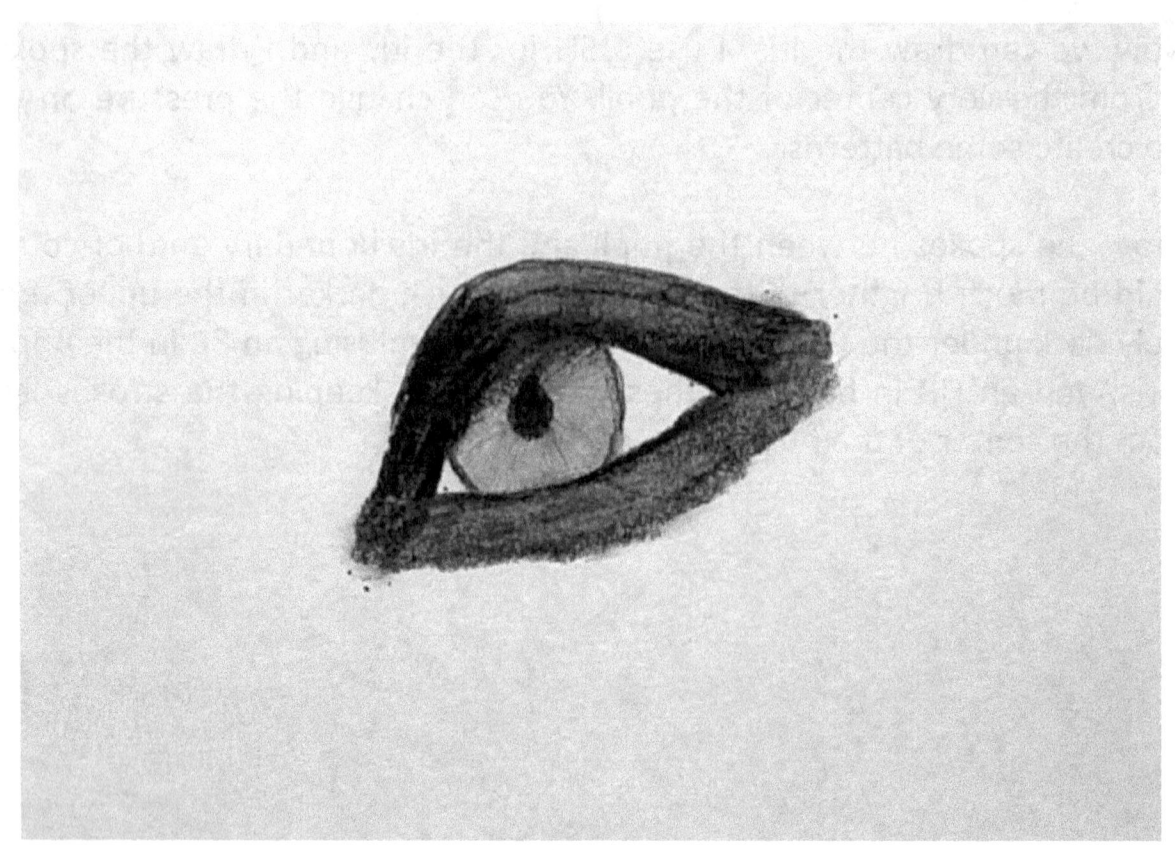

Next, blend the edge between the iris boundary and the spokes of the iris with an HB. Press harder next to the iris boundary and lighten the pressure as you shade into the spokes. The goal is to make the shade of the iris boundary gradually disappear into the tone of the spokes. There shouldn't be a clear visible edge between them.

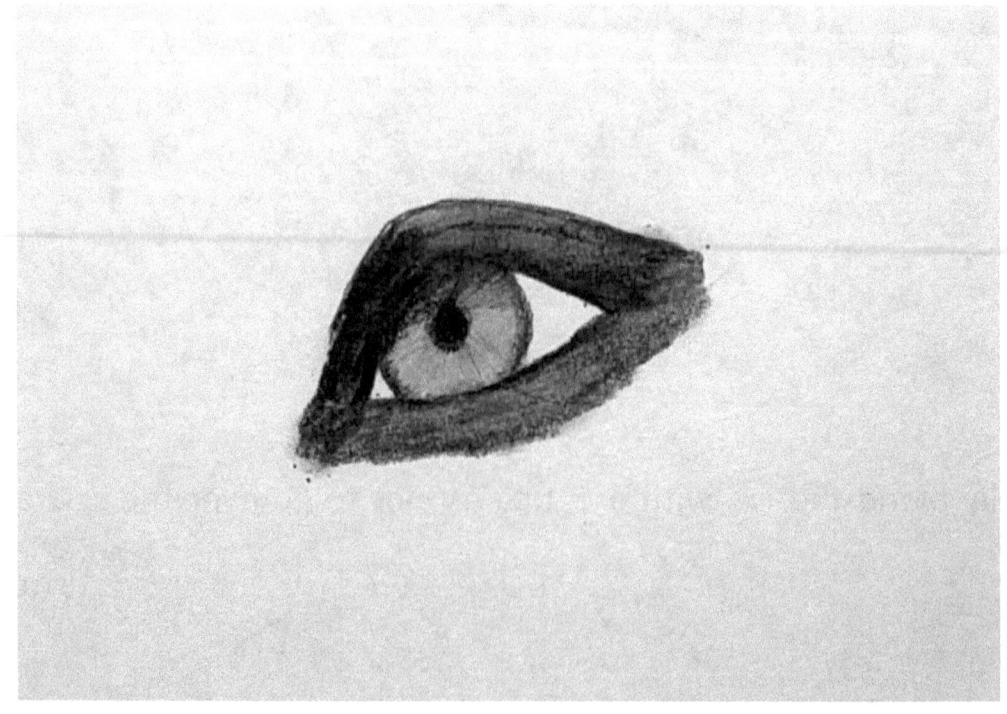

Start shading the sclera (the whites of the eye) on the right side with a 3H. We have to create a shadow that is cast by the upper eyelid over the sclera. The sclera shouldn't stay white, and although sometimes it can be totally white next to the iris boundary, the rest should always be shaded.

We should shade the sclera just the way we shaded the sphere because the eyeball has a round shape and we have to suggest it by shading the sclera. In the next image, you can see the area that I have shaded with a 3H.

Also, add some details with an HB, such as tiny eyelashes that grow downwards and the shadow that they cast over the sclera.

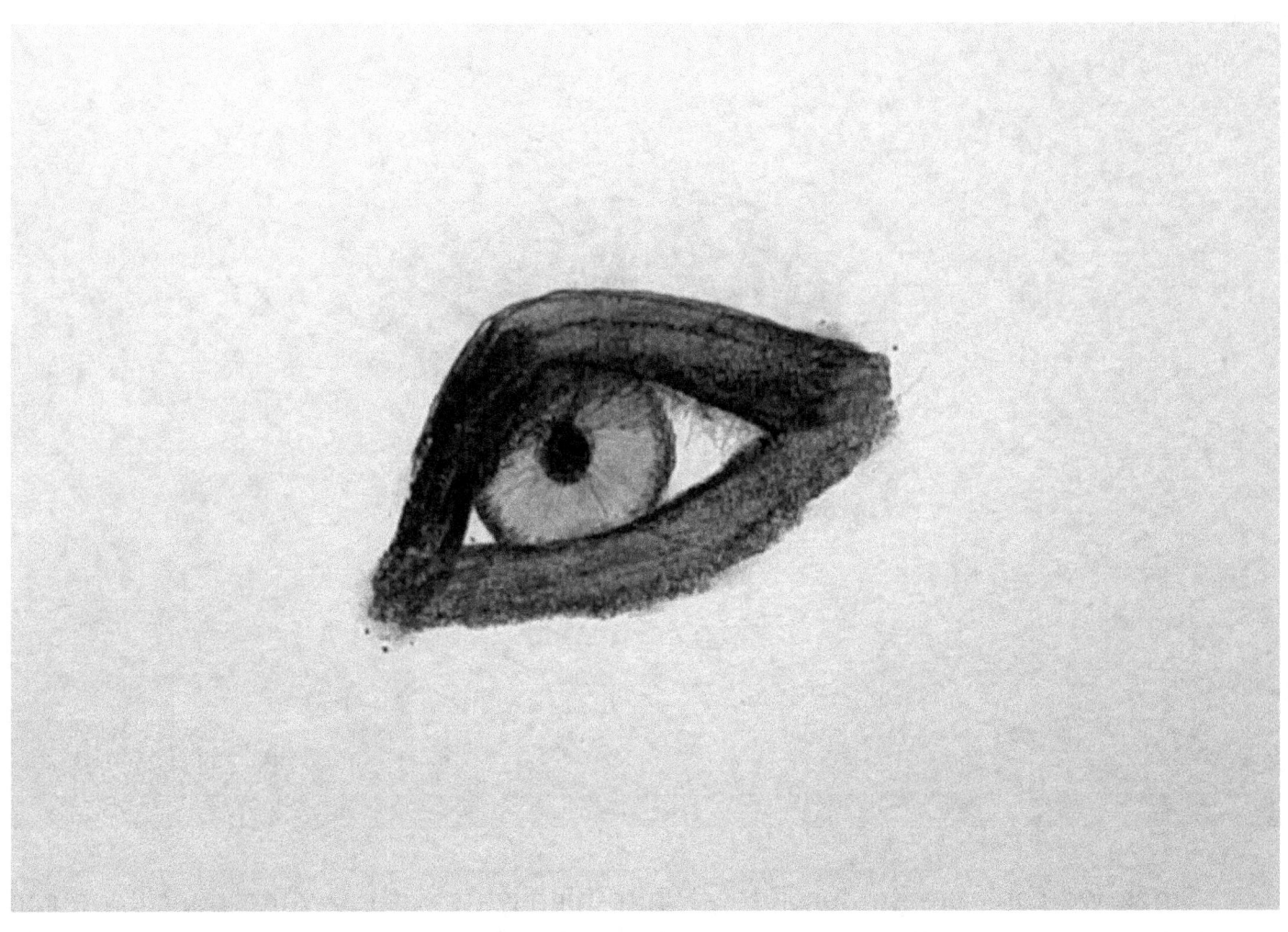

Now we can color the sclera next to the iris with a white pencil, and also create some highlights over the iris and even over the iris boundary. The white colored pencil can be easily applied over dark graphite pencils. Try to make the white colored pencil gradually disappear into the tone of the paper, somewhere in the middle of the sclera on the right side.

After having shaded the sclera, you can draw more eyelashes that grow downwards using an 8B. Analyze the next image to understand what I want to explain.

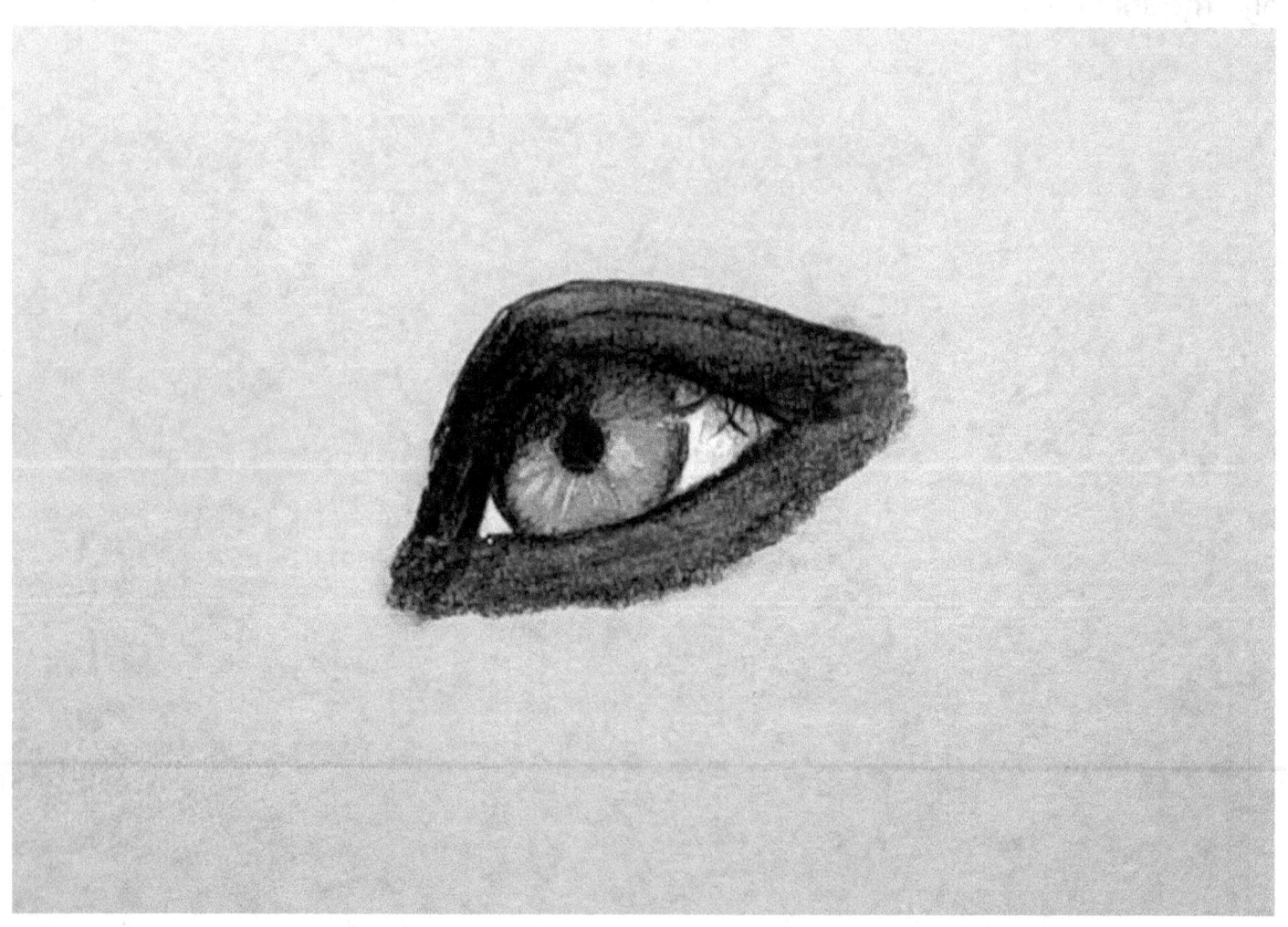

Since we can't create absolutely white highlights with a white pencil, we can now use an opaque white marker or a white ink gel pen over the iris and the pupil. When you apply the dot with a white marker, tap it with your finger to make the edges of the dot blurry.

Create the highlights wherever you want over the iris and the pupil. If you use the white marker by Uni Posca, you will be able to eliminate the highlights with your nail or with any other pencil while it's wet and even when it dries up.

Blend the edges of the highlights that you've created with a white marker or with a white colored pencil.

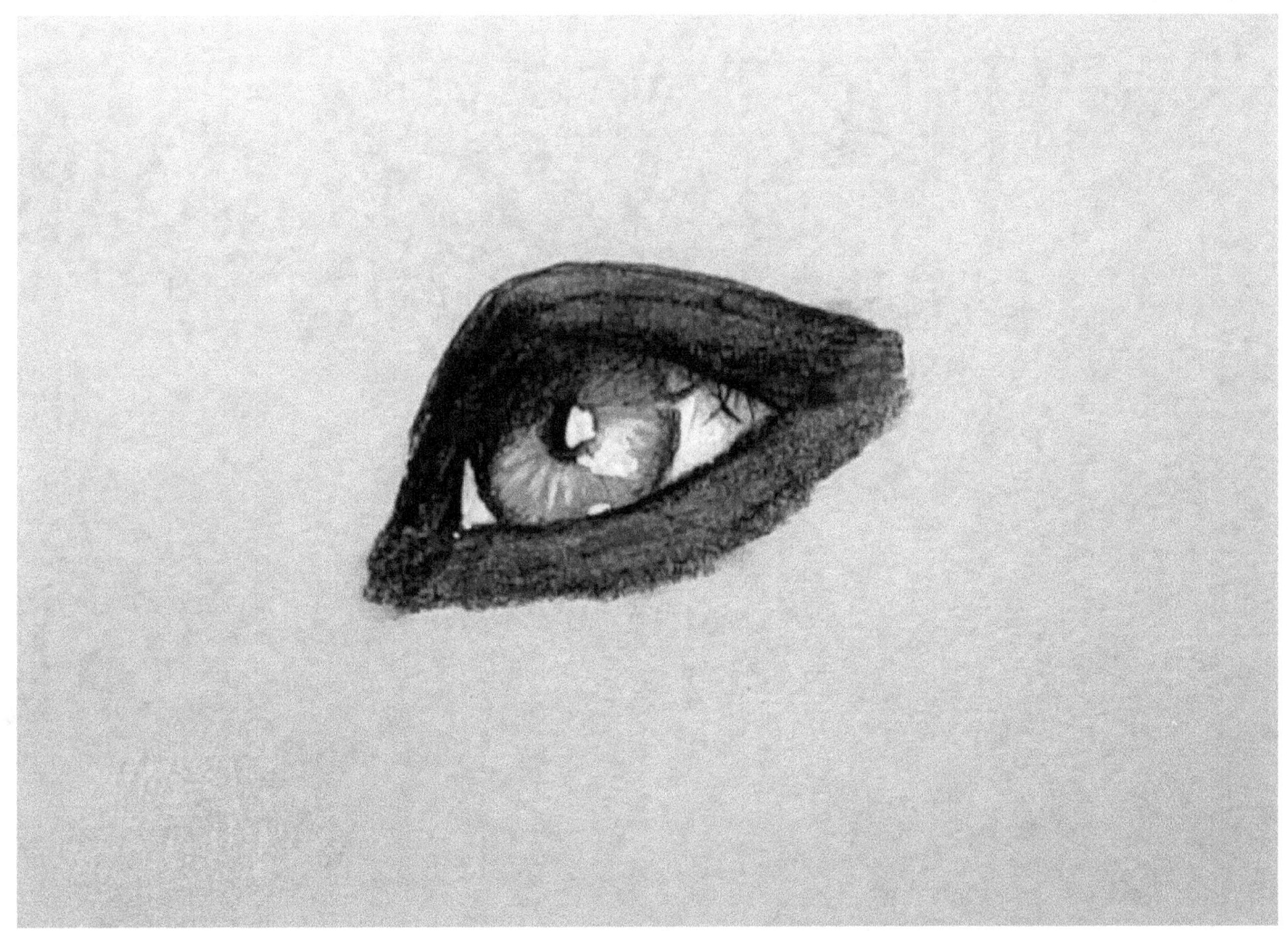

Before we draw the eyelashes, we should shade the skin above the eye. However, before that, let's draw the eyebrows so that we can shade the skin between the eye and the eyebrow. Also, the drawing of an eye looks better with an eyebrow.

I use an HB pencil to draw the eyebrow so that I can always darken it if I want. You can use any other shade of graphite; you don't have to use an HB. You can also draw any shape of the eyebrow. I wanted to draw a typical female arched eyebrow, and of course, we have to draw the strokes in the direction of the hair's growth.

Don't forget that the eyebrow should be somewhat shorter in a three-quarter point of view.

Analyze the next image to see where I have placed the eyebrow and notice the direction of the strokes that I have drawn. You can also check up on some reference photos or your own eyebrows in the mirror to see in which direction you have to draw the hairs.

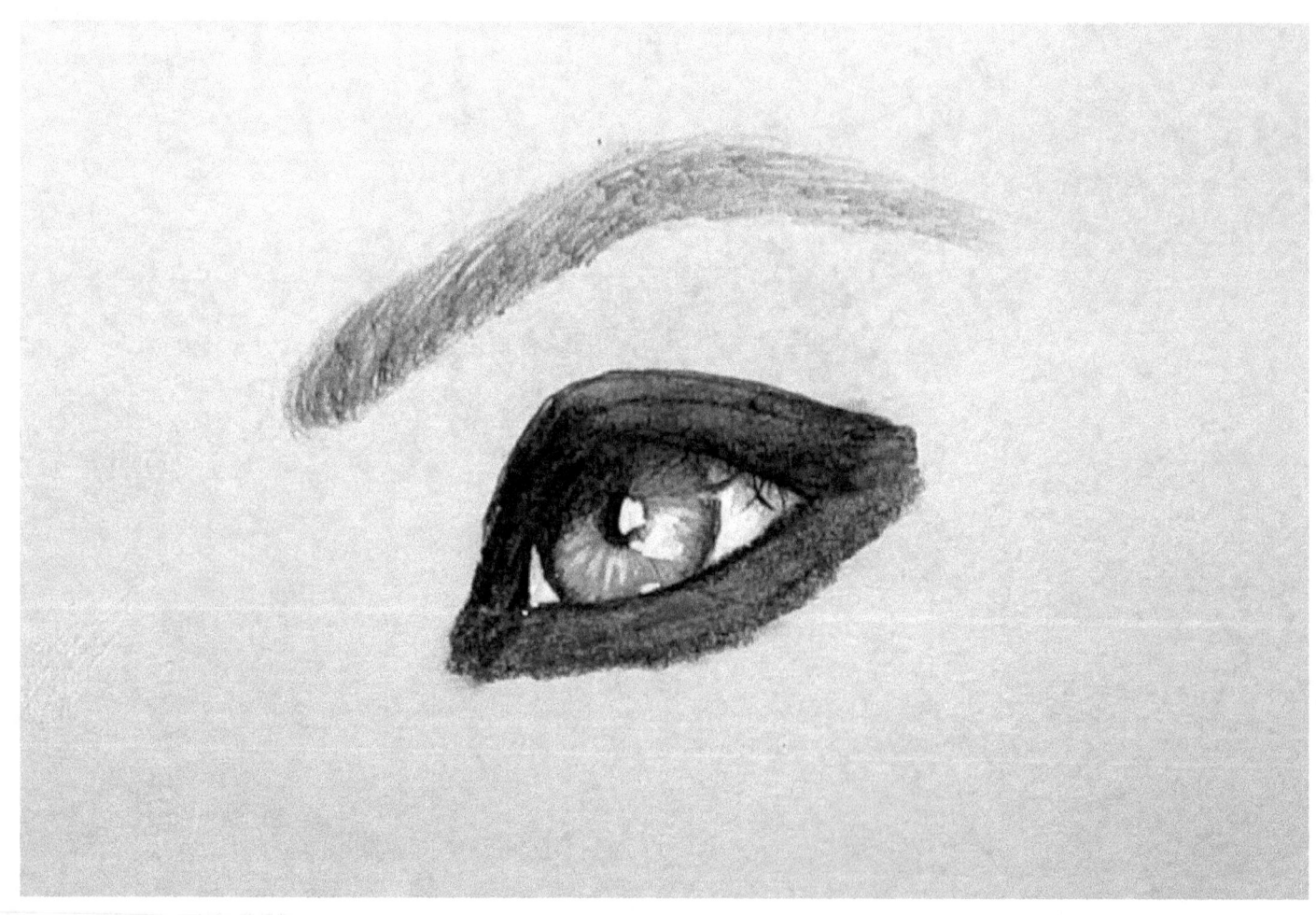

Blend the eyebrow with a Q-tip to impress the graphite into the paper and to make the hairs appear soft.

Compare the previous and the next image to see the difference that blending makes.

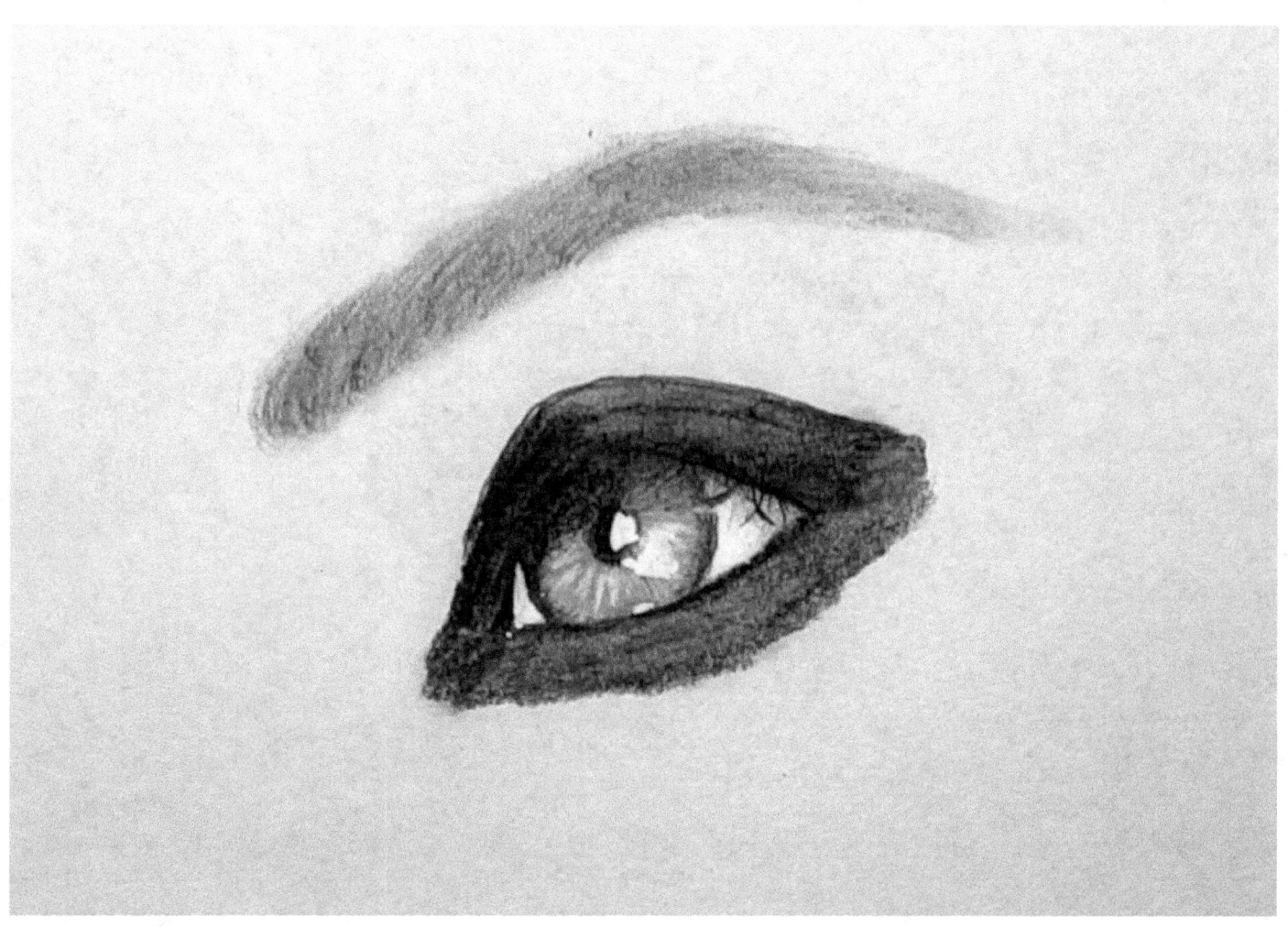

Next, use an 8B to draw the hairs that are found under the brow ridge because they get less light, and darken the eyebrows on the right side as well, next to the temple. This way, we will make the section in the middle brighter, which will suggest the roundness of the head.

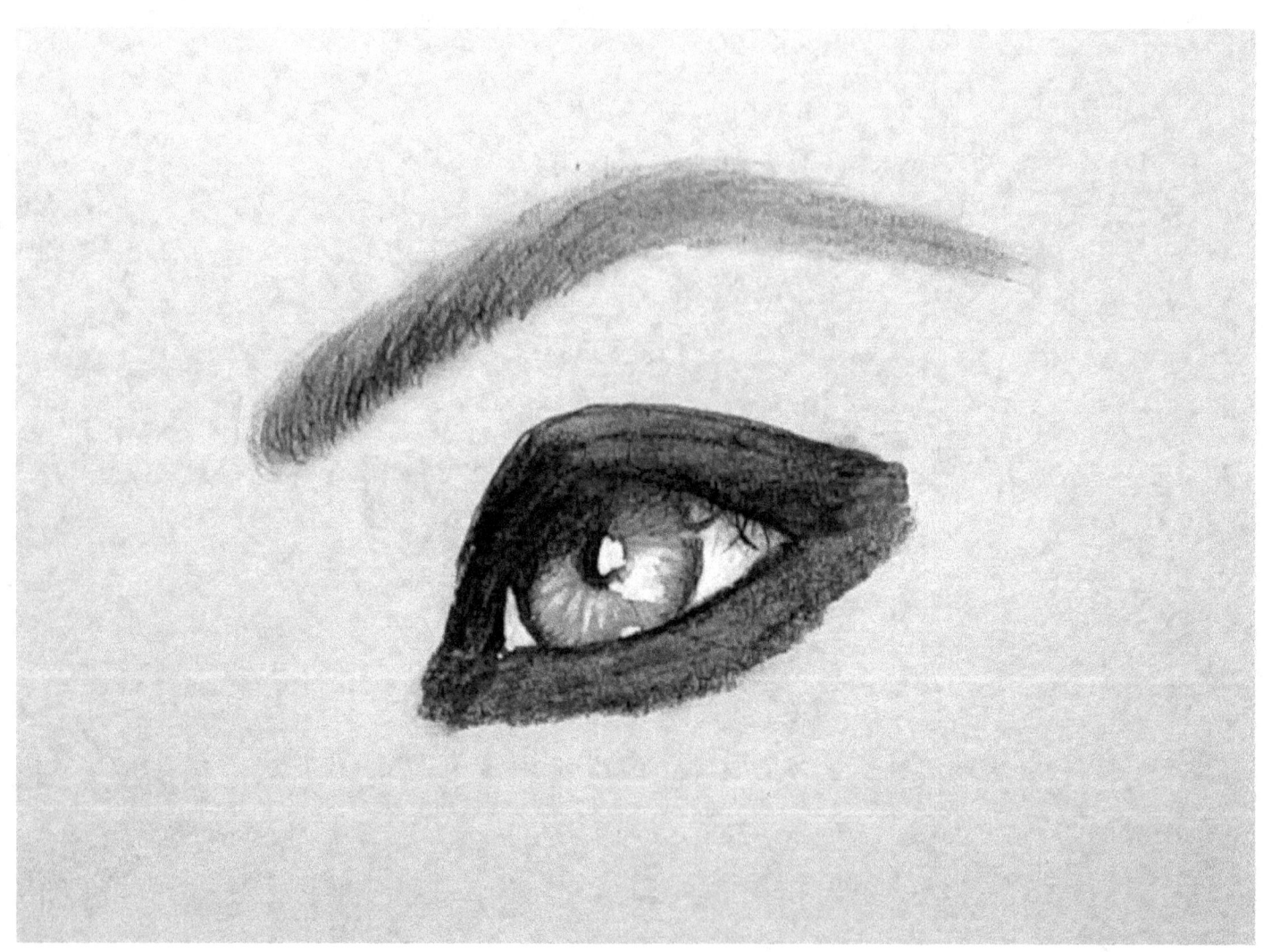

Now we can start shading the skin using a 2h and circular motions, the circulism technique, which means that you have to apply overlapping circles to create a smooth texture.

Shade the bridge of the nose a little, especially the right side of the nose so that the sunken area between the nose and the eye can be highlighted. Take a look at the next image to see which area I have shaded and how a 2H looks when applied over the grey paper. You can choose a brighter or darker shade.

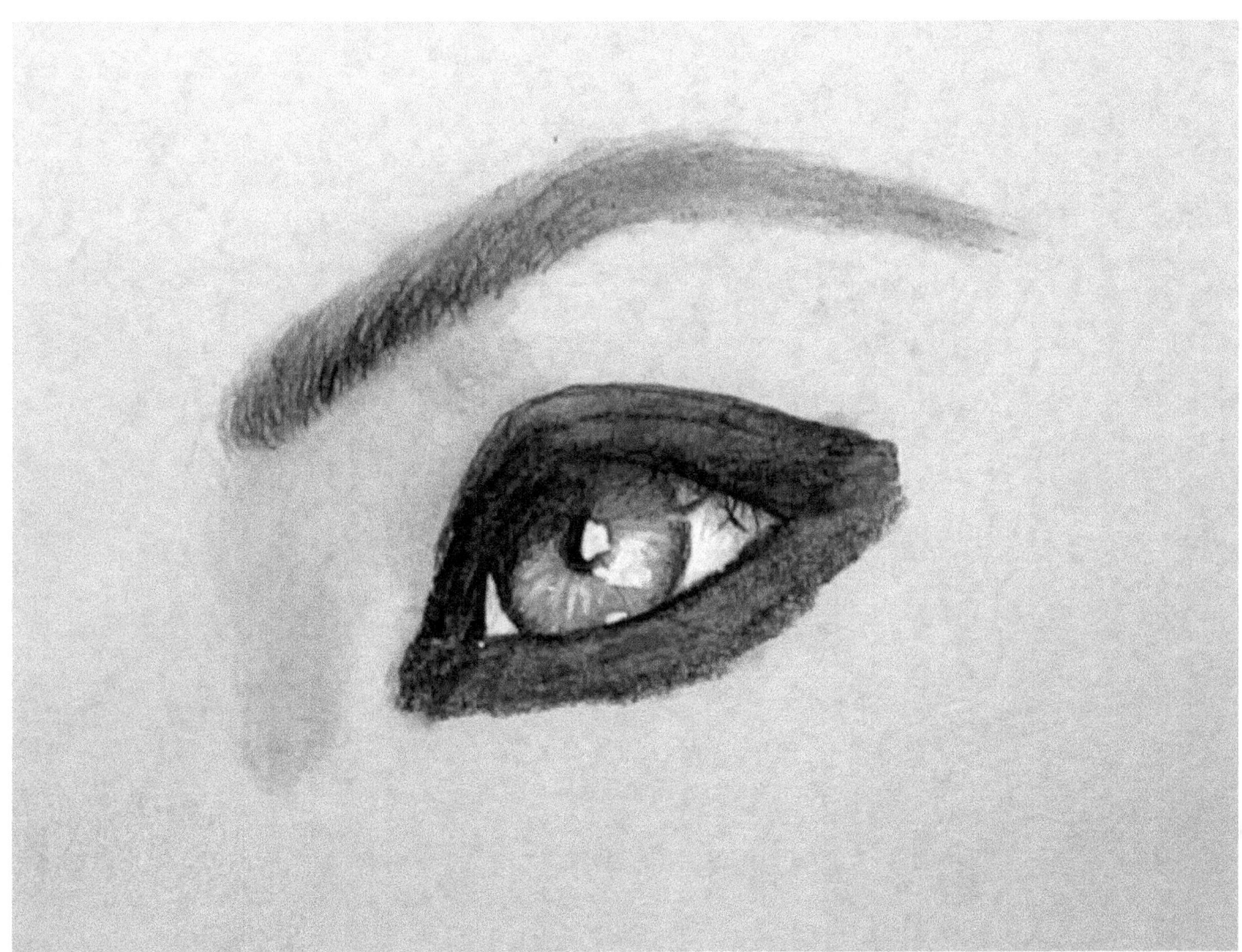

Blend this shaded area carefully with a Q-tip, and you will see how it becomes darker after blending. So, count on this alteration when choosing pencils for the skin and other textures.

Still using a Q-tip, shade the crease (the part between the eyelid fold and the eyebrow). Start by blending the eyelid fold and blend upwards, releasing the pressure. It is important to create a gradient transition from shadow to highlight. Also, shade the skin on the right side of the eye, next to the temple, as shown in the following image.

Go all around and blend the edges of the HB areas.

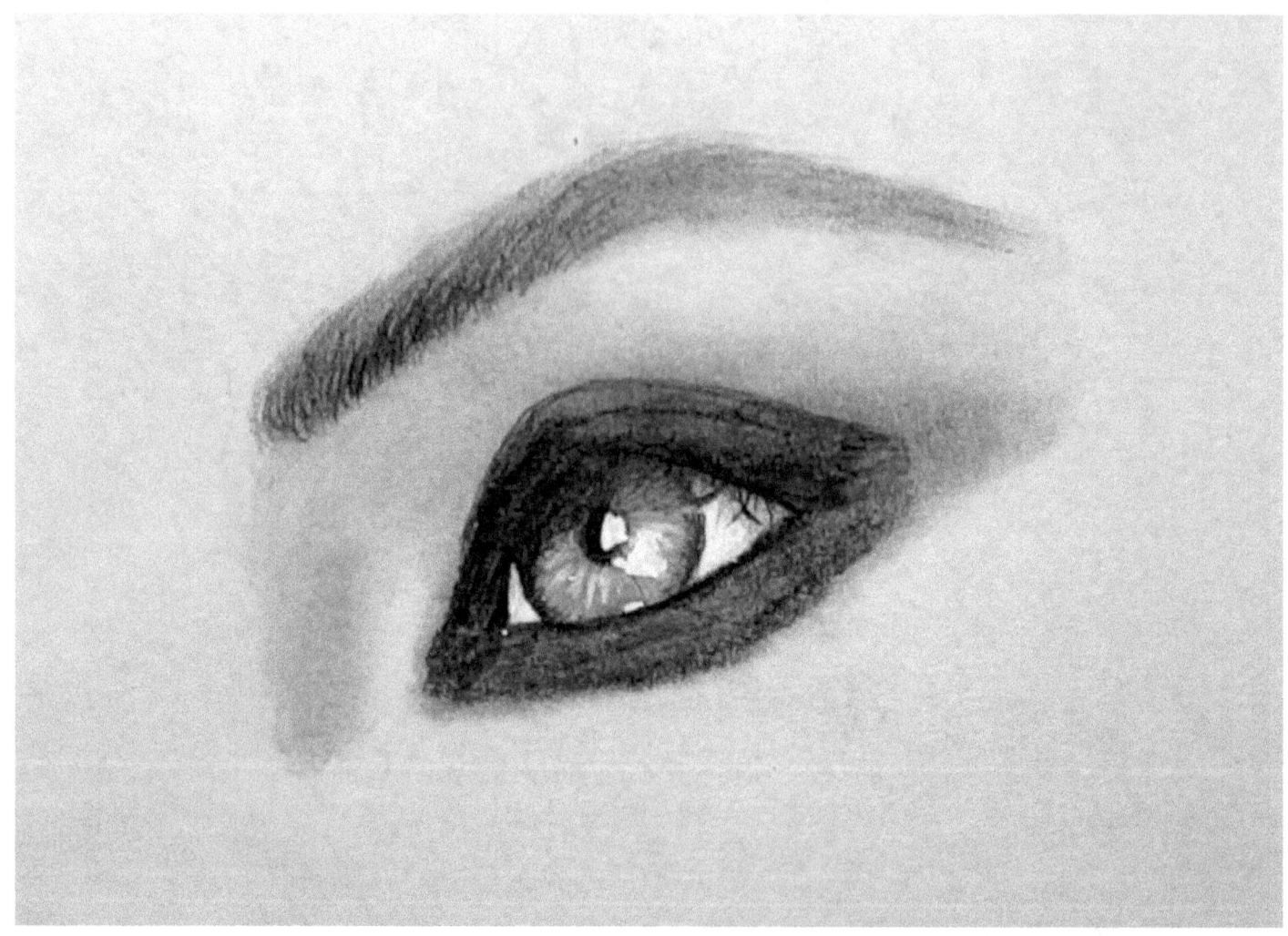

However, shading with a Q-tip won't be enough. We have to shade right above the eyelid fold with an HB using circular motions and pressing less and less as we work away from the eyelid fold, or actually upwards to create a gradient transition of the grey tones. The grey shade should gradually become brighter as we shade towards the highlight. So, the different shades should not have a clear edge between them, but they should flow into each other gradually.

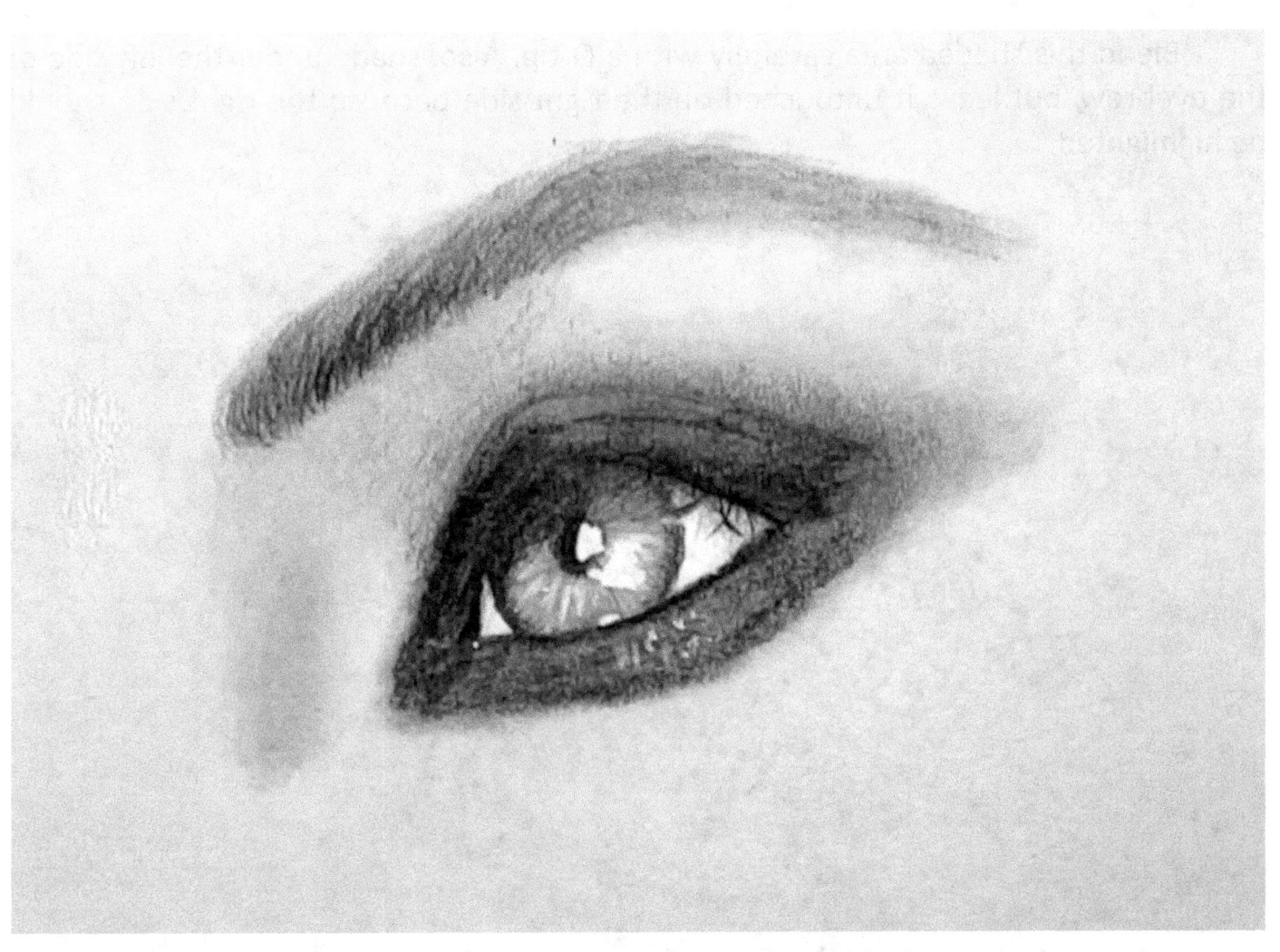

Tip

You need to find inspiration for drawing. Just as writers experience the writing block, artists can have the same creative block or so-called "art block." To avoid it happening to you, make a list of the things you want to draw and, when you're stuck, check that list. I even have a "to-draw" folder in my PC, containing reference photos and drawing ideas. When I don't know what to draw, I just take a look at those images, get inspired, and I am ready to start working on my next drawing.

Blend this shaded area carefully with a Q-tip. Also, shade under the left side of the eyebrow, but leave it untouched on the right side because the right side should be highlighted.

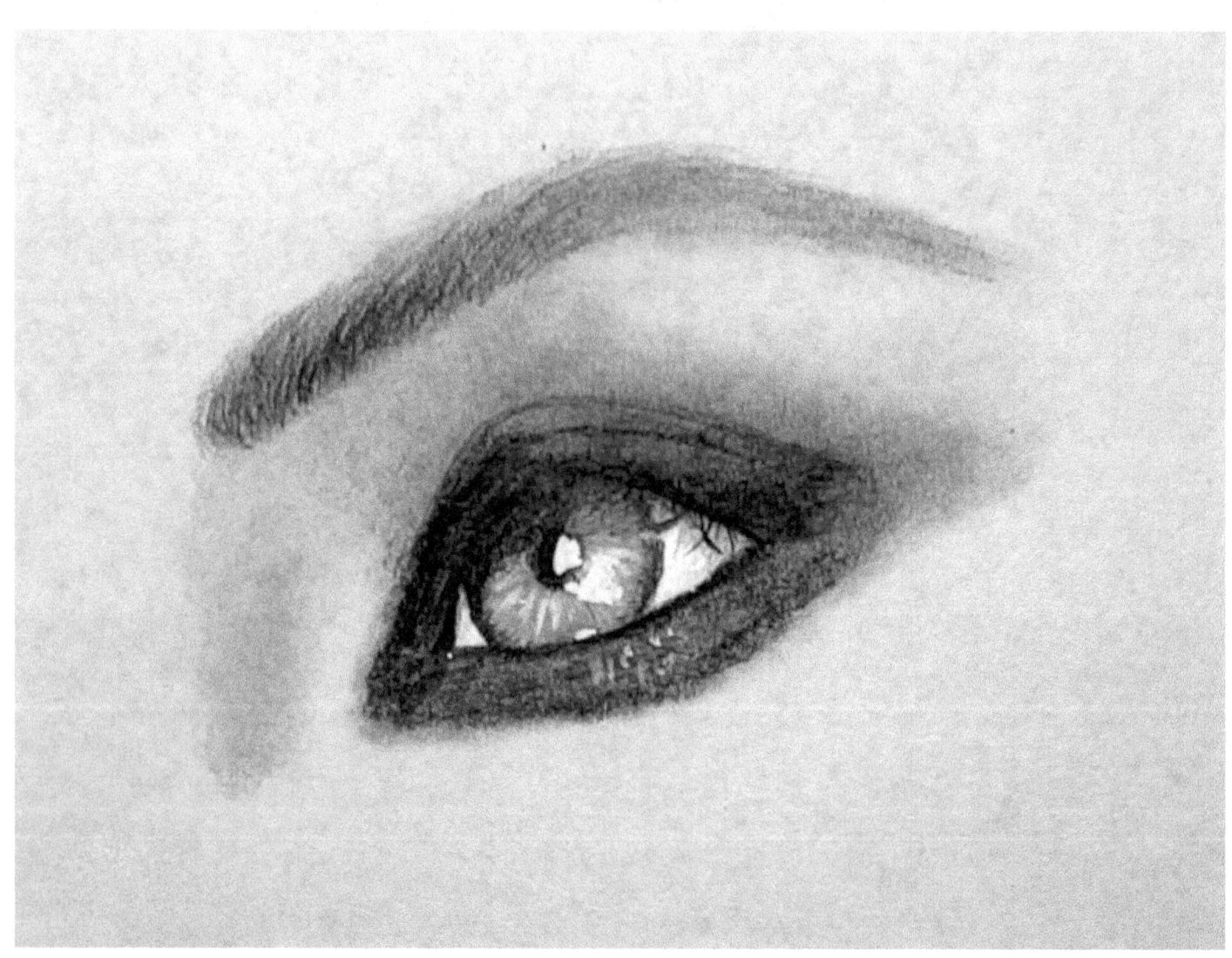

We can now create the highlight with a white colored pencil. Shade the skin right under the peaked part of the eyebrow, over the protruding bone, which is the brow ridge. Press harder over the middle of the highlight and lighten the pressure on your white pencil as you shade outward the highlight.

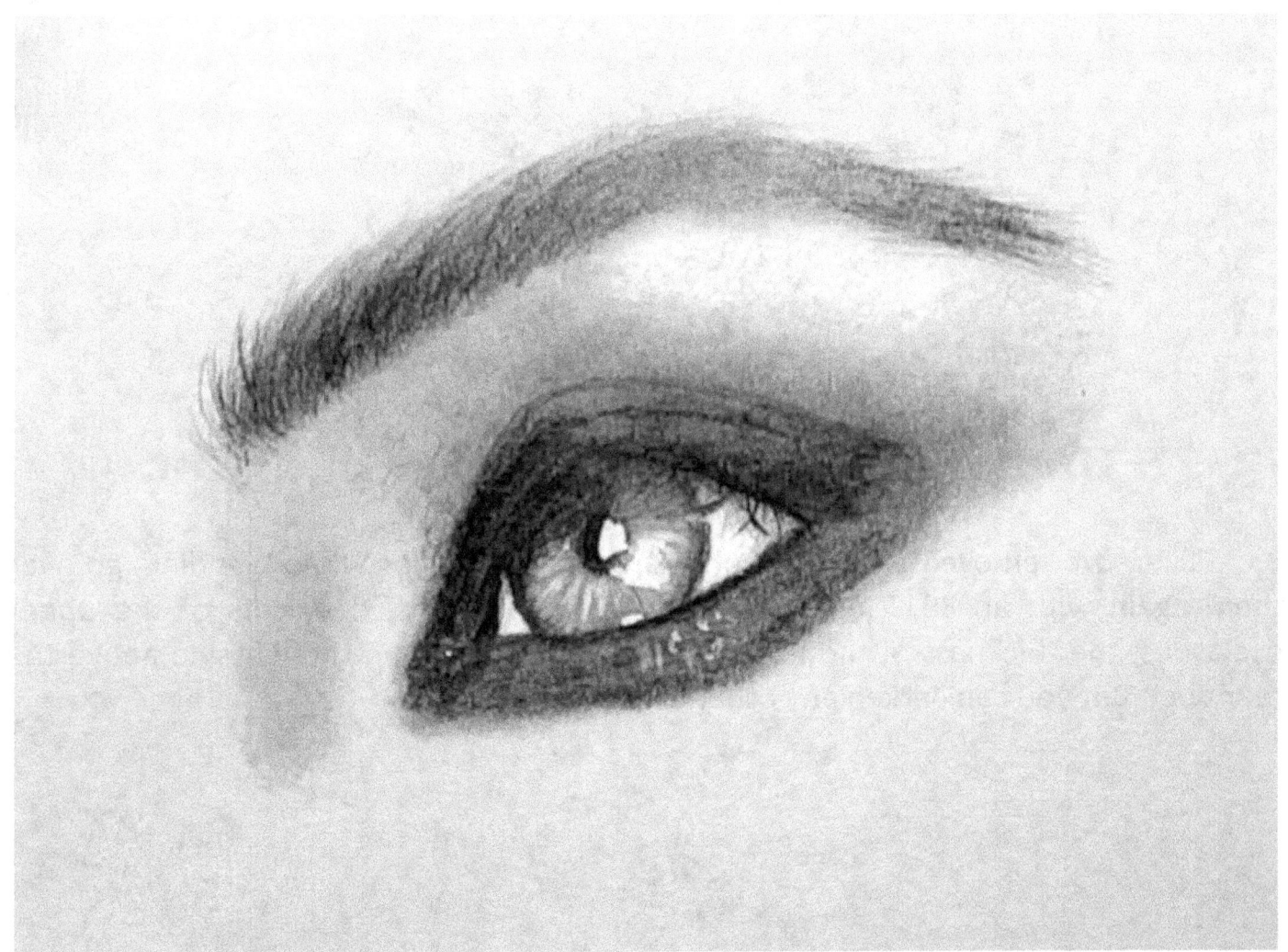

Now shade the area between this highlight and the temple with an HB. Use circular motions the entire time. This way, you will make the highlighted area even more prominent, and also because this section gets less light.

In this step, I went back to my eyebrow because I felt it was still too pale, and I wanted to darken it more with an HB. I also wanted to make the eyebrow darker so that a white colored pencil could be even more prominent. Now you can see the benefits of drawing on grey paper: the white areas pop and the eye is more striking.

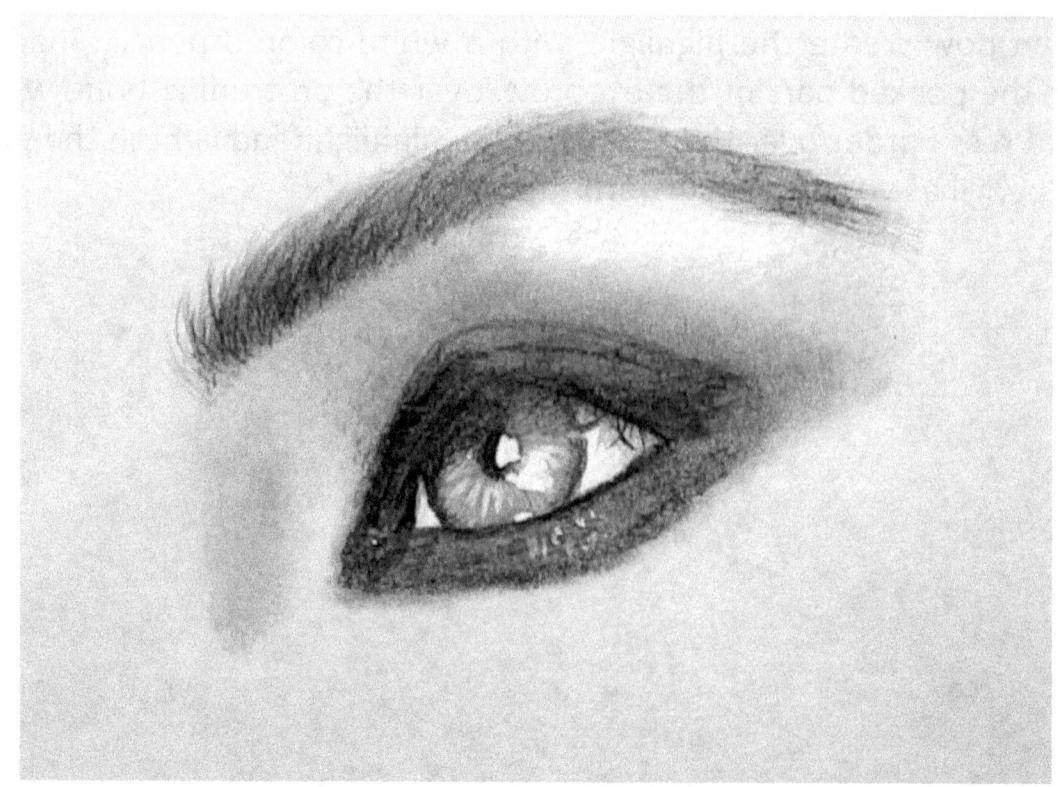

Since we removed a lot of graphite from the 8B areas when blending, go over them again with an 8B. These areas are the eyelid fold, the roots of the upper eyelashes, the thickness of the lower eyelid, and the skin on the left side above the tear duct. But you can darken any other area that you want.

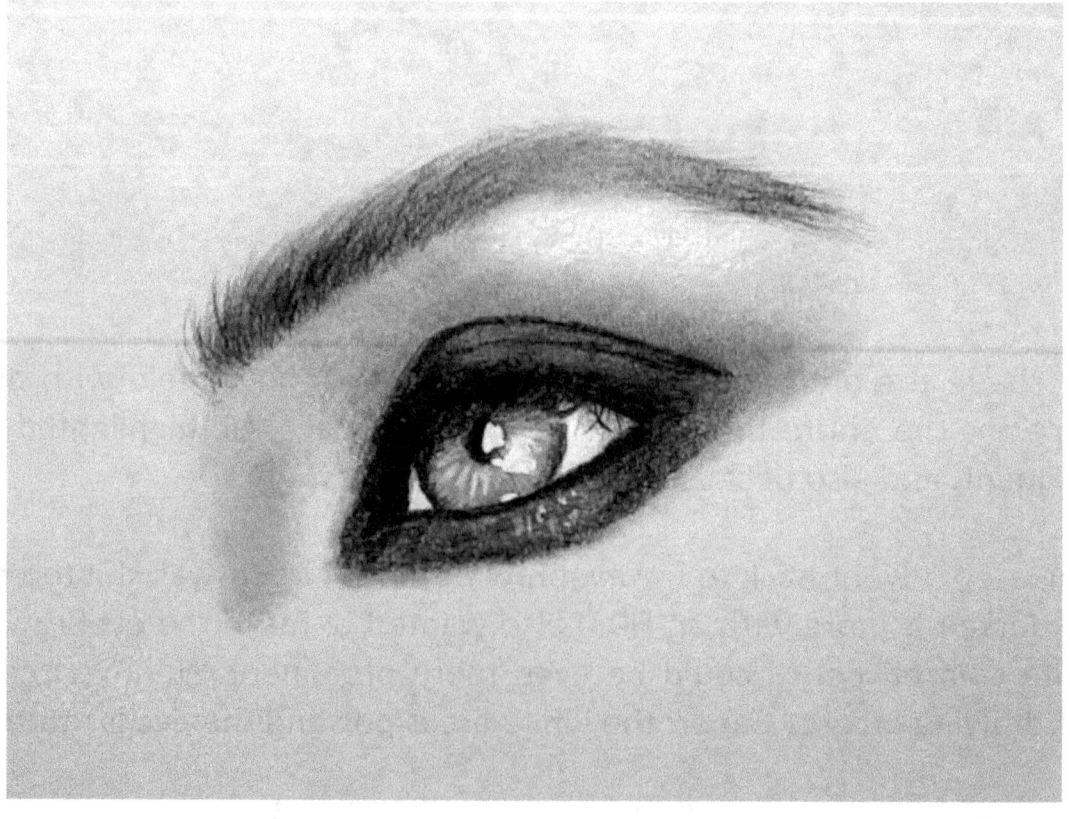

Next, blend the outer edges of the dark eyeshadow with the blending stump.

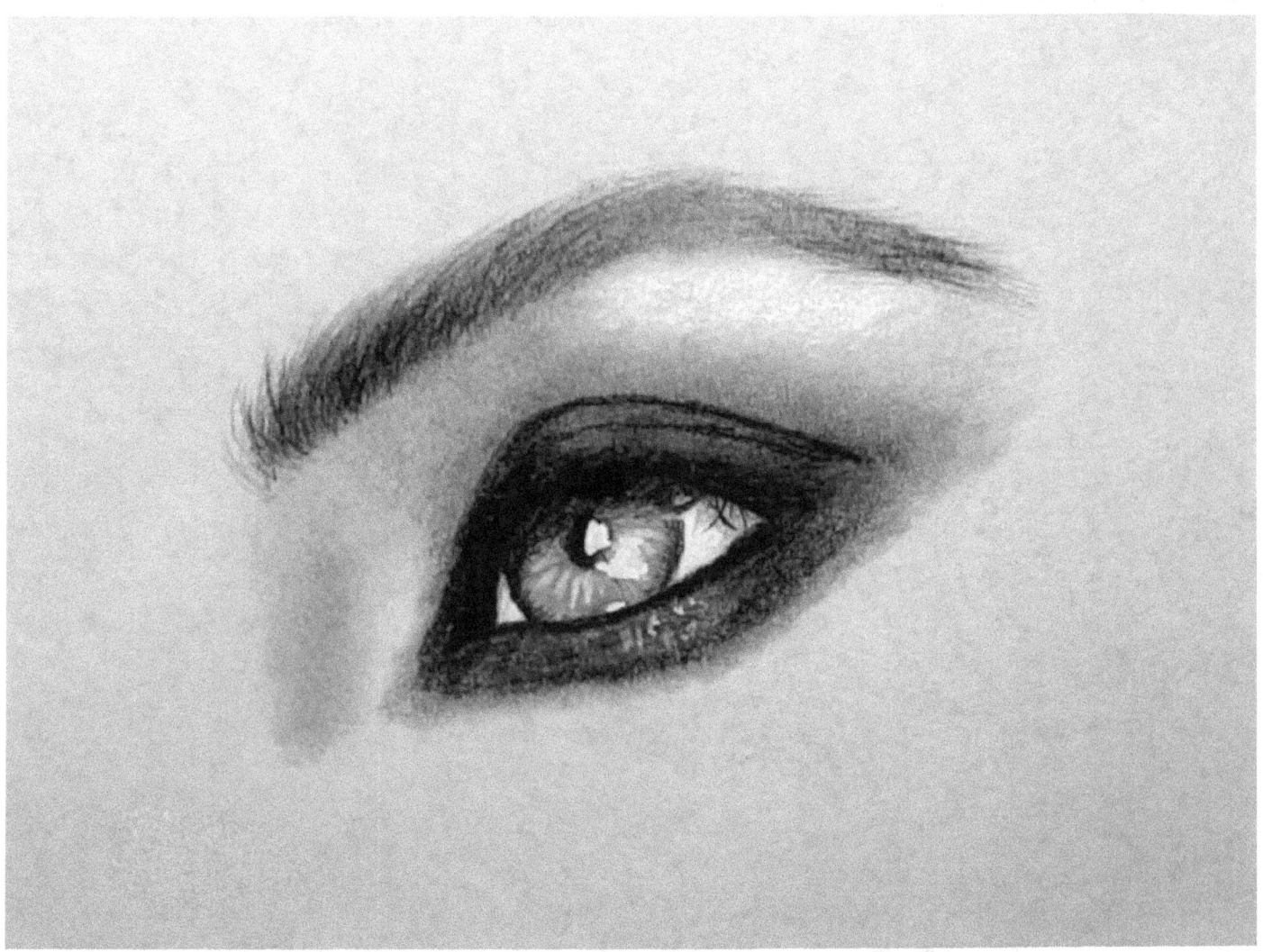

I have improved on the gradient transition above the eyelid fold because this area seemed to be too bright and I wanted to darken it with an HB and, as always, I blended it with a Q-tip.

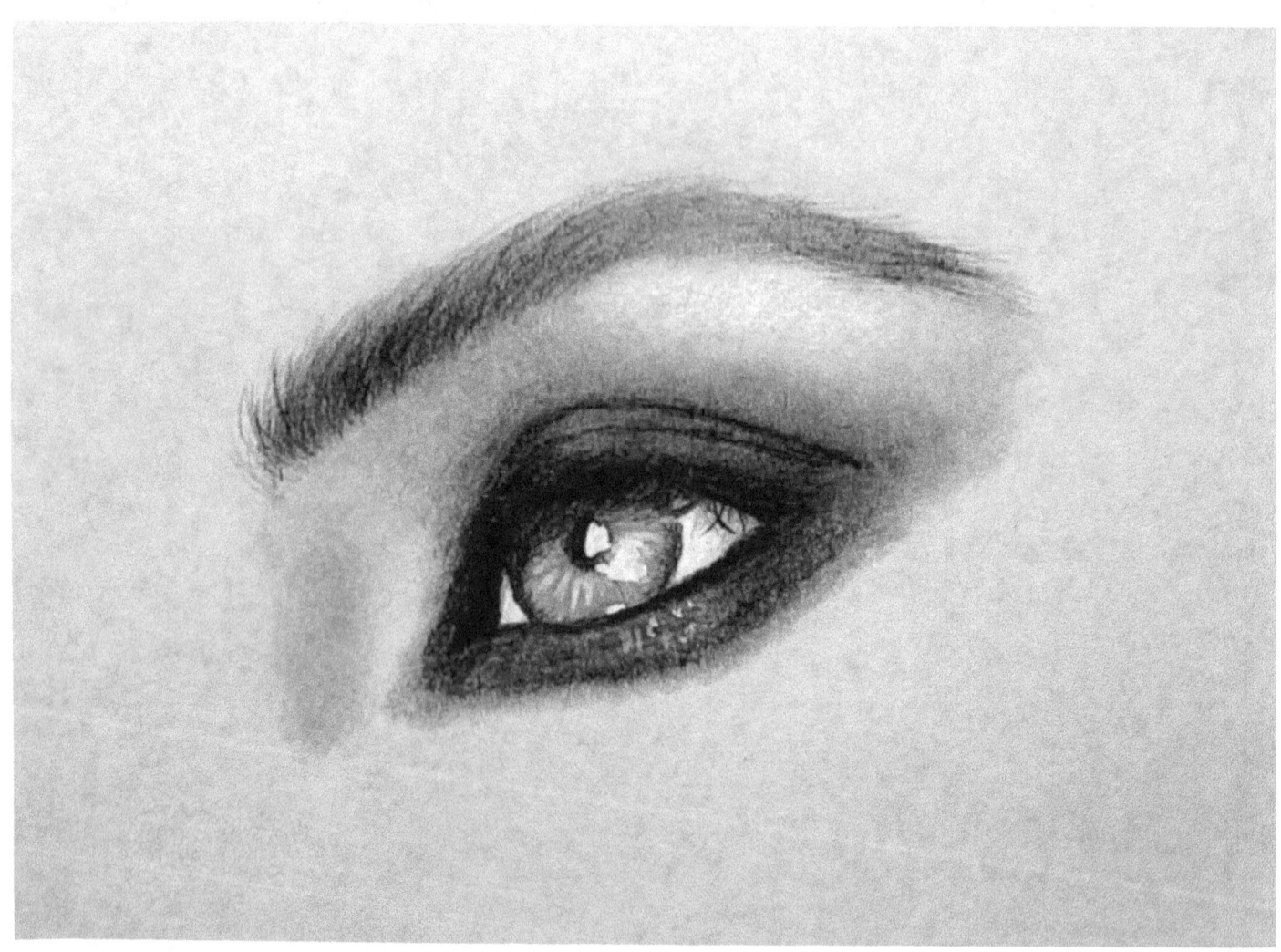

Finally, it's time for the eyelashes. I use an 8B for the eyelashes. We have to drive them with quick, confident strokes in one pass. I have drawn pretty long eyelashes because I want to draw fake eyelashes and those are much longer. In the next image, you can see the direction of the upper and the lower eyelashes.

I used an HB right above the tear duct because the eyelashes are pretty thin here.

The lower eyelashes are usually natural, but their ends can stick together when mascara is applied, so we have to draw them like this.

Blend the tops of the eyelashes with a blending stump.

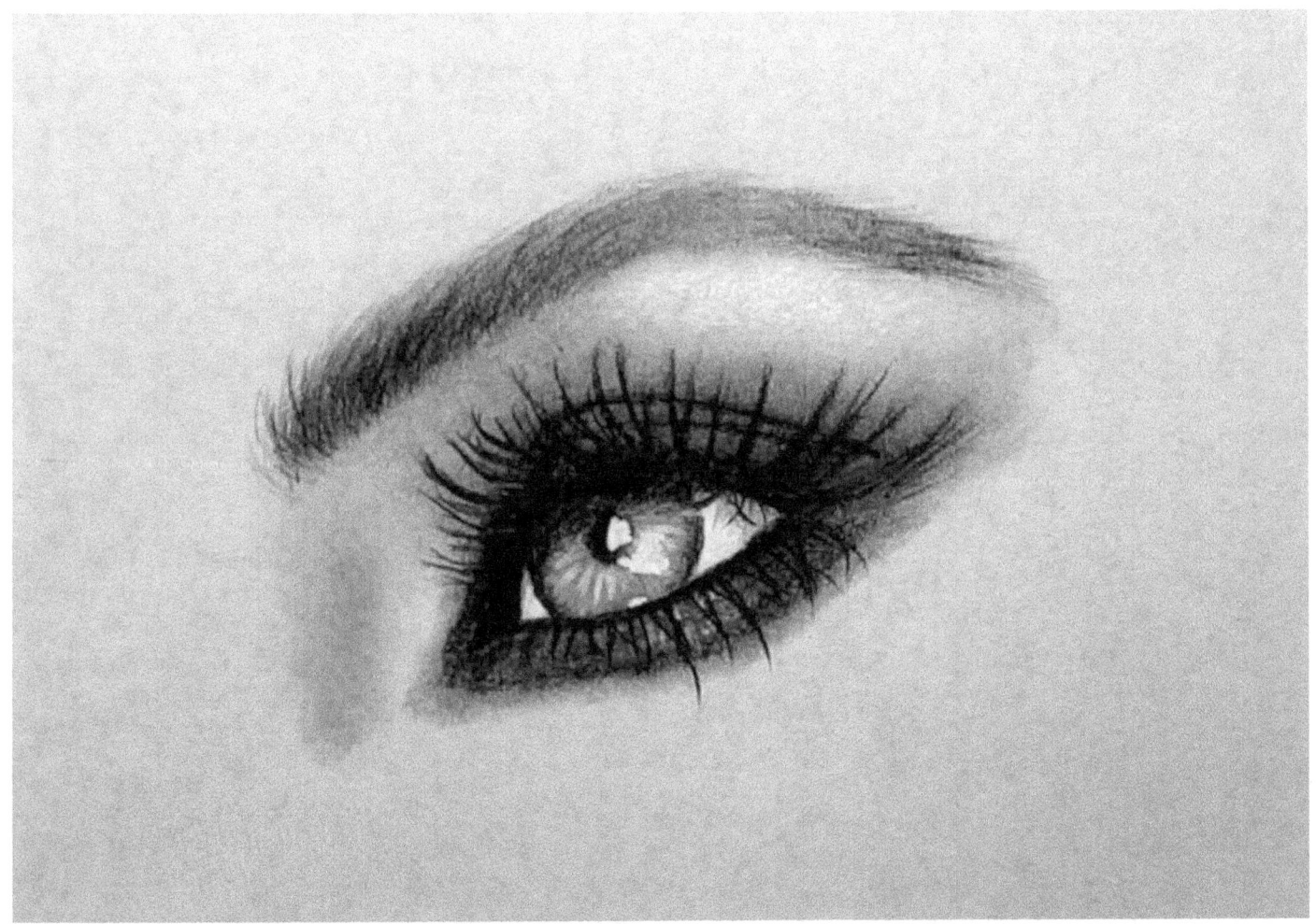

In this step, I shaded even more right above the eyelid fold with an HB, and I used a 2H above the HB in order to create the smooth gradient because the grey shade is darker right above the eyelid fold and it becomes brighter and brighter as we shade towards the highlight or upwards.

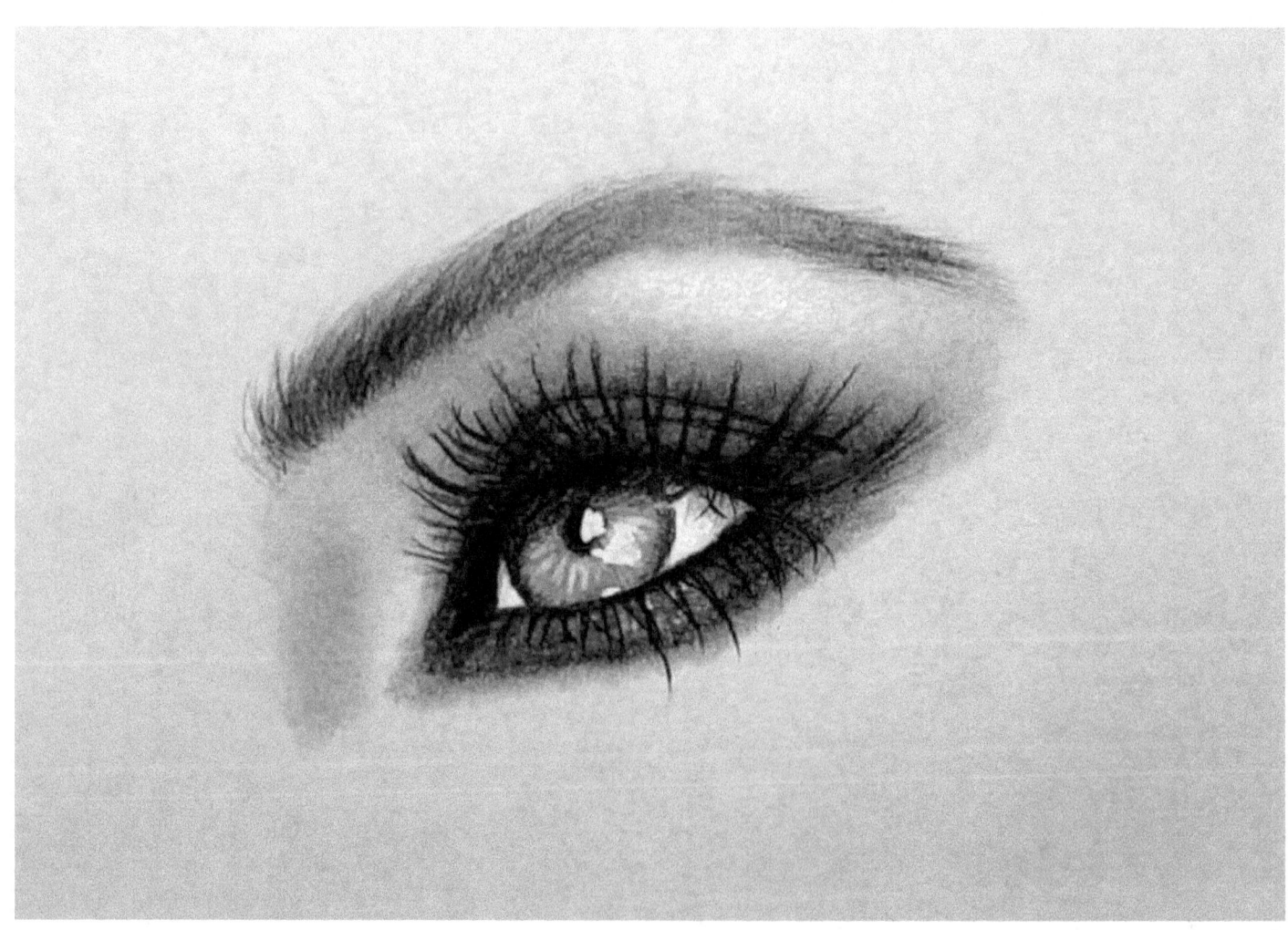

For the last step, we can use a gelly roll, a white ink gel pen, or a white marker. Create tiny dots somewhere in the middle of the lower and the upper eyelids because these areas are protruding and highlighted.

Also add some white dots over the sclera that you shaded right under the upper eyelid, and among the eyelashes that grow downwards.
If you think some dots are too white, simply go over them with a blending stump because some of them shouldn't seem too bright. The variety of the highlights and randomness of the created dots will add a lot to the realism.

Since makeup powder can shine even in sunken areas, add some white dots there too. Study the next image, the final drawing, to note where I have created the white dots.

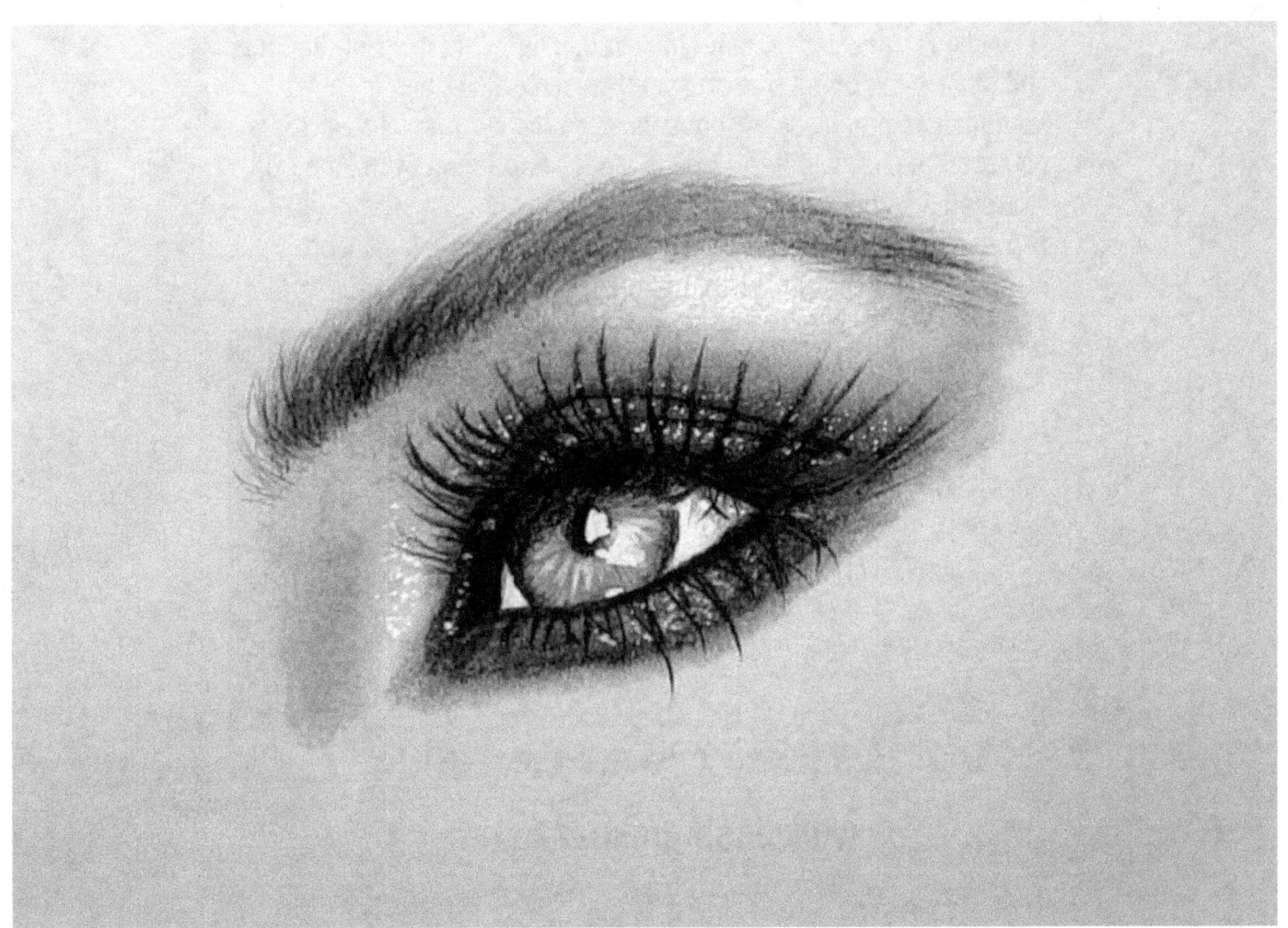

About the Author

Jasmina Susak is a self-taught, graphite and colored pencil artist, art teacher and author of more than 17 how-to-draw books. She specializes in creating photorealistic drawings of animals, people, superheroes and everyday objects.

Jasmina graduated and worked as a dressmaker for many years. Now she is a freelance, self-employed artist. It is her full-time job, and she's been doing it professionally since 2011.

Jasmina has hundreds of thousands of followers and subscribers on social media, and her drawing videos have tens of millions of views all around the world.

Jasmina loves animals, science, astronomy, technology, web designing, reading, listening to music.

Visit her website for more tutorials, her drawing gallery, art prints and more.

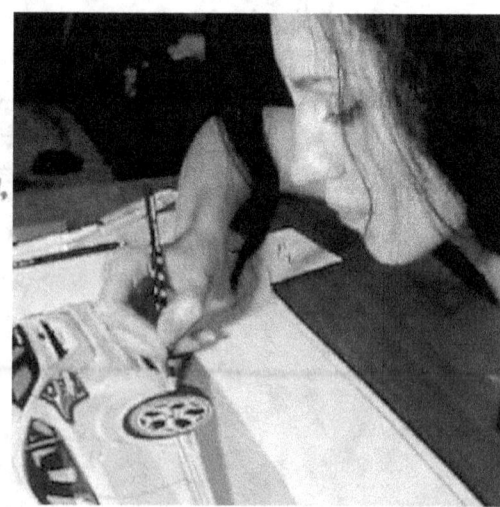

www.jasminasusak.com

If you want to learn faster and better, I recommend joining my website, **Pencil Drawing Tutor**. As a member, you'll learn through real-time narrated videos, step-by-step written tutorials with pictures, and have 24/7 access to **PenPick Graphite**. You can attach your drawings under any tutorial and chat with other members. The lessons are perfect for beginners, those looking to improve, or anyone who wants inspiration and fun.

Brand new tutorial every WEEK.
Come join us!

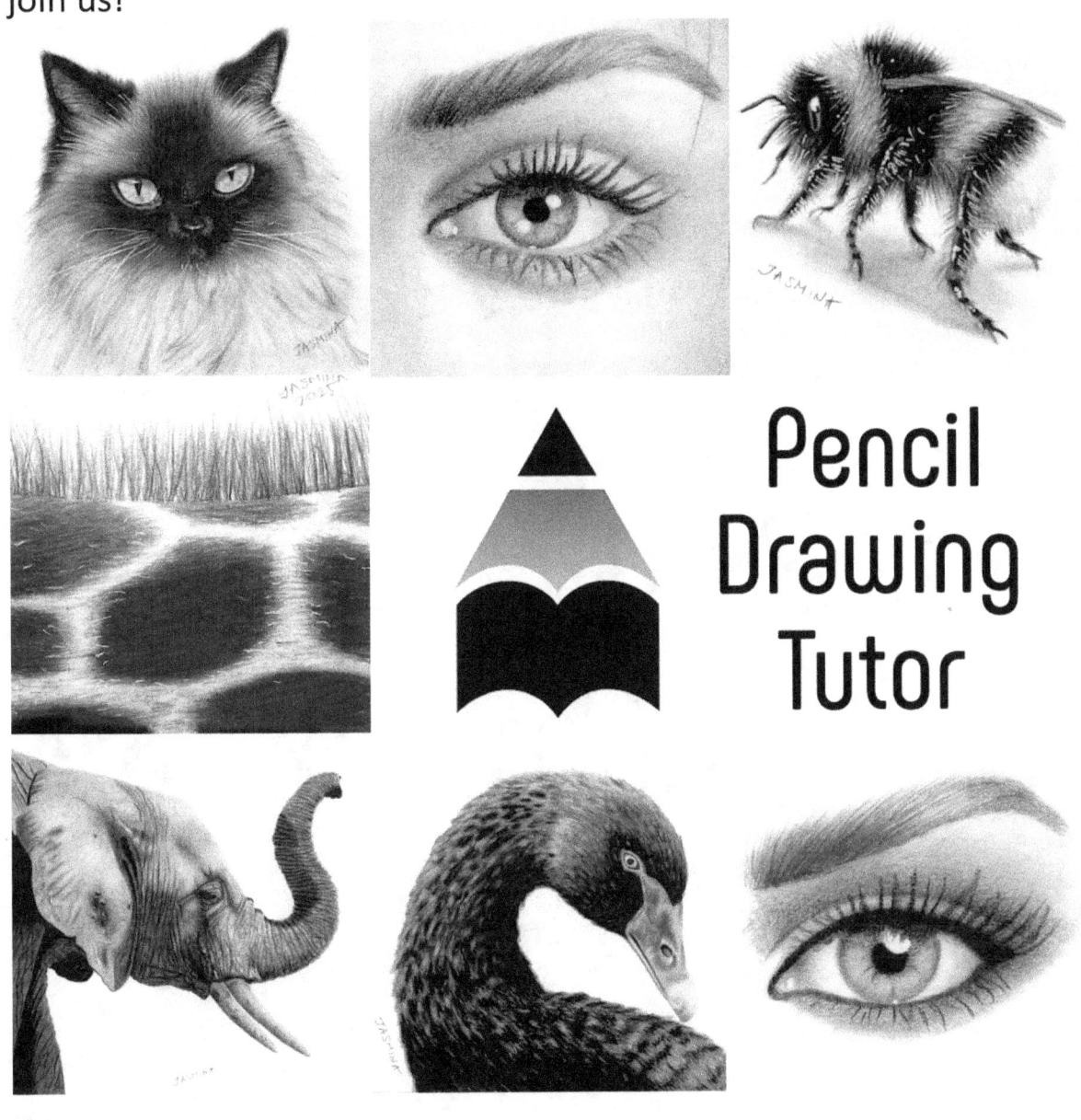

WWW.PENCILDRAWINGTUTOR.COM

www.ingramcontent.com/pod-product-compliance
Lightning Source LLC
Chambersburg PA
CBHW080453220526
45465CB00006B/2255